Michael Kirst

BROOKINGS PAPERS ON EDUCATION POLICY

2003

Diane Ravitch
Editor

Sponsored by
the Brown Center on
Education Policy

D0041831

BROOKINGS INSTITUTION PRESS
Washington, D.C.

Copyright © 2003
THE BROOKINGS INSTITUTION
1775 Massachusetts Avenue, N.W., Washington, DC 20036

Library of Congress Catalog Card No. 98-664027
ISSN 1096-2719
ISBN 0-8157-7361-7

BROOKINGS PAPERS ON EDUCATION POLICY

2003

BROOKINGS PAPERS ON EDUCATION POLICY contains the edited versions of the papers and comments that were presented at the fifth annual Brookings conference on education policy, held in May 2002. The conference gives federal, state, and local policymakers an independent, nonpartisan forum to analyze policies intended to improve student performance. Each year Brookings convenes some of the best-informed analysts from various disciplines to review the current situation in education and to consider proposals for reform. This year's discussion focused on the progress of high schools in providing all students an equal, high-quality education. The conference and journal were funded by the Herman and George R. Brown Chair in Educational Studies at Brookings. Additional support from the Miriam K. Carliner Endowment for Economic Studies and from the John M. Olin Foundation is gratefully acknowledged.

The papers in this volume have been modified to reflect some of the insights contributed by the discussions at the conference. In all cases the papers are the result of the authors' thinking and do not imply agreement by those attending the conference. Nor do the materials presented here necessarily represent the views of the staff members, officers, or trustees of the Brookings Institution.

Subscription Rates

Individuals $24.95
Institutions $39.95

For information on subscriptions, standing orders, and individual copies, contact Brookings Institution Press, 1775 Massachusetts Avenue, N.W., Washington, DC 20036. Call 202/797-6258 or 800/275-1447. E-mail bibooks@brookings.edu. Visit Brookings online at www.brookings.edu.

Brookings periodicals are available online through Online Computer Library Center (contact the OCLC subscriptions department at 800/848-5878, ext. 6251) and Project Muse (http://muse.jhu.edu).

Introduction

DIANE RAVITCH

In May 2002 the Brown Center on Education Policy at the Brookings Institution sponsored a two-day conference on the state of America's high schools. The discussion focused on new research about reform of these institutions that are so important in the lives of the nation's adolescents.

The participants considered the high school from a variety of perspectives—historical, international, sociological, and practical. The questions considered reflected the diversity of the participants' perspectives: How has the high school changed over time? What forces and ideas have promoted change? How does the American high school compare with similar institutions in other nations? What happens in high schools today to promote or suppress student achievement? What kinds of peer interactions create a culture that values achievement or one that spurns it? What accounts for the continuing gaps in achievement among students of different racial backgrounds? What can be done to reduce those gaps? How can high schools ensure that students are intellectually challenged? Is the high school as it has been known over the past century evolving? What reform strategies appear to be most promising in the near future?

For most of the twentieth century, the American high school suffered a prolonged identity crisis, much like the adolescents whom it serves. In the late nineteenth century, going to high school was still a fairly unusual experience. Most youngsters left school at the end of eighth grade and joined the work force or helped out at home or on the family farm. The high school at that time was widely perceived to be a college preparatory institution, and college was not necessary for entry to anything other than the learned professions. Less than 5 percent of adolescents attended high school in 1895, and even fewer went to college. In some towns and cities, until the 1920s, admission to high school was based on examinations. So long as the high school was considered a selective, college preparatory institution, its identity and its purposes were clear. The high school curriculum was determined largely by college admission requirements, which stressed mathematics, foreign languages, and close reading of literary classics. This curriculum set the pattern for almost all students, whether or not they intended to go to college.

The purposes of the high school became a matter for debate as high school enrollments spiraled upward. Beginning in 1880, the number of students who attended high school doubled every decade until 1930. In part this remarkable increase was driven by the growth of the population, but it far exceeded the rate of increase of the high school–age population. In 1900 about 10 percent of fourteen- to seventeen-year-olds were in high school; by 1930 nearly half of the age group attended high school.

Educators understood that the high school was changing from an elite institution to a mass institution, and they vigorously disagreed about what high schools should do. Almost all concurred that expansion of the high school was a good thing for a democratic society, but they parted company over how the high schools should meet the needs of a democratic society. Some maintained that the high school should offer the same academic programs, the same educational experiences to all students, regardless of their ultimate educational or occupational destination. This was the proper route for a democratic institution.

Other educators, who eventually prevailed, insisted that the high school in a democratic society should offer an academic education only for the few bound for college and an appropriate vocational education for the great majority heading for the workplace and homemaking. As enrollments expanded in the 1920s and 1930s, most high schools adopted a differentiated curriculum, with separate programs for future farmers, industrial workers, automobile mechanics, domestic workers, clerks, housewives, technicians, and other occupations. Few high schools attempted to provide a common academic experience for all students. Eventually, most students chose one of three tracks: academic, vocational, or general (which was neither academic nor vocational). The students' choices were influenced (or constrained) by guidance counselors, whose advice was based on students' social origins, their aspirations (which tended to reflect their social origins), and their intelligence test scores (which also tended to reflect their social origins).

For most of the twentieth century, the tripartite division of the high school population was unchallenged. Students were either college-bound, in which case they enrolled in the academic track; or they were bound for a specific occupation, in which case they enlisted in a vocational curriculum; or they did not know what they wanted to do, so they took a smorgasbord of courses in the general track that led neither to college nor to a skilled occupation.

In 1983, when the National Commission on Excellence in Education issued its landmark report *A Nation at Risk*, the dominant track in the American high school was the general one, in which 42 percent of students were enrolled. The commission took aim at the usual pattern of academic, vocational, and general tracks, blaming it for fostering a climate of low expectations and a curricular hodgepodge. The commission called on states to expect all students to take four years of English, three years of science, three years of mathematics, and three years of social studies. (It also recommended one-half year of computer science for all, but that proposal is obsolete now that students gain computer skills without the need for a specific course.)

With these recommendations, the National Commission on Excellence in Education directly challenged the regnant consensus of the previous several decades. High school, the commission implied, was not the time to sort students in accord with their future destinations, but a time to assure that all students have equal opportunity to get a high-quality education, either for postsecondary studies or for getting a good job in a technically advanced economy.

Nearly twenty years have passed since the commission called on states to reform their high schools and to raise graduation requirements. According to data gathered by the Department of Education, students today are taking many more advanced courses in mathematics and the sciences. Test scores, however, do not reflect the increases in enrollments in academic courses, and large score gaps remain among students from different social groups.

With this background in mind, participants at the Brown Center's discussions in 2002 debated the past, present, and future of the high school. As these discussions deepened, it was apparent to all that the high school does not exist in a vacuum. To one side are the elementary and middle schools that prepare students for the high schools; to the other are the postsecondary institutions for which most students are preparing. To what extent are the weaknesses of the lower schools hampering the effectiveness of the high schools? To what extent are the demands (or the absence of demands) of colleges and universities hampering the effectiveness of the high schools? The family, students' peers, and contemporary society also have roles to play in shaping adolescent behavior. Laurence Steinberg, in an address to the conference, discussed the social and cultural forces that influence students' attitudes, values, and behaviors and that encourage students to disengage from the educational goals of the schools. Steinberg and his colleagues reported in *Beyond the Classroom* that between 33 and 40 percent of students were disengaged from school. This disengagement was related not to teaching practices or course curricula but to the students' belief that, short of dropping out or failing, how they did in school did not much matter. Steinberg and his colleagues identified three out-of-school factors that negatively affected students' attitudes about school: (1) low level of parental engagement in their children's academic life; (2) peer group opinions that denigrate academic success; and (3) students' overinvolvement in nonschool activities, such as socializing with friends and working in part-time jobs. As Steinberg stated, "the problem of low student achievement needs to be viewed within a broader context that includes other institutions in addition to schools."

In his remarks, Steinberg reiterated his belief that it is not "possible to talk sensibly about high school reform without understanding the state of adolescence in America." Drawing from National Longitudinal Study of Adolescent Health data, he concluded that "American adolescents . . . lead the industrialized world in virtually every mental health problem social scientists collect data on, including suicide, drug and alcohol abuse, teen pregnancy, and violence." Furthermore, the data bore out Steinberg and his colleagues' findings that "a significant negative relationship [exists] between hours of employment and school achievement." While Steinberg agreed with the conference participants that "curricular reform and better trained teachers" are needed, he thought that "to improve high schools . . . a coordinated policy effort [is needed] that has as its focus adolescents, not secondary education."

The participants in the conference considered the broad web of institutions and forces in which the high school is embedded and acknowledged their importance. Independent scholar Arthur G. Powell, in "American High Schools and the Liberal Arts Tradition," reported on the changing relationship between high schools and the liberal arts tradition. This discussion provided a useful historical perspective for the rest of the conference participants' deliberations. Jeffrey Mirel of the University of Michigan School of Education and Richard J. Murnane of the Harvard University Graduate School of Education responded to Powell's presentation.

Barbara Schneider of the University of Chicago and the National Opinion Research Center, in "Strategies for Success: High School and Beyond," suggested that specific strategies—such as taking more rigorous academic course sequences and studying a foreign language—enable high school students to achieve higher levels of success. Michael Kirst of Stanford University and Frederick M. Hess of the University of Virginia School of Education responded to Schneider's presentation.

Maureen T. Hallinan, director of the Center for Research on Educational Opportunity, Institute for Education Initiatives, University of Notre Dame, pointed out in "Ability Grouping and Student Learning" that many high schools were setting expectation levels far too low for many of their students by assigning them to lower-ability groups. She suggested that ability groups are seldom as homogeneous as theory dictates and that many students are not intellectually challenged because of the group to which they are assigned. Eugene Bottoms of the Southern Regional Education Board and Aaron M. Pallas of Columbia University Teachers' College responded to Hallinan's presentation.

John H. Bishop and his team of researchers at Cornell University inquired into the student culture that permits the harassment of students who try to comply with the norms of the school. Such harassment, they suggested in "Nerds and Freaks: A Theory of Student Culture and Norms," depresses student achievement by stigmatizing those who take their studies seriously. Amy Ellen Schwartz of the New York University Wagner School of Public Service and David F. Labaree of the Michigan State University Department of Teacher Education responded to Bishop's paper.

Michael T. Nettles, Catherine M. Millett, and Douglas D. Ready, of the University of Michigan, discussed the extent and the possible causes of the performance gap between African American and white students on college admissions tests in "Attacking the African American–White Achievement Gap on College Admissions Tests." Jens Ludwig of the Georgetown University Public Policy Institute and James Forman of See Forever, the Maya Angelou Public Charter School in Washington, D.C., discussed the paper by Nettles, Millett, and Ready.

Two papers considered the American high school in an international context. William H. Schmidt, of the Michigan State University College of Education, reviewed the results of the Third International Mathematics and Science Study in "Too Little Too Late: American High Schools in an International Context." His findings highlighted the curricular incoherence in American high schools. Iris C. Rotberg of the George Washington University Graduate School of Education and Alan Siegel of the New York University Department of Computer Science commented on Schmidt's findings. David P. Baker, director of the Institute for Policy Research and Evaluation, Pennsylvania State University, Education Policy Studies Department, reached different conclusions from Schmidt in his review of international studies. He suggested, in "Should America Be More Like Them? Cross-National High School Achievement and U.S. Policy," that policy reforms that connect education to other domains may be more fruitful than changes in school practices. Jaekyung Lee of the State University of New York at Buffalo and Stephen P. Heyneman of Vanderbilt University, Peabody College, responded to Baker's presentation.

The final paper, "Accelerating Advancement in School and Work" by Hilary Pennington of Jobs for the Future, assessed the likelihood of structural changes in the high school experience, surveying a range of innovations now occurring in school districts across the nation. Sheila E. Murray of RAND Corporation and Marc Tucker of the National Center on Education and the Economy commented on Pennington's paper.

By the conclusion of the conference, after much dissent and debate, most presenters and discussants concurred that the high school would succeed to the extent that it focused on and strengthened its mission as an institution dedicated to the intellectual growth of its students. Some thought that the high schools were doing about as well as possible, given the range of social problems with which they deal. But most thought that the high school could do a far better job in preparing students for the demands of higher education and a complex and technologically advanced society. If a single theme emerged, it was that the high school must raise its expectations and challenge young people to use their minds well.

American High Schools and the Liberal Arts Tradition

ARTHUR G. POWELL

The term *liberal arts* usually conjures up one central idea; that is, effective liberal arts education as strong academic achievement. A second, less dominant, and frequently neglected notion regards effective liberal arts education as producing intellectual interests and habits that endure throughout adult life. The two ideas are complementary and not in opposition. But they are different.

The dominant idea associates the liberal arts with a collection of academic subjects or disciplines, most often divided into three broad and overlapping groups. For example, they are labeled by the National Center for Education Statistics as humanities, social and behavioral sciences, and natural sciences. The humanities embrace the imaginative and spiritual life of humankind. The social sciences address human institutions and relations as they have developed over time. The natural sciences cover the world of nature. The number of liberal arts has grown remarkably, in the form of area studies, gender and ethnic studies, other multi- and interdisciplinary fields, and entirely new subjects. The three subject areas are regarded as liberal because the knowledge they contain liberates and deepens understanding of life and because the methods they employ and the cognitive and other skills they teach make greater understanding more likely.[1]

Good performance in the liberal arts seems almost synonymous with good achievement in the study of academic subjects. The crucial indicators of performance are usually examinations—tests created by teachers, tests created and sometimes mandated by government, tests created by private organizations such as the International Baccalaureate or the College Board. Academic performance is usually assessed soon after instruction has occurred—at the end of a unit, project, term, or course. Performance is what

7

you can do shortly after you have been taught to do it. The typical assessment time frame is the close-in present. In addition, performance is what you can do when asked to do it by others. Some external compulsion or pressure is usually involved.

Boosting academic achievement for most high school students, and hence increasing the chances that large numbers of young Americans will acquire the beginnings of what a liberal education promises, has proven a difficult task. Only a century has passed since the goal was even imagined, much less undertaken seriously. The United States is now in the midst of the most sustained effort to foster academic achievement among the largest possible fraction of youth in its history. The genius of the American high school has resided in its capacity to avoid internal conflict by absorbing all conceivable purposes without embracing too strenuously any single one. The present effort, with its unmistakable tone of compulsion, potentially threatens, more than any other earlier school reform movement, the delicate internal balance that offers students endless opportunities but also allows them endless choices to engage or avoid engagement in learning. It is thus unusually ambitious and worthy of sustained public support.[2]

The second idea about the liberal arts tradition is that what begins as a required activity assessed just after instruction should become voluntary behavior engaged in for curiosity and pleasure. The ultimate agenda of the liberal arts is how a person lives his or her life—what that person is like as an adult and not merely as a youth at the time school graduation requirements have been met. The ultimate product of an effective liberal arts education is active reflection about serious ideas. Enduring intellectual interests are to be created and pursued long after required courses and examinations are over and done with.

An enduring intellectual interest sometimes involves activity in which doing something is readily visible to others—making a watercolor, writing a letter to the editor, leading a family discussion about an environmental issue, and participating in town or school board meetings. Activity also includes less visible, more private reflection—what people think about, what they read, how they read, what they watch or listen to, and what they make of these mental activities. Activity may be goal-directed, such as solving a problem, or it may have no obvious practical product except contemplative enjoyment.

Long-term, out-of-school, voluntary engagement in at least some aspects of the humanities, social sciences, or natural sciences has often been neglected as an educational purpose. Short-term academic achievement, after all, is a legitimate and valued objective in its own right and can be pursued in the absence of concern for intellectual enthusiasm and the life of the mind. Deborah Meier wrote an entire book chapter communicating the difference between academic achievement in school and intellectual behavior afterward. She felt the need to do so when a student expressed shock that Meier listened to Mozart for pleasure. To the student, such a motive was unfathomable. American attitudes about high school academic achievement have fluctuated greatly over time, while attitudes toward the place of intellectual values have remained stable. The latter are rarely visible in a positive sense or in any sense. The word *intellectual* suggests bloodless and bookish passivity far removed from the real world and active life. Anti-intellectualism, as Richard Hofstadter and many others have observed, remains pervasive in American society and in American schooling.[3]

For example, a longitudinal study of eighty-one high school valedictorians graduating in 1981 concluded that only about a half dozen developed enduring intellectual interests during the following decade. They were adept at getting high grades and motivated to get them for career success. But in later life they rarely engaged voluntarily in serious reading or thinking about anything outside the boundaries of their own vocations. In the field of reading, where considerable attention has been devoted to how school learning continues into adulthood, a whole new word—*aliteracy*—had to be invented to describe adults who could easily read but did not.[4]

In one field observation from a recent study of high schools, a small group of juniors argued loudly in the school cafeteria about the causes of the Civil War. Was the main factor slavery, were regional economic rivalries more crucial, or was extremism by a few zealots the true explanation? Some other juniors wandered by, overheard the raging debate, and proclaimed their puzzlement. "Why are you talking about this *here*?" they asked. "We're not in class anymore." The onlookers were willing to discuss the causes of the war in class or through out-of-class homework. They cared about good academic performance just as much as the cafeteria conversationalists did. But they were perplexed that a few peers cared enough about the issue to continue with it outside the classroom—when they did not have to, when they were not being assessed, and when no one but themselves even knew of their conversation. That good performance could be defined as voluntary activity never occurred to them.

In another field observation, several young women, exhausted but elated, had just finished their Advanced Placement chemistry exam. The preparation was extensive and few students in the school, and even fewer female juniors, were willing to exert the mental effort required. When they left the room, one threw up her arms in celebration and relief. She exclaimed, "Thank goodness. It's over. Just think. We will never, never again in our whole lives have to spend another second thinking about chemistry!" They all shrieked in knowing acknowledgment. Chemistry was over forever for them, except for picking up their exam scores in July. Their achievement was perceived as having no long-term impact on their lives or thoughts, except for the impact of their grades on college admission or placement.[5]

This essay explores both the academic achievement side of the liberal arts tradition and the enduring intellectual interests side as they have played out in American high schools. During the century beginning about 1890, American high schools saw an explosive enrollment growth. From an exclusive institution serving only about 6 percent of the age fourteen to seventeen population in 1890, high school participation rose decade after decade. By 1930 a majority of fourteen- to seventeen-year-olds were in high school; by 1950, 76 percent. Near universal participation—90 percent and above—was achieved in the 1960s and remained roughly around 94 percent through the end of the twentieth century. Furthermore, in the second half of the century, high schools were rapidly converted from mass terminal to mass preparatory institutions. Most adolescents not only graduated from high school, but they also continued with various forms of postsecondary education. The college preparatory experience became the rule rather than the exception.[6]

These historic shifts in institutional function profoundly affected each version of the liberal arts. Academic achievement marked school reform objectives of the last two decades of the twentieth century while enduring serious interests were largely ignored. Three historical windows further illuminate the interplay among ideas about the liberal arts. The work of Charles W. Eliot at the end of the nineteenth century first crystallized ideas about the content and purpose of modern high school academics. To a certain extent Eliot updated an older notion of academic purpose, conceived as developed mental capacity and acquired knowledge. He assumed that academic purpose was the only appropriate high school goal. He regarded the development of enduring interests as a central educational goal but saw interests in narrowly vocational terms.

A second historical window is the reaction against Eliot's work by the professional custodians of the rapidly expanding American high school. As high school enrollments mushroomed early in the twentieth century, Eliot's ideas were largely replaced by social efficiency. This emphasized preparation for specific adult roles, especially vocational ones. The idea that education should have enduring and specific effects was eagerly embraced, but the behavior that social efficiency endorsed was profoundly anti-intellectual.

A third window is the role of elite higher education, especially in the first half of the twentieth century, as guardian and primary generator of the liberal arts tradition. One conception of liberal education, known broadly as "liberal culture" or simply "culture," flourished after the turn of the century. Largely a revolt against university tendencies toward specialization, student electives, and vocationalism, this movement rarely touched high schools directly. But it contained a vision of the liberal arts that emphasized the role of intellectual interests in a life fully lived—a vision different from all the forces then contending for domination in high schools. That vision, however, also projected the impression that the liberal arts were the near-exclusive property of a moneyed class whose interests seemed more committed to establishing superiority to others than to the life of the mind. This association of class with the liberal arts created difficulties for those who sought, through high schools, to democratize culture.

The Contemporary Resurgence of Academic Achievement

After World War II, high school academics became a national priority for the first time in American history. As more students continued schooling beyond grade twelve, high school became increasingly focused on college preparation. Given that college prep in America meant a primarily academic secondary education, academics had to be taken at least somewhat seriously.

Academics also seemed suddenly relevant to national problems in a way they had not earlier in the century. Harvard University president James B. Conant, probably the most important high school reformer between the mid-1940s and mid-1960s, expressed several reasons for this change. By commissioning *General Education in a Free Society*, a 1945 report that defended school academics more forcefully than any major report since the National Education Association's Committee of Ten in 1893, Conant argued for the role of liberal education "not for the relatively few, but for a multitude." Depression and war had taught him how deep and dangerous social cleavages and perceived inequality could be. As a social conservative, he believed one function of liberal or general education was to help unify society.

A different concern that World War II and then the cold war impressed on Conant, and that coexisted with the unifying function of high schools, was the importance of highly educated manpower in science and technology. Discovering talent and establishing meritocratic values in school became another high priority developed fully in his 1959 report, *The American High School Today*. Well before Russia's launching of *Sputnik* in 1957 caused national hand-wringing about the neglect of academics, the federal government and private foundations began to make curriculum development and teacher education in math, science, and foreign languages a priority. If the emphasis on nurturing academic talent was stronger than that of dispersing liberal education to the multitudes, in Conant's writing and in the larger society, both tendencies existed in a somewhat reinvigorated academic tradition.[7]

Despite the subsequent national preoccupation with student unrest and social protest, these two traditions—dispersing educational opportunities widely and cultivating academic excellence—never disappeared and were in fact strengthened by events of the 1960s and 1970s. They became the dominant strains of academic concern about high schools in the early 1980s, and they remain so today. The remarkable tenacity of the high school academic reform movement—roughly twenty years have passed since the appearance of *A Nation at Risk* and the Boyer, Goodlad, and Sizer reports—is perhaps its most salient feature. The fundamental reason for that tenacity is the tight link between the ideas of equity and academic achievement. Usually in opposition, these ideas have remained in delicate balance.[8]

Two main factors explain this fairly durable alliance. First, the equity ideal largely grew from the civil rights movement of the 1960s and the subsequent War on Poverty. The civil rights movement tapped deeply held American values about fairness and opportunity, which had not been the focus of Depression-era concerns about class conflict and inequality. Political decisions in the 1960s were made to assault racial inequality and poverty mainly on the school battlefield. Subsequent equity battles involving special needs and gender have also been centrally addressed by schools. The schools, not other economic and social institutions, were largely entrusted with solving these problems and are still so entrusted at the beginning of the twenty-first century.[9]

Second, the way schools could advance equity was profoundly affected by the emergence of the new national economy in the 1970s and 1980s. In the new economy, Americans were told they had to learn to think for a living. Dropping out of high school, or even passing through high school without learning much, was no longer sufficient to guarantee middle-class jobs. Suddenly academic achievement was associated with vocational achievement and economic advancement far more than before. Academics mattered not just for the ever-increasing numbers who sought postsecondary education, but for everyone. The equity and academic lobbies could join in common cause.

One result of this alliance has been two decades of government intervention on behalf of systemic reform, in which teacher education, curriculum, and testing are aligned and in which the stakes for students themselves have become increasingly higher. Another result is the growing choice movement. All choice possibilities—from moving to a new town, to patronizing a charter school, to supporting themed environments within big public schools or private school vouchers—derive in large part from James Coleman's research-based insight that student body composition is a crucial determinant of school culture. A third result is the proliferation of bottom-up movements, which emphasize how freedom from bureaucracy can sometimes energize teachers to work better together to create effective and personalized school cultures.

What are the results so far? On dimensions such as academic course taking, data from the National Center for Education Statistics suggest that high schools are considerably more academic than they were two decades ago. Course taking in mathematics and science has substantially increased, while course taking in vocational-technical subjects has slightly decreased. But measured achievement, compared with international populations and with American elementary schools, indicates that high school performance has not dramatically improved. Reading achievement has remained stable for nearly three decades. Writing has declined in the past decade. Math performance increased in the decade after 1982 but has remained stable since. Science has gradually improved since 1982, but performance today is lower than in 1970. International comparisons indicate that, in the mid-1990s, American twelfth graders were among the lowest-performing students in science and math general knowledge.[10]

For an additional perspective on change, I compared 1982 catalogs from participants in a major study of high schools with 2002 catalogs from the same schools. One school, for example, is large, diverse, comprehensive, and comparatively affluent. It was in 1982 a prototypical "shopping mall high school" with an enormous curriculum and a deep commitment to student choice. In many ways it still is. Curriculum expansion continues and is dominated by three new growth areas—technology, bilingual education, and special education. Technology is everywhere—advanced television production, photography, computers. Where in 1982 the math department offered two computer courses, an entire page was needed in 2002 to summarize the different computer skills taught in thirty-six courses, notably in vocational-technical departments. A second growth area is bilingual education and English as a Second Language (ESL). Twenty years ago the school employed one teacher and offered one ESL course. Now a fully staffed department provides fifteen subject-specific ESL courses. The third area is special education. In 1982 three "learning skills" courses were listed in a miscellaneous catalog section called "Interdepartmental," which included other hard-to-categorize courses such as working on the stage crew. In 2002, nineteen courses and four distinct special education programs offering fifty additional credit courses were available.

The biggest difference between the two catalogs is tone. The 2002 school is more confident, more purposeful, and more academic. The 1982 statement of school philosophy acknowledged "deep concern about where the high school is and where it is heading." With considerable candor, the statement noted that the school contained committed students, disenchanted ones, and those who had not yet decided where they stood. To appeal to all, the school tried to provide something for everyone, including choice, an informal atmosphere, pass-fail grading, and an open campus. The 2002 statement drops this rhetoric of fragmentation and accommodation. The first part of the school's mission is to "require students to complete a rigorous academic program."

The sharp 1982 differentiation among academic curriculum levels was dramatically reduced by 2002. In addition, language stressing higher expectations for all students was introduced. Consider English as an example. In 1982 five curriculum levels were available in English in each grade. In 2002 only three levels remained. The middle Level B was described as follows in 1982: "The pace is slower and the materials and approaches more closely reflect the students' interests and practical needs." The 1982 description of Level B sophomore English advises students to choose the course "if you read and write only when you have to." Typical readings then were the

Reader's Digest and "one longer work" per semester. The 2002 description of Level B sophomore English, in contrast, abandoned the appeal to student preferences and established higher educational expectations. Level B English students—and this level is the lowest offered in 2002—"are expected to read all of the assigned texts and to devote, on average, at least one hour of homework time for each hour of class." Instead of two books a year, Level B sophomore English assigns at least five. Writing is also emphasized, including a major essay in which all sophomores write on a common theme.

Because the school will soon be affected by state-mandated examinations required for graduation, Level B students receive two more English classes a week than higher Level A students. And Level B students who wish to try the more challenging Level A English are encouraged to do so. Two extra periods per week ease their adjustment. Taken as a whole, these examples show efforts to increase expectations for all, reduce discrepancies among academic levels of the same subject, and provide concrete ways for students to move up or stay up. On the basis of catalog evidence alone, the bias toward academic work has increased notably over twenty years.[11]

The main energy that has sustained the contemporary school reform movement is the wish to boost achievement of poor and minority children. Additional energy came in the 1980s when reformers also believed that America was losing out economically to Germany and Japan because of an undereducated work force. The push was for tougher standards in all the academic subjects. In each instance, the reform motive was largely economic—helping individuals to get ahead and the country to stay ahead. Little attention was given to how education might develop enduring intellectual interests. That goal seemed a far-off luxury or frill compared with concrete measured student achievement. Few educators in the elementary-secondary sector have been seriously concerned about passive achievement and the resulting weak dispersion of enduring intellectual interests in the population.

Valedictorians who get ahead in life without using their minds outside their vocations, history students whose curiosity ends at the classroom door, and high achievers who drop chemistry like a hot potato when the test score is obtained are not considered national problems. Yet many teachers in schools and colleges report that students with satisfactory or even distinguished scholastic performance lack focus, direction, and passion. They seem burned out or stressed out, or perhaps were never lit up. But if they achieve enough to continue on to postsecondary education, complete it, and then enter the work force, their education is usually regarded as successful.[12]

Most educators, after all, are familiar and comfortable with tests and being judged by tests. Most believe, not without reason, that competent academic performance assessed soon after instruction is as good a proxy as now exists for predicting enduring performance such as interests. Most agree that a few basic skills such as reading are desirable outcomes for all. Beyond that, agreement begins to break down. People do not agree that all adults should be mature readers; they have not even reached consensus on what "mature" means. They are unlikely to support policies designed to press adolescents not merely to read but also to acquire the habits of mature readers. The more an interest is regarded as a desired educational habit that endures over time, the more commitment and resolve educators must show to develop that habit. But such resolve energizes opponents to criticize reform as undemocratic inculcation. So enduring interests can easily become the lowest of priorities.

The absence of a strong research tradition on enduring educational effects reinforces the invisibility of the issue. This is especially ironic, because no educational idea has been more popular in America for a century than interests. But what American educators have meant by interests is not desired outcomes, but preferences students bring initially to the educational process. Building on existing interests is a compelling idea because it is a tool to motivate students uninterested in interests of mind. In contrast, the creation of enduring interests has not attracted researchers in large numbers. Schools' lasting effects, aside from economic effects, are largely unknown. A 1997 review of several research literatures bearing on acquired serious interests revealed a fragmented endeavor in which enduring interests were a minor and peripheral concern.[13]

Charles W. Eliot and the High School Liberal Arts

Harvard University president Charles W. Eliot, the leading secondary school reformer at the end of the nineteenth century, believed the emerging American university could shape in its own image the new but still malleable institution called the high school. In purpose and organization, Eliot thought the high school should be the beginning stage of higher education, not the culminating phase of the lower schools. His chairmanship of the famous 1893 Committee of Ten on Secondary School Studies of the National Education Association had done much to identify a good high school curriculum with emerging mainline academic subjects: English, other modern languages, history, and science. These were the very subjects associated with the emergence of the modern university. The fullest study of the Committee of Ten concluded that its report "clearly dignified the new disciplines, raising them to a status that was well established even by the next generation."[14]

Eliot's major justification for a limited academic curriculum was its capacity to cultivate "mental power." By "power" he meant "a trained capacity to observe, to reason, and to maintain an alert attention." His distinction between the "false ideal of giving useful information" and the true ideal of "imparting power" were the terms by which he sought to shape discussion about the aims of liberal education. A practical man with little interest in psychology, Eliot used the term *power* in the same general sense that many contemporaries used *mental discipline* and many successors used *thinking, reasoning, understanding,* and *higher-order skills.* A chemist by training, his preferred conception of power emphasized scientific methods such as the gathering and evaluation of data. Although acquisition of intellectual power through study of academic subjects clearly required some knowledge of subjects, his point was that an educated person was defined by the power he could apply instead of by the information he possessed.

Thorough study of any academic subject conveyed the same educational benefits, Eliot believed, so nothing was lost if students were given wide discretion in what they selected. An important reason that high schools had improved, he felt, was their growing recognition that student choice—electives—complemented a limited academic curriculum covered thoroughly The more choice students experienced, the better chance their decisions would be governed by their interests and would act to inspire interest at deeper and more mature levels. The cultivation of enduring interests was thus a crucial part of Eliot's educational theory.

But the interests he had in mind were largely vocational. In his 1869 Harvard presidential inaugural address, he argued that every person possessed some sort of "natural bent or preference." A crucial job of high school (and any further schooling) was to help people discover their natural bents. Finding and pursuing one's true vocation was perhaps life's greatest satisfaction. For Eliot joy arose from productive labor. "When the revelation of his own peculiar taste and capacity comes to a young man, let him reverently give it welcome, thank God, and take courage. Thereafter he knows his way to happy, enthusiastic work, and, God willing, to usefulness and success."[15]

By 1899 the importance of allowing high school students to discover their natural bents led Eliot to advocate not only student choice of program of study or curriculum track (such as "English" or "Scientific"). He pushed further for the elimination of curriculum programs and for full election over individual classes. "The immense deepening and expanding of human knowledge in the nineteenth century" in combination with "the recognition of the profound individual differences of capacity and mental inclination" made uniform curriculum prescriptions "impossible and absurd." "Individual instruction is the new ideal," said Eliot.

What kind of student would be attracted to this vision of high schools? Eliot understood that few American youth then entered high school, fewer graduated, and fewer still went on to college. He expected high school attendance to expand somewhat—it had doubled in the 1890s to about one-half million—and he was deeply involved in making it easier and more desirable for high school graduates to enter colleges by altering admissions requirements. But he did not imagine high school as a destination for anyone but ambitious and fortunate middle-class strivers who did not need to work immediately after completing elementary education.

One implication was that high school should not prematurely lock students into separate destinations at an early age. Life futures should not be determined by choices made for pupils "without their participation or consent, by parents or teachers, sometimes on trivial grounds, or, at least, on imperfect knowledge of the pupils' capacities and tastes." Strongly committed to the idea that good education should arouse vocational interest, Eliot at this time opposed vocational education as premature sorting and as contrary to the prime goal of imparting mental power.[16]

Another implication of his selective view of the high school population was a strong emphasis on the similarities between the purpose of high school and college. An education that enabled a high school graduate to pursue college with intelligence and vigor "ought also to prepare him to grasp with rapidity the details of any business or mechanical occupation" and to pursue that work with "diligence and alertness." The high school education Eliot saw emerging would enable graduates, regardless of eventual life destination, to acquire the power that any of the mainline academic subjects could provide if studied thoroughly. He thought it wholly misleading to characterize high schools as "fitting or preparatory schools" for college.[17]

The influence of Eliot's high school vision waned quickly in his own day. A new and aggressively ambitious profession of education—professors of education, and city, state, and local administrators—is usually blamed for the abandonment of the ideal of a liberal education for all. Forces outside the humanistic tradition, with different conceptions of the role of high schools in an industrial democracy, pressed successfully for a reduction of academic emphasis in favor of focusing on the roles youth would play (such as vocation) in adult life. They also demanded that the individual differences Eliot noticed were good reason to differentiate students' school experiences, essentially by social classes. They rejected Eliot's proposal to provide a differentiated experience tailored to each individual but wholly within the academic tradition. But another important reason for the failure of Eliot's program was the program itself. Even without external opposition, Eliot's conception of the high school liberal arts contained serious internal problems.

He completely miscalculated how enormously popular the high school would become and how its increasing hold on most of the adolescent cohort would invariably complicate his ideas of high school purpose. He had no good answer to the sudden transformation of the high school from an exclusive institution serving a tiny minority to a mass institution serving, or wanting to serve, the entire age cohort. From about 203,000 public high school students in 1890, the population roughly doubled every decade until 1940. This growth created new education careers or professions, with powerful interests in shaping the modern high school. From the beginning, professional educators wanted to retain as many students as possible—the word *dropout* as synonym for high school failure dates to the beginning of the twentieth century.[18]

At first, Eliot thought high school growth vindicated his position that students considered the academic curriculum to be excellent preparation for jobs that did not require college attendance. But research suggested that youth dropped out of school not because parents needed their earnings but because the school curriculum seemed useless to reach vocational goals. In 1908 Eliot publicly embraced separate trade schools. "There is no such thing among men as equality of natural gifts, of capacity for training, or of intellectual power." It followed that some rational process was necessary to distribute students to schools appropriate to their talents. He proposed that elementary school teachers "ought to sort the pupils and sort them by their evident or probable destinies." Heavy criticism soon forced a retreat from these positions. Eliot's vacillation indicated, at the least, that an academic curriculum committed to mental power would be extremely difficult to defend as high schools increasingly included the entire range of American youth.[19]

Eliot remained in the thick of the battle over whether an academic curriculum for all should remain the central goal of high schools. But he retired from combat concerning the equally vexing question of how a high school academic curriculum provided the beginnings of liberal education for all as well as college preparation for a few. Mental training or power was important because it could be applied—transferred—from one situation to another. The assumption that serious academic subjects thoroughly taught could equally provide power rested on the notion that each had roughly equivalent educational value. Theodore R. Sizer's historical analysis concluded that the Committee of Ten "automatically assumed that there was no argument on their psychological position, and they did not even bother to spell out their rationale."[20]

In fact, Eliot never gave much thought to theories of faculty psychology. His favorite list for the faculties that made up mental power consisted simply of observation, reasoning, and expression, and he urged teachers to stress these capacities in whatever they taught. In advocating transfer of training and mental faculties, Eliot was using doomed language much more than he was espousing doomed ideas. The historian Hugh Hawkins gives a useful example of his approach. When speaking of developing the power of observation, Eliot wished a student to learn "how hard it is to determine with certainty even a simple fact" and "to distrust the evidence of his own senses." Such general ideas, habits, and methods could clearly be transferred from one situation to another. They were capacities that could be applied.[21]

But the image of nineteenth-century faculties—muscle-like mental entities that could be strengthened with use—thoroughly permeated understanding of what Eliot meant by mental power. Modern experimental psychology, in the hands of men such as Edward L. Thorndike, destroyed this dated psychology while at the same time claiming to destroy all conceptions of transfer. Where Eliot might have defended the transfer of ideas about, say, observation from one context to another, he had no interest in the new experimental psychology and remained silent.[22]

The demise of the idea of mental discipline also exposed Eliot's failure to defend academic subjects according to their content. Sizer's critical examination of the Committee of Ten especially lambasted its preoccupation with mechanical aspects of academic subjects (for example, how many times classes should meet per week) and neglect of why those subjects should be in the curriculum in the first place. Little attention was paid to "knowledge, skills, or values," and less attention to how subjects would accomplish what the committee report claimed for them. "How," for example, "does the required French syllabus cultivate a taste for reading?" It was simply taken for granted. Hawkins added that the Committee of Ten "barely mentioned any justification for school subjects besides mental training." That became a dangerous position when social efficiency critics were unwilling to take the value of academic subjects for granted.[23]

Eliot virtually never defended academic subjects by arguing they could generate valuable enduring interests in addition to vocational ones. On a few occasions, somewhat unexpectedly, he floated the idea of a broader view of interests. He spoke once, for example, of "implanting a longing or taste for some intellectual pleasure, like reading good literature, cultivating a natural science such as physics or chemistry, pursuing out of doors some branch of natural history, or studying history." He said that the "supreme object of all education, whether elementary, secondary, or higher, is to implant an intellectual longing that will continue to demand some satisfaction long after school days or college days are over." But these sentiments were not typical Eliot. Instead they expressed a lost opportunity to mount a potentially powerful defense of the liberal arts. By 1910 the liberal arts in schools needed all the arguments they could muster.[24]

All these developments challenged Eliot's basic justification of liberal arts in high schools—that high schools were the first leg on the majestic ladder of modern American higher education. As his Harvard presidency ended in 1909, the antiacademic revolt intensified. General power was discredited and academic content was undefended. In such circumstances, academic instruction seemed little more than college preparation. If that is all it meant, how could it be justified as the main diet for the vast majority of students who were not college-bound?

Eliot and the Committee of Ten were rediscovered and rehabilitated in the last two decades of the twentieth century by reformers and historians who saw parallels between efforts separated by nearly a hundred years. To these reformers, Eliot's use lay in how he tightly linked academic subjects, the cultivation of intelligence (power), and the commitment to provide the same demanding curriculum to all students. The ambitious late-twentieth-century movement to integrate the ideal of academic achievement with the egalitarian ideal that all children can learn had no more powerful historical benchmark than Eliot's ambitious late-nineteenth-century project. Thus David K. Cohen praised Eliot for arguing that "all high school students should be educated with equal seriousness in the great areas of human knowledge, and that occupational decisions should be put off until after graduation." Diane Ravitch contended that the Committee of Ten "endorsed the democratic idea that all students should receive a liberal education." Herbert M. Kliebard made Eliot a major leader of the "humanist" group, which, alone among the interests contending for influence over the twentieth-century high school, uncompromisingly defended the "ideal of a liberal education for all." David L. Angus and Jeffrey E. Mirel noted that the Committee of Ten represented the only back-to-basics movement led by professional educators.[25]

Eliot could never have been resuscitated in this way without the new legitimacy that post–World War II cognitive psychology gave the general features of his defense of academics. In his influential 1960 essay, *The Process of Education*, Jerome S. Bruner showed how the idea of mental power could be reinvented with new labels and new theoretical underpinnings. What Bruner called "general understanding" or "disciplined understanding" was "at the heart of the educational process—the continual broadening and deepening of knowledge in terms of basic and general ideas." Eliot would have concurred.

Where Eliot had gone wrong was his decision to separate power from knowledge and to devalue the latter as mere information. For Bruner, every discipline contained "fundamental ideas," which he famously labeled as the discipline's "structure." Knowing the structure—which meant knowing big ideas instead of disconnected facts—gave people the power to understand and apply what they learned. Structure arose from and was part of knowledge. After Bruner, it would be difficult for any educator to maintain dualisms such as deep understanding versus mere knowledge. The two were inevitably interconnected. Further, the proposition that different disciplines had different structures made academic content indispensable to any sort of general or liberal education. Finally, Bruner's dictum that any subject could be taught to any child at any age in some intellectually honest form gave an egalitarian flavor to his work, even though the curriculum reforms he pushed were primarily for the academically inclined.[26]

If Bruner legitimized Eliot's advocacy of mental power while correcting Eliot's devaluing of specific content, his work touched on enduring interests only indirectly. Neither Eliot's focus on finding a person's "natural bent" nor his rare vision of "implanting a longing or taste for some intellectual pleasure" were noticed or built on in the last decades of the twentieth century.

Schools could have done far more, for example, simply to detect individual interests that subsequently might be encouraged. An important step in developing interests of mind is to uncover embryonic curiosity and aptitude. But schools developed hardly any expectations, procedures, methods, or policies aimed at interest detection. Observed incipient interests, if written down and passed on over the years like a portfolio of student work, might provide clues for both teachers and students about student direction.

The healthy nurturance of virtually every interest of mind usually requires close contact of the young with adults who themselves have an interest of mind and have gained their respect. A young person must with his or her own eyes see adults who display interests of mind. The adults become models. The more visible the adult interest, the better. Whether in politics, the arts, science, or something else, being exposed to something portrayed as good for youth usually is insufficient. Many can recall the paradox of an unenthusiastic teacher of music appreciation. Teachers need to love and live their subjects. Creating enduring interests in the subjects they teach should be one central task of teacher education and subsequent professional development. Yet ideas such as these did not find widespread support at any time in the twentieth century.

Social Efficiency's Assault on the Liberal Arts

Critics of the academic tradition generally agreed on a utilitarian conception of high school purpose in which curriculum and school organization should be governed by the main roles people would play in adult life, such as worker, citizen, and family member. They focused on long-term or enduring educational outcomes, in specific ways that Eliot's equally utilitarian emphasis on academic subjects did not cover. The most influential proposal for changing secondary education along social utilitarian lines was the 1918 *Cardinal Principles of Secondary Education* report of the NEA's Commission on the Reorganization of Secondary Education. Almost always paired with the report of the Committee of Ten as the two seminal high school policy documents of the first half of the century, the *Cardinal Principles* was a major blueprint for high school expansion. It fully endorsed vocational education as the central purpose of high schools, while arguing that vocational education should occur under the same roof as other kinds of secondary education. This institution would be called the comprehensive high school and would be preceded by an intermediary three-year junior high school devoted mainly to vocational guidance.

Although a few extreme social efficiency reformers would happily have discarded academic subjects altogether and organized school studies wholly around life roles or functions, the *Cardinal Principles* did not take this position. It neither expelled the academic subjects nor demanded they justify themselves. The academic subjects were retained and assigned specific duties related to seven life-tasks of all adults (hence seven cardinal principles), which the report identified. Academic subjects in its view were not just for the college-bound but for everyone, although many subjects would need transformation to fulfill their new functions. "Worthy home membership," for example, was one cardinal principle. High school students should study the home as a fundamental social institution through a new amalgam of history and other social sciences (social studies). Literature should "interpret and idealize the human elements that go to make the home." Civic education, another principle, relied mainly on social studies but also on literature to "kindle social ideals and give insight into personal character as related to these conditions." "Command of fundamental processes," which meant basic skills, was retained as "tools in the affairs of life" instead of as "an end in itself."

From the viewpoint of the liberal arts, the most intriguing life-task was leisure. By 1918, the commission anticipated an American future of shorter working hours. A "margin of time" would exist for the cultivation of "personal and social interests," which the commission elevated into the principle of "worthy use of leisure." Heretofore, the report noted, American school purpose had rarely considered the idea of leisure time. The report blamed this neglect on the traditional pursuit of "intellectual discipline." Intellectual discipline promoted "sterility" remote from student experience and interest. It was the opposite of the engaged "recreational activities" the word *leisure* should properly suggest, such as using literature, or nonacademic subjects such as art and music, to "evoke right emotional response and produce positive enjoyment." The liberal arts had but a very modest contribution to make toward worthy leisure.

The domain of leisure, in short, largely banished intellectual pursuits while it simultaneously embraced the idea that schools should produce enduring leisure behavior. The commission defended the modest relevance of academic subjects to adult living largely on the basis of social control. They would help youth fit effectively into those specified adult roles that professional educators had determined for them. Leisure was less an opportunity for an individual to pursue passions or interests than a social duty to become "better able to meet his responsibilities." Literature functioned to evoke the right emotional response. A tone of passive spectatorship prevailed. Little emphasis was placed on how academic subjects could or should propel individuals to use their minds well to think for themselves as adults.

The emphasis on worthy leisure exposed the commission's main fear. Leisure time could just as easily be used unworthily. Leisure was more danger than opportunity. Although no list of unworthy leisure activities was supplied, they were well understood. "The unworthy use of leisure impairs health, disrupts home life, lessens vocational efficiency, and destroys civic-mindedness." The need to promote worthy leisure required high schools to invent a new administrative position, the director of preparation for leisure.[27]

In the face of this assault, the defense mounted by academic school people was surprisingly quiet. The historian Edward A. Krug was especially struck by how loath professional educators were to admit that knowing a subject could be in itself a good reason to study it. "Relatively few have dared to say that the purpose of studying history is to learn history." Eventually Krug became exasperated by how the mere mention of ideas and books could doom those who espoused them. Why should books, he wondered, give "so much offense to the community of modern pedagogy? . . . It has almost been taken for granted that books are in some way offensive. . . . The answer may well be the degree to which books symbolize academic education and become offensive to those with the anti-academic point of view." Krug concluded that the "reading of books, great or otherwise, for their intrinsic and internal values could win neither acceptance nor toleration" in American high schools.[28]

The relative silence of the defenders of the academic tradition owed much to the fact that the continuing expansion of high school enrollments offered a kind of protection to most academic subjects. Enrollments grew (excepting Greek and German) even if the percentages of students taking academic subjects declined. For example, the fraction of Latin students in the 1920s dropped from 28 percent to 22 percent, but that 22 percent was about 637,000 students—more than total high school enrollment in 1900. The expansion of vocational education in fields such as business education, industrial arts, agriculture, and home economics also conveyed a new elite status on academic subjects now more firmly identified than ever with the prestigious function of college preparation. And, as Eliot had hoped, the academic subjects organized as departments. These proved among the most politically durable features of high school structure.[29]

By the 1930s, doubts grew even among social efficiency proponents that vocational education for skilled occupations was appropriate for many youth. The intelligence testing movement brought new attention to individual and group differences in mental capacity. These differences seemed great. Professional educators sought a less vocationally oriented and more general program for students deemed unable to profit from either traditional academics or traditional vocational education. One obstacle to diffusing the liberal arts to a large population was educators' belief that most students could not handle these subjects. Consequently the *Cardinal Principles'* emphasis on life-needs and life-tasks remained but was brought closer to the day-to-day concerns of adolescents. The general curriculum increasingly stressed short-term concerns such as personal health, relationships, and dating. Broadly named "life adjustment education," the movement in the 1940s and early 1950s represented the nadir of respect for high school academic values in the twentieth century.[30]

All this was a sad outcome for those with a larger vision of the potential contribution of high schools to liberal education. During the debates that led to the 1944 National Education Association report *Education for ALL American Youth*, New York's frustrated state school chief, George Stoddard, complained about the growing curricular emphasis on social relationships, personal contacts, work, travel, and "being nice." These things, he said, could easily be learned outside school. But nobody would ever "teach anybody any algebra whatsoever outside of school." High schools should teach important things that most students would never have an opportunity to learn elsewhere.

Stoddard went on to call special attention to initiatives outside the high school—magazines, comics, radio, and movies—that increasingly competed with high schools for students' attention. He thought the special function of high school was to stand apart from and above the outside world. High school stood for the "glory of the human mind." The purveyors of a rapidly growing youth culture stood for "surface learning" instead of any "sense of theory or philosophy." High schools needed to guard against such external anti-intellectual influences. Almost poignantly, he proclaimed high school as society's "last little citadel" where intellectual values could be celebrated and cultivated.[31]

Near the end of the twentieth century the traditional antiacademic bias of vocational educators was softened by the reality that the emerging national economy required capacities that never occurred to the drafters of the *Cardinal Principles*. The idea of social efficiency in vocational education was retained. Curriculum emerged from an analysis of tasks that adult workers performed. But these tasks were viewed as more intellectually complex than before. The "new basic skills" proposed by Richard J. Murnane and Frank Levy, for example, are designed to help high school graduates enter the middle class. If high schools taught the new basic skills well, and if incentives existed for potential employers to assess their presence, vocational education might be transformed.

Murnane and Levy's new basic skills overlap but are not the same as the "Five New Basics" recommended in *A Nation at Risk* for all high school students. The latter recall the Committee of Ten in emphasizing the years students should spend in mainline academic subjects: English (four years), math (three years), science (three years), social studies (three years), and computer science (one-half year). Justifications for these are brief. Their value is assumed. And they are intended for all students, not just the college-bound. In contrast, Murnane and Levy begin, as did the social efficiency educators, with a kind of activity analysis of workplace skills needed by ambitious high school graduates. These skills were derived from observations of what new economy workers did. Murnane and Levy propose six new basic skills: minimal ninth-grade reading ability; minimal ninth-grade math ability; ability to "solve semi-structured problems where hypotheses must be formed and tested"; ability to work in groups with persons of various backgrounds; ability to communicate effectively both orally and in writing; and ability to use computers to do simple tasks such as word processing.

It is not difficult to imagine how someone such as Eliot, wishing high schools to help students discover vocational bents and not channel them prematurely into particular destinations, might be uneasy about a notion of basics that never mentions science or history or literature. Or how someone such as Stoddard might see in the emphasis on interpersonal skills the reemergence of life adjustment. But, taken as a whole, these new basic skills represent a remarkable broadening of what the *Cardinal Principles* perfunctorily described as command of fundamental processes. Now these cognitive skills constitute most of initial vocational education. One might hope that Murnane and Levy someday will utilize their activity analysis methodology to illuminate preparation for nonvocational adult roles, such as that of citizen, private intellectual, culture consumer, and the like.[32]

Liberal Culture and Intellectual Interests

Respect for the educational value of all academic subjects and faith in students' ability to make wise choices made Charles W. Eliot a prime target for social efficiency school reformers. Many in higher education, ironically, saw in those same qualities antiacademic vocationalism, utilitarianism, and narrow specialization. From the perspective of contending factions within high schools, the historian Herbert Kliebard considered Eliot a giant in the academic humanistic tradition. From the perspective of contending factions within higher education, the historian Laurence R. Veysey considered Eliot differently. Among three vital purposes of the modern university—research, utility, and liberal culture—Veysey placed Eliot firmly in the utilitarian camp. He was conspicuously not among the higher education giants who developed or advocated any coherent idea of the liberal arts.[33]

Veysey labeled the broad reaction against Eliot a celebration of "liberal culture." Liberal culture was not synonymous with liberal education. The latter was a more general notion that could and did embrace a variety of ideas. Liberal culture emphasized objectives perceived as goods in themselves and harder to label as either general capacities or particular knowledge. Characteristic goals were breadth of view, taste, and concern for heritage, for aesthetics, for the humanities, for standards, and for the importance of coherence and community in education.

Liberal culture was often associated with well-bred young people. Veysey suggested it required "a certain polish and elegance of style." The cultured gentleman was a gentleman of leisure. The vocationally oriented Eliot generally opposed all this. For him a gentleman was primarily a "worker, an organizer, and a disinterested laborer in the service of others." The heart of a college curriculum concerned with liberal culture, in contrast, was "civilization," which meant Western civilization: "a chain of artists and thinkers inhabiting a small part of the globe for approximately twenty-five hundred years." This judgment of what knowledge was of most worth was also in direct opposition to Eliot's.[34]

In one sense this internal reaction against the modern university further diminished the common cause Eliot hoped to make between higher education and the schools. The core of liberal culture was plainly exclusionary and aristocratic. The historian Frederick Rudolph, no enemy of the liberal arts, had few kind words for liberal culture. He said, "Art galleries, afternoon tea, and a self-proclaimed superiority to the masses and the bourgeoisie were components of culture's style, a style that, in some of its practitioners, came dangerously close to being effete. It did not intend to be democratic, for it clearly was an open and honest assertion of superiority."

These ideas had little influence on high schools, except to reinforce the notion that the liberal arts were the exclusive possession of the privileged classes and no friend of democracy. Instead of standing for the cultivation of interests of mind, the liberal arts seemed to stand for the cultivation of snobbery. Certainly when the historian Lawrence A. Cremin famously argued that "the case for popular education rests on the proposition that culture can be democratized without being vulgarized," he did not have the liberal culture movement in mind. Even within higher education, liberal culture never dominated. Rudolph concluded, "The vast majority of American college and university undergraduates by 1910 were enrolled in courses of study shaped by utilitarian and vocational values."[35]

But liberal culture had a saving grace. Its studied aversion to vocationalism, specialization, and utility offered a potentially fresh approach to the liberal arts tradition that was not inherently antidemocratic. It was mainly through liberal culture that intellectual values were gradually inserted into a revitalized twentieth-century postsecondary liberal arts tradition. This process happened, generally speaking, in two ways. First, emphasizing intellectual values raised academic standards. A common belief of liberal culture advocates, such as Eliot's Harvard successor, A. Lawrence Lowell, was that a wide variety of electives had led to lowered scholarship, easy courses, and a reduction of demanding academic work.

Second, and more important, the insertion of intellectual values into liberal culture contained an idea that went beyond higher academic standards. This was the conviction that, if liberal education were to be serious about intellectual matters, it had somehow to be visible and enduring in people's lives after college. That is, visible not only as personal style or gentlemanly taste, but also as active intellectual pursuit. Lowell profoundly cared how the experience of college, which he saw wasted on so many lazy rich boys, could be made to carry over into adult life. College had to affect later behavior. "The ordinary student is too apt to treat courses as Cook's tourists do the starred pictures in foreign galleries, as experiences to be checked off and forgotten," said Lowell. He became a pedagogical reformer equal to Eliot in producing imaginative educational inventions, although he made no attempt to connect his Harvard work with secondary education. Lowell is probably best known for replacing free electives with the major-minor scheme known as concentration and distribution. But the main thrust of his reforms was to press students to demonstrate that they could use their learning beyond passing course exams. Examples include culminating experiences such as honors theses and comprehensive or general examinations. The pedagogical implications were increased writing, oral demonstrations, independent scholarly work, and integration of materials from disparate sources. Above all, the intent was to encourage students to apply course knowledge to new situations. Lowell is not widely or admiringly remembered as a reformer who sought to integrate intellectual values with liberal culture. His aristocratic manner and narrow social prejudices have fixed his reputation as an antidemocratic conservative. But his educational policies, more than Eliot's, carried forward the theme Eliot had enunciated in 1899.[36]

By the early twentieth century, more and more higher education leaders connected intellect with enduring life activity. They reacted against the passive conception of liberal culture as a mere possession or status symbol. They opposed, as Veysey nicely put it, the notion that "ideas, particularly old ones, somehow seemed more attractive than did the underlying notion of aggressive, far-ranging intellect." More representative of this new look than the aristocratic Lowell was a young philosophy professor at Brown University, Alexander Meiklejohn. In 1908 Meiklejohn directly linked intellectual values with enduring intellectual activities. In so doing he helped expand liberal culture beyond the genteel tradition. For Meiklejohn, education should "broaden and deepen the insight into life itself, to open up the riches of human experience, of literature, of nature, of art, of religion, of philosophy, of human relations, social, economic, political, to arouse an understanding and appreciation of these, so that life may be fuller and richer in content." "In a word," he summarized, "the primary function of the American college is the arousing of interests."[37]

Meiklejohn later directly attacked the question of arousing intellectual interests, as president of Amherst College and of the Experimental College at the University of Wisconsin. The concerns he expressed were the beginnings of a broader effort to make enduring intellectual interests a priority within higher education. This effort was known as "general education" and flourished from the twenties through the fifties. The intention of general education—not to be confused with the "general" high school curriculum track—was to arouse genuine interest in what educated persons should share in common in a century in which knowledge was constantly proliferating. Given diminishing consensus about what intellectual knowledge was of most worth, a reality Eliot had anticipated and exploited, ideas about which intellectual enthusiasms educated people should share were largely a matter of what consensus might be achieved in individual colleges.

If the elective idea legitimized curriculum variety and broad student choice, the general education idea mandated close faculty cooperation, creative curriculum development, and serious attention to pedagogy. General education never came close to eclipsing higher education's relentless embrace of specialization and electives. General education, to Rudolph, was only a "freakish exception" to the broader trends. It is interesting today because it demonstrates what individuals and institutions committed to arousing intellectual interests in college developed.[38]

General education in practice typically meant two different initiatives. The first created new institutions that celebrated intellectual interests of varying sorts by providing an intense, common experience (for example, Black Mountain College, the undergraduate college of the University of Chicago, Bennington College, St. John's College). In general, the more cohesive, enveloping, and idiosyncratic an institution's version of general education, the smaller the student market and the greater the problem of financial survival. They were magnets mainly for students already attracted by their focus. They reinforced existing interests more than they aroused new ones.

The second type of general education occurred in courses or groups of so-called core courses. Daniel Bell hoped general education courses would serve to "free a student from provincialism and to lead him to self-discovery through an awareness of tradition, to confront him with the persistent issues of morals and politics, and to give him an understanding of the interconnectedness of knowledge." Columbia's "Literature Humanities" and "Contemporary Civilization" courses are perhaps the best-known examples. Student surveys suggested, Bell reported, that these courses played a "transforming role" in many lives. They were often "a 'conversion experience,' a shock of ideas that gave them a new appreciation of the dimensions of thought and feeling—a conversion, so to speak, to culture."[39]

What explains how these and similar courses could "provoke interest and excite the imagination"? One factor is that they needed not only to be special but also to be perceived as special. It helped if they acquired legendary or mythic status in the minds of students. Another factor is that serious intellectual content seemed a necessary condition to arouse serious intellectual interest. A third theme is that the chief breeding ground for ideas and course materials, pedagogy, and objectives was the work course staffs did together. The existence of a staff made possible ongoing professional conversation and debate about a course's substance. Regular staff meetings were crucial to maintain self-criticism and an intellectual edge. Bell believed that the Columbia core staff created "a small intellectual college within the college itself."[40]

General education as a movement was in full decline by the 1960s. The attractions of individual choice and of academic specialization were greater than the forces favoring carefully planned introductions to mankind's intellectual heritage. It is not that enduring interests were regarded as unimportant in the academy. Instead, intellectual interests were regarded as less able to catch the attention of college youth than courses that were directly vocational, pre-professional, or closely connected with popular culture or current social issues. Bell's deeply pessimistic end to his 1966 *The Reforming of General Education* presciently anticipated the final coup de grâce administered to general education by the cultural and intellectual revolution of the 1960s and 1970s. The authority claimed by some ideas, fields, and texts as essential grounding from which serious intellectual interests emerged was challenged as illegitimate, racist, sexist, classist, or all of the above. Between 1970 and 2000 the percentage of bachelor's degree majors in the liberal arts dropped from about 45 percent to about 40 percent.[41]

In light of the brief heyday and narrow institutional base of the general education movement in colleges, little of it not surprisingly affected schools. Few of its leaders, with the notable exception of Chicago's Robert M. Hutchins, articulated its ideals to a broader public or cared much about schools. The notion of interests penetrated school discourse not because of general education (or the different perspective of Eliot) but because of the philosopher John Dewey.

But Dewey's focus was always on how to build upon and use existing interests of young children as a means to their growth. He had less to say about creating interests, especially those that were specifically intellectual. And much of his work, and most of his accessible examples, came from children below high school age. Even the most upscale progressive high schools, which often seemed more seriously concerned with arousing enduring interests than more traditional academic high schools, rarely gave intellectual interests primary attention. The headmaster of John Burroughs School, author of the history of the famous eight-year study of progressive high schools and college performance in the 1930s, asserted that the academic high school curriculum was out of touch with the "real concerns" of youth. This was a reasonable point to make in the 1930s. But then he went on to describe those real concerns in terms that meshed poorly with the objectives of general education or any education concerned with enduring intellectual interests. He said, "Young people wanted to get ready to earn a living, to understand themselves, to learn how to get on with others, to become responsible members of the adult community, to find meaning in living."[42]

Since the 1950s little has changed concerning higher education's inability to suggest to schools imaginative models that emphasize enduring intellectual interests as a crucial part of liberal education. One of the few projects in which a group of schools and colleges jointly examined how students perceived the liberal arts education they were receiving led to depressing conclusions. The "greatest single failure" of six participating elite schools and colleges, the authors concluded, was providing no sense of what a liberal education was. Students passed through "unaware and unawakened." They were not aroused intellectually, and many did not "care about their education" at all.

When these conversations took place in 1952, the issue of liberal education was at least discussable by high schools and colleges. It was discussed because it was considered problematic by the participants. At stake was lack of coordination between curriculum in the last two years of high school and the first two years of college, the fact that students often repeated what they had studied earlier, and a sense of educational purposelessness in those years. The conversations contributed significantly to the creation of the Advanced Placement program, which addressed important issues of standards and overlap but neglected issues such as curriculum coherence and education's enduring effects. Such intellectual issues seem even further removed from the priorities of contemporary school reform than they were in 1952.[43]

Perhaps schools, colleges, and broker institutions such as the College Board should revisit the older college idea of general education. General education was perhaps the last moment when coherent conceptions of the liberal arts were imagined and tried out. Some lessons from that movement bear close examination. For one thing, total institutional commitment to specific purposeful ideals did occur in some places and were a powerful influence on members of those institutions. But these places failed to attract many more than the already committed few. A second, more potent lesson—Columbia is perhaps its best example—was the commitment of groups of teachers to work together on courses that stimulated them as much as they subsequently stimulated students. The collegial stimulation of staffed courses, the time commitment given to debates within staffs, the effects of teachers on each other through dialogue about practical teaching, all seem to have worked together to produce successful general education courses. Perhaps an analogous reconstruction can be imagined of the work lives of high school teachers. Perhaps, to paraphrase Daniel Bell, teachers can be envisioned creating small "intellectual schools" for themselves within larger high schools. By combining enduring passion for intellectual interests with contemporary concern for collegial process, a new era of cultural infiltration might begin.[44]

Yet the liberal arts in higher education have been in crisis during the past four decades. The colleges were previously assumed to be the custodians of the liberal arts tradition. But, as evidenced by the intellectual disarray reported by Alvin Kernan, Robert Orrill, and many others, they have been unwilling and unable to carry out that role. As a model for high school, higher education today seems little more than a vaster, more specialized, and more contentious version of high school—the shopping mall college or university. This situation places a large and ironic burden on high schools. They may become, by default, the source of whatever liberal education Americans will receive—not vocationally driven, not particularly specialized, not wholly elective, and concerned with immediate academic achievement as well as with enduring habits and interests of mind.

Why Care about Enduring Intellectual Interests?

The most practical reason to care about enduring intellectual interests is that persuading students that learning can be interesting and pleasurable—

beyond the undoubted satisfaction that comes from passing tests—adds an enormously powerful set of incentives to those available to educators in their quest to motivate children. Boosting incentives of all sorts is a crucial means to boost achievement. Economic incentives such as teaching children the dollar benefits of increased educational attainment are important. So are the incentives inherent in government-mandated achievement as enforced by high-stakes testing. But these incentives do not seem sufficient. Students should also learn that academic subjects provide a partial entry not only to the business of making a living, but also to the business of making an informed and examined life. Academics are not something to be endured because economic mobility is a happy reward after attending boring classes and passing boring tests. Academics are to be engaged in because they lead to enduring habits of mind, which give meaning and pleasure to life.[45]

A second reason to care is that mobilizing positive incentives to engage in the liberal arts has become increasingly difficult. Weakly valued though they are in both school and society, major pressures exist to weaken them further. Activities unquestionably more immediately interesting and pleasurable than academic study are within the reach of more adolescents than ever before. High schools no longer are the only major social institution besides the family and church committed to the deliberate and conscious education of adolescents. In the second half of the twentieth century, organized and professionalized for-profit purveyors of youth culture joined school, family, and church as deliberate educators. The youth culture industry now directly competes with schools for the time and attention of students. But the products, values, and habits being sold are very different.

The educative function of institutions besides schools was the central theme of Lawrence Cremin's monumental history of American education. One of Cremin's most trenchant criticisms of John Dewey was Dewey's excessive faith that schools were the only educative agency worth serious attention. Dewey never understood that the youth culture industry could educate teenagers—shape enduring tastes and habits—often more effectively than schools. Youth culture celebrates the passive consumption of immediate pleasure, which is easy and wonderful, to sell products and make money. In contrast, education emphasizes the long-range benefits of hard work, deferred gratification, and mental exertion.[46]

In 1982 the first market research company was founded exclusively devoted to adolescents, Teenage Research Unlimited (TRU). A youth culture and an adolescent society existed long before 1982, but the success of

TRU was built around the fact that teenagers had developed both enormous consumer appetites and the economic means to satisfy them at unprecedented levels. According to TRU's president, teens were "a consumer segment too powerful and a marketing opportunity too profitable to ignore. . . . In the last decade the collective knowledge about teens and the understanding of how to reach them have grown enormously, allowing more companies to create relevant and compelling marketing communications." TRU data indicate that the average teen consumer spent $104 per week in 2001. Using sophisticated polling and focus group data provided to paying corporate subscribers, TRU reported that entertainment, fun, and social activity dominate teen spending and all aspects of their lives. In 1998 very high percentages of teens spent almost forty-six hours a week listening to music, watching TV, and hanging out with friends. Far smaller percentages spent far fewer weekly hours on studying (3.3 hours) and reading books for pleasure (3.8 hours).

Director Steven Spielberg, a captain of the youth culture industry, has admitted the irony of his success on educational values ranging from length of attention span to delayed gratification. Father of the children's blockbuster movie, Spielberg in 2002 noted that a new film of his was atypically "challenging" and hence required viewers "to pay attention to it, listen to what people say, . . . pay attention to the story." Spielberg admitted this was a tough demand to make on young audiences in the twenty-first century. He felt that his quarter-century-old hit *Jaws* would not "do as well today as it did in 1975 because people would not wait so long to see the shark. Or they'd say, there's too much time between the first attack and the second attack. . . . We have an audience now that isn't patient with us." With a smile and a shrug he concluded, "They've been taught, by people like me, to be impatient with people like me."[47]

Teens regard school as the "ultimate social environment." But when asked in 1996 to list three favorite activities about school, only 12 percent mentioned teachers and only 10 percent classes. Being with friends "is by far teens' favorite thing about school." Comparisons over the past decade suggest that teens have become more negative about their teachers and less likely to rate them among top role models. Media advertisers are cautioned to avoid portrayals of "the dark side of school," such as classes, unless presented with humor. Otherwise adolescents become alienated from the message. In the competition to shape teen values and behavior, the youth culture industry has an increasing advantage over high school, especially the dark side of high school concerned with education. High schools tend to ignore or repress this situation. The market research from TRU, for example, is available in the reference library of the Harvard Business School, but it is not available anywhere in the library of the Harvard Graduate School of Education.[48]

If high schools wish to fight back against passive and mindless consumption, they must commit themselves to value the life of the mind in daily life outside school as much as they value academic achievement within school. A commitment to academic achievement, while necessary, is insufficient. Students who read, write, and think only to pass a test are unlikely to read, write, or think after the test is over. Schools must aim to integrate achievement with lasting serious interests. They must explicitly value, model, and promote the rewards of lifelong engagement with the liberal arts. When students are in close contact with teachers, classes, and institutional climates that strongly value the enduring uses of the liberal arts, the chances that they themselves will value them increase.

Comment by Jeffrey Mirel

In a famous passage in *The Souls of Black Folk*, W. E. B. DuBois declares, "I sit with Shakespeare and he winces not. Across the color line I move arm in arm with Balzac and Dumas, where smiling men and welcoming women glide in gilded halls."[49] The passage envisions an educational paradise, where access to the best of Western knowledge and culture is open to all regardless of race, color, or creed. But DuBois did not believe that access alone was enough. He saw the primary goal of education as encouraging young people to embrace "ideals, broad, pure, and inspiring ends of living, not sordid money getting, not apples of gold."[50]

Arthur G. Powell envisions education in a similar way. He longs for high schools that celebrate the liberal arts and the intellectual values embodied in them. It is impossible to quarrel with that goal. Who in education would not be thrilled at the prospect of large and increasing numbers of young Americans reading and enjoying great literature, seriously debating vital issues in history and philosophy, or understanding and considering the consequences of new discoveries in the sciences? Who would not want young people to develop a love of the liberal arts so deep and abiding that it would sustain and challenge them throughout their lives?

Despite this worthy goal, Powell's essay troubles me in several ways. His breezy overview of the history of the American public high schools misses or misconstrues how and why high schools have largely abandoned their mission of providing access to the liberal arts. Consequently, he underestimates how hard it is to challenge the anti-intellectual character of the high schools, and he overestimates the degree to which the current academically focused reforms have succeeded in reshaping the institution. Finally, Powell fails to consider the enormous challenge the country faces in finding and preparing the kind of teachers he believes could inspire students to embrace the liberal arts and make high schools avenues to the life of the mind.

Powell devotes a considerable amount of his essay to a reevaluation of the work of Charles W. Eliot, the president of Harvard University who chaired the Committee of Ten in 1893. Eliot has become an important figure in the current debate about what the nature of high school curricula should be. Powell is correct that a growing number of current historians view Eliot and members of the committee as important but unappreciated educational leaders who advocated both equity and excellence. Specifically, these historians applaud the conclusion of the Committee of Ten report that urged all high school students to follow a rigorous liberal arts curriculum regardless of their backgrounds or their future educational or vocational plans.

Powell does not directly challenge this view of Eliot. Instead he argues that current problems with the American high schools arose in part because Eliot and the committee failed to adequately defend the cause of liberal arts education in three crucial ways. First, he claims that Eliot and the committee believed only a small number of young people could benefit from a strong liberal arts education. Second, neither Eliot nor the committee provided a strong intellectual argument to counter progressive educators' attacks against the liberal arts in favor of social efficiency, particularly vocational education. Third, neither Eliot nor the committee explicitly urged high schools to promote the life of the mind as opposed to the mere mastery of academic subject matter. Each of these criticisms is only partially accurate, and their inaccuracy contributes to the broader problems I have with Powell's essay.

In 1893, when Eliot and the other members of the committee issued their report, none of them believed that the high school would become a mass institution. How could they? At the time, despite the rapid growth of the institution, only about 6 or 7 percent of American fourteen- to seventeen-year-olds were enrolled in high schools. Nevertheless, the fact that the committee believed high schools would serve only a small proportion of American youth led critics at the time, and others today, to label it as simply a group of undemocratic elitists. As one recent critic writes, "Rather than envisioning secondary education for all youth as the progressives later would do, the Committee of Ten viewed the high school as an elite, albeit not an exclusively college-prep, institution."[51]

Powell does not go that far but he does claim that Eliot "completely miscalculated" how popular the high school would become. Consequently, Powell argues that Eliot "had no good answer" for whether the liberal arts curriculum promoted by the committee was right for high schools serving a large and growing proportion of American youth. But both the explicit charge of elitism and the criticism that Eliot and the committee lacked foresight seriously miss the point. To dismiss the report of the Committee of Ten for failing to imagine the high school as a mass institution is akin to rejecting the Declaration of Independence for failing to foresee the civil rights movement. In both cases the documents provide ideals that transcended and ultimately corrected flaws in the originals.[52]

Equally as important is that in the ensuing decades Eliot appears to have abandoned the idea that only a small proportion of American youth deserved the kind of education advocated by the Committee of Ten. Other than his lapse in 1908 in supporting trade schools for some students, in the years following the release of the report, Eliot continued to defend the idea that all high school students should follow the curriculum guidelines laid out by the committee. He maintained this position even as high school enrollments grew. In 1905, for example, in response to criticism of the Committee of Ten by G. Stanley Hall, Eliot explicitly rejected Hall's charge of elitism by quoting the passage from the Committee of Ten report that declared:

> the secondary schools of the United States, taken as a whole, do not exist for the purpose of preparing boys and girls for colleges. Only an insignificant percentage of the graduates of these schools go to colleges and scientific schools. . . . A secondary-school program intended for national use must therefore be made for those children whose education is not to be pursued beyond the secondary school.[53]

The ellipses before the last line in that quote are crucial. The main sentence from the original report that Eliot left out reads as follows: "Their main function is to prepare for the duties of life that small proportion of all children in the country—a proportion small in number, but very important to the welfare of the nation—who show themselves able to profit by an education prolonged to the eighteenth year, and whose parents are able to support them while they remain so long at school."[54] In leaving out that sentence, Eliot essentially was revising the committee's report to reflect the changing times, specifically revising it, one might assume, to acknowledge the fact that the percentage of fourteen- to seventeen-year-olds in high school had doubled between 1893 and 1905. Put simply, as high school enrollments grew well beyond what the committee had envisioned, Eliot still endorsed the approach to high school curriculum espoused by the committee.

In 1921 Eliot returned to that proposition in what was probably his last major speech on education before his death. Reviewing the development of American education since the end of the Civil War, Eliot devoted over 40 percent of the talk to the work of the Committee of Ten. He reaffirmed his belief in the fundamental wisdom of the ideas advanced by the committee, particularly the assertion made in its report that "every subject which is taught at all in a secondary school should be taught in the same way and to the same extent to every pupil as long as he pursues it, no matter what the probable destination of the pupil may be, or at what point his education is to cease." After quoting that line, he added the following.

> This statement is still having a strong effect on discussions about the point at which determinations of the probable life career should be allowed to determine the school career. A democracy naturally desires to postpone as much as possible the parting of the ways.[55]

If, as Powell argues, Eliot was a keen observer of educational trends, one must assume he knew that as he spoke nearly a third of all fourteen- to seventeen-year-olds were in high school. That speech, given nearly three decades after he wrote the Committee of Ten report (and thirteen years after his talk on trade schools), provides strong evidence that Eliot was not the educational elitist that later generations of educationists claimed he was. Nor was he, as Powell contends, unsure about whether the Committee of Ten's curricular recommendations were appropriate for large numbers of American youth. He obviously still thought they were.

Even if Eliot supported a strong liberal arts education for large numbers of American youth, did he, as Powell argues, fail to adequately defend such education in the face of attacks by advocates of social efficiency and vocational education? This is a more difficult question in part because Powell seems to accept the conventional historical argument that social efficiency advocates succeeded in vocationalizing the high school in the first third of the twentieth century. Supporters of vocational education and proponents of *Cardinal Principles of Secondary Education* undoubtedly wanted to reshape high school along vocational lines. But as David Angus and I argue, in terms of student course taking, the vocational revolution failed. Specifically, throughout the twentieth century such highly touted vocational courses as home economics and shop never accounted for more than single digit percentages of student course taking. As late as 1930, the course-taking patterns of most high school students were closer to those of the Committee of Ten than those proposed by supporters of social efficiency.[56]

Powell is correct that proponents of progressive-style school reform routinely attacked the academic curriculum. But such attacks were motivated more by the broad disdain that progressive educators had for disciplinary knowledge than they were by the goals of social efficiency. In addition, Powell's suggestion that teaching the liberal arts declined in high schools because Eliot defended them using outmoded conceptions of faculty psychology misses how broad and unrelenting the progressive attack on discipline-based subject matter was. The progressive critique of American high schools rested less on psychological beliefs about learning and knowledge and more on the sociological argument that the traditional academic curriculum was elitist, irrelevant, and undemocratic. By about 1915, such denunciations had become routine among such progressive thinkers as William H. Kilpatrick, Harold Rugg, and, at times, even by John Dewey. For example, in their book *Schools of To-Morrow*, John Dewey and Evelyn Dewey described academic subjects as holdovers from an aristocratic past. These subjects, they declared, were designed "for people who did not earn their own livings, for people who wished to be accomplished, polished, and interesting socially, so the material was abstract, purposefully separated from the concrete and the useful." In the eyes of progressive leaders, traditional academic subjects were largely compilations of organized facts that were unrelated to the interests or lives of children.[57]

Typical of how such criticism got translated into recommendations about high school curricula is a 1934 article by an education professor from New York University who argued that

> high-school authorities placed a halo around certain subjects—which might not have been so reprehensible in itself—but they insisted upon a content in these subjects that in only a small way touched upon the lives these pupils were living and were destined to live. Only mention need be made of the mathematics, the

formal literature, the absurd emphasis on foreign language to convince any fair-minded observer of the total inadequacy of the offering from the point of view of the typical adolescent.[58]

These ideas eventually became the conventional wisdom, or more accurately the conventional folly, of large numbers of high school educators for most of the twentieth century.

How should Eliot or later defenders of the liberal arts have responded to attacks that so contemptuously dismissed disciplinary knowledge? These were not calls for reform or for debate about the different approaches to education, but instead were ungrounded assumptions that disciplinary learning was at best an absurd waste of time and at worst aristocratic in its pretensions. At the time when an increasingly powerful group of educational reformers was institutionalizing structures that severely restricted access to the liberal arts for most American secondary students, defending the life of the mind instead of fighting for equal access would seem frivolous at the very least.

The anti-intellectual character of the American high school owes far more to the belief that traditional academic subject matter was irrelevant and undemocratic than to specific attempts to lure students into vocational courses. By the mid-1930s most American educational leaders thoroughly rejected the educational ideal that all students should have access to the liberal arts. They even rejected the idea that most of the new students flooding the high school could benefit from vocational education. Instead these leaders began relegating most students to a second- or third-rate education that was long on relevance and short on disciplinary or vocational substance. Between 1940 and 1980, the amorphous general track, not the college prep or vocational track, became the defining program of American high schools.

Powell notes these developments but does not dwell on them, apparently viewing them as aberrations instead of the norm. Yet by the mid-1950s the rise of the general track had effectively foreclosed access to in-depth study of the liberal arts for most high school students. This restriction was based on the widely held belief that the way to educational democracy was assigning most students into tracks or programs that would keep them in school for longer periods of time while requiring less of them intellectually. Such curriculum differentiation became the organizing principle of American high schools, and according to educational leaders such as James B. Conant it was the key to equal educational opportunity (that is, everyone got to go to school, but each student followed a different regimen of courses).

Few educational leaders were more responsible for legitimizing curriculum differentiation than Conant. Even though Conant commissioned *General Education in a Free Society*, I find little support for Powell's assessment of him as a leader who sought to balance access to liberal knowledge for the supposedly mediocre many with providing better educational opportunities for the gifted and talented few. Conant's main interest was better education for the few, period. One of his most telling suggestions in *The American High School Today* was that guidance counselors must aggressively deter the "overambitious [sic] parent" of supposedly less capable children from trying to get these children into the college preparatory track. He justified this stand because if such children were placed in high track classes they would hold back the education of the talented.[59] If any Harvard president deserves the label of elitist insofar as his recommendations about K–12 education are concerned, it is James Conant, not Charles Eliot.

By the mid-1960s, curriculum differentiation had transformed American high schools, particularly those in urban areas, into vast warehouses for huge numbers of teenagers. In Michigan, for example, the percentage of student course taking in core liberal arts subjects (English, foreign languages, math, science, and social studies) fell from almost 73 percent in 1924–25 to about 57 percent in 1960–61, and the content of many of these courses was seriously diluted.[60] Offering growing numbers of relevant but vacuous electives and watered-down general education courses, these schools were institutions that students accurately recognized as places where socializing with friends was more important than what was taught in class.

This situation stemmed not just from the rise of an anti-intellectual youth culture. The trend was given additional impetus by the development of an anti-intellectual school culture. The 1960 Sam Cooke hit that begins "Don't know much about history, don't know much biology" ends with him wanting to become an "A student" so he could win his love's affection. Ironically, if he were an "A" student in this era in the general track of most urban high schools, he still probably would not know much about history or biology.

Throughout the 1950s and 1960s, exposés about the poor quality of high school education and the limited skills of large numbers of urban high school graduates had become both frequent and frequently ignored. In March 1965, for example, the *Detroit Free Press* reported that many Detroit public school graduates were showing up at antipoverty job training programs reading on average at a seventh-grade level. Some were almost illiterate. Instead of promoting greater equality, the differentiated educational system that leaders such as Conant espoused was increasing social class and racial stratification. Despite an angry denunciation of this educational double standard by the one black member of the school board, Detroit school leaders, arguably among the most liberal in the nation, took no action to change the situation.[61] Educational leaders in other major cities were equally as complacent, having accepted the assessment by experts such as Conant that the differentiated American high school was fundamentally sound.

Powell is correct that the civil rights movement and later the women's movement helped raise people's consciousness about the problems of educational inequality. But in terms of changes in policy and practice (particularly regarding high school course offerings and graduation requirements), real reform did not begin until the mid-1980s. This leads to my last problem with Powell's overview of the history of the high school. He seems to believe that the reform effort begun in the 1980s has been largely successful and that it is now time to turn to more important concerns such as nurturing the life of the mind.

Despite some impressive results, the reform campaign that envisions modern high school programs akin to those described by the Committee of Ten is still far from the norm. Moreover, the success of that reform effort is hardly assured. Many states and school districts have toughened graduation requirements. But such policies as requiring three years of mathematics for graduation instead of one or two can be—and are—easily sidestepped by allowing students to fulfill the requirement with a series of general math courses, not algebra, geometry, and trigonometry. In addition, state-mandated high school curriculum standards in core liberal arts subjects frequently are so broad and so vague that they provide little guidance to curriculum designers or teachers. Finally, many educational leaders often housed in schools and colleges of education continue to assert the progressive mantra that discipline-based curricula amount to little more than forcing students to pile up mountains of useless facts.

The primary problem facing American high schools today, as Eliot intuited more than a century ago, is providing students access to the knowledge, skills, and values contained in the liberal arts. That Eliot may have failed to proclaim a ringing defense of the life of the mind probably had more to do with his basic practicality than it did with the failure of vision that Powell implies. Without access to the liberal arts in the first place, students cannot discover the life of the mind. Improving access to the liberal arts for all American high school students must remain the top priority for educational reformers.

Like DuBois almost a century ago, Powell is right in asserting that access to the liberal arts is insufficient. Students might "sit with Shakespeare" long enough to score well on Advanced Placement tests but then roughly push the Bard aside in their pursuit of "apples of gold." Powell is also correct that the people who can inspire students to see the liberal arts as more than just a ticket to the Ivy League are great teachers, "adults who themselves have an interest of mind and have gained their respect."

But here again is a practical problem that Powell does not address. Large numbers of American high school teachers have neither a major nor even a minor in the core liberal arts subjects that they are teaching. Such teachers are unlikely to be the role models that Powell envisions. They will not be teachers who are deeply committed to the liberal arts and who "love and live their subjects." Many of these teachers barely know their subjects. Before anyone imagines, as Powell does, groups of inspiring teachers creating "intellectual schools" within schools, large numbers of teachers who know their subjects must find their way into classrooms.

It is well and good for Powell to recall the great goals that high schools must strive to reach. It is, however, counterproductive to focus on those goals without attending to the difficult and practical but necessary steps that must be taken to reach them.

Comment by Richard J. Murnane

A growing number of states require students to pass common English language and math exams to obtain a high school diploma. In the midst of frenzied efforts in many schools to prepare students to pass the exams, one can easily lose perspective on the roles that American high schools have played over the last 120 years. Arthur G. Powell's essay provides this important historical perspective. He recalls that high schools have changed from institutions that prepared a small percentage of adolescents for college to places where almost all Americans spend their teenage years. As high schools grew to serve a growing number of Americans from all walks of life, they were asked to serve many functions. In Powell's words, "the genius of the American high school has resided in its capacity to avoid internal conflict by absorbing all conceivable purposes without embracing too strenuously any single one." As Powell says, a Golden Age never existed in which the American high school concentrated on developing the academic skills of all the nation's teenagers.

From his perspective as a historian, Powell sees two aspects of the American high school as new. The first is the "sustained effort to foster academic achievement among the largest possible fraction of youth" in American history. While Powell does not emphasize this, the current focus on developing academic skills is in large part a response to dramatic changes in the American economy. These changes have drastically reduced the number of jobs in which workers can earn a decent living by carrying out routine tasks. They have also increased the skill requirements for jobs that pay a middle-class wage.

The second relatively new aspect of the high school scene is that changes in pop culture, many of which have been facilitated by new technology, have increased the number of nonacademic, enjoyable activities competing for the time of American teenagers. American high schools are being asked today to develop the academic skills of teenagers more than they ever have in the past and to do this at a time when it is more difficult than ever to harness the attention of their clientele. As Powell points out, one element of the current situation that is not new is that the burden of preparing students to live in a changing economy rests squarely on the nation's schools.

Powell believes that fostering academic achievement among all American youth is a goal worthy of public support. However, he asks whether the policy instruments states have embraced to pursue this goal—standards-based educational reforms—will elicit unequivocally constructive responses. To understand this concern, consider the four elements of standards-based educational reforms.

1. Content standards that specify what students should know and be able to do, and performance standards that describe how students should demonstrate their knowledge and skills and what levels of performance constitute meeting the standard

2. Assessments that measure the extent to which students meet performance standards

3. Instructional materials and professional development that provide teachers with the knowledge, skills, and materials needed to prepare all students to meet the performance standards

4. Incentives for educators to do the hard work required to prepare all students to meet the performance standards, and incentives for students to devote the time and energy needed to meet the performance standards

Standards-based reforms create incentives for educators to focus instruction on the skills that are measured on the exams. When the exams are of high quality and are well aligned with content standards, earning high scores on the exams may mean that students have acquired significant knowledge and skills. However, Powell points out that scores on exams taken as teenagers are not what matters. He provides a number of anecdotes illustrating that mastery of subject matter sufficient to do well on standardized tests is no assurance that students will develop sustained intellectual interests—an important goal for schooling in Powell's view and in mine. Powell is concerned that, because standards-based educational reforms cannot base rewards and penalties on what matters—the quality of lives students lead—and instead base them on scores on exams that students take as high school students, this might be a situation of "On the Folly of Rewarding A, While Hoping for B."[62]

In a creative research approach, Powell looks for evidence on the effects of standards-based reforms by examining changes over the last twenty years in the course catalog of a suburban high school. While the school still offers classes at several difficulty levels for core subjects at each grade level, the number of options is smaller in the 2002 catalog than in the earlier one. Even more important, students in lower-level classes in 2002 are expected to read more difficult material and to write more than was the case in 1982. This is good news. However, one cannot learn from the catalog what instruction looks like in the lower-level classes and whether it entices students to develop sustaining intellectual interests.

I wish that Powell could have compared the 1982 and 2002 catalogs for some urban schools serving primarily low-income children of color. Standards-based reforms are likely to have their greatest impact in these schools. In many states, including Massachusetts, more than half of the students in urban high schools today are in danger of leaving without diplomas because they did not succeed in passing the mandatory English language arts and mathematics exams. The response to this problem in many schools has been to focus instruction on the skills measured on the exams. This need not be a dysfunctional response if the mandatory assessments are well designed and if the teachers know how to help students develop the requisite skills and to do so in a way that the skills are worth learning. However, the professional development needed to improve instruction is the component of standards-based reforms that is lagging in most states.

Whether standards-based educational reform will improve the education provided to urban students is a topic of considerable dispute among civil rights advocates. For example, the civil rights lawyer William L. Taylor writes:

> Today, new forms of accountability and assessment are the best tools we have to ensure quality education for all children. When schools and districts are held accountable for the achievement of all students, the means are at hand to force them to improve the quality of schooling provided for previously neglected students. Standards and accountability expose the sham that passes for education in many heavily minority schools and provide measurements and pressure to prod schools to target resources where they are needed most.[63]

Other important voices advocating better education for low-income children see standards-based reforms differently. Debbie Meier, a pioneer in developing schools that have been remarkably effective in educating low-income students of color, writes:

> It will not help to develop young minds, contribute to a more robust democratic life, or aid the most vulnerable of our fellow citizens. By shifting the locus of authority to outside bodies, it undermines the capacity of schools to instruct by example in the qualities of mind that schools in a democracy should be fostering in kids—responsibility for one's own ideas, tolerance for the ideas of others, and a capacity to negotiate differences.[64]

Given that almost every state is engaged in standards-based reforms that are having major impacts on urban schools, one can only hope that Taylor's prognosis proves more correct than Meier's. This will only happen if high schools become places that, in Powell's words, "value, model, and promote the rewards of lifelong engagement with the liberal arts." Few urban high schools fit this description today. The success of standards-based reforms in improving the education of urban students depends on a rapid growth over the next decade in the number that do.

Notes

1. Thomas S. Snyder and Charlene M. Hoffman, *Digest of Education Statistics, 2001* (Washington: National Center for Education Statistics, March 2002), table 250.

2. This is a central theme in Arthur G. Powell, Eleanor Farrar, and David K. Cohen, *The Shopping Mall High School: Winners and Losers in the Educational Marketplace* (Houghton Mifflin, 1985).

3. Deborah Meier, *The Power of Their Ideas: Lessons for America from a Small School in Harlem* (Beacon Press, 1995), pp. 161–73; and Richard Hofstadter, *Anti-Intellectualism in American Life* (Vintage Books, 1962), pp. 299–309. See also Daniel J. Boorstin, *The Americans: The Democratic Experience* (Vintage Books, 1974), pp. 449–522.

4. Karen D. Arnold, *Lives of Promise: What Becomes of High School Valedictorians* (Jossey-Bass, 1995), pp. 35, 62–64.

5. These examples are from academically oriented private schools observed by the author in 1992.

6. Thomas S. Snyder and Charlene M. Hoffman, *Digest of Education Statistics, 2000*, 2001–034 (Washington: National Center for Education Statistics, March 2001), tables 38 and 57.

7. Harvard Committee on the Objectives of a General Education in a Free Society, *General Education in a Free Society* (Harvard University Press, 1945), p. ix; and James Bryant Conant, *The American High School Today* (McGraw-Hill, 1959).

8. National Commission on Excellence in Education, *A Nation at Risk: The Imperative for Educational Reform* (Government Printing Office, 1983); Ernest L. Boyer, *High School: A Report on Secondary Education in America* (Harper and Row, 1983); John I. Goodlad, *A Place Called School: Prospects for the Future* (McGraw-Hill, 1984); and Theodore R. Sizer, *Horace's Compromise. The Dilemma of the American High School* (Houghton Mifflin, 1984).

9. Ellen Condliffe Lagemann, *An Elusive Science*: *The Troubling History of Education Research* (University of Chicago Press, 2000), p. 161.

10. Snyder and Hoffman, *Digest of Education Statistics, 2000*, tables 110, 117, 122, 128, 138, 141, 404, 405.

11. The catalogs reviewed were from some of the schools participating in field research for Powell, Farrar, and Cohen, *The Shopping Mall High School*.

12. An unusually thorough overview of the issues facing American high schools ran in six issues of *Education Week* (vol. 20) between April 11 and May 16, 2001. Almost every conceivable high school issue was discussed, but no mention was made of intellectual engagement with the curriculum or enthusiasm about what was being studied. Instead, much attention was given to the "ambitious academic agenda" of high schools and the problems associated with that agenda.

13. Arthur G. Powell, "Interests of Mind: Mapping the Territory," Brown University, Annenberg Institute for School Reform, 1997. The project reviewed several disparate research literatures, including vocational interests and guidance, adult reading, the psychology of motivation and interests, the development of gifted and talented youth, long-term effects of higher education, the idea of building upon rather than creating interests, and the general education movement in higher education. The essential question was, "What do these very different fields tell us about how enduring serious interests are acquired and emerge, and how can they be created and nurtured?"

One exception to the general neglect of long-term educational outcomes is research on higher education effects. Higher education is rarely held accountable for student academic achievement or any short-term effects. Assessment of large groups of college students hardly exists. Perhaps because of this striking difference from high school practice, a rich research tradition exists within higher education concerning long-term educational effects. But this tradition is invisible to school people. "Higher education" as a research field is hardly ever included within "education research," which is presumed to refer exclusively to the elementary-secondary sector. For example, Ellen Lagemann's *An Elusive Science: The Troubling History of Education Research* is exclusively about school research. The vast materials on higher education effects can be sampled in two classic and complementary literature reviews. See Ernest T. Pascarella and Patrick T. Terenzini, *How College Affects Students: Findings and Insights from Twenty Years of Research* (Jossey-Bass, 1991); and Kenneth A. Feldman and Theodore M. Newcomb, *The Impact of College on Students* (New Brunswick, N.J.: Transaction Publishers, 1994, originally published 1969). The most relevant longitudinal studies, of 320 members of the Stanford University class of 1981, are Herant A. Katchadourian and John Boli, *Careerism and Intellectualism among College Students* (Jossey-Bass, 1985); and Herant Katchadourian and John Boli, *Cream of the Crop: The Impact of Elite Education in the Decade after College* (Basic Books, 1994). I am grateful to the Annenberg Institute for its generous support of my work on enduring interests and effects.

14. Louis Menand, "The Demise of Disciplinary Authority," in Alvin Kernan, ed., *What's Happened to the Humanities?* (Princeton University Press, 1997), p. 202; and Theodore R. Sizer, *Secondary Schools at the Turn of the Century* (Yale University Press, 1964), p. 129. For an argument that the liberal arts did not simply descend from colleges to schools but often existed side by side in both institutions, see Jurgen Herbst, *The Once and Future School: Three Hundred and Fifty Years of American Secondary Education* (Routledge, 1996). To make his point, Herbst relies heavily on a few unusually elite nineteenth-century public high schools. See, in particular, David F. Labaree, *The Making of an American High School: The Credentials Market and the Central High School of Philadelphia, 1838–1939* (Yale University Press, 1988).

15. Charles W. Eliot, "Inaugural Address as President of Harvard College, October 19, 1869," in *Educational Reform* (New York: Century Company, 1898), pp. 11–12; and Hugh Hawkins, *Between Harvard and America: The Educational Leadership of Charles W. Eliot* (Oxford University Press, 1972), p. 91.

16. Hawkins, *Between Harvard and America*, p. 236.

17. Charles W. Eliot, "Recent Changes in Secondary Education," in Edward A. Krug, ed., *Charles W. Eliot and Popular Education* (New York: Teachers College, 1961), pp. 117–38.

18. Snyder and Hoffman, *Digest of Education Statistics, 2000*, tables 38 and 57.

19. Charles W. Eliot, "Industrial Education as an Essential Factor in Our National Prosperity," *NSPIE Bulletin*, no. 5 (1908), pp. 11–13. This section draws heavily on Hawkins, *Between Harvard and America*, pp. 246–51; and Arthur G. Wirth, *Education in the Technological Society: The Vocational-Liberal Studies Controversy in the Early Twentieth Century* (Scranton, Pa.: Intext Educational Publishers, 1972), pp. 98–102.

20. Sizer, *Secondary Schools at the Turn of the Century*, p. 142.

21. Hawkins, *Between Harvard and America*, pp. 85–91.

22. Lagemann, *An Elusive Science*, pp. 58–59; and Diane Ravitch, *Left Back: A Century of Failed School Reform* (Simon and Schuster, 2000), pp. 61–69.

23. Sizer, *Secondary Schools at the Turn of the Century*, pp. 106–07, 116; and Hawkins, *Between Harvard and America*, p. 257.

24. Eliot, "Recent Changes in Secondary Education," pp. 122–23; and Hawkins, *Between Harvard and America*, p. 237.

25. Powell, Farrar, and Cohen, *The Shopping Mall High School*, p. 241; Ravitch, *Left Back*, p. 43; Herbert M. Kliebard, *The Struggle for the American Curriculum 1893–1958*, 2d ed. (Routledge, 1995), p. 14; and David L. Angus and Jeffrey E. Mirel, *The Failed Promise of the American High School 1890-1995* (New York: Teachers College Press, 1999), p. 10.

26. Jerome S. Bruner, *The Process of Education* (Vintage Books, 1963, originally published 1960), pp. 1–7, 17–19, 33.

27. *Cardinal Principles of Secondary Education*, Bulletin 35 (Department of the Interior, Bureau of Education, 1918), pp. 10, 12–15, 20–22.

28. Edward A. Krug, *The Shaping of the American High School* (Harper and Row, 1964), pp. 314, 347–48, 353–61. See also Edward A. Krug, *The Shaping of the American High School: 1920–1941*, vol. 2 (University of Wisconsin Press, 1972), pp. 303–06.

29. Krug, *The Shaping of the American High School: 1920–1941*, pp. 24, 40, 55–56, 105. Until recently, the importance of high school departments as centers of faculty power and identity has been overlooked. Recent research sheds new light on departmental cultures, their differences across subjects, and their capacities for survival. See Milbrey W. McLaughlin and Joan E. Talbert, *Professional Communities and the Work of High School Teaching* (University of Chicago Press, 2001); Leslie Santee Siskin, *Realms of Knowledge: Academic Departments in Secondary Schools* (London: Falmer Press, 1994); and Leslie Santee Siskin and Judith Warren Little, eds., *The Subjects in Question: Departmental Organization and the High School* (New York: Teachers College Press, 1995).

30. Krug, *The Shaping of the American High School: 1920–1941*, pp. 108–17.

31. Robert Hampel, *The Last Little Citadel: American High Schools since 1940* (Houghton Mifflin, 1986), pp. 35–41.

32. Compare Richard J. Murnane and Frank Levy, *Teaching the New Basic Skills: Principles for Educating Children to Thrive in a Changing Economy* (Martin Kessler Books, Free Press, 1996), pp. 31–33, with National Commission on Excellence in Education, *A Nation at Risk*, pp. 24–26.

33. Kliebard, *The Struggle for the American Curriculum*, pp. 8–11; and Laurence R. Veysey, *The Emergence of the American University* (University of Chicago Press, 1965), pp. 86–98.

34. Much of this discussion is taken from Veysey, *The Emergence of the Modern University*, pp. 184–96, 205, 248; Hawkins, *Between Harvard and America*, p. 264; and Frederick Rudolph, *Curriculum: A History of the American Undergraduate Course of Study since 1636* (Jossey-Bass, 1977), pp. 188–96.

35. Lawrence A. Cremin, *The Genius of American Education* (Vintage Books, 1966), p. 74; and Rudolph, *Curriculum*, pp. 189, 210.

36. Few important figures in American higher education require a modern biography more than does A. Lawrence Lowell. His educational ideas are broadly discussed in Henry A. Yeomans, *A. Lawrence Lowell, 1856–1943* (Harvard University Press, 1948).

37. Alexander Meiklejohn, "College Education and the Moral Ideal," quoted in Veysey, *The Emergence of the American University*, pp. 208, 210–11.

38. Rudolph, *Curriculum*, p. 191; and Russell Thomas, *The Search for a Common Learning: General Education, 1800–1960* (McGraw-Hill, 1962), pp. 61–91.

39. Daniel Bell, *The Reforming of General Education: The Columbia College Experience in Its National Setting* (Columbia University Press, 1966), pp. 50–51, 210, 224.

40. Bell, *The Reforming of General Education*, pp. 32, 225. See also David Denby, *Great Books: My Adventures with Homer, Rousseau, Woolf, and Other Indestructible Writers of the Western World* (Simon and Schuster, 1996).

41. Bell, *The Reforming of General Education*, pp. 307–12. A thoughtful, modestly conservative memoir of the liberal arts in elite universities since the 1950s is Alvin Kernan, *In Plato's Cave* (Yale University Press, 1999). A sense of the intellectual ferment, disagreement, and sometimes chaos in thinking about liberal education in higher education can be found in Bruce A. Kimball, with Robert Orrill, ed., *The Condition of American Liberal Education: Pragmatism and a Changing Tradition* (New York: College Entrance Examination Board, 1995); and Robert Orrill, ed., *Education and Democracy: Re-imagining Liberal Learning in America* (New York: College Entrance Examination Board, 1997). The tabulation of liberal arts majors comes from *Digest of Education Statistics, 2001*, table 255.

42. Wilford M. Aikin, *The Story of the Eight-Year Study* (Harper and Brothers, 1942), p. 7.

43. *General Education in School and College: A Committee Report by Members of the Faculties of Andover, Exeter, Lawrenceville, Harvard, Princeton, and Yale* (Harvard University Press, 1952), pp. 12, 15. Robert Orrill develops the idea that the liberal arts have been nearly forgotten as a high school concern or a concern connecting the upper secondary and lower college years. See Robert Orrill, "Grades 11–14: The Heartland or Wasteland of American Education?" in Michael C. Johanek, ed., *A Faithful Mirror: Reflections on the College Board and Education in America* (New York: College Entrance Examination Board, 2001), pp. 81–101.

44. The research on high school departments cited in note 29 is relevant here. In general the authors do not like departments. More often than not, departments seem to reinforce traditional notions of academic education that the authors criticize from a neo-progressive viewpoint. Their books demonstrate how powerful and entrenched departments are. The collegial "staff course" work modeled on how certain staff courses used to work in higher education probably requires major rethinking about how members of school departments work with or might work with each other. The department thus seems a crucial structure for proponents of enduring intellectual interests to understand.

45. Susan H. Fuhrman and Jennifer A. O'Day, ed., *Rewards and Reform: Creating Educational Incentives That Work* (Jossey-Bass, 1996).

46. Cremin, *The Genius of American Education*, pp. 8–11.

47. Rick Lyman, "Spielberg Challenges the Big Fluff of Summer," *New York Times*, June 16, 2002, section 2, p. 26. The new film was *Minority Report*.

48. Teenage Research Unlimited, "Teens Spent $172 Billion in 2001," press release, January 25, 2002; and Peter Zollo, *Wise Up to Teens: Insights into Marketing and Advertising to Teenagers*, 2d ed. (Ithaca, N.Y.: New Strategist Publications, 1999), pp. 6, 98–99, 242, 276–78, 337.

49. W. E. B. DuBois, *The Souls of Black Folk* (Vintage Books, 1990, originally published in 1903), p. 82.

50. DuBois, *The Souls of Black Folk*, p. 67.

51. William G. Wraga, "Left Out: The Villainization of Progressive Education in the United States," *Educational Researcher*, vol. 30, no. 7 (October 2001), pp. 34–35.

52. Another way to look at this is to imagine opponents of secondary education for black youth using W. E. B. DuBois's appeal for the education of the Talented Tenth to claim that he never intended or hoped for high-quality high school education for all black youth.

53. Charles W. Eliot "The Fundamental Assumptions in the Report of the Committee of Ten," *Educational Review*, vol. 30 (November 1905), pp. 340–41.

54. *The Report of the Committee of Ten on Secondary-School Studies,* in Sol Cohen, ed., *Education in the United States: A Documentary History*, vol. 3 (Random House, 1974), p. 1942.

55. Charles W. Eliot gave the speech in June 1921. It is reprinted in *Charles W. Eliot, A Late Harvest: Miscellaneous Papers Written between Eighty and Ninety* (Boston: Atlantic Monthly Press, 1924), pp. 121–48, quote on p. 138.

56. Angus and Mirel, *The Failed Promise of the American High School*, pp. 18–56.

57. John Dewey and Evelyn Dewey, *Schools of To-Morrow* (New York: E. P. Dutton and Company, 1915), p. 140. For more on this trend in educational thought, see Ravitch, *Left Back*, pp. 162–201; and Jeffrey Mirel, "Old Educational Ideas, New American Schools," *Paedegogica Historica* (forthcoming).

58. Forrest E. Long, "The High School in Competition," *Journal of Educational Sociology*, vol. 7, no. 4 (May 1934), p. 576.

59. Conant, *The American High School Today,* p. 93.

60. Angus and Mirel, *The Failed Promise of the American High School*, pp. 122–61, 225.

61. Editorial, "Poverty War Turns Up a School Embarrassment," *Detroit Free Press,* March 26, 1965, p. 6A.

62. This is the title of an insightful article about the difficulty of getting the incentives right. See Steven Kerr, "On the Folly of Rewarding A, While Hoping for B," *Academy of Management Journal*, vol. 18, no. 4 (1975), pp. 769–83.

63. William L. Taylor, "Standards, Tests, and Civil Rights," *Education Week*, vol. 20 (2000), pp. 56, 40–41.

64. Debbie Meier, *Will Standards Save Public Education?* (Boston: Beacon Press, 2000), pp. 3–31, quote on pp. 4–5.

Strategies for Success: High School and Beyond

BARBARA SCHNEIDER

The majority of American adolescents today are extraordinarily ambitious. In contrast to previous generations, more of them aspire to become physicians, lawyers, and business managers; few would consider working as machinists, office assistants, or plumbers. Not only do most teenagers hold high occupational aspirations, but they also have high educational expectations. Most adolescents expect to graduate from college, and a surprisingly significant proportion of them expect to earn graduate degrees. Such ambitions are widely held by teenagers from all different types of families and ethnicities—rich, poor, Asian, black, Hispanic, and white.[1] Although highly ambitious, many of these teenagers will not fulfill their expectations, not because they are unwilling to work hard for grades or believe that school is unimportant to their future lives, but because they lack important information that would help them form effective strategies for successfully navigating their educational experiences in high school and the transition process after graduation. This is particularly the case for teenagers whose families have limited economic and social resources.[2]

Ambitions are an essential component of adolescents' development, for they can help teenagers chart a life course and provide direction for how and where to invest their time and efforts. Prior research clearly demonstrates that one important predictor of social mobility is how much schooling an adolescent expects to obtain.[3] Students who expect to attend college are more likely to graduate from high school and enroll in postsecondary school than students with similar abilities and family background characteristics who expect to obtain only a high school diploma. Occupational aspirations are another component of ambition. When consistent with educational expectations, such aspirations demonstrate an adolescent's knowledge of

55

the world of work and educational pathways to different occupations. Not knowing how much education is needed for a given occupation makes it difficult to construct realistic plans for reaching one's goals. Ambitions formed in adolescence can have lifelong significance, influencing career choices as well as future earnings.

Even though economists have differing opinions on the labor market needs for the twenty-first century, most agree that entry-level credentials for stable jobs paying more than the minimum wage will most likely continue to rise.[4] This is evident in the types of jobs now requiring postsecondary degrees. For example, to do police work in some major cities, the required credential has changed from a high school diploma to a college degree. While what the long-term earnings trajectories will be for young people who hold only a high school diploma is unclear, being able to support a family and maintain a reasonable life-style with only a high school degree seems unlikely, at least in the near future.

Teenagers appear savvy about the economic returns of entering the labor force with only a high school diploma. The jobs available to high school graduates tend to be low skill, low wage, and in the service sector, with limited possibilities for stable long-term employment. The ambitions of today's adolescents are, in part, a response to the lack of work opportunities and dire prospects awaiting young people who do not attend college.[5]

Over the past twenty years the percentage of high school graduates who immediately began working full time instead of enrolling in postsecondary school has steadily declined. Young adults who do not enroll in college immediately after high school graduation are more likely to be male and minority—Hispanic, African American, or Asian American. The number of nonwhite students entering the labor market following high school graduation nearly doubled (from 14 to 27 percent) between 1980 and 2000. Despite widespread concerns about the academic performance of American high school students, analyses of longitudinal data indicate that students entering the labor force directly after graduation do not have lower cognitive skills than students in similar circumstances ten years ago. Instead, the most significant differences between those who enter college and those who enter the labor force tend to center on behavioral problems. This is somewhat disconcerting as national committees have recommended that, in addition to being technically proficient, young workers should possess strong social skills, such as being cooperative and a team player.[6] Yet, young people who enter the labor force full time after graduation appear to be those individuals who lack such skills and are more likely to have been suspended from school and considered to be troublemakers by their classmates than those who go on to college.[7]

Choosing the College Path

The high ambitions of most adolescents are realized to some extent, given that the majority of high school graduates today will enroll in some type of postsecondary institution immediately after high school graduation.[8] Sixty-three percent of the high school class of 1999 attended college in the fall after graduating, an increase of nearly 20 percent over college matriculation rates in the 1970s.[9] This number will likely continue to increase. Recent census data show that the median number of years of schooling among young adults ages twenty to twenty-four is thirteen years.[10]

Although the number of high school graduates entering postsecondary school has increased substantially, the proportion of students entering two-year versus four-year colleges has remained relatively stable over the past thirty years. Among those students who matriculate to college immediately after graduating from high school, approximately two-thirds enroll in four-year institutions and the remaining one-third enroll in two-year institutions.[11] The decision to attend a two-year instead of a four-year institution is not necessarily based on the desire to obtain an associate's degree instead of a bachelor's degree. Today, 70 percent of recent high school graduates who begin their college careers at two-year institutions expect to earn a bachelor's degree compared with less than 50 percent twenty years ago.[12]

Despite having high ambitions, students who enter two-year institutions are unlikely to reach their goals. Those who expect to receive a bachelor's degree but begin their postsecondary education at a two-year institution take longer to attain their educational goals than those who begin at four-year institutions. Using standard statistical methods, David Stevenson and I estimated the likelihood of receiving a bachelor's degree for those who began their postsecondary education in a two-year institution. We found that the odds of these students transferring to a four-year institution and earning a bachelor's degree are low. They are 28 percent less likely to receive a bachelor's degree than comparable students who began their postsecondary career at a four-year institution. Our analyses indicate that students who transferred to a four-year institution took a year and a half longer to com-

plete their degrees than comparable students who entered a four-year institution immediately after graduation. Stevenson and I referred to these students as being caught in an "ambition paradox"; that is, they have high
expectations, but their plans for achieving them are fraught with problems.
Some of these problems are financial, and the remainder are directly related
to high school academic preparation and the academic advisory process in
high school and college.

For many teenagers, attending college immediately after high school is a
choice supported by their friends, teachers, and parents. Research has
shown that parents as well as school personnel view college as the most
appropriate transition for nearly all students.[13] This preparation for college
begins early in a high school student's schooling career, for it is in high
school that teenagers build the academic record that eventually will be used
by colleges in making admissions decisions. The building blocks of the academic record are the courses the students take, their grades, and the
extracurricular activities they participate in. Assembling these blocks into a
viable structure is not straightforward, for blueprints are often not available
for many students. And if they are available, they are often incomplete and
fail to reveal the importance of taking rigorous academic courses or the per-
ils of poor time management, such as spending long hours on sports, clubs,
or paid work at the expense of schoolwork.

The academic record is not solely constructed by the students themselves, because schools and parents also influence students' high school
careers by providing guidance and resources. Consequently, the process of
creating an academic record requires that students, their parents, and
schools become strategic, if their goal is to have the students enroll in college. Becoming strategic is a process that requires both organizational skills
and the willingness to commit to a course of action to achieve specific
goals.[14] This course of action needs to be coherent, detailed, and realistic. It
is more likely to be realized when adolescents and their parents regulate
what they do, mobilize personal resources, and sustain high levels of effort.
Schools need to be fully involved in the process, articulating formal and
informal messages to students and their parents about the importance of
forming effective postsecondary plans matched to students' abilities and
goals—and, if that plan includes college, recognizing the steps that need to
be taken long before the senior year of high school. For example, secondary
schools can encourage students to take rigorous courses by emphasizing the
links between high school courses and college matriculation and by clarify-

ing why such courses are more likely than others to adequately prepare students for college. They can also play important roles by providing extensive information on college programs and financial aid.

When students, parents, and schools work in unison, students' goals are most likely to be achieved. However, students' desires, parents' support, and schools' organizational efforts are often at odds with one another. Students may believe that college is important but be unwilling to take difficult courses that require them to work hard. Parents may also believe that their children should attend college but may be overly dependent on high schools to help their adolescents choose the right college and program of study. And high schools, with the many responsibilities they have, are often ill equipped to provide individual college counseling for all of their students.

Helping Students Become Strategic

One of the most noticeable consequences of *A Nation at Risk,* published in 1983 by the National Commission on Excellence in Education, was the response to the report's recommendation to increase the number of academic courses required for high school graduation.[15] Within several years, nearly every state had adopted plans that increased the required number of courses to graduate from high school. As a result, the percentage of high school students taking four years of mathematics and science increased from 13 percent in 1983 to more than 60 percent in 1997 [16]

Instead of strengthening the curriculum, however, the increases in state graduation requirements seem to have intensified the "shopping mall" character of American secondary schools.[17] In response to state mandates, many high school districts added academic courses that varied considerably in content and difficulty. A high school, for example, may increase its offerings in mathematics but offer remedial courses such as basic mathematics or pre-algebra, not advanced courses. Analyses of high school transcripts show a 10 percent increase in the number of different courses taken by high school students between 1980 and 1990.[18] Yet research by Christopher Swanson, Catherine Riegle-Crumb, and myself indicates that only rigorous, advanced-level mathematics and science course taking in high school is strongly predictive of four-year college attendance and continuation.[19] Although taking advanced courses in foreign languages was also predictive of attending a four-year college, similar effects were not observed for students taking advanced-level courses in other subjects such as history or the humanities.

When researchers have examined student course choices, some have concluded that students have little agency in determining what classes they will take in high school. Clearly schools play a role in course selection by determining what courses will be offered, establishing the procedures for allowing students into certain courses, and creating a climate whereby teachers and counselors are encouraged to adopt either a universal (advocating college for all students) or a selective (recommending college for a chosen few) approach to student counseling and academic planning. But if researchers place students entirely on the receiving end of school policies, teacher and counselor predilections, and parent influence, they underestimate the role students play in their own educational careers.

Students have their own educational goals and plans, which may be dissimilar to those of their peers or the adults responsible for their education. Studies show that high-ability students—that is, those who work hard and are interested in the subject matter—are more likely to pursue advanced courses in particular subjects.[20] These intrinsic factors are also complemented by external incentives, such as anticipating applying to certain types of postsecondary institutions and courses of study. If more students are made aware that competitive colleges consider advanced-level course taking in making admissions decisions, they may be more likely to take an additional year of mathematics or science.[21]

Given these facts, arguably one way to increase achievement and college attendance is to help students become more strategic by having them take more rigorous courses and providing them with information about the college admissions process. Using the high school transcript file from the National Education Longitudinal Study of 1988–94 (NELS:88–94), a nationally representative sample of eighth graders first surveyed in 1988, with follow-ups conducted in 1990, 1992, and 1994, Catherine Riegle-Crumb constructed high school course sequences for grades nine through twelve for mathematics, science, foreign language, English, and history or social science. Subject-specific course sequences are progressions of courses that can be hierarchically organized with respect to their complexity and academic rigor.[22] Overall, she finds that while high school requirements have increased since the 1980s, only 12 percent of high school seniors take the highest mathematics course sequence, 22 percent take the highest science course sequence, and 7 percent take the highest foreign language course sequence.[23] And among those who enroll in these advanced sequences, females, minorities, and students in families with constrained economic and social resources are underrepresented.[24] Perhaps most important, she finds that course sequences have sizable and significant effects on academic performance and admission to postsecondary schools.

One of the most widely used admission requirements for postsecondary school is the college entrance examination, either the SAT or the American College Test (ACT). Despite recent public debates concerning the value and reliability of these tests (particularly the SAT) for predicting college success, most colleges and universities continue to give considerable weight to the test scores, along with other information such as high school transcripts, in making admissions decisions.[25] Recognizing that colleges continue to rely on entrance examinations, Fengbin Chang, Lori Hill, Robert Petrin, Catherine Riegle-Crumb, Christopher Swanson, and I were interested in determining the extent to which different combinations of courses taken in high school influenced one's score. We assumed that more advanced-level courses would increase a student's performance on these tests. Abstracting college examination scores from high school students' transcripts and placing the SAT and ACT scores on a single metric, Riegle-Crumb investigated the relationship between advanced-level courses and college entrance examinations. Using standard ordinary least squares (OLS) regression procedures and accounting for several student background characteristics, such as gender, race, and ethnicity, parent education, parent income, and prior ability, she examined the association between entrance exam scores and taking high course sequences in both mathematics and science, taking a high course sequence in either mathematics or science, and taking a high course sequence in history or English but not mathematics or science, against taking no advanced sequences.

Riegle-Crumb finds that more rigorous course taking, particularly in science and mathematics, seems to have the greatest influence on SAT performance (see table 1).[26] A student who takes rigorous mathematics and science courses in high school can potentially gain 265 points on the SAT compared with a student who takes no advanced courses. Even taking a high sequence in either mathematics or science (but not both) has a positive effect, increasing one's score by 161 points. However, taking a high sequence in history or English without more course work in mathematics and science accounts for only a 99-point gain on the SAT.

Table 1. Coefficients from OLS Regression Model for Combined (Verbal + Math) SAT Score

	Combined SAT score	
Independent variable	Unstandardized coefficient	Standardized coefficient
Student background		
Female	−20.46 ***	(−0.05)
Black	−87.91 ***	(−0.13)
Hispanic	−57.87 ***	(−0.07)
Asian	4.25	(0.01)
Parent education	34.26 ***	(0.17)
Family income (natural logarithm)	30.15 **	(0.04)
Eighth-grade composite math and reading test score	4.60 ***	(0.31)
Sequence combinations[a]		
Math and science high sequences	265.35 ***	(0.47)
Math or science high course sequence	161.51 ***	(0.35)
High sequence not including math or science	99.75 ***	(0.21)
Constant	497.09 ***	
Adjusted R^2	.53	
Number of observations	4,130	

Source: Department of Education, National Center for Education Statistics, National Education Longitudinal Study of 1988–94.
Note: Data are weighted to produce results generalizable to the population of U.S. high school students. The weight applies to 1994 sample members for whom transcript data are available. OLS = ordinary least squares.
a. In comparison with taking no high sequences.
Probability > |t|: ** = 0.01, *** = 0.001.

While other student attributes and resources have significant effects on test score performance, they pale in comparison to the effects associated with course sequences. On average, being a male student increases one's SAT score by 20 points (see the unstandardized coefficient column). Other family background characteristics, such as parent education, also increase SAT scores. These scores appear to be influenced by family income, but the effect is not as strong as parent education or high course sequences in mathematics and science. Prior ability, as measured by the eighth-grade test score, is also related to higher SAT performance, but the overall test score gain is not as substantial as other measures (see the standardized coefficient column).

But the most compelling evidence for advocating higher-level courses for ambitious students is found by examining the relationship between enrollment in rigorous courses and students' odds of attending postsecondary school. In a separate analysis, using multinomial logistic regression techniques, Chang, Hill, Petrin, Riegle-Crumb, Swanson, and I estimated the effect of taking different advanced-level courses on two-year versus four-year college attendance. Using the same basic set of demographic controls as those included in the Riegle-Crumb analyses, and controlling for the students' SAT or ACT test scores, we found that taking high-level course sequences in both mathematics and science is a stronger predictor of attending a four-year institution than any other combination of lower-level course sequences. Course sequences in mathematics and science were among the strongest overall predictors of enrollment in a two- or four-year postsecondary institution. Students who complete high-level mathematics and science courses, even after taking into account prior ability in these subject areas, are likely to be among the most competitive college applicants.

A significant gender effect is evident on college matriculation, with female students being about 1.2 ($e^{.20}$) times as likely as males to attend four-year instead of two-year institutions (see table 2). African Americans are nearly twice ($e^{.66}$) as likely to attend a four-year versus a two-year institution compared with white students, when other variables are controlled. Again, a strong effect is found for parent education, with a smaller effect for family income. While these background factors are important, the effects for course sequence could be considered staggering. Compared with students who take no advanced courses, those who take high mathematics and science courses are seventeen ($e^{2.81}$) times more likely to attend a four-year than a two-year college. Essentially, the data in table 2 show that students who take higher course sequences greatly increase their chances for college admission to any type of postsecondary institution. This is especially the case for blacks with respect to their enrollment in four-year institutions (results of partial regressions not shown).

Although students with higher academic abilities are more likely to be enrolled in higher-level courses, if average students take these courses and persist in them, they are likely to receive the same matriculation benefits as students who begin high school with higher test scores. Thus encouraging all students to take higher-level courses is one key way to help them become competitive college applicants.

Extracurricular Participation

One of the ways students make themselves more competitive with respect to college admissions is by engaging in a variety of extracurricular activities.

Table 2. Multinomial Logistic Model for Postsecondary Matriculation, October 1992

Independent variable	Two-year college versus not in school	Four-year college versus not in school	Four-year college versus two-year college
Student background			
Female	0.34 ***	0.54 ***	0.20 **
Black	−0.33 **	0.33 ***	0.66 ***
Hispanic	−0.07	0.04	0.11
Asian	0.04	−0.01	−0.04
Parent education	0.26 ***	0.63 ***	0.38 ***
Family income (natural logarithm)	0.70 ***	1.02 ***	0.32 *
Eighth-grade composite math and reading test score	0.01 **	0.02 ***	0.01 ***
Sequence combination[a]			
Math and science high sequences	0.27	3.07 ***	2.81 ***
Math or science high course sequence	0.60 ***	1.92 ***	1.32 ***
High sequence not including math or science	0.69 ***	1.50 ***	0.81 ***
Constant	−3.17 ***	−5.40 ***	−2.23 ***
−2 log-likelihood	14,263.10		
Chi-square (df)	2932.92 (20)		
Number of observations	8,122		

Source: Department of Education, National Center for Education Statistics, National Education Longitudinal Study of 1988–94.
Note: Data are weighted to produce results generalizable to the population of U.S. high school students. The weight applies to 1994 sample members for whom transcript data are available.
a. In comparison with taking no high sequences.
Probability > |t|: * = 0.05, ** = 0.01, *** = 0.001.

Faced with a wide variety of choices for spending time outside the classroom, young people today can choose to participate in a range of activities, including sports, academic or hobby clubs, music, theater, art, social service, student government, and religious organizations. Some argue that these activities can reinforce traditional academics and aid students in achieving key educational goals. However, others indicate that too much participation, including spending considerable hours at paid work, has deleterious effects on student academic performance and subsequent college admission.

Activity groups can be distinguished from the fluid peer groups to which most adolescents belong. Research shows that students in high school often move from one friendship group to another, changing friends within a few weeks or months. Best friends are few, and students frequently refer to peers as acquaintances or associates.[27] Young people travel in groups of as many as twenty whom they consider to be close friends. Building close ties with a boyfriend or girlfriend that could lead to a long-term relationship is often viewed as undesirable. Few teenagers date. Instead they go out with someone, which can mean anything from spending time together to a casual relationship that is recognized by peer groups as a form of special emotional attachment.

In contrast to these social groups, activity-based groups are easily recognizable and sustained over time even when their membership changes. Unlike peer groups, which are organized around socializing, activity-based groups have well-defined functions, clear boundaries of membership, and established procedures for joining. Membership requirements vary from a simple commitment to participate in the activities of the group, such as community service, to highly competitive tryouts for the tennis team, school newspaper, or orchestra. In addition to taking high levels of academic courses, participating in these activity groups is another way strategic students build portfolios for college admission. The idea of being a well-rounded student today means being both academically strong and participating and excelling in some type of extracurricular activity.

Christopher Swanson, also using the NELS:88–94 data set, has estimated the impact of extracurricular participation on college admission. Using a series of hierarchical linear models, he finds that in addition to taking high-level course sequences, students who are more likely to attend college participate in school-sponsored extracurricular activities such as interscholastic sports, performing arts groups, honor societies, academic clubs, or school publications. These activities significantly improve a student's prospects of attending a four-year college by a margin of approximately 8 percent. Involvement in specific types of out-of-school activities show an even smaller relationship with attending a four-year versus a two-year college, apart from a modest positive effect for volunteering and community service after controlling for student background characteristics and academic preparation. Paid employment has a consistently negative, although nonsignificant effect on attending a four-year institution even after controlling for other factors such as ability and the types of jobs students hold in high school. Thus Swanson finds that the one aspect of students' academic record that provides the strongest and most consistent advantage for college attendance is academic course taking, followed by extracurricular school activities, and then outside school activities.[28]

Employing a two-level hierarchical linear model that includes student-level terms for family background, academic performance, mathematics

Figure 1. Effects of Math Course Sequence and School Extracurricular Participation on Predicted Probabilities of Four- versus Two-Year Postsecondary Matriculation

Percent change in predicted probabilities

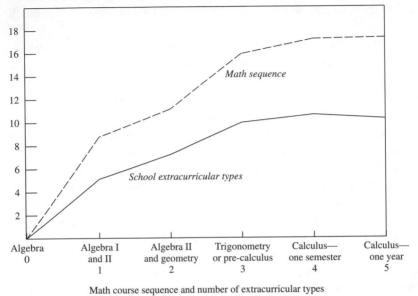

Math course sequence and number of extracurricular types

Source: Department of Education, National Center for Education Statistics, National Education Longitudinal Study of 1988–94.

course taking, hours of paid work, educational and sociability attitudes, and school-level controls for program offerings, school structure, and community context, Swanson also calculates the probability of attending a four-year college for an average student who participates in various extracurricular activities versus a similar student who does not participate. The baseline probability of matriculating to a four-year institution for an average student is approximately 78.5 percent.

Figure 1 presents the change in an average student's predicted probabilities for attending a four-year institution if that student increases the level and difficulty of his or her mathematics course taking. As the top line in figure 1 shows, the more difficult the courses an average student takes, the higher his or her predicted probabilities for matriculating to a four-year college. The effect for participating in extracurricular activities is not as strong. The bottom line represents the change in predicted probabilities for an average student attending a four-year institution if he or she increases the level of participation in extracurricular activities. If a student increases his or her participation by four or more activities there is no additional effect on the probability of attending a four-year institution. These findings suggest that additional participation does not necessarily increase a student's chances of matriculating to college, whereas taking more advanced-level courses increases a student's chances of attending a postsecondary school. This is especially the case when instead of completing one's mathematics course taking with algebra II and geometry, a student goes on and takes trigonometry and pre-calculus.

Adolescents should participate in activities outside of school to help them develop social skills. However, students often participate in certain activities merely to portfolio build. That is, they join clubs and associations that will look good on their college applications. Community service clubs are a prime example of this type of activity, in which the number of hours and activities a student has to perform is minimal, yet indicates to others an interest in civic and social concerns. Students participate in extracurricular activities not to boost admission to four-year versus two-year institutions but to boost admission to highly selective versus less selective colleges. Extracurricular activities at best should be viewed as a valuable complement to academic performance but not as a viable substitute in the increasingly competitive college market.

Strategic Actions by Teachers and Schools

The idea that most high school students should attend postsecondary school is shared by teachers and administrators, even in schools in which the number of students matriculating to college is lower than the national average. College counselors and teachers, often criticized for labeling students and directing them to consider employment after high school graduation, have recently adopted a "college for everyone" rhetoric. In spite of this, Chang, Hill, Petrin, Riegle-Crumb, Swanson, and I expect that teachers and school personnel would vary in how they planned to accomplish this goal given a variety of school-level professional and structural influences. We suspect that teachers, particularly in more advanced-level courses, would take extra steps to help students acquire knowledge and skills that would increase their academic performance and ability to successfully complete college coursework. We also assume that some schools would be more proactive in the types of activities they support to encourage students to attend college.

With respect to the teachers and their pedagogical practices, Robert Petrin, using data from the NELS:88–94 first follow-up sample, examines how authentic instruction varies within the types of courses that are essential for college admission, mainly mathematics and science.[29] Limiting his analysis to sophomores enrolled in one of two mathematics courses (algebra and geometry) and in one of two science courses (biology and chemistry), he uses student reports of their experiences to construct measures of classroom instructional environments. He then uses teacher reports of their professional qualifications and their class preparation activities, as well as measures of school academic press and professional environment, to generate an overall image of the determinants and effects of instruction at the student level. He uses a number of data imputation and structural equation techniques not only to retain representation of traditionally underrepresented students in the analysis and generate robust parameter estimates, but also to capture variations in instructional types and school and teacher effects across courses.

Petrin finds, first, that classroom instructional environments can be organized into three separate pedagogical components. He defines instructional practices by their locus of agency—teacher, student, or shared. In teacher-focused instructional practices, students are heavily engaged in note taking and listening to teachers lecture. Here teachers control discourse and pedagogical content. In student-focused instructional practices, students are directly engaged with material and participate in more self-directed activities, such as formulating methods to solve problems, conducting their own experiments, and choosing their own topics of study. In these environments, students directly influence the nature of inquiry in the classroom. In shared-type instructional practices, students are involved in instruction, although much of what transpires in the classroom is heavily influenced by teacher input. Students spend a considerable amount of time engaged in conventional approaches to performing experiments, writing laboratory reports, and watching teacher demonstrations. More discussion takes place among teachers and students than in teacher-focused instructional practices. The use of these instructional practices varies across the curriculum and is a defining feature of curricular content. Petrin finds that these different pedagogical practices are related to differences in achievement gains across subjects. Teacher-focused instruction has positive effects on student achievement in algebra and geometry, but no effect in biology. The achievement effects for student-focused instruction are modest and positive in algebra only, having no effect in geometry and a slightly negative effect in biology. Shared-instruction is the least successful, having a slight statistically significant negative effect on achievement in algebra and geometry and no effect on achievement in biology.

With respect to motivational and other psychological measures, Petrin finds that teacher-focused instruction shows the most significant and consistently positive associations between student reports of working hard, feeling challenged, and being asked to show that they understand the material in algebra, geometry, and biology. The effects for student-focused instruction are similar to those found for teacher-focused instruction, although they are not as robust. Minor yet statistically significant positive associations are found for working hard in algebra, geometry, and biology, with feeling challenged in biology and algebra and being asked to show one understands science in biology. Shared instruction was not associated with working hard in any subject. It was, however, positively associated with challenge in biology and with being asked to show one understands the material in algebra and geometry.

Although students in more advanced-level mathematics and science classes appear to benefit from teacher-focused instructional types, they do not necessarily feel more challenged. Students in higher-level courses, while experiencing greater achievement gains, report working less hard and feeling less challenged than students in lower-level courses. This seems to suggest that even when high-ability students are in advanced-level courses they are more likely to feel disengaged and less challenged.[30]

Feelings of engagement and challenge are found, however, in predominately minority schools, where the majority of students have parents with low levels of education and income. Petrin finds that minority students perform slightly less well on achievement tests than whites, even though they indicate that they work harder and feel more challenged. In both types of mathematics courses, minority students in predominately minority schools are more likely than whites and minorities in suburban schools to report that they are asked to demonstrate their understanding of class material. Teachers in schools targeted for reform may be trying to engage students by using innovative instructional approaches. Perhaps the idea of showing that one understands the material has limited value, especially in classrooms where many students may not grasp the content. Assuming students listen to one another, they may be exposed to their classmates' confused or incorrect solutions to problems. Students could be less able to articulate novel solutions to problems without first having some mastery of more conventional approaches to problem solving. While such techniques have widespread appeal among educators, deriving their legitimacy from research on motivation, the variation in performance levels in classrooms hinders mastery of the material.

While several researchers have examined the school's role in creating an environment that encourages academic performance, Lori Hill has studied how schools, especially those serving minority students with limited economic and social resources, can encourage college matriculation.[31] Using a subsample of NELS:88–94 high schools in predominately urban areas, Hill examines how high schools can increase the chances that more graduates will attend four-year institutions. Employing two-level hierarchical linear models, she finds that high schools can significantly increase the proportion of minority students who attend college in three ways. First, high schools need to implement a foreign language requirement. Second, they need to hold college fairs so that college representatives can meet and talk with students. Third, and most important, high schools need to provide assistance with the college admissions process, including help with financial aid forms. Hill concludes that providing these types of information and resources to an average student in a high-minority high school will create a 35 percent change in the odds that such a student will apply to college.

In a more qualitative study, where Stevenson and I conducted longitudinal observations of the counseling process, we found that one high school was able to encourage more of its students to attend college by engaging in a comprehensive college advisory program.[32] The high school uses its advanced-level courses as a way to help students develop plans for college and beyond. Counselors work closely with the students and explain the consequences of not taking certain courses on college admission. Special attention is given to those students who are the first in their families to attend college. As the counselors explain, these students sometimes have a stereotypical idea of what college is about that is often drawn from television or the movies. The high school stresses the importance of taking the SAT, notifies students when it is being offered, and suggests courses to take to improve one's scores. Help is also provided for writing the college essay. Finally, the school works with the parents and the student in securing financial support for college and completing financial aid forms. This convergence of qualitative and quantitative findings suggests an active role for urban high schools in the college planning process, a role that is often undertaken in suburban communities by parents who typically have attended college themselves.[33]

The Importance of College Reputation

Although high schools can promote college attendance, students themselves have to make a commitment to attend, and their parents must commit to supporting their efforts. Robert Petrin has examined changes over time in the values and attitudes students have in selecting their college using data from three longitudinal data bases—the National Longitudinal Study of 1972, High School and Beyond, and the National Education Longitudinal Study of 1988–94. He finds that students have become more academically focused in their orientations toward postsecondary education. Over the past thirty years students applying to college have become increasingly concerned with academic prestige and less concerned with college social life or selecting colleges that are easy to get into. Students who plan to attend two-year institutions are increasingly concerned with the curricular offerings in various institutions, whereas students who plan to attend four-year institutions have become more concerned with the overall academic reputation of the college.

The student who expects to attend a four-year institution may perceive college as only a first step toward graduate school, and the reputation of one's college takes on the same importance as taking advanced courses does in high school. Despite the increase in the numbers of students needing financial support for college, securing financial assistance seems less important to four-year college applicants than it was in the past. However, finances remain a primary concern for those attending two-year institutions.

The importance of academic reputation in the college application process reflects to a certain extent the rise in educational expectations among adolescents, the importance of building an academic record, and the extensive college information network supported in some high schools. Even though teenagers may be becoming more discriminating academic shoppers, their choice of college is constrained to some extent by the involvement of their parents in the process, simply because most colleges, even two-year institutions, have become increasingly costly, a cost that teenagers cannot bear themselves. The role of parents in the postsecondary application process has received limited attention except by economists who have focused on parent assets and debt burden as independent constraints on sending children to college. Being a strategic parent, Chang, Hill, Petrin, Riegle-Crumb, Swanson, and I argue, constitutes more than contributing to a student's educational college costs.

Being a Strategic Parent

Much like the adolescents, most parents today expect their children to attend college. As is the case for students, parents' expectations remain high regardless of their income level, educational background, and race and ethnicity. While parents may have high educational expectations for their children, they are unlikely to allocate their social and financial resources in uniform ways. Some parents may be willing to expend a sizable proportion of their accumulated wealth on their children's postsecondary education, while other parents in similar economic situations may be less willing to make the same financial sacrifices. These allocations, however, can have appreciable effects on students' postsecondary careers.

Clearly, many parents, regardless of their financial assets, will set limits on the economic and social sacrifices they are willing to make for their children's college careers. However, even those parents with few resources may be willing to take extra steps so their child can attend postsecondary school. Parents' resource allocation decisions are likely in part determined by their perceptions of the educational promise of the child. Further, that educational promise will be more salient to parents with fewer economic resources than those who are willing to send their child to college to maintain their social status. Thus the social exchange for parent investment is predicated not only on accumulated wealth but also on the assessment parents make of their child's potential for future educational success.

The decision to allocate resources on the part of the parents is influenced by several factors, among which are parents' evaluations of their adolescents' high school performance, the social resources they devote to their children's education (such as time spent discussing college plans), and the financial strategies they pursue to pay for educational expenses. Because students allocate resources through the time and effort they direct toward their schoolwork, the more positive actions an adolescent takes toward becoming a competitive candidate for college, the more likely the parents are to allocate economic and social resources to that end. But not all parents respond to a given level of student performance in the same way, even if they have similar levels of economic and social resources.

Several aspects of student academic performance may factor into parents' evaluations and decisions to allocate resources for further education. Course taking, for example, can be a signal to the parent of both the student's level of effort and potential for succeeding at more challenging coursework in the future. A student who takes and excels in more rigorous courses, particularly in such core subjects as science and mathematics, indicates that he or she is up to the cognitive challenge these courses present and the amount of work they require. Rigorous course taking in high school can be viewed as an indicator of a student's academic dedication and ability to persevere in achieving long-term educational goals. Course-taking behaviors are highly visible to parents and are likely to be taken into account when parents determine the level of resources to commit to their adolescent's current and future education.

Grades are another indicator of a student's performance in high school. However, relying only on teacher-awarded grades as an indicator of ability and perseverance risks inaccuracies because of grade inflation and the practice of assigning grades for reasons other than academic performance. Studies of high schools show that students are often given higher grades for behaving well in class or turning in extra homework assignments. Regardless of these concerns, parents continue to consider grades to be important indicators of their child's academic performance.

Parent-child discussions have been described as a form of social capital, in that parents and students spend time interacting with each other around a common positive goal. These interactions can be thought of as a form of investment that serves to reinforce mutual interests and formulate strategic plans. For example, parent-adolescent discussions of the teenager's courses, grades, college plans, preparations for entrance exams, and application to college are all indicators of the strategic planning process. Parent-child discussions are a social resource that families are willing to expend so that their child's chances for attending college are optimized.

And finally, the last component of the strategic process includes parents' financial plans, debt liability, and willingness to commit additional resources to their child's education. These measures take into account how extensively parents seek information on financial aid, apply for loans, ask for contributions from relatives, take on second jobs, borrow money, or re-mortgage their homes. This willingness to commit high or low levels of social and financial support for the child's education can be seen as a culmi-nation of long-term educational investment strategies and evaluations of a student's academic potential.

Again using data from NELS:88–94, Fengbin Chang, Christopher Swan-son, and I estimated the influence parent strategies have on student matricu-lation to four-year or two-year institutions, controlling for student perfor-mance, parent-student discussions, and parent financial strategies. The analysis is limited to those students who graduated from high school in spring of 1992 and matriculated to college in fall of that same year. The analysis sample is divided into two groups of students: those from families at or above and those below the sample mean household income level of approximately $45,000. Employing logistic regression procedures, Fengbin Chang estimated the importance of parent strategies for both high- and low-income families.

For the high-income group, several student indicators of performance—grades, mathematics course sequence, and standardized college admission score—are directly related to four-year college attendance (see table 3). What is perhaps most surprising is how strong the effect for mathematics course sequence is in relation to the other indicators of student performance. If a student takes high sequences in mathematics and science, he or she is four times more likely to attend a four-year college than a student who has no high course sequences.[34]

Social strategies appear to have no effect on college admissions to four-year institutions among the higher-income group. However, if parents con-sult with knowledgeable persons about financial aid, their adolescents are more likely to attend four-year institutions. Probably because of their ample financial resources, if their teenager attends a four-year institution, these parents are less likely to cover college expenses with current earnings, debt financing, or state and federal loans. However, when parents have financial resources, they seem willing to expend them, even when the costs to attend college are significant.

Parents in the low-income group show a commitment to education and, even though their resources are constrained, strategically work with their children to maximize their chances for college attendance. As shown in table 4, black students are more likely than other groups to attend four-year institutions, holding all other factors constant. With respect to student per-

Table 3. Logistic Regression Model for Matriculation to Four- versus Two-Year Institutions for High-Income Group, October 1992

	Four-year versus two-year		
Independent variable	*Model 1*	*Model 2*	*Model 3*
Student background characteristic			
Female	–0.61 **	–0.67 **	–0.60 **
Asian	–0.57	–0.78	–0.81
Black	0.76	0.85 *	1.06 *
Hispanic	0.21	0.25	0.35
Nontraditional versus mother-father family	0.13	0.17	0.15
Number of siblings	0.00	0.02	0.02
Family socioeconomic status			
Family income (thousands of dollars)	0.00	0.00	0.00
Parent educational attainment	0.20 *	0.24 *	0.20 *
Student performance			
Student educational expectations	0.04	0.02	0.02
Grades	0.56 **	0.52 **	0.39 *
Math course sequence	0.30 ***	0.31 ***	0.27 ***
Science course sequence	0.05	0.06	0.04
Social strategy			
Frequency of parent-child academic discussions	–0.01	–0.02	–0.02
Financial strategy			
Total amount currently spent on educational expense (thousands of dollars)	0.04	0.01	0.01
Level of family financial sacrifice	0.21	0.12	0.10
Consulted written sources and persons about financial aid	0.69 ***	0.60 **	0.58 **
Number of expected funding sources internal to family	–0.40 ***	–0.46 ***	–0.45 ***
Number of expected funding sources external to family	0.07	0.01	–0.01
Parent commitment to provide financial support			
Low support (less than $5,000) versus no support	–0.09	0.22	0.18
High support ($5,000 and more) versus no support	2.12 ***	2.17 ***	2.14 ***
Expected college tuition (thousands of dollars)	—	0.18 ***	0.17 ***
Standardized college admission score	—	—	0.32 *
Constant	–3.59 ***	–3.85 ***	–3.02 **
–2 log-likelihood	836.50	797.30	793.10
Chi-square (df)	438.17 (20)	477.37 (21)	481.57 (22)
Number of observations	1,437	1,437	1,437

Source: Department of Education, National Center for Education Statistics, National Education Longitudinal Study of 1988–94.
Note: Data are weighted to produce results generalizable to the population of U.S. high school students. The weight applies to 1994 sample members for whom transcript data are available. High-income group: Family income ≥ $45,000. — = Not in the model.
Probability > |t|: * = 0.05, ** = 0.01, *** = 0.001.

Table 4. Logistic Regression Model for Matriculation to Four- versus Two-Year Institutions for Low-Income Group, October 1992

	Four-year versus two-year		
Independent variable	*Model 1*	*Model 2*	*Model 3*
Student background characteristic			
Female	0.12	0.20	0.23
Asian	−0.05	−0.02	0.03
Black	1.00 ***	0.94 ***	1.05 ***
Hispanic	0.56	0.62 *	0.72 *
Nontraditional versus mother-father family	−0.02	−0.03	−0.02
Number of siblings	0.09	0.08	0.08
Family socioeconomic status			
Family income (thousands of dollars)	0.00	0.00	0.00
Parent educational attainment	0.11	0.10	0.08
Student performance			
Student educational expectations	0.23 *	0.20 *	0.19 *
Grades	0.38 **	0.39 **	0.31 *
Math course sequence	0.26 ***	0.27 ***	0.25 ***
Science course sequence	0.13 **	0.10 *	0.09 *
Social strategy			
Frequency of parent-child academic discussions	0.09 *	0.12 *	0.12 *
Financial strategy			
Total amount currently spent on educational expense (thousands of dollars)	0.09 **	0.08 **	0.08 **
Level of family financial sacrifice	−0.32 **	−0.39 **	−0.40 **
Consulted written sources and persons about financial aid	0.41 *	0.35 *	0.35 *
Number of expected funding sources internal to family	0.12	0.12	0.13
Number of expected funding sources external to family	0.14	0.10	0.10
Parent commitment to provide financial support			
Low support (less than $5,000) versus no support	−0.25	−0.16	−0.18
High support ($5,000 and more) versus no support	0.90 **	0.74 **	0.73 **
Expected college tuition (thousands of dollars)	—	0.15 ***	0.14 ***
Standardized college admission score	—	—	0.20
Constant	−5.15 ***	−5.48 ***	−5.06 ***
−2 log-likelihood	1,438.04	1,385.21	1,382.24
Chi-square (df)	373.16 (20)	425.99 (21)	428.96 (22)
Number of observations	1,616	1,616	1,616

Source: Department of Education, National Center for Education Statistics, National Education Longitudinal Study of 1988–94.
Note: Data are weighted to produce results generalizable to the population of U.S. high school students. The weight applies to 1994 sample members for whom transcript data are available. Low-income group: Family income < $45,000. — = Not in the model.
Probability > |t|: * = 0.05, ** = 0.01, *** = 0.001.

formance, those measures that are in the control of the student—expectations, grades, mathematics and science course sequence—all have a positive and significant effect on college attendance at a four-year institution. In contrast to the high-income group, standardized college admission score does not significantly influence whether they will attend a four-year institution. This finding raises several questions about the viability of the SAT in predicting admissions for students in low-income families. What does matter, and significantly so, are course sequences, grades, and student expectations. Thus a more reasonable route for minority students and students in low-income families to increase their college attendance would be to take more rigorous courses.

The findings for parent financial strategies for low-income families are in the expected directions. Families that already have limited incomes are less likely to incur substantial financial sacrifices for their children to attend college. Similar to the high-income group, low-income parents whose children attend college are likely to be strategic, consulting with knowledgeable persons regarding financial aid. Although these parents have smaller incomes than those in the high-income group, they would be willing to commit additional financial resources so that their children could attend four-year institutions. This willingness is a clear sign of the value that parents place on the college degree. For both groups the importance of these intangible commitments points to the dynamic social processes through which some families, irrespective of income, support and create opportunities for their children's learning (see table 5).

The Value of Being Strategic

Nicholas Lemann points out that by the 1990s the SAT had become deeply woven into the fabric of higher education and into the lives of American upper-middle-class parents who were prepared to financially extend themselves to ensure that their children were admitted to the most prestigious colleges. He describes the SAT in Durkheimian terms as a powerful totem, a scientific numeric assignment of worth that symbolized potential access to higher education.[35] This is certainly the situation for families with considerable resources, but not for those with constrained social and economic means. Students in families with fewer economic resources believe that a college education will bring a level of economic prosperity and suc-

Table 5. Selected Coefficients from Multinomial Logistic Regression Models for Matriculation to Highly Competitive versus Less Competitive Colleges, October 1992

	High-income group (family income ≥ $45,000)		Low-income group (family income < $45,000)	
Independent variable	(I) Competitive versus less competitive	(II) Highly competitive versus less competitive	(I) Competitive versus less competitive	(II) Highly competitive versus less competitive
Student performance				
Student educational expectations	−0.18	−0.24	0.07	0.36 *
Grades	0.16	0.52 *	−0.05	−0.13
Sequence combination				
Math and science high sequences	−0.73 *	0.58	1.66 ***	1.85 ***
Math or science high sequence	−0.08	0.64 *	0.49 *	0.33
High sequence not including math or science	−0.07	0.62 *	0.27	0.07
Standardized college admission score	0.13 *	0.82 ***	0.40 **	0.94 ***
−2 Log-likelihood	1,966.84		2,193.59	
Chi-square (df)	557.42 (46)		303.20 (46)	
Number of observations	1,222		1,185	

Source: Department of Education, National Center for Education Statistics, National Education Longitudinal Study of 1988–94.
Note: Data are weighted to produce results generalizable to the population of U.S. high school students. The weight applies to 1994 sample members for whom transcript data are available. Both models also control for the other independent variables included in table 3 and table 4 (student background, family socioeconomic status, social strategies, financial strategies, and expected college tuition).
a. In comparison with taking no high sequences.
Probability > |t|: * = 0.05, ** = 0.01, *** = 0.001.

cess that having only a high school diploma cannot. They have invested their time and effort in tangible markers over which they have control—grades and taking advanced-level courses—to a greater extent than those in high-income families.

The lack of a relationship between the SAT and four-year college attendance for students in low-income families signifies, to some extent, that the SAT marker is less effective for differentiating the winners and losers in the educational college marketplace for these students than for those whose families are more economically advantaged.[36] The SAT appears to matter most to those with the resources to hire tutors, buy computer software practice tests, and enroll in commercial preparation courses. If the SAT is discontinued as an indicator for college admissions, some other measure likely will surface that parents with resources can purchase to ensure that their children obtain places in the most competitive colleges and universities.

The results pertaining to the effects of taking high-level course sequences are important to emphasize because they suggest that a single course is unlikely to make a difference in a young person's schooling career. A high school program should be created around a series of courses that have intellectual integrity; that is, that increase in cognitive challenges and demand enhanced skills over time. With most students seeing themselves in the college track in high school, what differentiates their curricular placements are the advanced sequences in mathematics, science, and foreign language.

As society continues to promote educational consumption, a college diploma takes on the same significance that a high school diploma did some fifty years ago. To ensure access to college, students, especially those in families with limited resources and who attend high schools serving predominately minority and economically disadvantaged students, need to be directed to take advanced-level courses. Moreover, schools need to allocate resources to assist students with college planning. Schools should provide information on the importance of entrance exams and mechanisms for taking them as well as information on different colleges and their programs of study. Students, particularly those who are the first in their families to attend college, also need assistance in completing applications, including financial aid forms. In turn, high schools should create an academic climate in which students can visualize their educational lives after high school graduation as unfolding not only in a dorm room but also in classrooms where the subject matter is challenging, engaging, and personally interesting.

Comment by Michael Kirst

Barbara Schneider has written an important and well-researched paper. The key conclusions concerning essential high school courses and parent-student strategies that increase postsecondary attendance and completion are based on solid longitudinal data. Little argument can be raised in terms of what Schneider presents, but much is available to expand upon in terms of policy implications. Much of Schneider's paper focuses upon students who go to selective postsecondary education institutions.

As she suggests, however, the biggest student preparation problems are evidenced in the approximately 80 percent of the students who go to minimal or nonselective institutions, including community colleges.[37] These students are accepted because they are eighteen years old or have passed the required high school courses to be admitted. These institutions may require the SAT but rarely use it for admissions decisions.[38] More than 50 percent of their students are in remediation, and their completion rates are low.[39] The students who attend these institutions face many obstacles. High school counseling resources are minimal, parents know little about higher education, and high school teachers in the middle- and lower-ability groups do not provide much college knowledge. Because admission is certain, the de facto key academic standard for these students is a placement test once they enroll in postsecondary education.[40]

Baltimore City Community College (BCCC) provides an extreme example but illustrates the depth of the problems.[41] Of 1,350 first-time students who entered BCCC in fall 1996, only 13 had received a vocational certificate, an associate's degree, or transferred to a bachelor's degree–granting college. Ninety-five percent needed remediation, and 45 percent required three math courses to reach the credit level. The math placement test, Accuplacer, was not matched to state high school math standards that emphasized authentic problem solving (for example, word problems with applications to real-life scenarios). The BCCC placement exam included content beyond algebra 2.

Schneider's paper primarily takes a bottom-up view of the educational system from secondary to postsecondary schooling. Improvements in the system, however, require looking down from higher education to secondary schools as well. The most relevant four-year postsecondary schools for Baltimore high schools are Choppin State, Morgan State, and the University of Baltimore, not the selective schools that receive most of the media attention. What signals do these types of schools send secondary school students about what they need to know and be able to do for completion of their college programs? Interviews reveal many students believe their high school graduation requirements are sufficient, and they have scant information on placement standards that direct them to postsecondary remediation.[42]

While the reality for high school graduates is that 70 percent will likely continue past the secondary years, state and institutional policies continue to reflect a significant separation between K–12 and postsecondary education. The current organization of secondary schools and postsecondary institutions is such that communication and information dissemination between levels is often difficult. For instance, students—especially those who are economically disadvantaged or whose parents did not attend college—often do not know what colleges expect of them in terms of meeting their admission or placement requirements. Many students believe that nonselective four-year institutions and community colleges do not have academic standards. This is not the case as is evidenced by the widespread use of placement tests for access to credit-level courses. Also, policies across the segments—particularly those concerning the transition from high school graduation to college admission—are fragmented and confusing.

Education standards have swept across the United States, engulfing almost every state. Forty-six states have created K–12 academic content standards in most academic subjects, and all but Iowa and Nebraska have statewide K–12 student achievement tests. At the state level, progress has been made toward focusing on, and clarifying, what students must be able to know and to do in the K–12 grades and how to align standards, assessments, textbook selection, and accountability measures at the K–12 level. A gaping hole in this reform strategy, however, is the lack of coherence in content and assessment standards between higher education institutions and K–12 systems. Unless this standards gap is closed and K–12 and postsecondary education policies are aligned, students and secondary schools will continue to receive a confusing array of signals and will not be able to prepare adequately for higher education. The current scene is a babel of standards, not a coherent strategy.

The roots of this problem go deep in the history of American education. The United States created two separate mass education systems (K–12 and universities and colleges) that rarely collaborated to establish consistent standards. Universities pay little attention to K–12 standards or assessments. Universities emphasize that they were not involved in the process of creating or refining K–12 standards. Moreover, state K–12 standards keep changing because of political or technical problems. The K–12 assessments are not evaluated to see how well they predict freshman grades (although this is not difficult to do). Universities hope that the SAT and the American College Test (ACT) will make adjustments to accommodate these new K–12 standards and feel more comfortable with the two assessments they know and can influence.

These disjunctures will be hard to fix without new K–12 and postsecondary educational institutions being at the center of reform. Few states have any policy mechanism that can deal with K–12 and postsecondary standards alignment. As president of the California State Board of Education for several years, I never met with my higher education counterparts. Higher education coordinating bodies do not include K–12 and postsecondary standards alignment within their purview. In short, few regular opportunities are available for K–12 educators to discuss standards issues with college and university faculty or policymakers. The professional lives of K–12 and higher education proceed in separate orbits. In some states, the governor's office is the most logical place to put these fractured systems together, but higher education leaders want to guard their political independence from gubernatorial and legislative specification of admissions criteria. Because each state has a distinctive K–12 standards and assessment system, what can be done nationally is not clear. President Bill Clinton's advocacy of a national voluntary test died after protests arose about states' rights in education.

Signaling theory suggests that streamlined and aligned high-quality and appropriate content messages have a positive impact on students' learning and achievement and that mixed signals—the current state of affairs—have the opposite effect.[43] Crucial aspects of appropriate signals and incentives are simplicity, clarity, and consistency.[44] Consistency is enhanced when signals, incentives, and institutional policies are aligned—for example, the alignment of format and content of state and local student assessments with SAT I. If incoherent and vague signals and incentives are sent by postsecondary education institutions and state agencies to students, then students will be less adequately prepared for postsecondary education. Minority students are often placed in low academic high school courses and tracks that decrease both motivation and preparation.[45]

J. Rosenbaum found that Chicago-area counselors do not want to give low-achieving students negative information about their future prospects, so they advocate college for all without stressing necessary academic preparation.[46] Because gaining admission to many four-year and two-year schools is easy, scant incentives exist to work hard in high school.[47] Once students enroll they face challenging placement exams, faculty expectations, and general education and graduation requirements that they often do not know about. They end up taking remedial noncredit courses that better signals may have prevented, such as the two-thirds failure rate of placement exams by first-year students entering the California State University System from high school.

A conceptual framework guides Bridge Project research questions and provides an analytical lens. Bridge Project concentrates on whether K–12 exit-level and postsecondary entrance-level signals and incentives for students are delivered in isolation from one another or through interaction and reinforcement. Three possible scenarios for signal delivery are postsecondary education drives policy (option A), K–12 drives policy (option C), and combined efforts of K–12 and postsecondary education drive policy (option B). The preferred delivery is option B.

Signals and incentives sent along through either a separate postsecondary education or a K–12 system will result in less student preparation, college knowledge, and postsecondary outcomes. Strong signals have positive impacts on desirable outcomes, while confusing or weak signals provide a negative influence. Combined efforts between K–12 and postsecondary especially help disadvantaged students, while honors students can succeed with less K–12 and postsecondary cooperation. Clear and consistent signals are related to outcomes such as less remediation and more completion of a student's desired postsecondary program.[48]

Joint efforts between postsecondary and lower education are crucial in creating positive outcomes for more students, particularly those from economically disadvantaged families, those from families in which a parent did not attend college, and those who face stigmatization and racism as they proceed through school. If there is no interaction and reinforcement of signals, then the more advantaged students will receive ample signals and incentives to prepare for postsecondary education. But the more educationally disadvantaged high school graduates will enroll at lower rates, require remediation, and experience lower postsecondary completion rates.

Combined efforts by postsecondary education and K–12 will improve college knowledge that is essential for student aspiration and preparation. College knowledge is acquired and possessed unequally among students and families of different social classes and racial/ethnic backgrounds. College knowledge by secondary school students and parents includes knowledge of tuition, curricular requirements, placement tests, financial aid, and admission procedures and selection criteria. A high school's collegiate preparation culture cannot be fully measured via simple, visible, or discrete indexes such as standardized test scores, honors and Advanced Placement courses, and postsecondary placement. Collegiate culture also encompasses the less tangible, more elusive qualities that can best be described through narratives that reveal the sustaining values or ethos of a high school.

For example, in Oklahoma, eighth graders take ACT Explore and tenth graders take a PLAN assessment (part of ACT) that tests English, math, reading, and science reasoning.[49] Since this policy was implemented, Oklahoma reports more students taking college preparation courses, increased enrollment in postsecondary education, and lower remediation rates. The California State University System in 2002 approved dropping its internal math and English placement tests and, instead, will be using the high school California Standards Test for placement. This will provide secondary students with early indicators of their probable placement before they reach a California state university. The Georgia Hope Scholarship Program is a simple but powerful signal that is reaching most secondary pupils who now know that a "B" high school average will result in a guaranteed state scholarship.[50] By middle school (grades six to eight), 51 percent of Georgia students and 59 percent of the parents knew the specific requirements for obtaining a Georgia state Hope scholarship. This knowledge was present in 1997—only four years after Hope scholarships started. These young pupils knew that only college preparation courses were computed as part of the "B" average required for a Hope scholarship.[51] These examples are incomplete, but they offer a positive step toward K–12 and postsecondary education articulation.

If K–12 schools are left largely alone to carry the brunt of college knowledge and preparation signals, then more students will receive vague signals and lesser incentives for adequate preparation. For example, a Metropolitan Life Survey in 2000 found that 71 percent of the students expected to go on to a four-year college, but teachers expected only 32 percent of their students to attend a four-year school.[52] A survey of twenty-six thousand high school teachers in twelve southern states found that only 38 percent believed that it was "very important" to "help all high school students master the essential content taught in college preparatory language arts, mathematics, and science courses." The Southern Regional Education Board determined that in the thirteen southeastern states it covers, from 21 to 42 percent of high school students finished a college preparatory curriculum.[53]

Many factors have led to the current problems with preparation for college, and better aligned policy signals are not a panacea. However, if the signals and incentives to students concerning needed postsecondary education preparation are optimal, several positive outcomes will follow. These include substantial increases in higher student and parent aspirations and actions to prepare and enter postsecondary education, increased student mastery of college preparatory content and skills, and better outcomes such as reduced need for postsecondary remediation, increased college and university persistence, and improved time to degree rates for postsecondary students.

Comment by Frederick M. Hess

Barbara Schneider is to be congratulated on presenting a most interesting paper. Parents, taxpayers, and voters would all regard the questions tackled in her paper as obviously significant. The question of how to help children make it through school successfully and learn material that will improve the quality of their lives is probably the central question for high school reform. So Schneider conducts a valuable exercise in trying to operationalize these concerns and draw explicit linkages between pedagogical practice, curricular structure, and outcomes for children.

The paper helps to illustrate the challenges that emerge when scholars seek to use large data sets to draw specific prescriptions regarding policy or practice. The questions and cautions are similar to those regarding the effects of private schooling or school choice, as researchers are forced to wrestle with issues of omitted variable bias and similar concerns that are difficult to get one's hands around. This paper is also useful as an opportunity to discuss some of those analytic challenges, primarily for the purpose of guiding other scholars who will seek to build upon Schneider's valuable work.

In terms of the actual policy prescriptions that Schneider lays out, she offers nothing that I would quibble with. Giving students better information, counseling, and advice and encouraging them to take more challenging courses can only redound to their benefit. All of these strike me as relatively commonsensical. High schoolers in the last thirty or forty years have been done a disservice in being provided with a take-out menu of course options that are too often academically inadequate.

Schneider's policy prescriptions resonated strongly with me on a personal level. I used to be a high school social studies teacher in Baton Rouge, Louisiana. Every time a ninth or tenth grader moved out of remedial classes into a more challenging course, I felt that he or she was being given at least a fighting chance to have post–high school choices beyond dry cleaning or food delivery.

That said, a couple of assumptions embedded in the proposed policy recommendations are worth thinking about. First, assuming the presence of linear effect in this context means that course taking is presumed to have a consistent and incremental effect on all children. This suggests that if those students not enrolled in the advanced sequences of math or science are placed in those classrooms, then they would accrue the same kinds of benefits as those gained by the students already enrolled in the advanced courses.

A potential problem is self-evident. It is not clear that the students currently in the lower tracks have the preparation or ability to benefit from more advanced courses in the same way that students currently in those courses do. For instance, it is not clear that all students would become better football players if placed on the varsity team or better musicians if placed in the district symphony. Some might improve under the heightened demands, but others might recoil or give up in frustration. Achievement always takes a certain amount of natural ability and a certain degree of preparation. Proponents of lower-level courses and offerings have always made this claim, which is that some students might come out worse if enrolled in advanced tracks than in their relatively mediocre offerings. All of this merely suggests a need to be careful about generalizing too readily about the benefits of enrolling students in advanced classes.

The benefits that accrue to those currently in these classes would not necessarily accrue to other students. In particular, the students who complete high-sequence courses are different from their peers. They are the students who, for whatever reason, chose to enroll in more challenging classes and then managed to pass those courses. They are not the students who failed out of earlier math classes or who were counseled out of more challenging math classes after receiving a "D" in algebra or geometry. As somebody who was counseled out of a number of college preparatory classes when I was a kid, I can say that my life has probably turned out better than if I had enrolled in them and racked up a string of failing grades.

So such cautions need to be kept in mind when educators and policymakers analyze survivors—the kids who make it through these tracks—and then try to impute the outcomes to everybody else. The bottom line is that here, as in all analysis, care must be taken in how findings are generalized.

Second, an acknowledged omitted variable bias problem is familiar to anyone who has followed the debates regarding private school effects or the impact of choice-based reforms. In that line of work, researchers can control for race, family income, mother's education, and so forth, but they may be unable to capture why one family chooses to use a private school while another seemingly identical family does not. If a systematic factor both explains this choice and affects subsequent student performance, such as the degree to which parents value education, then the findings may misrepresent the true effect of the treatment (whether the treatment involves enrolling in private school, receiving a voucher, or signing up for advanced courses).

The same dilemma is present here. Schneider and her associates have done an excellent job trying to address these issues. They have controlled in most of these analyses for parental education, parental income, race, prior student performance, and so on. Nonetheless, the question remains: Does this model capture everything that differentiates a student who takes a high-level sequence of math or science through high school from those who do not? One can readily argue that it does not, that some other intrinsic difference is not fully captured. If that is the case, the findings reported here would provide a poor guide to policy. Again, this caution is not intended as a criticism of the impressive work done here but is a general question and caution.

Third, one of the findings I found especially interesting is that the math sequence is strongly related to many other effects. This raises intriguing questions of how much of this effect is math-specific and how much is a case of math standing in as a proxy for something else. For instance, high school curricula often are driven by a student's placement in math courses. Care must be taken in distinguishing the effects of math-specific instruction and preparation from other instruction or preparatory effects that may be only incidentally related to a student's math instruction.

Fourth, Schneider discusses the effect of information and counseling on college matriculation. Again, this makes sense. For students in inner-city school systems who know few people who have ever made it out, who do not consider college part of the daily calculus, and who are unsure about the whole complex process of pursuing postsecondary education, enhanced guidance and information should have significant effects.

However, the systematic analysis, as presented here, poses some tricky analytic questions. For instance, the research suggests that mentoring and counseling have a direct impact on the likelihood a student will attend college. But might the effect point the other way? After all, higher levels of teacher attention are probably not meted out at random. Students in the highly advanced sequences tend to receive more attention and more mentoring from teachers. Whether or not teachers do it intentionally, they often work more closely with, and invest a little more after-school time in, those students who are particularly promising and appear likely to succeed. So, there might be a triage effect at work, a self-fulfilling prophecy.

A particular course sequence may not necessarily make a difference. Instead, students enrolled in these courses may enjoy other benefits, such as increased teacher attention. If that is the case, as more students are encouraged to take advanced sequences, the benefits of being in those classrooms likely would be diluted. Again, caution is necessary when generalizing about which effects are instruction-specific and therefore replicable and which could be watered down or diffused if the size or academic profile of the high-sequence cohort were to change.

A final point worth thinking about is the degree to which improved performance by students in advanced sequences represents a net gain in human capital versus a manifestation of queue-jumping. If participating students are primarily getting into better colleges, graduate schools, and jobs because of the counseling or assistance, then that outcome is very different from a fundamental increase in the knowledge and talent of American youth. To the extent that advanced courses are better preparing a generation of students, they are producing real systemic benefits to their communities and the nation. If, however, strategies for success are largely about determining who gets positioned for the most attractive avenues to success, then the discussion is primarily about how to reshuffle existing opportunities.

To the degree that the discussion is about democratizing opportunity rather than systemic benefits, a political conundrum arises. Pouring resources into bolstering high-sequence coursework under such conditions essentially requires advantaged taxpayers to subsidize more challenging sequences of instruction for other people's children. More specifically, by asking these taxpayers to subsidize more counselors and so forth, they are being asked to pay a premium to ensure that their children get fewer shots at getting ahead. This is a political reality that attends any redistributive policy proposal, but it seems especially poignant in this case.

There is one other related issue that I would like to raise. Schneider's work has important implications for the whole question of tracking and the de-tracking movement that has had such a widespread impact in the past two decades. De-tracking may be thought of in two ways. One approach is to think of tracking as a way to deny large numbers of low socioeconomic status (SES) and minority children access to the educational opportunities being reserved for middle- and upper-class children. This critique is made most famously by Jeannie Oakes, and it has enjoyed widespread popularity in recent years. Such critics argue that if the vestiges of tracking are limited and disadvantaged children are given a shot at the same educational opportunities enjoyed by their more privileged peers, then progress would be made in democratizing American education and enhancing social equity.

An alternative hypothesis provides an equity-based justification for tracking. One key argument offered by proponents of tracking is that it can help schools effectively serve at-risk children by placing them in classroom environments where success is modeled and expected. Where students are being tracked most aggressively, the children who benefit the most may not be the high SES students who wind up in the advanced tracks—because those students are more likely to already know the strategies for success and to have support and resources available—but those children from low SES families. These children would otherwise be surrounded by friends and peers who do not understand the rules for getting ahead and thus would be less likely to work toward high school graduation and college attendance. In such a framework, tracking becomes a way to steer low SES children with good habits or high aspirations into academic tracks and courses where they are going to learn strategies for success and be insulated from more destructive influences.

If this second dynamic helps to explain Schneider's findings regarding the effects of sequencing, then de-tracking schools might have adverse consequences for those low SES and disadvantaged students who have nurtured a desire to succeed. The push to de-track schools, by fracturing the concentrated benefits currently present in high-sequence courses, might undercut a route that helps some children escape circumstances where both mentoring and role models are in short supply. While I am uncertain as to the merits of such an argument, it does pose a challenge that ought to be considered.

Notes

1. The rising educational expectations and occupational aspirations of America's teenagers are discussed in Barbara Schneider and David Stevenson, *The Ambitious Generation: America's Teenagers Motivated but Directionless* (Yale University Press, 1999). For more recent information on the increase in numbers of young people now aspiring to and matriculating to postsecondary institutions, see National Center for Education Statistics, *Condition of Education, 2001* (Washington, 2001).

2. For the past five years, Fengbin Chang, Lori Hill, Robert Petrin, Catherine Riegle-Crumb, Christopher Swanson, and I have been working on identifying strategies that help young people matriculate to college. Several papers on this topic have been given at profes-

sional conferences, and selected findings are discussed in a White Paper prepared for the National Science Foundation, "Transitioning from High School" (University of Chicago, 1999). Many of the findings are included in this paper and our book, *Strategies for Success*, forthcoming.

3. A comprehensive sociological literature links student educational expectations and occupational aspirations with later adult success. This model, described in William Sewell, Archibald O. Haller, and George W. Oblendorp, "The Educational and Early Occupational Attainment Process: Replication and Revisions," *American Sociological Review,* vol. 35 (1970), pp. 1014–27, has been replicated with various samples over the past thirty years. Reviews of this model and recent research can be found in Robert Dreeben, "The Sociology of Education: Its Development in the United States," in Aaron Pallas, ed., *Research in Sociology of Education and Socialization*, vol. 10 (Greenwich, Conn.: JAI Press, 1994), pp. 7–52. See also William H. Sewell and Robert M. Hauser, "A Review of the Wisconsin Longitudinal Study of Social and Psychological Factors in Aspirations and Achievements 1963–1992," Working Paper 92–02 (University of Wisconsin–Madison, Center for Demography and Ecology, 1993); and Alan C. Kerckhoff, "Institutional Arrangements and Stratification Processes in Industrial Societies," *Annual Review of Sociology*, vol. 21 (1995), pp. 323–47.

4. The increasing wage gap between college graduates and high school graduates has been documented by several economists. See, for example, Chinhui Juhn and Kevin Murphy, "Inequality in Labor Market Outcomes," *Economic Policy Review,* vol. 1 (1995), pp. 26–34.

5. For further explanation of changes in the role of education for understanding wage differentials, see Marvin H. Kosters, ed., *Workers and Their Wages: Changing Patterns in the United States* (Washington: American Enterprise Institute Press, 1991).

6. Secretary's Commission on Achieving Necessary Skills (SCANS), *Learning a Living: A Blueprint for High Performance* (Department of Labor, 1992).

7. These analyses can be found in David Stevenson, Julie Kochanek, and Barbara Schneider, "Making the Transition from High School: Recent Trends and Policies," in Kathryn Borman and Barbara Schneider, eds., *The Adolescent Years: Social Influences and Educational Challenges*, National Society for the Study of Education Yearbook (University of Chicago Press, 1998), pp. 207–26.

8. Over the past decade, the number of students receiving a college degree has not grown at the same pace as the number of students who enter postsecondary institutions. This is particularly the case for minorities, who now constitute the fastest-growing proportion of entering college freshmen, but whose completion rates remain considerably lower than their white counterparts'. See *Condition of Education.*

9. *Condition of Education.*

10. Bureau of the Census, "Educational Attainment of the Population 15 Years and Over by Age, Sex, Race, and Hispanic Origin: March 2000," 2000 U.S. Census (www.census.gov/population/www/socdemo/education/p20-536.html [December 19, 2000]).

11. These analyses were conducted on national longitudinal databases from 1972, 1982, and 1992. See Schneider and Stevenson, *The Ambitious Generation.*

12. See Schneider and Stevenson, *The Ambitious Generation.*

13. See Schneider and Stevenson, *The Ambitious Generation*; and Mihaly Csikszentmihalyi and Barbara Schneider, *Becoming Adult: How Teenagers Prepare for the World of Work* (Basic Books, 2000).

14. The strategic process is described in Schneider and Stevenson, *The Ambitious Generation.*

15. National Commission on Excellence in Education, *A Nation at Risk: The Imperative for Educational Reform* (Government Printing Office, 1983).

16. Stevenson, Kochanek, and Schneider, "Making the Transition from High School."

17. "Shopping mall" in reference to high schools was coined by Arthur Powell, David K. Cohen, and Eleanor Farr, in *The Shopping Mall High School: Winners and Losers in the Educational Marketplace* (Houghton Mifflin, 1985). The term refers to the vast array of courses that are available to students for meeting their high school graduation requirements. Many popular, trendy courses are substituted for academic or higher-level courses.

18. Stevenson, Kochanek, and Schneider, "Making the Transition from High School."

19. This analysis can be found in Barbara Schneider, Christopher Swanson, and Catherine Riegle-Crumb, "Opportunities for Learning: Course Sequences and Positional Advantages," *Social Psychology of Education*, vol. 2 (1998), pp. 25–53.

20. Sally B. Kilgore and William W. Pendleton, "The Organizational Context of Learning: Framework for Understanding the Acquisition of Knowledge," *Sociology of Education*, vol. 66 (January 1993), pp. 63–87.

21. A more comprehensive discussion of these points can be found in Catherine Riegle-Crumb's chapter, "Course Strategies: Equitable Strategies for Learning," in *Strategies for Success.*

22. David Stevenson, Kathryn Schiller, and Barbara Schneider, "Sequences of Opportunities for Learning," *Sociology of Education*, vol. 67 (1994), 184–98.

23. The highest course sequence in mathematics includes trigonometry, pre-calculus, and one or more semesters of calculus; the highest course sequence in science includes chemistry and physics; and the highest course sequence in foreign language consists of four or more years of a foreign language.

24. For this analysis, see Riegle-Crumb, "Course Strategies."

25. Barbara Whitaker, "University of California Panel Suggests Abandoning SAT," *New York Times*, January 31, 2002, p. A22; and Tamar Lewin, "College Board to Revise SAT after Criticism by University," *New York Times*, March 23, 2002, p. A10.

26. For convenience, Fengbin Chang, Lori Hill, Robert Petrin, Catherine Riegle-Crumb, Christopher Swanson, and I use SAT instead of SAT or American College Test (ACT).

27. For distinctions among best friends, cliques, and crowds, see Laurence Steinberg, B. Bradford Brown, and Sanford M. Dornbusch, *Beyond the Classroom: Why School Reform Has Failed and What Parents Need to Do* (Simon and Schuster, 1996).

28. These results are based on analyses conducted by Christopher Swanson, "Opportunities to Shine: Student Involvement in Activities outside the Classroom," in *Strategies for Success*. The idea that students can overextend themselves in extracurricular activities is discussed in Christopher Swanson, "Spending Time or Investing Time: Participation in High School Curricular and Extracurricular Activities as Strategic Action," *Rationality and Society*, forthcoming. Research on the effects of paid employment on academic achievement continues to grow since the seminal work of Ellen Greenberger and Laurence Steinberg, *When Teenagers Work: The Psychological and Social Costs of Adolescent Employment* (Basic Books, 1986). More recent studies demonstrate a negative relationship between paid work and achievement, especially if teenagers work more than twenty hours a week. A review can be found in Jeylan T. Mortimer and Monica Johnson, "Adolescents' Part-Time Work and Educational Achievement," in Kathryn Borman and Barbara Schneider, eds., *The Adolescent Years: Social Influences and Educational Challenges,* National Society for the Study of Education Yearbook (University of Chicago Press, 1998), pp. 183–206.

29. Robert Petrin's results can be found in the chapter "The Distribution and Effects of Instruction for 10th Grade Mathematics and Science" in *Strategies for Success*. A version of this paper was presented at the annual meeting of the American Sociological Association, Chicago, August 6-10, 1999.

30. Similar results have been found using the experience sampling method. See David Shernoff, Shaunti Knauth, and Eleni Makris, "The Quality of Classroom Experiences," in Mihaly Csikszentmihalyi and Barbara Schneider, *Becoming Adult: How Teenagers Prepare for the World of Work* (Basic Books, 2000).

31. For additional studies on the positive effects of schools supporting strong academic press environments, see Roger Shouse, "Academic Press, Sense of Community, and Student Achievement," in James S. Coleman and others, *Redesigning American Education* (Boulder, Colo.: Westview Press, 1997). Lori Hill's chapter in *Strategies for Success* is titled "High School Resources and Post Secondary Outcomes: Implications for a Changing Student Population."

32. For complete descriptions of the Alfred P. Sloan Study of Youth and Social Development, see Schneider and Stevenson, *The Ambitious Generation;* and Csikszentmihalyi and Schneider, *Becoming Adult.*

33. This idea is more fully developed in Hill's chapter, "High School Resources and Post Secondary Outcomes: Implications for a Changing Student Population," in which she employs latent class measures that are modeled in a hierarchical linear analysis.

34. In additional analyses, Chang, Hill, Petrin, Riegle-Crumb, Swanson, and I specify various types of course-taking behaviors using different scales. Table 3 provides the results for using mathematics and science sequences as continuous variables. For convenience of interpretation, we used the same model as represented in table 3 with high mathematics and science sequence entered as a categorical variable. The odds reported in the text are based on the model that used this categorical variable.

35. Nicholas Lemann, *The Big Test: The Secret History of the American Meritocracy* (Farrar, Straus, and Giroux, 1999).

36. In a separate analysis where Chang, Hill, Petrin, Riegle-Crumb, Swanson, and I distinguish between students attending less competitive and highly competitive four-year colleges, we find that the SAT does matter for black students expecting to attend highly competitive institutions. These students, much like other students, appear to be motivated by the same academic markers.

37. C. Adelman, "Putting on the Glitz: How Tales from a Few Elite Institutions Form America's Impressions about Higher Education," *Connection: New England's Journal of Higher Education and Economic Development,* vol. 15, no. 3 (2001), pp. 24–30; and Department of Education, *Condition of Education* (National Center for Education Statistics, 2001).

38. Carnegie Foundation for the Advancement of Teaching, *The Carnegie Classification of Institutions of Higher Education* (Menlo Park, Calif., 2001).

39. American Council on Education, *Access and Persistence* (Washington, 2002).

40. See Bridge Project website at www.stanford.edu/group/bridgeproject/.

41. Abell Foundation, *Baltimore City Community College at the Crossroads* (Baltimore, Md., 2002).

42. M. Kirst and A. Venezia, "Bridging the Great Divide between Secondary Schools and Postsecondary Education," *Phi Delta Kappan* (September 2001), pp. 92–97.

43. J. Rosenbaum, *Unrealistic Plans and Misdirected Efforts: Are Community Colleges Getting the Right Message to High School Students?* (New York: Teachers College Press, 1998).

44. G. T. Henry and R. Rubenstein, "Paying for Grades: Impact of Merit-Based Financial Aid on Education Quality," *Journal of Policy Analysis and Management,* vol. 21, no. 1 (2002), pp. 93–110.

45. J. Oakes, "Can Tracking Research Inform Practice? Technical, Normative, and Political Considerations," *Educational Researcher* (May 1992), pp. 12–21.

46. Rosenbaum, *Unrealistic Plans and Misdirected Efforts.*

47. D. T. Conley, "Where's Waldo? The Conspicuous Absence of Higher Education from School Reform and One State's Response," *Phi Delta Kappan*, vol. 78, no. 4 (1996), pp. 309–15.

48. Henry and Rubenstein, "Paying for Grades."

49. D. Mize, "Oklahoma Education Planning and Assessment System," speech prepared for the annual meeting of EdTrust, Washington, D.C., 2000.

50. Henry and Rubenstein, "Paying for Grades."

51. Henry and Rubenstein, "Paying for Grades," p. 96.

52. Metropolitan Life Survey of the American Teacher, *Are We Preparing Students for the Twenty-first Century?* (New York: Metropolitan Life, September 2000).

53. Gene Bottoms, *Report of the SREB: High Schools That Work, 1998 Secondary School Survey* (Atlanta, Ga.: Southern Regional Education Board, 1998).

Ability Grouping and Student Learning

MAUREEN T. HALLINAN

Many school practices and policies are built on the assumption that students learn best when the curriculum is well matched to students' learning abilities. The belief is that when students understand what they are being taught, they are more likely to be actively involved in the learning process and less likely to disengage from classroom instruction and activities. The common practice of age-grading, which assumes that student age correlates with learning ability, enables teachers to present a curriculum designed to interest and challenge students at a particular age. Similarly, the practice of curriculum differentiation found in most secondary and middle schools and some elementary schools is based on this belief. Teachers assign students to ability groups to ensure that the curriculum they receive is suitable for their academic preparation and to expose them to new material at a level that they can comprehend.

Ideally, ability grouping should maximize student learning. In practice, ability grouping falls far short of its goal. Limitations in the process of assigning students to ability groups and in the pedagogical techniques utilized at different ability group levels seriously restrict the learning opportunities that are provided to students in some ability groups.

Empirical research reveals several of the limitations in the practice of ability grouping that account for its failure to maximize learning opportuni-

I gratefully acknowledge support for this research from the Institute for Educational Initiatives at the University of Notre Dame, the Spencer Foundation, the National Science Foundation, and the American Educational Research Association (RED–9452861). I also am grateful to Warren Kubitschek for significant contributions to the analysis and to Stephanie Arnett, Kim Galipeau, Jason Maki, Gail Mulligan, and Sylvia Phillips for research and editorial assistance.

ties for students. Studies show that the criteria schools use to assign students to ability group levels do not always produce groups that are homogeneous with respect to ability. Schools generally rely on some combination of standardized test scores, grades, teacher and counselor recommendations, student and parent choice, and college and vocational requirements to assign students to ability groups. This implies a certain subjectivity in the assignment process and leaves open the possibility that nonacademic factors may play a significant role in determining the ability group level to which a student is assigned. To the extent that this is the case, a student may be placed in an ability group that has a curriculum that is easier or more difficult than the student's learning level. That is, the assignment process may produce a poor match between student learning ability and the curriculum to which the student is exposed. As a result, the student may not learn as effectively or efficiently as would occur in a different level group.

Empirical research also shows that, on average, students assigned to higher-ability groups attain higher test scores than those placed in lower groups. Both survey and observational studies suggest reasons for this ability group effect. Studies show that students in higher-ability groups are given higher-quality instruction, a more challenging and interesting curriculum, and more teaching time than those in lower-ability groups. Further, students in high-ability groups are immersed in a more academic climate, are more academically minded, and attain higher social status than those in lower-ability groups. These characteristics of ability groups increase learning opportunities for the students assigned to them. In contrast, the research suggests that students in low-ability groups are offered a less challenging and less interesting curriculum, are assigned more boring academic tasks, have less experienced teachers and fewer academic role models, and endure a more disruptive classroom atmosphere. As a result, they are offered fewer opportunities to learn.

While a negative effect of ability grouping on the achievement of students assigned to lower-ability groups has been noted frequently, no empirical research has looked at the effect on academic achievement of moving a student from one ability group level to a higher or lower group. This paper reports on an empirical study that demonstrates that students would generally attain higher test scores if they were moved to a higher-ability group than if they remained in the one to which they were assigned. Conversely, they would perform more poorly if moved to a lower-ability group. What is remarkable about this finding is that it holds regardless of the student's ability. That is, assigning a student to a higher-ability group increases the student's learning regardless of the student's ability level. This finding raises critical questions about whether American schools sufficiently challenge students to attain optimal performance and suggests a way to increase achievement for all students, and especially for slower learners.

Determinants of Student Learning

The belief that a good fit between the curriculum and student ability is critical for learning is supported by an understanding of how students learn. Educational literature identifies several factors that promote learning. These factors include the quantity and quality of instruction, social-psychological processes governing student motivation and effort, and the academic climate of the learning environment. These three determinants of learning are believed to vary across ability group level.

Quantity and Quality of Instruction

Several conceptual models explain why increasing the quantity and quality of instruction increases student learning. J. B. Carroll relates learning to student characteristics, to the quality of instruction, and to the amount of time allowed for learning. He argues that high-quality instruction enables students to better understand what is being taught and increases the likelihood that they will retain the material and be able to build on it. Further, he claims that optimal learning occurs when schools provide adequate time for students to learn. F. M. Newmann relates learning to teacher qualifications. He states that increasing the competence and confidence of teachers improves the quality and quantity of instruction, which, in turn, raises student achievement. His argument that the professional development of teachers is crucial is based on his conviction that teacher competence influences how well students comprehend instruction.[1]

A. Brown's model of learning directs attention to student involvement in the learning process. He claims that students learn best when they take an active role in instruction and when they are encouraged to use higher-order thinking skills. High-quality instruction, which demands intellectual engagement on the part of students, results in greater achievement. A. B. Sørensen and M. T. Hallinan depict learning as dependent on student ability, effort, and opportunities to learn. In their model, learning is interactive, not additive, implying that even with an increase in ability or effort, a student will not learn unless provided with opportunities to learn. They argue that a primary component of opportunities to learn is the quantity and quality of instruction presented to the student.[2]

Empirical research supports the theoretical arguments that relate student learning to the quantity and quality of instruction. B. Heyns looks at quantity of instruction in terms of attendance at summer school and finds that students who attend summer school have significantly higher achievement levels the following academic year than those who do not. D. Wiley shows that the longer the school year, the higher the students' achievement test scores. This result is also seen in cross-national analyses of the Department of Education's Third International Mathematics and Science Study (TIMSS) data. R. Barr and R. Dreeben demonstrate that increasing the pace of instruction without decreasing the length of a lesson has a positive effect on the reading scores of first-grade students. Other studies show that higher achievement is related to teaching students higher-order thinking skills, engaging students in the instructional process, and providing a variety of tasks designed to engage student interest.[3]

Student Motivation

Most conceptual models of learning identify student motivation as a major determinant of learning.[4] They posit that motivation increases student effort to learn. Increased effort, in turn, raises academic achievement.

Conceptual models identify several mechanisms that link motivation to learning. Carroll posits that both extrinsic and intrinsic motivators influence student behavior. He suggests that students are extrinsically motivated when they seek the approval of a teacher, the affirmation of parents, the esteem of friends, the satisfaction of receiving good grades, or the recognition of external rewards and honors. Students are intrinsically motivated when they study to increase self-confidence in their abilities, to build self-esteem, or to avoid the embarrassment of failure. Carroll argues that increasing intrinsic and extrinsic rewards increases student achievement. B. Schneider, M. Csikszentmihalyi, and S. Knauth also stress the importance of intrinsic motivation, saying that it is supported by activities that enhance a student's self-esteem.[5]

Another conceptualization of the relationship between student motivation and learning focuses on the importance of self-regulated learning; that is, learning that is independent and academically effective. V. Vauras and others argue that intrinsic motivation leads to self-regulated learning. C. Waronsky and A. Waronsky claim that extrinsic motivators should be replaced by intrinsic motivators as soon as possible to ensure long-term commitment to learning. P. Pintrich holds that intrinsic motivation increases with self-efficacy beliefs, belief in the value of the task, and goal orientation. Similarly, F. M. Newmann and G. G. Wehlage assert that student motivation grows with intellectual involvement in a task and when a student judges the task to be relevant for the future.[6]

A third conceptualization of student motivation and learning focuses on teacher expectations. J. Dusek claims that teachers form expectations for student achievement in response to cues students provide about their ability and commitment to learning. R. Rosenthal and L. Jacobson argue that teacher expectations for student performance become a self-fulfilling prophecy, with students modifying their behavior to make it consistent with teacher expectations. J. Eccles and A. Wigfield link teacher expectancies to student motivation and assert that teacher expectations have a direct effect on student self-concept and self-expectations, which are determinants of motivation.[7] Each of these models suggests that the higher a teacher's expectations, the harder the student will study and the more likely the student will be academically successful.

Several empirical studies support the conceptual associations between student motivation and learning.[8] Research on instructional grouping shows that assigning students to groups in which tasks are intellectually challenging and related to future goals increases their motivation to learn. Students whose teachers provide complex and interesting activities, opportunities to make decisions, and occasions to evaluate their own and peers' work show greater motivation and higher achievement than students whose teachers provide fewer of these opportunities. Students whose teachers use cooperative learning techniques and allow students to work together on common activities with a shared goal show lower anxiety, more positive social behavior, and greater responsibility in task performance.

Empirical research also shows a positive relationship between external rewards and achievement.[9] Students who are given positive feedback for satisfactory performance make more impressive gains on subsequent performance. Student participation in athletics and clubs is seen to increase academic motivation in schools that recognize excellence in extracurricular activities. Athletic participation, in particular, is positively correlated with academic outcomes.

While some empirical studies fail to find a relationship between teacher expectations and student achievement, a number of other studies find evidence of a self-fulfilling prophecy.[10] Students whose teachers have high expectations for their performance tend to attain higher academic achievement. W. Meyer reports that teachers make fairly accurate judgments about student capabilities, implying that teachers do not expect more of their students than their capabilities allow. P. Peterson and S. Barger demonstrate that teacher expectations remain fairly stable over time.[11] This finding suggests that teachers may not take into account the sporadic patterns of cognitive growth evidenced by some students.

Academic Climate

The third condition that affects student learning is the academic climate of the school or classroom. Two important dimensions of the academic context may be identified: school or teacher norms governing student learning and peer norms about academic performance. A strong academic climate is one in which teachers strongly emphasize the importance of learning and students hold norms that support academic success.

J. Coleman claims that, in schools where educators stress the importance of academic success and reward student achievement, students develop positive attitudes toward learning. These attitudes are reflected in good learning habits, such as paying attention in class, participating in the instructional process, studying, completing homework assignments, and attaining good grades. P. A. Cusick holds that classrooms with a strong academic climate support students' determination and effort to succeed. A. S. Bryk, V. E. Lee, and P. B. Holland argue that schools with high academic standards set in motion social-psychological processes that support learning. Students grow in self-esteem and in the confidence that they are capable learners and that they experience an increase in achievement-based social status. E. L. McDill, G. Natriello, and A. M. Pappas state that a school that is committed to academic excellence and that encourages individualized learning and rewards academic proficiency promotes student learning.[12]

Normative reference group theory provides an understanding of how peer norms influence student learning.[13] The theory states that over time a group establishes norms that become the standard or reference point for members' behavior. A normative reference group exerts its influence on an individual through processes of compliance and internalization. A group member complies with a group norm to be rewarded and to avoid sanction. Individuals gradually internalize the group norms and begin to conform through personal commitment and choice. If a student wants to be part of a group whose norms include studying hard and striving for academic success, the student initially will conform to these norms to attain group membership. Eventually, the student will internalize the group's norms, leading to improved academic performance.

Several empirical studies relate academic climate to student learning. Bryk, Lee, and Holland report a positive effect of academic climate (as measured by such factors as time spent on homework and academic orientation of the school) on student achievement. C. Hill finds that schools with stronger academic climates have lower dropout rates. Empirical studies also demonstrate the effects of peer norms on student achievement. In an early review of research on academic climate, W. G. Spady reports several studies showing a positive effect of a strong academic climate on student learning. Cusick finds that a strong academic climate has a positive effect on the achievement of all students, not just members of an academic clique.[14]

The three determinants of learning—the quantity and quality of instruction, student motivation, and academic climate—are interrelated. The strength of an academic climate is dependent on the quantity and quality of instruction, and both of these factors influence student motivation. When these three factors co-vary in a way that fosters learning, students are provided with rich educational opportunities and experiences, and they are most likely to attain high achievement. When one or more of these determinants of learning is weak, student performance is expected to suffer.

Variation in Learning Opportunities across Ability Groups

Empirical studies provide evidence that opportunities to learn created by the quantity and quality of instruction, influences on student motivation, and academic climate vary across instructional groups in ability grouped schools. A number of studies show that higher-ability groups are characterized by high quantity and quality of instruction, strong student motivation to learn, and an academic climate that fosters learning. Controlling for student ability, the research reports that students in higher-ability groups attain higher achievement than those in lower-ability groups.

Several studies demonstrate the superiority of high-ability groups in terms of the quantity and quality of instruction. In high-ability groups, teachers devote more time to instruction and less time to management and discipline, cover more of the curriculum at a faster pace, and are more experienced and skilled.[15]

Empirical research also shows that ability group level influences student motivation. Students in high-ability groups have higher social status, command more teacher and peer respect, develop greater self-confidence and self-regulation, and devote more time to studying than students in lower-ability groups. Teachers have higher expectations for the performance of students in high-ability groups than for equally talented students assigned to lower-ability groups or to heterogeneous groups. Similarly, teachers have lower expectations for the achievement of students in low-ability groups than for pupils of equal ability in higher-ability groups.[16]

Research also reveals differences in academic climate across ability group levels. Teachers spend less time dealing with disciplinary problems and devote more time to instruction in higher groups. In lower-ability groups, teachers tend to praise minor accomplishments of students, seemingly satisfied with minimal performance. In addition, students in high-ability groups tend to be more serious about learning and to share more positive attitudes toward schooling with their classmates. Meanwhile, students in lower-ability groups are more apt to adopt norms and standards of behavior that detract from learning.[17]

These studies provide compelling evidence that high-ability groups generally are characterized by higher quantity and quality of instruction, stronger student motivation, and a stronger academic climate than low-ability groups. By channeling more and better opportunities for learning to students, high-ability groups are more conducive to student learning and act as a more positive influence on student achievement than low-ability groups.

Criteria for Assigning Students to Ability Groups

Selecting an ability group that will best foster a student's learning is a major consideration in making ability group assignments. Three research streams support a policy of assigning students to the highest ability group level at which they can perform successfully. The first body of research includes theoretical and empirical studies showing that higher-ability groups provide greater academic benefits than lower-ability groups. These benefits are likely to offset any risk of student discouragement at the difficulty of the work in a higher-level group. Moreover, the benefits of high-ability group assignment, in terms of teacher expectations and peer support, are likely to increase student motivation, leading to greater effort and higher academic performance.

A second body of research focuses on the way students are assigned to ability groups. Studies show that schools typically rely on several criteria in making ability group placements. These criteria include grades, test scores, teacher and counselor recommendations, parental preference, and student choice. While many of these criteria are designed to ensure a good fit between ability group level and a student's capabilities, nonacademic considerations often enter into consideration. For example, students may select a class because their friends are taking it, because they like a particular teacher, or because the class meets at a preferred hour. In addition, scheduling constraints may necessitate that a student take a class at an ability level different from the one for which he or she is best suited. Limitations on enrollment created by class size and the availability of teachers also affect placement decisions.

The subjectivity of some of the criteria schools use to assign students to ability groups introduces the likelihood that some students will be assigned to classes that are above or below their learning level. As a result, ability groups arc likely to be more heterogeneous in practice than by design. Moreover, the distributions of achievement are likely to overlap across groups. Students at the high end of the ability distribution in one ability group may have higher test scores than students at the low end of the distribution in the next highest ability group. This overlap suggests that the most capable students in one ability group likely would succeed if they were advanced to the next highest ability group level.

An effect of heterogeneity within ability groups is that, even in ability grouped classes, teachers must take into account a fairly wide distribution of ability when presenting the curriculum. To instruct students in a class with a broad range of abilities requires that some of the curriculum be taught at a higher or lower level than the mean. This instructional accommodation has the unintended consequence that students in any given ability group are likely to receive approximately the same level of instruction, some of the time, as students in the adjacent higher- or lower-ability groups.

A third body of research that supports a policy of placing students in as high an ability group as possible compares the academic achievement of students in Catholic and public schools. Studies show that, on average, Catholic school students attain higher academic achievement than their public school counterparts.[18] Researchers attribute the Catholic school advantage, in part, to characteristics of the academic program of these schools. Catholic schools tend to provide all their students, regardless of ability group level, with a strong curriculum, and Catholic school teachers hold high expectations for student performance. The success of Catholic school students, especially low-ability students, is evidence that taking solid, academic courses increases the achievement of students at all ability levels.

Strategies for Studying Ability Group Effects

In empirical studies of ability group effects on student achievement, researchers have taken one of two analytical approaches. In the first approach, researchers ask whether students in ability grouped schools perform differently from students in ungrouped schools.[19] These studies typically find no mean difference in achievement between schools with homogeneous and heterogeneous groups. However, the variance in achievement tends to be greater in ability grouped schools. This suggests that ability grouping has a differential effect on student achievement by level. Students in high-ability groups attain higher achievement or students in low-ability groups have lower achievement, or both, than similar peers in ungrouped schools.

In the second analytical approach to studying ability group effects, researchers compare the effects of ability groups across group level.[20] When cross-sectional data are analyzed, the studies generally show that the higher the ability group, the higher the mean achievement. With longitudinal data, the research generally demonstrates that students' growth in achievement is greater in high-ability groups than in lower groups.

These two approaches to the study of ability grouping are methodologically sound and yield important information about the magnitude and direction of ability group effects. Nevertheless, they are limited in that they focus only on group differences in achievement and fail to highlight the impact of ability grouping on the performance of an individual student. This paper attempts to overcome this limitation of previous research by comparing the achievement of a student in a particular ability group with the performance of a student with the same characteristics in a higher- or lower-ability group.

The aim of the analysis is to examine whether a student would attain higher (or lower) achievement if placed in a higher- (or lower-) ability group than the one to which the student was assigned. This analytic strategy is similar to Coleman and others' approach in comparing the achievement of students in Catholic and public schools.[21] It permits an examination of the achievement of a student in different ability group contexts. The theoretical appeal of this analytical strategy is that it provides a better understanding of the differential learning opportunities that are offered across ability group levels. Its practical appeal is that it should assist educational personnel, parents, and students who are faced with decisions about choice of courses and ability group placement.

Methodology

The analysis presented here is part of a longitudinal study of the effects of ability grouping on students' growth in academic achievement. The five public high schools and one Catholic high school in a Midwestern city and a single public high school in an adjacent city participated in the study.

Sample

Survey information was obtained on more than four thousand students in two cohorts: the students in the seven high schools in the sample who entered high school in either the 1988–89 or 1989–90 school year. The present study is based on students in the six public high schools in the sample. The single Catholic high school in the study is excluded because its ability group structure differs from that of the public schools. The combined total population of Hispanics, Asians, Native Americans, and other nonwhite, nonblack students in these schools is less than 5 percent of the sample. These students are treated as white in the analysis. Students who took special education courses and English as a second language courses and those not taking English or mathematics in the particular grade being studied are excluded.

Variables

The dependent variable in the analytic models is student achievement in English and mathematics in the spring of ninth, tenth, and eleventh grades. Achievement is measured by a student's percentile score in English and mathematics on a statewide standardized test. This test was designed and scored by a national testing company that used a national sample as the reference group. Public school students took this test in the spring of their eighth, ninth, and tenth grades, and the first of the two cohorts also took it in the eleventh grade.

The independent variables include several exogenous and control variables. Ability group level for each student was obtained from school records at four points over each school year. In this study, ability group assignment at midyear is used because group assignments are fairly stable by then. The schools in the sample had four ability group levels in English: Advanced, Honors, Regular, and Basic. They had five levels in mathematics: Advanced, Honors, Regular, Basic, and Very Basic. (The terms *Basic* and *Very Basic* were not used by the school, but examination of the curriculum indicated that these names are appropriate.)

Other independent variables in the analysis are students' previous percentile test scores in English and mathematics, students' final grade in their previous English and mathematics classes, and absenteeism. Previous grades follow the usual four-point scale, from "A" = 4.0 to "F" = 0.0. Absenteeism is measured by the total number of days the student missed school during the first semester of that year. Background variables for the analysis include gender, race, whether the student participated in the free lunch program (an indicator of socioeconomic status), and age (measured in years minus an appropriate integer for that year). Cohort is added as a control variable, as are dummy variables for school attended.

Statistical Model

The dependent variable, student percentile test score in English and mathematics, is censored at both ends of the distribution; no student can obtain a test score lower than 1 or higher than 99. Because this censoring violates the assumptions of the ordinary least squares (OLS) regression model, OLS coefficient estimates would be biased toward zero by the resulting floor and ceiling effects. Therefore, a two-limit tobit model is employed, which provides consistent coefficient estimates for censored dependent variables with this type of distribution.[22] The tobit model estimates the underlying and unobservable, uncensored error distribution, transforms the observed dependent variable into this uncensored distribution, and computes coefficients based on that transformation. The statistical program used for these analyses (LIMDEP) provides an estimate of the standard deviation of the estimated uncensored error distribution, identified as σ in the appropriate tables.

Unless the proportion of censored cases is large, the values of the transformed dependent variable provided by the tobit model are virtually indistinguishable from those of the observed dependent variable for most of the distribution of the dependent variable. Thus tobit coefficient estimates can be and usually are interpreted as if they were ordinary regression coefficients. Similarly, predictions made from tobit models can be interpreted in the metric of the observed dependent variable. Given the limited amount of censoring present in the data used in these analyses, such interpretations will not be substantively misleading.

Because of the nature of the tobit model, the transformed dependent variable will differ somewhat from the observed dependent variable at the ends of the distribution. For example, if a student in the sample had an observed value of 99 on an achievement test, the transformed variable might be as large as 105. Thus, while predictions from the tobit models provide completely accurate predictions of the transformed variable, they slightly overestimate any values at the upper end of the achievement distribution and slightly underestimate any values at the lower end.

Furthermore, the models will be estimated separately for each ability group because the effects of previous achievement, background, and other factors on learning are expected to vary by group. This variation is expected because of interactions with unmeasured factors associated with each ability group, such as the quantity and quality of instruction and the social-psychological dynamics and academic climate that distinguish the groups.

These models and estimates will be used to predict student achievement for students with various combinations of characteristics. Theoretically, these models provide consistent estimates for the effect of prior factors for any student and accurate predictions for any combination of measured student characteristics. In practice, the calculated estimates are based on the particular, observed sample of students and the combination of characteristics they happen to have. For example, the prediction equation for the Regular English ability group is based on the characteristics of the students who happened to be in that group that year. As with any modeling, because of sampling variability, the calculated estimates and thus the predictions derived from those estimates will be most accurate for students with characteristics similar to those of the typical student in the sample. The calculated estimates and predictions are likely to be less accurate for students with combinations of characteristics that are rare in the sample, and they are likely to be least accurate for students with combinations of characteristics outside the range found in the sample.

In this analysis, student achievement is predicted for various students hypothetically placed in various ability groups. That is, the analysis predicts the achievement of students with different combinations of characteristics, had they been placed in the Regular group, had they been placed in the Honors group, and so forth. When the student characteristics are similar to students in the ability group in which they are placed, the predictions are likely to be accurate. When the student characteristics are not similar to students in that ability group, the predictions are less accurate. As a result, the farther one moves from a student's group assignment, the less reliable the predicted mean achievement score will be. For example, predicting how well a typical student from the Basic group would achieve in the Regular group will be more reliable than predicting that same student's achievement in the Honors group. The prediction will be most accurate when one estimates how well that student would achieve in the Basic group.

One important characteristic of the sample analyzed for this study is the overlap across ability groups in the measured characteristics of the students, especially measures of achievement. Not only is this true for students in adjacent ability groups, but noticeable overlap also exists in characteristics of students in groups even two levels apart. That is, most students have a number of counterparts, students with similar measured characteristics, in a wide range of ability groups. The favorable statistical consequence of this overlap in student measured characteristics, and especially achievement, is to reduce any unreliability of the predictions.

One might argue that students who are similar in prior achievement but are placed in different ability groups likely differ on unmeasured characteristics such as motivation, effort, and ambition; otherwise, they would have been assigned to the same ability group. Moreover, these unmeasured factors might also affect student achievement, reducing the accuracy of the predictions. While that argument is true in general, any such effects here should be small. This can be viewed as a sample selection issue. The analysis includes multiple controls for prior achievement known to reduce or eliminate sample selection effects in general and does so in these data (results not shown).[23] Therefore, any error in the mean predictions due to unmeasured factors is expected to be small.

Results

Descriptive and inferential analyses were conducted to determine the effects of ability group level on student achievement.

Descriptive Analysis

Table 1 presents the means and standard deviations of the dependent and independent variables for the ninth-grade students in the analysis. Given that the descriptive statistics are similar for tenth and eleventh grades, the results are not included. The data in table 1 indicate that the average student test scores were slightly higher than the national mean in both English and mathematics. Their mean grade was a "C" in both subjects. Students were absent five and a half days, on average, during the first semester. The sample was evenly divided by gender. Twenty-two percent of the sample was black and 20 percent participated in the free lunch program. Students were fairly evenly distributed across the six public high schools in the study. The majority of students were assigned to the Regular English and mathematics ability groups in eighth grade, with Honors being the next largest previous ability group placement.

Figures 1 and 2 present the distribution of eighth-grade standardized test scores in English and mathematics for the ninth-grade students in the sample by their ninth-grade ability group placement. To create a more readable graph, that is, one without a large number of spikes, a moving average was calculated over an interval of 7 percentile points. For example, if two students had test scores between 1 and 7, the point (4, 0.27) was plotted, with 4 being the midpoint of the interval from 1 to 7 and 2/7 = 0.27 being the number of students with test scores in the interval and 7 the number of possible test scores in this interval. If seven students had test scores between 2 and 8, the point (5, 1) was plotted, where 5 is the midpoint of the interval and 7/7 = 1 being the number of students divided by the number of possible test

Table 1. Descriptive Statistics

Variable	English, ninth grade (N = 2,581)		Mathematics, ninth grade (N = 2,574)	
	Mean	Standard deviation	Mean	Standard deviation
Ninth-grade English test score	54.70	24.44	—	—
Ninth-grade mathematics test score	—	—	56.78	26.19
Eighth-grade English test score	57.92	23.87	58.02	23.87
Eighth-grade mathematics test score	61.26	25.75	61.34	25.70
Eighth-grade English grade	2.18	1.10	2.19	1.10
Eighth-grade mathematics grade	2.00	1.12	2.00	1.12
Days absent first semester	5.43	6.70	5.43	6.65
Cohort 2 = 1	0.50	0.50	0.50	0.50
Age in years	−0.03	0.52	−0.03	0.52
Female = 1	0.50	0.50	0.50	0.50
Black = 1	0.22	0.41	0.22	0.41
Free lunch = 1	0.20	0.40	0.20	0.40
School 1.1 = 1	0.15	0.36	0.15	0.35
School 1.2 = 1	0.15	0.36	0.15	0.36
School 1.3 = 1	0.19	0.39	0.19	0.39
School 1.4 = 1	0.13	0.33	0.13	0.34
School 1.5 = 1	0.18	0.38	0.17	0.38
School 2.1 = 1	0.21	0.41	0.21	0.41
Eighth-grade ability group				
Very Basic = 1	—	—	—	—
Basic = 1	0.09	0.28	0.10	0.30
Regular = 1	0.57	0.50	0.57	0.49
Honors = 1	0.28	0.45	0.20	0.40
Advanced = 1	—	—	0.10	0.30
Special Program = 1	0.01	0.11	0.01	0.08
Eighth-grade not ability grouped = 1	0.01	0.12	0.02	0.13
Eighth-grade ability group info missing = 1	0.04	0.20	0.01	0.10

Figure 1. Frequency of Standardized Test Scores by Ability Group Level, Ninth-Grade English Students
Frequency (moving average over 7 percentile points)

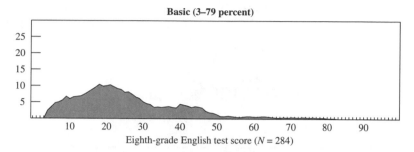

Basic (3–79 percent)

Eighth-grade English test score (*N* = 284)

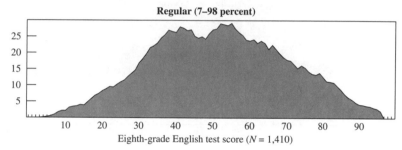

Regular (7–98 percent)

Eighth-grade English test score (*N* = 1,410)

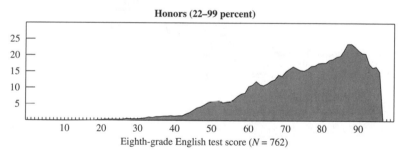

Honors (22–99 percent)

Eighth-grade English test score (*N* = 762)

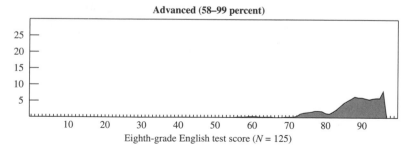

Advanced (58–99 percent)

Eighth-grade English test score (*N* = 125)

Figure 2. Frequency of Standardized Test Scores by Ability Group Level, Ninth-Grade Mathematics Students

Frequency (moving average over 7 percentile points)

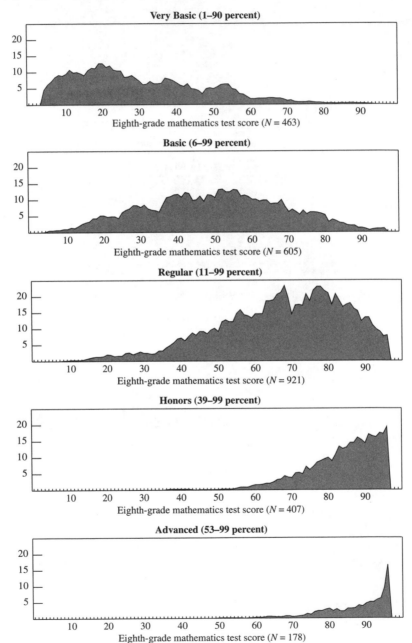

scores in this interval. A consequence of using this method is that the scores of the lowest- and highest-scoring students do not appear per se in the figure, but they are included in the first and last average, respectively. For example, while several Advanced English students achieved test scores at the 99th percentile, their frequency is averaged with those of students who scored between 93 and 99.

Different measures of achievement could be used for the analysis, such as normal curve equivalents. However, whether the dependent variable is percentiles or normal curve equivalents or other related measures, the distributions would all reveal significant overlap across groups and thus lead to the same conclusions about the effects of ability group placement.

While some overlap of the test scores of students across ability groups was expected, given the criteria schools use to assign students to ability groups, figures 1 and 2 reveal far greater overlap than anticipated. Overlap is found even between ability groups two or more levels apart. In other words, the ninth-grade ability groups in the high schools in this sample are far less homogeneous than one might expect, with extensive overlap in standardized test scores across English and mathematics groups. The tenth- and eleventh-grade test scores, which are not shown, have considerable overlap as well.

The high degree of overlap across ability groups has several consequences for the students in these schools. In the first place, overlap makes determining appropriate group placement difficult. For example, if a student were to receive a ninth-grade English test score of 60 percent, the student could reasonably be assigned to any one of the four ninth-grade ability groups. A student who scored at the 90th percentile in ninth-grade mathematics could conceivably be placed in the ninth-grade Basic, Regular, Honors, or Advanced mathematics ability group.

Moreover, the figures show that the distribution of English and mathematics scores of some groups is virtually contained within the distribution of another ability group. For example, the distribution of scores of the students in the Basic English group is almost completely contained within the Regular English group distribution and the Basic mathematics distribution encompasses the Regular, Honors, and Advanced distribution of scores. This suggests that the curriculum differences across some groups must be small, given the heterogeneity of the students with respect to ability.

Another consequence of the overlap across ability groups is that nearly every student in the ninth grade, regardless of actual ability group assignment, could have been placed in the next higher ability group in English or mathematics, without being at the bottom of the ability distribution of the higher group. Similarly, nearly every student could have been assigned to the next lower ability group without being at the top of the lower distribution. This degree of heterogeneity within ability groups suggests that students could easily be assigned to a higher-ability group with their capabilities being indistinguishable from many of the other students in the higher group.

The extent of the overlap in the ability group distributions also suggests that not all the assignment criteria used by schools are designed to maximize group homogeneity. While it is often believed that schools rely primarily on test scores and grades to make ability group placements, these data suggest a heavy influence of nonacademic criteria as well. Groups that are heterogeneous with respect to test scores could be homogeneous with respect to grades. However, the means and standard deviations of student grades by ability group indicate that this is not the case in these data. The considerable degree of heterogeneity within ability groups in the sample likely weakens the benefits of ability grouping by making it more difficult for teachers to tailor the curriculum and instruction to the ability level of their students.

Inferential Analysis

The central aim of this study is to measure the effect of ability group level on student achievement. The strategy is to determine whether a student would receive a higher or lower test score if assigned to a different ability group. To accomplish this requires a two-stage analysis. First, prediction equations must be estimated for the effects of ability group level on English and mathematics achievement. Second, a predicted test score must be calculated for each student for each possible ability group to which the student could be assigned.

Alternatively, one could perform a propensity score matching analysis in which comparisons are made between the achievement of similar students in different ability groups. This approach has the advantage of avoiding distortions that may result in comparing dissimilar students. However, it is less theoretically grounded than the method used here because it fails to fully utilize the previous achievement histories of students in making predictions. In practice, both methods should yield similar results for students in adjacent tracks.

Table 2. Tobit Models Predicting Ninth-Grade English Achievement

Variable	Students in Basic (N = 284) b	Students in Regular (N = 1,410) b	Students in Honors (N = 762) b	Students in Advanced (N = 125) b
Eighth-grade English test score	0.59***	0.78***	0.80***	0.79***
Eighth-grade mathematics test score	0.02	0.06***	0.12***	0.15*
Eighth-grade English grade	−0.62	0.92**	0.64	0.84
Eighth-grade mathematics grade	0.10	0.33	−0.32	−0.09
Days absent first semester	0.03	−0.02	0.03	0.29
Cohort 2 = 1	1.00	1.45**	1.03	1.37
Age in years	−2.54***	−2.10***	−0.37	−2.22
Female = 1	1.03	0.55	0.21	1.10
Black = 1	−1.43	−0.61	0.04	−5.81**
Free lunch = 1	0.68	0.10	−1.42	−0.15
School 1.2 = 1	−2.00	2.67**	−0.87	−3.73
School 1.3 = 1	−1.29	1.83*	−1.30	1.04
School 1.4 = 1	−0.40	0.16	−2.22	−4.96**
School 1.5 = 1	−2.39	2.32**	−0.19	—
School 2.1 = 1	−3.54	4.02***	1.19	1.08
Eighth-grade ability group Basic = 1	−0.05	−2.85*	−11.97	—
Honors = 1	—	1.80	1.94*	2.15
Advanced = 1	—	—	—	—
Special Program = 1	−0.44	−1.34	−0.90	3.45
Eighth-grade not ability grouped = 1	—	5.39	3.92*	5.39
Eighth-grade ability group info missing = 1	−0.86	−2.87*	−1.83	1.30
Constant	10.46***	−1.09	1.81	−1.37
σ	7.53***	9.34***	8.28***	5.33***
Log-likelihood	−976.33	−515.30	−2,678.98	−372.14

* = $p < 0.05$; ** = $p < 0.01$; *** = $p < 0.001$.

Table 2 presents a tobit model predicting English test score at the end of ninth grade by ninth-grade ability group. The independent and control variables are previous test scores, previous grades, absenteeism, background information, school, and previous ability group level. Table 2 shows that eighth-grade test score in English has a statistically significant positive effect on ninth-grade English achievement in all ability groups and that eighth-grade mathematics test score has a statistically significant positive effect on ninth-grade English achievement for all but the Basic group. English and mathematics eighth-grade grades have only a weak effect on English achievement. The bivariate correlations between English eighth-grade test score, mathematics eighth-grade test score, English eighth-grade grade, and mathematics eighth-grade grade are all positive both in the full sample and within each ability group.

Being older has a significant negative effect on English achievement in the Basic and Regular groups, likely because older students in these groups tend to have repeated a grade for poor performance. Being black has a significant negative effect on English achievement in the Advanced group. Because only ten black students were in this ability group in all six schools combined, it is not clear that this result is meaningful. Assignment to the Basic English ability group in eighth grade has a significant negative effect on English achievement in ninth grade, while assignment to the Honors English ability group in eighth grade has a significant positive effect, compared with the Regular ability group. Previous attendance at a heterogeneously grouped school has a significant positive effect on English achievement, likely because these students are mostly from Catholic schools and tend to score higher on standardized tests than the students in public schools in the sample.

Table 3 presents a similar analysis using mathematics test score as the dependent variable. The results show that eighth-grade test score in mathematics has a positive effect on ninth-grade mathematics achievement in all ability groups. English eighth-grade test score has a positive effect on ninth-grade mathematics achievement in the Basic and Regular ability groups. Like mathematics eighth-grade test score, mathematics grade in eighth grade has a significant, positive effect on ninth-grade mathematics test score in all five ability groups. However, English grade in eighth grade has a significant negative effect on ninth-grade mathematics achievement in the Basic and Regular ability groups. This negative effect is likely the result of multicollinearity among grades and test scores, and it serves to compensate for the relatively large positive effect of English test score on mathematics in these groups. Being older has a significant negative effect on mathematics achievement in the Basic and Regular group, again likely because older students in these groups tend to have a history of poor academic performance. As with English, assignment to the Basic mathematics group in eighth grade has a significant negative effect on ninth-grade mathematics

Table 3. Tobit Models Predicting Ninth-Grade Mathematics Achievement

Variable	Students in Very Basic (N = 463) b	Students in Basic (N = 605) b	Students in Regular (N = 921) b	Students in Honors (N = 407) b	Students in Advanced (N = 178) b
Eighth-grade mathematics test score	0.56***	0.51***	0.56***	0.51***	0.60***
Eighth-grade English test score	0.06	0.19***	0.14***	0.07	0.03
Eighth-grade mathematics grade	2.39**	2.13**	2.69***	2.80***	2.11**
Eighth-grade English grade	-0.35	-1.54*	-1.18*	-0.54	0.13
Days absent first semester	-0.19**	-0.15	0.03	0.09	0.23
Cohort 2 = 1	3.01**	0.24	2.91***	-0.02	-1.92
Age in years	-1.90*	-1.40	-1.83*	-0.14	1.91
Female = 1	0.97	-1.87	-1.28	-1.46	-1.97
Black = 1	-0.98	-1.11	-2.71*	-1.69	-3.22
Free lunch = 1	0.36	1.03	-0.20	-0.51	0.65
School 1.2 = 1	1.51	2.19	-0.49	-0.94	-1.43
School 1.3 = 1	0.82	6.93***	1.73	3.55*	-2.98
School 1.4 = 1	-3.95*	-0.94	-1.01	-8.22***	-4.02*
School 1.5 = 1	-0.35	2.15	-4.94***	-5.56**	-2.46
School 2.1 = 1	-10.48***	5.38**	1.83	-2.42	-5.43*
Eighth-grade ability group					
Basic = 1	-3.40**	-0.68	4.96	—	—
Honors = 1	-0.36	6.60	7.08***	6.57**	—
Advanced = 1	—	—	17.60*	11.61***	0.33
Special Program = 1	-4.42	4.54	8.23	-9.86	—
Eighth-grade not ability grouped = 1	-0.16	0.96	4.86	10.22**	—
Eighth-grade ability group info missing = 1	-0.19	-5.65	-0.15	-13.73	4.94
Constant	10.91***	6.88*	8.83***	24.32***	33.23***
σ	10.45***	12.49***	11.44***	8.70***	5.79***
Log-likelihood	-1,738.13	-2,386.07	-3,540.28	-1,403.42	-462.92

* = $p < 0.05$; ** = $p < 0.01$; *** = $p < 0.001$.

achievement while assignment to the Honors or Advanced group has a significant positive effect on ninth-grade mathematics achievement.

To determine the effect of moving from one ability group to another, means and standard deviations of the predicted scores were calculated for each ability group. The predicted means can be interpreted as the test score a typical student assigned to a specific ability group would receive if that student were placed in a different ability group. These predicted means and standard deviations, as well as the observed means for each ability group, are presented in table 4.

The results show a general pattern with some deviations for both English and mathematics. In general, a student's standardized test score in English at the end of ninth grade would increase if the student were assigned to a higher-ability group than the group to which the student was assigned. This is seen for the Regular, Honors, and Advanced English groups. For example, the average student in ninth-grade Regular English receives an English test score of 47.3. If that student were assigned to the Honors group instead of the Regular group, the student's predicted test score would be 49.5; if the student were assigned to the Advanced group, it would be 50.1. Similarly, students in the Honors group would do better in the Advanced group, less well in the Regular group, and even worse in the Basic group. However, the farther a student moves from the original placement, the less reliable the predication. Hence the predicted test score of Regular group students, if they were assigned to the Advanced group, may be slightly less reliable than if they were assigned to the Honors group because the Advanced Group is two groups away from the Regular group to which the students were assigned.

The Basic English students form a slight exception to the pattern that a student's test score increases with placement in a higher-ability group. If a Basic student were assigned to the Regular group, the model predicts that the student's score would drop slightly, less than a percentile. If a Basic student were assigned to the Honors group, the student's score would drop a little more than 2 percentile points. While these differences are not large, any loss in achievement associated with organizational factors is reason for concern. At the same time, the small differences in the predicted means for Basic students assigned to higher-ability groups might simply be the result of random error.

Moving a student to a lower-ability group in English from a Regular, Honors, or Advanced group has the opposite effect of an upward move and

Table 4. Predicted Ninth-Grade English and Mathematics Achievement by Ability Group

Ability group	Actual test score	*Predicted test score if students were assigned to*				
		Very Basic	*Basic*	*Regular*	*Honors*	*Advanced*
		English				
Basic (N = 284)						
Mean	22.9	. . .	22.9	21.5	18.8	23.1
Standard deviation	11.9	. . .	9.1	12.5	14.7	14.8
Regular (N = 1,410)						
Mean	47.3	. . .	40.1	47.3	49.5	50.1
Standard deviation	18.6	. . .	11.6	16.0	17.5	18.4
Honors (N = 762)						
Mean	74.6	. . .	55.0	71.5	74.6	76.2
Standard deviation	15.9	. . .	9.2	12.9	13.6	14.7
Advanced (N = 125)						
Mean	88.8	. . .	63.4	82.7	86.5	88.6
Standard deviation	10.1	. . .	5.0	7.0	7.3	8.9
		Mathematics				
Very Basic (N = 463)						
Mean	27.2	27.2	28.4	31.9	40.4	51.0
Standard deviation	16.0	12.1	12.6	13.2	12.0	12.4
Basic (N = 605)						
Mean	43.6	42.3	43.6	46.4	54.0	64.1
Standard deviation	18.6	12.4	13.7	14.1	12.7	12.6
Regular (N = 921)						
Mean	61.3	55.6	57.5	61.4	67.6	76.1
Standard deviation	18.3	11.9	13.7	14.4	13.0	12.1
Honors (N = 407)						
Mean	84.2	67.1	73.2	81.7	84.5	88.5
Standard deviation	12.1	8.9	8.9	10.2	9.0	7.5
Advanced (N = 178)						
Mean	92.2	73.4	73.5	94.5	91.9	93.4
Standard deviation	8.2	8.5	7.9	8.9	9.7	7.4

Note: The mean of the observed test scores for students in an ability group does not exactly equal the predicted mean for students with those characteristics if they were in that ability group because of the nonlinearities of the tobit model.

lowers the student's English standardized test score. A student who received a test score of 47.3 in the Regular group would attain a score of only 40.1 in the Basic group. As another example, the test score of a typical student in the Advanced English group would decrease by 2.1 percentile points if assigned to the Honors group, from 88.6 to 86.5. An Honors student moved to the Regular group would lose 3.1 percentile points, from 74.6 to 71.5. The test score of a student in the Regular group would decrease 7.2 percentile points if placed in the Basic group, dropping from 47.3 to 40.1. The biggest decrease in test scores would occur if a student were moved to the Basic group from any other ability group, suggesting that the greatest obstacles to learning English are found in the Basic English ability group.

The predictions for mathematics achievement reported in table 4 provide further evidence that assigning students to higher-ability groups increases their achievement. With only two exceptions, moving a student to a higher-ability group increases the student's mathematics standardized test scores while moving a student to a lower group decreases the student's test scores. For example, students assigned to the Very Basic mathematics group would gain slightly over 1 percentile by assignment to the Basic group, almost 5 percentiles by assignment to the Regular group, over 13 percentiles by assignment to Honors group, and almost 25 percentiles by assignment to the Advanced group.

The one exception to the observed pattern of improved mathematics test scores with higher ability group placement is found for students assigned to the Advanced mathematics group. If these students were placed in the Regular group instead of the Advanced group, their test scores would increase more than 1 percentile. This oddity is likely due to unwarranted weight being given to the effect of being in the Advanced mathematics group in the eighth grade for students in the ninth-grade Regular group. As shown in table 2, the coefficient for eighth-grade Advanced group is extremely large ($b = 17.60$). However, it is based on only two students who moved from an Advanced group in eighth grade to a Regular group in ninth grade. Almost all (94.4 percent) of the students in ninth-grade Advanced mathematics were in eighth grade Advanced mathematics and thus receive the full weight of this effect in their predicted Regular scores. If the true effect of being in an Advanced instead of a Regular ability group in eighth grade for students in the Regular group in ninth grade is merely as large as the estimated effect for students in the Honors group ($b = 11.61$, well within one standard error of the Regular estimate), the pattern of improved test scores by group for mathematics is without exception.

A result that raises considerable alarm is the difference between actual and predicted mathematics scores for students in the Very Basic mathematics group. The data show that students' test scores improve dramatically as they move from Very Basic to higher-ability groups. Again, the further one moves from a student's assigned ability group, the less reliable the predictions become. Nevertheless, the marked difference between the test scores of students in the Very Basic group and the predicted test scores for the same students in higher-ability groups suggest that very little learning is occurring in the very low mathematics groups. Assigning a student destined for the Very Basic group to a higher group virtually ensures higher achievement.

In general, a pattern of higher predicted test scores associated with higher ability group placement is clear for both English and mathematics. These findings are consistent with the belief that greater learning opportunities are available in higher-ability groups. More important, the results support the argument that, regardless of ability, and given the way ability groups are currently formed in secondary schools, students generally would attain higher test scores if provided with the greater learning opportunities that characterize higher-ability groups.

Conclusions

This study examines the effects of ability grouping on student achievement. The research builds on the widely held belief that a good fit between the curriculum and a student's academic ability facilitates learning. The common practice of assigning students to ability groups for instruction rests on this belief. The rationale underlying ability grouping is that students learn more when teachers design a curriculum and adopt instructional practices geared to the students' ability level. The goal in assigning students to ability groups is to create the best match between instruction and student ability. The more homogeneous the ability group, the easier it is for a teacher to achieve this goal. Students in homogeneous ability groups should attain their learning potential regardless of the level of their ability group assignment.

In practice, ability groups are seldom as homogeneous as theory would dictate. The study reported here reveals considerable heterogeneity at all ability group levels in English and mathematics. Moreover, ability groups are not discrete entities with respect to ability. In every ability group in this study, the distribution of student ability overlaps with the distribution in the next highest or next lowest ability group, and in most cases, both. Most students assigned to the Regular group, for example, could as easily be assigned to the Basic, Honors, or Advanced groups and still not be an outlier in any group. In a few cases, the ability distribution of one group was completely contained within the distribution of another group. These data suggest that educators rely not only on student ability, but on other criteria as well, in making ability group assignments. To the extent that these additional criteria are nonacademic, ability groups become more heterogeneous, contrary to the theoretical rationale that motivates their use.

When ability groups are heterogeneous, teachers have more difficulty targeting instruction to the ability level of the students in the class. Teachers are forced to adopt the approach used in ungrouped classes, namely to direct instruction to the mean of the group. When this occurs, students at both ends of the ability distribution in the group, the fastest and the slowest learners, are disadvantaged. The wider the distribution, the less appropriate is the level of instruction for students not in the middle range.

Teachers may rely on an alternative approach to dealing with a range of ability in a somewhat heterogeneous ability group—spending some time directing instruction at each of the high, middle, and low parts of the distribution. While this technique addresses each student's learning needs at least some of the time, it results in students' being exposed to a considerable amount of instruction that is more advanced or less advanced than appropriate for their ability level.

The overlap in the distribution of achievement across ability groups suggests that, other things being equal, a student at the high end of the distribution in one ability group would be at least as capable of doing the work in the next highest ability group as the students at the low end of the higher group's distribution. The greater the overlap between ability groups, the more likely that students will find peers in the group whose ability level is similar to their own and who can provide academic and social support to each other.

These considerations lead to the policy recommendation that students should be assigned to the highest ability group commensurate with their academic abilities. However, the strategy of biasing ability group assignments upward must be tempered by an awareness of the social-psychological consequences of student discouragement. Students who find academic work too difficult eventually lose motivation and withdraw effort to learn. Consequently, teachers must take on the delicate task of weighing the benefits of academic challenge against the potential costs of student disengagement. If teachers can enable students to maintain a positive attitude toward learning in a higher-ability group, the student is likely to learn more than in a lower group.

A second policy recommendation emerging from this study is related less to the heterogeneity and overlap of ability groups and more to differential learning opportunities across groups. Past research shows that ability groups vary in three critical conditions for learning: the quantity and quality of instruction, factors affecting student motivation, and the academic climate of the group. Several empirical studies show that higher-ability groups offer a greater quantity and higher quality of instruction, provide stronger motivational factors for students to learn, and offer a more stimulating and supportive learning climate than lower-ability groups. As a result, students assigned to higher-ability groups are given greater opportunities to learn than those assigned to lower-ability groups.

The differences across ability groups in conditions for learning raise serious concerns about the equity of ability grouping. If higher-ability groups are more conducive to learning, students placed in low-ability groups are doubly disadvantaged. Not only do their weaker academic abilities make learning more difficult for them, but they are also disadvantaged by the poor learning environment found in lower-ability groups.

If ability grouping creates inequities in learning opportunities across students, then policy governing learning conditions across ability groups is imperative. Reform efforts need to be directed at improving the quantity and quality of education in the lower-ability groups, providing greater motivation to learn for students in these groups, and creating a serious academic climate in all ability groups to ensure that students are not disadvantaged by placement in lower groups. If learning opportunities can be made independent of ability group level, then teachers are free to create more homogeneous groups to better gear instruction to the learning level of the students.

Increasing ability group homogeneity would require teachers and counselors to carefully select criteria for making ability group assignments. Current practice in many schools is to rely primarily on academic criteria, but to allow certain other considerations as well. The academic bases for assignment typically include standardized achievement test scores, grades, teacher and counselor recommendations, prior curricular history, and requirements for graduation and college entrance. In addition, schools may permit parental and student choice, which may or may not be academically motivated. Schools also take into account constraints that the schedule of courses might place on a student's ability to take cocurricular classes, such as chorus, band, or debate, which may occur in only one time slot each day. They also may consider a student's employment schedule and work-study demands on a student's time. Use of some of these criteria results in greater ability group heterogeneity and greater overlap in ability between groups.

Because different selection criteria have different impact on the homogeneity and overlap of ability groups, educators should choose assignment criteria strategically to best meet a school's goals. If academic achievement is the highest priority of a school and if higher-level ability groups provide greater opportunities to learn, then school personnel should give greatest weight to academic selection criteria and less weight to nonacademic considerations. In this case, one would expect the resulting groups to be homogeneous with little overlap. Students assigned to lower groups should be given a challenging curriculum and as high a quality of instruction as those in higher-level groups. If schools stress the importance of cocurricular and extracurricular activities as well as academic achievement, they need to be flexible in their ability group assignments. If necessary, they should place a student in a lower-ability group to permit the student to participate in an activity that meets at the same time as the higher-ability group class. The school must ensure that learning opportunities are distributed equally across all ability groups, lest students lose ground academically by assignment to a lower group.

Finally, the findings reported here do not lead to a policy recommendation that ability grouping should be abandoned. The way ability grouping is currently practiced can be legitimately criticized, primarily because it channels unequal educational opportunities to students who vary by ability and related characteristics. These limitations can be avoided by improving educational opportunities in the lower-ability groups. The theory of ability grouping suggests that the practice has pedagogical advantages over heterogeneous grouping. Moreover, many teachers prefer to arrange students by ability for instruction because they find the practice to be more efficient and effective. Consequently, retaining ability grouping but reforming its practice is the preferred educational policy.

Comment by Eugene Bottoms

Based on my years of experience in working with high schools to improve the academic achievement of the students who upon leaving high school will go to work, go to a community or technical college, or go to a second-tier four-year university, no justification can be made for maintaining the practice of grouping as it presently exists in schools. The present system sorts poor and minority youth into low-level, watered-down courses. In my view, middle-class parents in most communities will not permit grouping based solely on levels of academic achievement because they will insist that their children be enrolled in higher-level courses. Therefore, as is recommended in Maureen T. Hallinan's paper, pure homogeneous grouping based on academic ability is impossible to create. The assumption that academic ability is fixed underestimates the intellectual ability of poor and minority students. If educators and policymakers are serious about closing the achievement gap by getting more students up to a standard level of achievement, a new approach is needed.

Southern Regional Education Board's *Making Middle Grades Work* initiative recently tracked more than three thousand students from grade eight to grade nine in forty-four middle schools and thirty-eight high schools across ten states. From eleven of the middle schools, about 75 percent of the students were placed in college preparatory or honors-level core academic courses in language arts, mathematics, and science in high school. In the remaining thirty-three middle schools, between 25 and 30 percent of the students were placed in the advantaged college preparatory or honors curriculum. Based on the eighth-grade National Assessment of Educational Policy (NAEP)-linked exams in reading, mathematics, and science, the achievement of students from the eleven middle schools with a high percentage of students in college prep courses (eleven high schools) matched closely the achievement of students from the remaining thirty-three middle schools. In the middle schools with high enrollment in college prep courses, the percent of students who were minority ranged from 1 to 89 percent and on free and reduced-price lunches ranged from 14 to 84 percent. The percent of students who made at least a grade of "C" or higher was virtually the same in the two groups of schools.

Regardless of students' reading, mathematics, and science achievement levels in grade eight, in both groups of schools the ninth graders placed in higher-level courses had lower failure rates than students with similar achievement levels who were placed in lower-level courses. Two exceptions were found: Students scoring in the lowest quartile in mathematics and science achievement when placed in higher-level mathematics and science courses had a failure rate slightly greater than students placed in lower-level mathematics and science courses. However, students scoring at the remaining three quartiles when placed in higher-level mathematics and science courses had a failure rate much less than students placed in lower-level courses. The present system of grouping in high schools underestimates the intellectual ability of many students.

High schools with the greatest number of students enrolled in college preparatory classes are more likely to require students with a grade of "C" or lower to attend extra-help sessions (62 percent) than schools with fewer students enrolled in higher-level classes (36 percent). Therefore, schools do not need a program of extra help when they use a placement system that is designed to find a comfortable niche for each student. Hallinan seems to endorse an approach to placement that would fail to challenge students. Students need extra help and academic support when they are enrolled in challenging classes that require them to achieve at a higher level.

Hallinan's paper fails to address the impact of socioeconomic and racial factors on current placement practices. In a study of the course-taking patterns of more than forty-two hundred graduating seniors from fifty-one rural high schools, *High Schools That Work* found that a white student whose mother finished high school or less had a 49 out of 100 chance of completing an advantaged academic curriculum. If the student's mother had finished high school and beyond, chances increased to 66 out of 100. However, an African American student whose mother finished high school or less had a 42 out of 100 chance of completing an advantaged academic curriculum. If the student's mother finished high school and beyond, chances were 55 out of 100.

Current placement practices filter out many students. I know of many students who upon entering grade nine stated that they intended by the end of grade ten to go to the vocational center to study a program such as automobile mechanics, carpentry, machining, electronics, and so on. As a consequence, these students are automatically enrolled in low-level courses in high school. It is assumed that they are not ambitious and that they do not have the ability to do higher-level work. The lucky few who insist on taking the advantaged academic core will be more successful. One former career-technical student I interviewed took four years of challenging mathematics and science in high school and after completing a degree in engineering is now employed as an engineer with General Motors. The present grouping system allows too many such capable students to enter into a series of courses that fail to adequately prepare them for both work and further study.

In most American high schools with the current grouping system, career-oriented male students have a much better chance of being placed in lower-level basic or regular English courses than do career-oriented female students. *High Schools That Work* visits to more than 150 high schools per year for the past several years and its database of more than one thousand high schools show that a disproportionate number of the career-oriented male students are enrolled in lower-level basic and regular English courses instead of college preparatory or honors English courses.

Given an information-based economy, all students in high school need a challenging language arts curriculum, one that engages them in reading many materials in a variety of forms, in analyzing information and expressing it in their own words, and in preparing high-quality short and long papers. But most high schools continue to sort too many students, especially males, into lower-level language arts courses—not because they cannot do the higher-level work, but because schools have created a series of differentiated courses that enable enterprising students to follow an easy path through high school.

Major differences exist in the quantity and quality of what is expected of students in the college preparatory language arts versus regular, basic, or below basic courses. Presumably students are placed in lower-level language arts courses because they do not read, comprehend, and write at an acceptable level. Yet these students are placed in language arts courses that require them to perform at that same unacceptable level. That is, they read fewer books, write fewer papers, and revise their papers less often, and also many never complete a major research paper. The opportunity to advance their ability to read, process, and organize information into writing assignments is simply not available to them in the present grouping system.

It would have been interesting if, for her study, Hallinan had chosen high schools where the faculty under enlightened leadership worked with their middle grades schools to place 75 percent or more of the students coming into grade nine into college preparatory or honors-level academic classes. Then she could have compared the achievement of students in these schools with students in schools that still place no more than about one-third of incoming ninth graders in such courses.

An alternative to ability grouping is to look at the concept of acceleration. Some states have developed end-of-course exams in core academic subjects such as algebra, biology, and English. Students in these states tend to take algebra in grade seven and thus pass the exam at that grade level. As courses with challenging standards and end-of-course exams in core academic areas are developed, some students could take these courses and pass the exam in grade seven, others in grade eight, and still others in grade nine. Thereby, all students are engaged in learning the same challenging algebra course, all have to meet the same standards tested on an end-of-course exam, and the different versions of algebra in grade nine no longer exist. Similar patterns of acceleration can be developed in other academic areas.

In my experience, the more high schools sort students into different lower-level courses, the lower their achievement levels. The sorting process places more poor and minority students in low-level classes, often taught by the least experienced teachers. Many of these teachers believe that they can do little to accelerate the achievement of their students, that their students are controlled by factors outside the school, and that trying to create quality learning for them is virtually impossible.

Based on my own years of experience in visiting high schools and analyzing data on more than 200,000 high school graduates, I have reached a set of recommendations different from those presented in Hallinan's paper. First, states and districts should set a goal for high schools to move toward having 85 percent of students complete the advantaged academic core. The advantaged academic core is at least a series of mathematics courses through algebra II and beyond; three laboratory sciences such as chemistry, physics, college preparatory biology, and so on; and four years of college prep or honors English. Some students will take more courses than those listed in the core, and some will begin their core program much earlier than others. But rising workplace requirements and the increased need for most students to go on to further study demand that the old notion that only a few students can complete this type of curriculum be adandoned and that all students be required to complete a rigorous core of academic courses that will prepare them for postsecondary education.

Some students, to complete an advantaged academic core, will need to combine their studies with high-quality career-technical studies. The intent of their technical studies will be to advance their technical literacy—their ability to read, interpret, and comprehend technical materials, to use mathematics in the context of the broad career field, and to increase their understanding of fundamental technical concepts. This program provides the connection between the academic world and the real world that many students need to recognize the meaning and purpose of their high school studies.

Other students need to be encouraged to complete a concentration of studies in mathematics and science or the humanities. Even students who are pursuing a technical concentration in high school need encouragement to spend at least half their time in the senior year in core academic subjects, including a higher-level mathematics or science course. If they must choose between mathematics or science, they should choose mathematics.

The integration of academic and career-technical studies demands that schools have the flexibility to use time differently. For example, some schools use a semester block schedule, so that students can earn thirty-two credits upon graduation. This type of scheduling allows schools to require that all students take four years of mathematics and science, thus increasing the likelihood that more students will complete the advantaged academic core. In fact, the schools making the most progress in student academic achievement are those that use some sort of block schedule and that require students to complete four years of mathematics and science.

Second, records need to be kept regarding whether students from a given high school are completing a solid academic core. By asking students a series of questions about their high school experiences, it can be determined whether they completed a college preparatory or honors curriculum or a series of low-level courses. Then, for example, the achievement levels could be compared between those students who took a one-year basic algebra course and those who took a two-year algebra course. A series of indicators needs to be developed in all subject areas that inform students and parents whether the students are experiencing a challenging curriculum, quality instruction, and quality extra support to meet these high standards. States must support schools in this effort.

Third, the honors or college preparatory program of courses with well-aligned standards and common assessments should be made the foundation for all students. This means that the Advanced Placement classes would become the new honors-level classes for the more advanced students in grades eleven and twelve. Most of these students will begin their high school–level studies in grades seven and eight, while other students will begin in grade nine.

End-of-course exams in a few core academic subjects appear to contribute to the improvement in achievement of poor and minority students. These exams can also help ensure that core academic courses are taught to college preparatory or honors standards for all students. Forty percent of students at *High Schools That Work* sites in North Carolina are African American, and they have significantly higher reading, mathematics, and science achievement scores than do African American students in any of the other *High Schools That Work* states. End-of-course exams, particularly in algebra, geometry, biology, and language arts, have set a basic standard to which all students in North Carolina are taught.

High-quality exams in a few core academic areas can ensure that poor and minority students receive the same instruction when placed in the advantaged academic core curriculum. This means that all below basic academic courses will be eliminated and, over time, all basic and regular sections will be as well. Schools can eliminate 20 to 25 percent of these sections each year until they no longer exist. To do this, schools must have sufficient resources so that they can make more effective use of summer school and create, particularly in grades eight and nine, a series of catch-up courses designed to prepare students to be successful in more challenging courses.

Fourth, to move more students into higher-level courses means providing quality extra help and catch-up support opportunities. Low-level courses are designed to keep performance below standard. Catch-up courses aimed at raising standards should begin as early as grade seven. This means a new kind of working relationship between high schools and middle grades, and it means that states must support the two levels of education working together.

Some high schools are abandoning the strategy of differentiating the curriculum by enrolling many students into lower-level courses. Instead, students who are not ready upon entering grade nine for college preparatory algebra or English take a noncredit course for eighteen weeks to get ready or they go to summer school. Schools that take the time to help students catch up are getting more students to the level necessary to be successful in a more demanding series of core academic courses. Many students score below basic on NAEP-like exams because often schools have created a curriculum and instructional program that gives them below basic- and basic-level assignments and tests them with below basic- and basic-level exam questions.

Student achievement will never rise above the level of assignments students are asked to do or the quality of the exams they are given. However, when the curriculum is realigned so that assignments are at the proficient level or above and high-level exams are given, quality extra time and help before school, after school, on Saturday, or during the summer must be provided. Quality extra help requires using different methods to reteach material. Too often, reteaching in low-performing high schools means repeating the same teaching strategies over and over and using numerous drill sheets on the same concepts.

Fifth, an effective guidance and advisement system, one that gives parents and students factual information, is needed. If students take regular and basic courses, they will be more likely to take remedial courses in college, and they will be less likely to pass employers' exams for access to decent jobs. Often neither students nor their parents know about these outcomes because they lack the information they need to make informed decisions.

Based on my interviews of hundreds of seniors, most plan to attend college, but they are unaware that they will have to take a placement exam upon arriving at college or that they are at risk of spending most of their freshman year in remedial or developmental classes. A policy that informs parents and students will require that college placement exams be given to students by the end of grade ten or at least by the middle of grade eleven. The results will show parents that their children cannot coast through the senior year or else students will have to learn in their first year of college what they should have learned in high school. These placement exams can help parents and students understand the need to make the senior year count.

In a *High Schools That Work* follow-up study of seventy-six hundred career-oriented students who finished high school in 2000, 72 percent enrolled in college. About one-third of these students are angry that their high schools did not prepare them adequately and that they were not pushed, informed, and encouraged to take the right courses while in high school. These students would have been better prepared if they had received higher-quality instruction, had gotten positive encouragement to take the advantaged academic core curriculum, and were instructed in a climate of higher academic standards. Unfortunately, ability grouping and sorting students as Hallinan recommends make it impossible for students to get high-quality learning in low-level courses. The secondary education system must break free of this differentiated curriculum and create the opportunity and support that allow more students to succeed in the advantaged academic core.

Sixth, incentives and strategies must be put in place to get the best teachers to teach challenged students in grades nine and ten and to work with teams of teachers on how to get the most challenged students to meet course standards. The best teachers must be turned into leaders who can guide other teachers in common planning, in developing common exams, in examining student work and teacher assignments, and in fashioning successful extra-help strategies.

Policies that encourage incremental progress toward having more students complete a solid academic core—accelerating students in the early grades and requiring all students to finish some kind of concentration beyond a solid academic core in high school—will result in less student apathy and disruptiveness and lower student dropout rates.

The quality of instruction at all levels must be improved. That means supporting teachers with more time to plan and with opportunities to learn better strategies and classroom practices to engage students in meaningful learning. Teachers must believe that all students can learn at high levels.

Policies are needed that gradually and successfully give more students access to the advantaged curriculum. It will take time and support for teachers to learn how to teach more intellectually challenging content to many more students, but the result will be higher student achievement and graduates who are prepared to be successful in careers and in postsecondary education.

Comment by Aaron M. Pallas

When I was a senior in high school, I was placed in a remedial English class. My guidance counselor was very apologetic. It could not be helped, she said. I was taking three classes that each had but a single section—honors French, honors biology, and an honors course in modern algebra for the students the math department felt were not strong enough for Advanced Placement calculus. Plus, I was the features editor for the school newspaper. And when all of these constraints were taken into account, the only available English class was a remedial class held during the last period of the school day.

I recognized how incongruous this placement was. I was thrust into a class of students whom I had barely seen in gym class, let alone other core academic classes. I spent much of the year cracking jokes that went over the heads of most of my classmates, but the teacher seemed to get a kick out of them.

I do not recall mentioning the situation to my parents. Even if I had, they likely would not have complained or taken any other action. On academic matters, they were content to defer to the authority of the school. From Maureen T. Hallinan's paper, however, I have come to fully appreciate the damage that was done to me. I enjoyed the relaxed pace of the class and basked in the presence of amiable, drug-addled classmates who were fans of

Ozzy Osbourne when he was a founding member of the band Black Sabbath, three decades before mainstream America discovered him. I now know that I was shortchanged and that my academic achievement would likely have been higher had I been placed in a class that was more challenging academically.

But I am not bitter. To the contrary, my misassignment, and the group assignments of many other students, may not be easily manipulated via building-, district-, or state-level education policies.

I want to say something about the technical features of Hallinan's analysis, because she is a wise researcher and her approach deserves to be highlighted. I appreciate her care in describing some of the limits of her estimates of group effects. For example, she says that the predicted achievement of students hypothetically placed in a particular group is likely to be accurate when the characteristics of those students are similar to the actual characteristics of students in that ability group. When the student characteristics are not similar to students in that ability group, the predictions are less accurate. As a result, the further one moves from a student's actual group assignment, the less reliable the predicted mean achievement score will be.

What this suggests is that the overlap across groups in students' characteristics is critical to the ability to estimate group effects. It is fortunate that there is so much overlap in Hallinan's sample. If the groups were homogeneous with respect to prior achievement and other student characteristics, a persuasive argument could not be made that a student in one group would have performed better or worse if he or she had been in a different group.

The gold standard here, not surprisingly, is random assignment of students to groups, which would ensure, subject to sampling variation, that the measured and unmeasured characteristics of students are distributed identically across groups. But students have never been randomly assigned to basic, regular, honors, and advanced groups, and they probably never will be. Schoolteachers and counselors believe that the most capable students belong in the honors and advanced groups, and savvy middle-class parents want to position their children in the higher groups, thinking that this will enhance their children's chances for attending a prestigious selective college. Even if the process by which students are assigned to groups cannot be fully specified, the process clearly is not at all random.

To take account of the nonrandom selection of students into groups, Hallinan uses multiple regression methods, a time-honored tradition on which many social scientists rely. A supplemental analysis, not necessarily better, but equally defensible, is worth exploring. Propensity score matching has become common in recent years and has been used in a variety of education policy contexts, including Stephen L. Morgan's studies of the Catholic schooling effect.[24]

I also would prefer to see within-school analyses of track overlap—that is, the extent to which students' performance levels overlap across groups—and within-school analyses of assignment processes. The models that Hallinan reports pool the data across the schools, representing differences across schools simply through a main effect. But the process by which students are assigned to groups is not common to all schools. It is likely to differ from one school to the next. For example, the number of curricular groups and the size of those groups can vary from one school to the next. It is likely that some high schools have a great deal of overlap in the prior achievements of students in different groups and other high schools have little overlap.

The analyses could be enriched by estimating group effects on achievement separately for each school. Perhaps the samples within schools are not large enough to produce reliable estimates. Matching students within schools is definitely more difficult than matching students by drawing on all of the schools. But the approach that Hallinan is using treats schools more or less interchangeably. An analyst should be fairly sure that schools can be treated interchangeably before comparing, for example, a basic group student at Washington, D.C.'s Cardozo High School, where 90 percent of the students score below basic proficiency on the mathematics portion of the Stanford Achievement Test, with a similar regular group student at Washington, D.C.'s Banneker High, where only 9 percent of the students score below basic proficiency.

The policy recommendation that Hallinan proposes is that students should be assigned to the highest ability group commensurate with their academic abilities. A second proposed policy is to equalize learning conditions across ability groups. But a desired result is only a part of the policy puzzle. Equally important is considering what kinds of policy instruments can produce these desired results. Policymakers typically have an array of approaches that include mandates, incentives, capacity building, system changing, and persuasion.

Many social scientists are comfortable with persuasion as a policy instrument. Persuasion uses information to suggest what should be done. Policymakers relying on persuasion encourage a target audience to act in certain ways, instead of coercing these actions. Hallinan, for example, is relying on the force of her empirical findings to persuade school personnel to assign students to the highest ability group appropriate to a student's academic abilities.

As with any policy instrument, conditions exist under which persuasion is likely to be more effective and other circumstances under which persuasion might be less effective. Many scholars argue that persuasion is likely to work only if the information that is being disseminated is credible to the target audience; in this case, schoolteachers, counselors, and administrators who are responsible for assigning students to groups.

I wonder whether this would be so, on two grounds. First, I am unsure that school personnel would believe that research can reveal that many students would perform better if they were assigned to higher groups. The logic of the regression analyses may simply escape them. After all, how can one tell whether a student would do better if he or she were assigned to a higher group? In point of fact, a student is not assigned to a higher group. A student is assigned to a particular group, and not arbitrarily.

Second, I am skeptical that school personnel will believe that students would do better based on an assignment process that supersedes their own judgment. Many school staff are suspicious of the validity of standardized achievement tests, preferring instead to rely on their own observations and those of trusted colleagues. Teachers and counselors are privy to a much richer sample of a student's academic performance than can be discerned from a standardized test, even a well-constructed one. Teachers and counselors may not be easily persuaded by information that says, "Don't trust your own professional judgment, or that of your friends and colleagues." So I am not persuaded that persuasion is likely to work. Furthermore, persuasion does not have a good track record as an education policy instrument.

Suppose that a school district or a state mandated that students be assigned to the highest group commensurate with their academic abilities. Mandates assume that widespread uniform behavior is desirable and that a mandate is enforceable. As with persuasion, a mandate is likely to be a good policy instrument under some conditions and less likely to be successful under others.

Mandates are more likely to be successful if the rules are perceived as fair; if the mandate is precise, yet flexible; and if the mandate is not in conflict with other mandates. Is the mandate that students be assigned to the highest group commensurate with their academic ability enforceable? How a rule-maker could judge whether a particular assignment was academically challenging, but not so challenging as to spur demoralization and disengagement, is not clear. It is not even that easy to tell in hindsight, let alone prospectively. Part of the problem is that the mandate obliges school personnel to operationalize both academic ability and the ability demands of a particular classroom.

The term *academic ability* is troubling, and the term *ability group* applied to high school courses is somewhat jarring. In school subjects in which knowledge is organized hierarchically, such that a learner must have mastered some foundational knowledge before exposure to advanced knowledge, it certainly makes sense to group students homogeneously on the basis of what they know. But I would not want to characterize grouping on the basis of academic performance as ability grouping.

Hallinan acknowledges other bases on which students might be grouped for instruction, such as their interests. Ordering, for example, biology, chemistry, physics, and geology on a unidimensional scale of scientific ability would be difficult. At the least, then, consideration needs to be given to what school subjects are amenable to a unidimensional hierarchy of knowledge.

Interests raise another potential problem with mandates. American public education has a strong tradition of curricular choice. Most high schools do not prescribe the entire curriculum but afford students, and especially their parents, some opportunities for choice. In some cases, these choices are largely illusory. But as a practical matter, high schools are often responsive to parental preferences.

In a study of urban high schools that I carried out with Gary Natriello and Carolyn Riehl, we found that school staff were responsive to parents' requests for particular course placements for their children. As the head of scheduling in one school told us, "You're entitled to fail any course you want." In the urban high schools we studied, the schools had to be responsive to their students' parents, lest these parents vote with their feet and withdraw their children from the school. It may be rational for schools to do so, and satisfying a mandate to assign students to particular curricular groups may be in tension with other pressures and values to which high schools of all stripes must respond.

Finally, I want to consider incentives as a policy instrument to promote the assignment of high school students to groups that are academically challenging. Incentives are rewards and sanctions that are exchanged for particular actions. They are held to be effective policy instruments when the cause of a problem is purposive action and when the desired behavior is specific.

If the cause of a problem is not purposive action, then attempting to induce particular behaviors will not have the desired result.

And here I think is the rub. My being placed in a remedial English class in my senior year of high school was not the result of purposive action. This placement resulted from an attempt to balance a variety of forces shaping the process by which students are assigned to classes.

In the past decade or so, Brian DeLany; Jeannie Oakes and her colleagues; Gary Natriello, Carolyn Riehl, and I; and Hallinan have demonstrated that the process of matching students to school resources, particularly curriculum resources, is an organizational process that responds to a variety of deeply felt values held by educators and the broader public, as well as an array of environmental resources and constraints.[25] It is not clear that an optimal rational solution exists to the problem of matching students to courses, or that it is evident what set of steps would lead to such a solution.

So I am led to wonder whether mandates, inducements, or persuasion could be effective in promoting better matches between students' academic performance and their courses. But I am persuaded by Hallinan's analyses that better matches, in the form of more challenging academic standards, are desirable.

Notes

1. J. B. Carroll, "A Model of School Learning," *Teachers College Record,* vol. 64 (1963), pp. 723–33; and F. M. Newmann, "Beyond Common Sense in Educational Restructuring: The Issues of Content and Linkage," *Educational Researcher*, vol. 22 (1993), pp. 4–13.

2. A. Brown, "The Advancement of Learning," *Educational Researcher*, vol. 23 (1994), pp. 4–12; and A. B. Sørensen and M. T. Hallinan, "Effects of Ability Grouping on Growth in Academic Achievement," *American Educational Research Journal*, vol. 23 (1986), pp. 519–42.

3. B. Heyns, *Summer Learning and the Effects of Schooling* (New York: Academic Press, 1978); D. Wiley, "Another Hour, Another Day: Quantity of Schooling, a Potent Path for Policy," in R. M. Hauser, W. H. Sewell, and D. L. Featherman, eds., *Schooling and Achievement in American Society* (New York: Academic Press, 1976), pp. 225–65; Department of Education, *Third International Mathematics and Science Study* (Washington: National Center for Education Statistics and National Science Foundation, 1996); and R. Barr and R. Dreeben, *How Schools Work* (University of Chicago Press, 1983). Other studies include Brown, "The Advancement of Learning"; and F. M. Newmann, H. M. Marks, and A. Gamoran, "Authentic Pedagogy and Student Performance," *American Journal of Education*, vol. 104 (1996), pp. 280–312.

4. Brown, "The Advancement of Learning"; Carroll, "A Model of School Learning"; and Sørensen and Hallinan, "Effects of Ability Grouping on Growth in Academic Achievement."

5. Carroll, "A Model of School Learning"; and B. Schneider, M. Csikszentmihalyi, and S. Knauth, "Academic Challenge, Motivation, and Self-Esteem: The Daily Experiences of Students in High School," in M. T. Hallinan, ed., *Restructuring Schools: Promising Practices and Policies* (New York: Plenum, 1995), pp. 175–95.

6. V. Vauras and others, "Motivation Vulnerability as a Challenge for Educational Interventions," *International Journal of Education Research*, vol. 31, no. 6 (1999), pp. 515–31; C. Waronsky and A. Waronsky, "Motivation: A Key to Reaching Educational Objectives," *Journal of Physical Education, Recreation, and Dance*, vol. 71, no. 1 (2000), pp. 13–15; P. Pintrich, "The Role of Motivation in Promoting and Sustaining Self-Regulated Learning," *International Journal of Education Research,* vol. 31, no. 6 (1999), pp. 459–70; and F. M. Newmann and G. G. Wehlage, "Five Standards of Authentic Instruction," *Educational Leadership*, vol. 50, no. 7 (1993), pp. 8–12.

7. J. Dusek, ed., *Teacher Expectancies* (Mahwah, N.J.: Lawrence Erlbaum, 1985); R. Rosenthal and L. Jacobson, *Pygmalion in the Classroom: Teacher Expectations and Pupils' Intellectual Development* (New York: Holt, Rinehart, and Winston, 1968); and J. Eccles and A. Wigfield, "Teacher Expectations and Student Motivation," in J. Dusek, ed., *Teacher Expectancies* (Mahwah, N.J.: Lawrence Erlbaum, 1985), pp. 185–228.

8. See M. T. Hallinan and W. N. Kubitschek, "Curriculum Differentiation and High School Achievement," *Social Psychology of Education,* vol. 2 (1999), pp. 1–22; Pintrich, "The Role of Motivation in Promoting and Sustaining Self-Regulated Learning"; N. Perry and J. VandeKamp, "Creating Classroom Contexts That Support Young Children's Development of Self-Regulated Learning," *International Journal of Education Research*, vol. 33, no. 7–8 (2000), pp. 821–43; R. E. Slavin, "Ability Grouping in Secondary Schools: A Best-Evidence Synthesis," *Review of Educational Research*, vol. 60 (1990), pp. 471–99; and R. E. Slavin and E. Oickle, "Effects of Cooperative Learning Teams on Student Achievement and Race Relations: Treatment by Race Interactions," *Sociology of Education*, vol. 54 (1981), pp. 174–80.

9. K. Alexander, D. Entwisle, and S. Bedinger, "When Expectations Work: Race and Socioeconomic Differences in School Performance," *Social Psychology Quarterly*, vol. 57, no. 4 (1994), pp. 283–99; J. D. Finn, "Withdrawing from School," *Review of Educational Research,* vol. 59 (1989), pp. 117–42; H. W. Marsh, "Extracurricular Activities: Beneficial Extension of Traditional Curriculum or Subversion of Academic Goals?" *Journal of Educational Psychology*, vol. 84 (1992), pp. 553–62; and E. Snyder and E. Spreitzer, "Social Psychological Concomitants of Adolescents' Role Identities as Scholars and Athletes: A Longitudinal Analysis," *Youth & Society*, vol. 23, no. 4 (1992), pp. 507–22.

10. H. Cooper and D. Tom, "Teacher Expectation Research: A Review with Implications for Classroom Instruction," *Elementary School Journal*, vol. 85, no. 1 (1984), pp. 77–89; R. L. Thorndike, "Review of the Book *Pygmalion in the Classroom*," *American Education Research Journal*, vol. 5 (1968), 708–11; S. W. Raudenbush, "Magnitude of Teacher Expectancy Effects on Pupil IQ as a Function of the Credibility of Expectancy Induction: A Synthesis of Findings from 18 Experiments," *Journal of Educational Psychology,* vol. 76 (1984), pp. 85–97; S. S. Wineburg, "The Self-Fulfillment of the Self-Fulfilling Prophecy: A Critical Appraisal," *Educational Researcher*, vol. 16, no. 9 (1987), pp. 28–37; and L. Jussim, J. Eccles, and S. J. Madon, "Social Perception, Social Stereotypes, and Teacher Expectations: Accuracy and the Quest for the Powerful Self-Fulfilling Prophecy," *Advances in Experimental Social Psychology*, vol. 28 (1996), pp. 281–388.

11. W. Meyer, "Summary, Integration, and Prospective," in J. Dusek, ed., *Teacher Expectancies* (Mahwah, N.J.: Lawrence Erlbaum, 1985), pp. 353–70; and P. Peterson and S. Barger, "Attribution Theory and Teacher Expectancy," in J. Dusek, ed., *Teacher Expectancies* (Mahwah, N.J.: Lawrence Erlbaum, 1985), pp. 159–84.

12. J. Coleman, "Achievement-Oriented School Design," in M. T. Hallinan, ed., *Restructuring Schools: Promising Practices and Policies* (New York: Plenum, 1995), pp. 11–30; P. A. Cusick, *Inside High School* (New York: Holt, Rinehart, and Winston, 1973); A. S. Bryk, V. E. Lee, and P. B. Holland, *Catholic Schools and the Common Good* (Harvard University Press, 1993); and E. L. McDill, G. Natriello, and A. M. Pallas, "A Population at Risk: Potential Consequences of Tough School Standards for Student Dropouts," *American Journal of Education,* vol. 94 (1986), pp. 135–81.

13. H. H. Kelley, "Two Functions of Reference Groups," in G. E. Swanson, T. M. Newcomb, and E. L. Hartley, eds., *Readings in Social Psychology* (New York: Holt, Rinehart, and Winston, 1947), pp. 410–14; R. Merton, *Social Theory and Social Structure* (Glencoe, Ill.: Free Press, 1957); T. D. Kemper, "Reference Groups, Socialization and Achievement," *American Sociological Review,* vol. 33 (1968), pp. 31–45; and G. Peterson, B. Rollins, and D. Thomas, "Parental Influence and Adolescent Conformity: Compliance and Internalization," *Youth and Society,* vol. 16 (1985), pp. 397–420.

14. Bryk, Lee, and Holland, *Catholic Schools and the Common Good;* C. Hill, "Capacities, Opportunities, and Educational Investments: The Case of the High School Dropout," *Review of Economic Statistics,* vol. 61 (1979), pp. 9–20; W. G. Spady, "The Impact of School Resources on Students," in F. Kerliner, ed., *Review of Research in Education* (Itasca, Ill.: Peacock, 1973), pp. 135–77; and Cusick, *Inside High School.*

15. T. L. Good and S. Marshall, "Do Students Learn More in Heterogeneous or Homogeneous Groups?" in P. L. Peterson, L. C. Wilkinson, and M. T. Hallinan, eds., *The Social Context of Instruction: Group Organization and Group Processes* (New York: Academic Press, 1984), pp. 15–38; Barr and Dreeben, *How Schools Work;* and J. Oakes, *Multiplying Inequalities: The Effects of Race, Social Class, and Tracking on Opportunities to Learn Mathematics and Science* (Santa Monica, Calif.: RAND, 1990).

16. Pintrich, "The Role of Motivation in Promoting and Sustaining Self-Regulated Learning"; M. Patchen, *Black-White Contact in Schools: Its Social and Academic Effects* (Purdue University Press, 1982); J. E. Rosenbaum, *Making Inequality: The Hidden Curriculum of High School Tracking* (Wiley, 1976); J. E. Rosenbaum, "Social Implications of Educational Grouping," in D. C. Benlinger, ed., *Review of Research in Education,* vol. 7 (Itasca, Ill.: American Educational Research Association, 1976), pp. 361–401; J. Oakes, *Keeping Track: How Schools Structure Inequality* (Yale University Press, 1985); J. Brophy and T. Good, *Teacher-Student Relationships: Causes and Consequences* (New York: Holt, Rinehart, and Winston, 1974); P. S. Fry, "Pupil Performance under Varying Teacher Conditions of High and Low Expectations and High and Low Controls," *Canadian Journal of Behavioral Science,* vol. 14 (1982), pp. 219–31; L. Jussim and J. Eccles, "Teacher Expectations II: Construction and Reflection of Student Achievement," *Journal of Personality and Social Psychology,* vol. 63 (1992), pp. 947–61; and Good and Marshall, "Do Students Learn More in Heterogeneous or Homogeneous Groups?"

17. F. Schwartz, "Supporting or Subverting Learning: Peer Group Patterns in Four Tracked Schools," *Anthropology and Education Quarterly,* vol. 12 (1981), pp. 99–121; J. Oakes, A. Gamoran, and R. N. Page, "Curriculum Differentiation: Opportunities, Outcomes, and Meanings," in P. W. Jackson, ed., *Handbook of Research on Curriculum* (Macmillan, 1992), pp. 570–608; and Patchen, *Black-White Contact in Schools.*

18. Bryk, Lee, and Holland, *Catholic Schools and the Common Good;* J. S. Coleman and T. Hoffer, *Public and Private Schools: The Impact of Communities* (Basic Books, 1987); A. M. Greeley, *Catholic Schools and Minority Students* (New Brunswick, N.J.: Transaction Books, 1982); T. B. Hoffer, "Accountability in Education," in M. T. Hallinan, ed., *Handbook of the Sociology of Education* (New York: Kluwer Academic/Plenum Publishers, 2000), pp.

529–44; and V. E. Lee and A. S. Bryk, "Curriculum Tracking as Mediating the Social Distribution of High School Achievement," *Sociology of Education,* vol. 6 (1986), pp. 78–94.

19. For a review, see Slavin, "Ability Grouping in Secondary Schools."

20. M. T. Hallinan and W. N. Kubitschek, "Curriculum Differentiation and High School Achievement," *Social Psychology of Education,* vol. 2 (1999), pp. 1–22; and Rosenbaum, *Making Inequality.*

21. J. S. Coleman and others, *Equality of Educational Opportunity* (Department of Health, Education, and Welfare, 1966).

22. See, for example, G. S. Maddala, *Limited-Dependent and Qualitative Variables in Econometrics* (Cambridge University Press, 1983).

23. A. Gamoran and R. D. Mare, "Secondary School Tracking and Educational Inequality: Compensation, Reinforcement, or Neutrality?" *American Journal of Sociology,* vol. 94 (1989), pp. 114–83.

24. See Stephen L. Morgan, "Counterfactuals, Causal Effect Heterogeneity, and the Catholic School Effect on Learning," *Sociology of Education,* vol. 74 (2001), pp. 341–74.

25. See Brian DeLany, "Allocation, Choice, and Stratification within High Schools: How the Sorting Machine Copes," *American Journal of Education,* vol. 99 (1991), pp. 181–207; Maureen Hallinan, "How Schools Work: School Response to Unpredicted Events," paper presented at the Institute for Educational Initiatives Conference on Stability and Change in Education, University of Notre Dame, November 2001; Jeannie Oakes and Gretchen Guiton, "Matchmaking: The Dynamics of High School Tracking Decisions," *American Educational Research Journal,* vol. 32 (1995), pp. 3–33; and Carolyn Riehl, Aaron M. Pallas, and Gary Natriello, "Rites and Wrongs: Institutional Explanations for the Student Course-Scheduling Process in Urban High Schools," *American Journal of Education,* vol. 107 (1999) pp. 116–54.

Nerds and Freaks:
A Theory of Student
Culture and Norms

JOHN H. BISHOP, MATTHEW BISHOP,
LARA GELBWASSER, SHANNA GREEN,
and ANDREW ZUCKERMAN

B y a two-to-one margin (60 to 28 percent), American parents say that "if forced to choose, they would prefer their sons or daughters to make C grades and be active in extracurricular activities rather than make A grades and not be active."[1] Why do parents think it so important for their children to participate in extracurricular activities? Certainly, they are not expecting their child to make it into the National Football League or the National Basketball Association. They probably believe extracurricular activities teach teamwork, time management, self-discipline, and other skills that are important in later life. Those students who participate in sports during high school do spend more time doing homework and less time watching TV, are less likely to drop out of high school, are more likely to attend college, and earn 3 to 11 percent more as an adult. Controversy exists, however, about whether the association between sports and earnings reflects a causal relationship or a selection effect. Deborah Anderson's analysis of the issue concluded that while sports had causal effects on schooling, effects on earnings were probably selection effects.[2] Regardless, getting "A's" instead of "C's" has much larger effects on high school and college completion rates and labor market success than participating in extracurricular activities. Nearly 99 percent of students with "A" averages (and comparably higher test scores) in eighth grade complete high school; only 80 percent of the "C" students graduate.[3] For seniors who in 1982 planned on getting a bachelor of arts degree or higher, chances of achieving that goal during the next decade

141

were four times greater for "A" students than "C" students.[4] Norton Grubb's analysis of High School and Beyond data found that, holding years of schooling constant, earnings at age thirty-one by males with an "A" average in high school were $5,549 (20 percent) more than those with a "C" average; for females, $2,906 (17.7 percent) more.[5]

If parents knew these facts, one would think that they would choose "A" grades over participation in extracurricular activities. Probably, many are ignorant of just how important academic achievement is to future labor market success, but we think that is not the whole answer. We suggest the parents responding to the Gallup survey interpreted "makes A grades and not be active" as code for "nerd" or "dork." They remember how unpopular nerds were and perceive them as unhappy with their position in the high school social system. The parents chose the alternative that meant their child would not suffer what the nerds of their era had suffered.

What were the peer culture and norms of the 1960s and 1970s like? James Coleman was the first sociologist to examine adolescent status systems. In all ten of the Illinois high schools he studied in 1958, athletic achievement was the single most important criterion for high status.[6] Abraham J. Tannenbaum conducted a similar study at a predominantly Jewish high school in New York City in 1960.[7] He asked students to react to written descriptions of eight fictitious students. The ratings from most positive to most negative were as follows:

1. Athlete—Brilliant—Nonstudious
2. Athlete—Average—Nonstudious
3. Athlete—Average—Studious
4. Athlete—Brilliant—Studious
5. Nonathlete—Brilliant—Nonstudious
6. Nonathlete—Average—Nonstudious
7. Nonathlete—Average—Studious
8. Nonathlete—Brilliant—Studious

Being smart was OK, if it was not combined with studiousness. Getting good grades did not get one into trouble with one's peers, but trying to get good grades did.

In 1972 D. Stanley Eitzen replicated Coleman's study using nine high schools in Illinois, Indiana, and Kansas.[8] Students were asked, "If you could be remembered here at school for one of the three things below, which would it be?" "Brilliant student" was selected by 31 percent of the male students in Coleman's 1958 sample and only 23 percent of Eitzen's 1972 sam-

Table 1. Criteria for Male Popularity in High School

	1958 James Coleman study		*1972 D. Stanley Eitzen study*	
Criterion for status	*Popular with boys*	*Popular with girls*	*Popular with boys*	*Popular with girls*
Be an athlete	2.2	2.2	2.06	1.94
Be in the leading crowd	2.6	2.5	2.10	2.12
Leader in activities	2.9	—	2.82	—
Have a nice car	—	3.2	—	2.81
High grades, honor roll	3.5	4.0	3.73	3.87
Come from the right family	4.5	4.2	3.98	3.89

Note: Male students were asked what made boys popular with other boys and what made them popular with girls. The figures in the table are mean rankings on a one-to-five scale. A low score implies a high rank. — = Not available.

ple. "Athletic star" was selected by 44 percent of Coleman's sample and 47 percent of Eitzen's sample. "Most popular" was selected by 25 percent of Coleman's sample and 30 percent of Eitzen's sample. Boys were asked what makes one popular with other boys and what "makes a guy popular with girls around here." They were to choose from several positively valued traits (see table 1). In Eitzen's 1972 data, "high grades, honor roll" came out only slightly ahead of "come from the right family" and well behind "have a nice car" and "leader in activities." "Be an athlete" and "be in the leading crowd" were the achievements that contributed to popularity the most. In the popularity contest, being accepted into the leading crowd is almost as important as being an athlete and substantially more important than being a leader in activities.

Laurence Steinberg, Bradford Brown, and Sanford Dornbusch's 1996 study of nine high schools in California and Wisconsin suggests that academic excellence is still not highly valued by peers in most schools.

> Less than 5 percent of all students are members of a high-achieving crowd that defines itself mainly on the basis of academic excellence. . . . Of all the crowds, the "brains" were the least happy with who they are—nearly half wished they were in a different crowd.[9]

Parents know that adolescents can be cruel. They do not want their child to be rejected by his or her peers. What is it like to be given a denigrated identity by one's middle school classmates? Don E. Mertens's ethnography of Cronkite Junior High School provides a rich and perceptive description of how four seventh graders (named Morton, William, Les, and Scott), designated "Mels" by the rest of the middle school, interpreted and dealt with their outcast status.

"For some reason they just hear about me [Morton] and say 'Hey let's bug the kid or let's chase him.' I don't know, that always seems to amaze me—like kids that I've never seen before know my name, know about half the things about me; some of them I don't know." Morton was correct that he was known (by reputation) throughout the school. Once agreement existed that an individual was a Mel, peers who knew him only by reputation felt free to harass him. . . . Even more than school, the bus was dominated by peer group standards. . . . "I never get a good seat—good seats are in the back. I had to sit in the front [with the younger students]. I just kinda stay where no one wants to be (Morton in 7th grade)." . . . He followed the same strategy in the lunch room by seeking interstitial space and thereby reducing his social visibility.[10]

[According to Becky, a popular student who could help William escape Mel status,] "A lot of people make fun of him. He is really nice to me. But sometimes I'm mean to him. One time, it was really so nice of him. . . . He took my punishment for me. Sitting in the seat all period. I didn't even thank him. I was spitting on him. I don't know why. I felt like it. He was really upset. He goes, 'Becky what have I done to you? I mean I even made up that time for you in art.' I told him I was sorry and I spit on him again."[11]

What do the Mels perceive causes their outcast status?

"I ask them why they tease and they start giggling. My mother has already tried to call their parents. . . . I don't tell her to call anybody because the next day they call me a narc. The way we figured it out is that narc probably means like a tattletale or a squealer (Les)."[12]

William knew what it took to be popular. As he saw it, one needs to: "pay no attention and talk [in class]. Don't listen to the teacher and tell jokes all day. . . . Yeah, really not pay attention and goof around." Despite having recognized some of the elements that made a person cool. . . . William still preferred to be the sort of person he valued. . . . "Les Renault is my friend. . . . Nobody ever really liked us because we like to stay straight. There's Mr. Muscular and Mr. Cool. We don't like doing that—we're acting how we want to act. . . . Why can't anyone act themselves in school? I'm a goodie-goodie. I want to be straight—I want to do good things in my life. I don't want to be bad (William in the second semester of 7th grade)."[13]

[Scott said,] "One thing, he [Les] is more like a teacher's pet. He always hangs around teachers. That I don't like. I don't know how to say this but it looks like you look at teachers as your friends. They [one's peers] got to think that a teacher is not your friend."[14]

Is there a way out? At the beginning of eighth grade, William decided that he did not "want to be the little kid pushed around any more" and tried to change. "I've been taking a lot of people's punishments, to get them out of trouble. Or say they flunk a test. I grade it 100%. It's how everybody does it. Everybody fits in better. I don't tattle like I used to."[15] Les's perspective on William's transformation was as follows.

"This year he [William] does not want to be teased. So what he is doing is challenging kids who are younger than him to fight. I think it is super stupid because he didn't like it when everybody was bugging him, so why is he going around bugging everyone else. I'm just strickly [*sic*] in the middle. I'm not going to be any bully or any wimp."[16]

William intentionally defied adult authority. He stopped associating openly with his Mel friends. At the end of eighth grade, William said, "Now everybody likes me. . . . I would say I'm in the top 10. I mean everything has changed. I know it's the best I've ever felt in my life." The efforts of the other three Mels to escape their outcast status were unsuccessful.

William's jouney from Mel to "top 10" illustrates the power of peer norms in middle school. To fit in at school, William cast away the norms and values he had lived by in elementary school and had defended in seventh grade: empathy, helping others, being good. He adopted instead the more predatory antiteacher persona promoted by the dominant and popular students in junior high school. Many of the norms and values that William's parents taught him and that most people would probably hope him to have appear to have been put in the attic along with his GI Joe and *Star Wars* figures.

How common is the predatory antiteacher peer culture of Cronkite Junior High School? Does it typically last into senior high? How do the peer norms of the different crowds within a school get established? Who sets them? How are they enforced? Most high schools have a variety of crowds with different views about what is normative behavior. Why are some crowds and individuals more influential in establishing the peer norms that apply generally to all students? Why do some crowds have higher status than others? What happens to the crowds and individuals who challenge the normative dominance of the popular crowds? What are the long-term effects of being popular or unpopular during secondary school? What effects do context and educational policy have on the norms that prevail in the youth culture? These are a sample of the questions being addressed by the research program of the Educational Excellence Alliance (EEA). The alliance is a consortium of schools and school districts that are interested in learning how to more effectively help all their middle and high school students to achieve at higher levels and to respect individual differences.

This paper looks at the relationship between the study behavior and academic engagement of individual students, the norms and attitudes of close friends, and the peer culture of school. We are particularly interested in how the academic orientation of a student and his or her close friends invites or protects him or her from harassment by peers. Our description of the peer culture is based on a review of ethnographic studies of adolescent peer cultures, structured and unstructured interviews we conducted, and responses to survey questionnaires completed by nearly 100,000 middle school and high school students from 1998 to 2001.[17] Our qualitative data are the memories of the paper's authors (most of whom had only recently graduated from New York State high schools when work on the paper was started) and our taped winter 1998 interviews with tenth graders in eight secondary schools serving predominantly white upper-middle-class suburbs in New York.[18] We felt we would get a more accurate picture of peer cultures if we matched the gender of interviewers and respondents. The time available for interviewing was limited, so we were able to study both genders in only one school, the culture of male students in another school, and the culture of female students in six schools. The characteristics of the high schools and middle schools we visited can be found in appendix A. The survey data on the attitudes and behavior of secondary school students were collected in more than four hundred schools by the Educational Excellence Alliance.[19] The multivariate analysis employs data from surveys completed between May 1998 and December 1999 by thirty-five thousand students attending 134 schools. A copy of the Ed-Excel Student Culture survey used during this period is provided in appendix B.

The descriptions and hypotheses developed from our qualitative research have been used to develop a simple theory of how crowd and school norms influence peer harassment, student engagement in school, how students choose their crowd, and why crowds and schools have the norms that they have. Because the interview data are limited to public schools in predominantly white upper-middle-class neighborhoods, the theory will require revision before it can be applied to schools in working-class neighborhoods or minority communities.[20]

What Students Say about Peer Pressure

The literature on school peer groups draws a distinction between cliques and crowds. Cliques are small groups of friends who hang out together a great deal and are personally close. Crowds, by contrast, are larger, "reputation-based collectives of similarly stereotyped individuals who may or may not spend much time together. . . . Crowd affiliation denotes the primary attitudes and activities with which one is associated by peers. . . . Whereas clique norms are developed within the group, crowd norms are imposed from outside the group and reflect the stereotypic image that peers have of crowd members."[21]

Cliques

Members of a clique often have similar attitudes and behavior patterns. This similarity stems in part from the influence that clique members have on each other. It also arises from selective entry and selective exit from the clique. Sociometric studies that ask students to list their closest friends typically find that friendship nominations often change by the end of a school year. These studies also find that students are often part of more than one friendship circle or clique.[22] Students who are uncomfortable with the norms and behavior of a particular clique need not join it. If they find that the other members of their clique are heading down a path they do not like, they can shift their time and attention to one of their other circles of friends or they can try to develop new friends. Consequently, high school students must be viewed as choosing the normative environment of their clique. However, selection is not the sole reason that clique members are similar in attitudes and behavior.

A great deal of evidence exists that pressures to conform to the norms of one's clique and crowd are quite strong. Some examples follow.

—Rule 2 in Jessica's clique: "Parties. Of course, we sit down together and discuss which ones we're going to go to. . . . No getting smacked at a party, because how would it look for the rest of us if you're drunk and acting like a total fool? And if you do hook up with somebody at the party, please try to limit it to one. Otherwise, you look like a slut and that reflects badly on all of us. Kids are not that smart: they're not going to make distinctions between us."[23]

—Some students we interviewed said that just about everybody at their school felt pressured to keep their distance from outcast groups. David E. Kinney got a similar response from one student he interviewed: "[We] always had that one group—we had all the good-looking girls and that is the one [group] that everybody wanted to be in. At lunch we sit at our own table

[but] if you go out to lunch with the wrong person, rumors would go around that you went to lunch with a geek!"[24]

—Sandra B. Damico studied the effects of clique membership on academic achievement at a small school run by one of Florida's state universities. Through forty hours of observation over a six-month period and interviews with teachers and students, she charted the clique structure of the school's ninth grade. Aptitude test scores were unrelated to clique membership. Nevertheless, she found that clique membership was a better predictor of a student's grade point average (GPA) than an aptitude test taken during the year.[25]

—Laboratory studies employing confederates and experimental designs find strong conformity pressures among adolescents. Vernon D. Gifford and Douglas H. Colston's experimental work, for example, led them to conclude that "secondary school students are affected significantly by group pressure emanating from their peer group in a majority-versus-one situation and a majority-versus-two situation."[26]

—Studies of the influence of randomly assigned college roommates on each other also clearly establish that peer effects are significant.[27]

Crowds

Some stereotypic identities or crowds are respected by most of the rest of the students in the school. In most schools, the Jocks, Preppies, and Populars are identities that carry prestige and bring power. Some of the other crowds—Freaks, Goths, Losers, Druggies, Nerds—are at the bottom of the status hierarchy. There are also typically other crowds whose status varies across schools. In the schools we studied the majority of the student body were either floaters or did not classify themselves as members of a distinctive crowd. They were in the middle in terms of status and popularity. Researchers who study peer cultures often refer to this category of students as "the normals."[28]

Boundaries exist between crowds and cliques. As one girl said, "I usually sit at the same place, with the same people. But then we usually walk around and talk to other people. I'll go and talk to the guys. But then the other girls, I don't really talk to 'cause it's weird. It's weird 'cause they're them and we're us. I can't explain it."[29]

Crowds represent different "identity prototypes" reflecting "different lifestyles and value systems."[30] Crowd affiliation is most fluid at transitions between schools—for example, entry into middle school or transferring between schools. Many of the students we talked to said they were aware of their crowd assignment (and the assignment of most of their friends) only a month or so after they started middle school. Many were not happy with the stereotypic identity—loser, nerd, dork—they were assigned and tried for the next couple of years to escape it.

Once classmates have categorized a student, changing their minds about who the student is can be difficult. In small schools, to change crowds essentially involves convincing classmates that the student has become a different person. Downward mobility is easy for them to recognize. Upward mobility is harder to pull off.

The barriers to entry into high-status crowds are often substantial. Most of the student leaders of the predominantly white upper-middle-class suburban high schools we studied were from one of the school's high-status, all-rounder crowds (called "Preps" in many of these schools). These crowds are probably the hardest to get into. Entry typically requires that one demonstrate achievement in both academics and a respected extracurricular activity. At most schools, president of the Science Club was not good enough. For most of the Preps we interviewed, their participation in interscholastic athletics rounded out their resume and made them eligible for the prep crowd. Cool clothes were also necessary. This was probably a barrier for students from modest circumstances, but most of the families in these well-off communities could handle the modest additional cost of fashionable clothes.

Some activity-based crowds are built around teams—cheerleaders, traveling soccer teams, auditioned choirs, Thespians, Math Olympics, the Debate Team, and the Chess Team—that have tryouts and auditions. Most high school athletic teams, by contrast, are open to anyone. Joining a team and showing up regularly at practice may gain one admission to the crowd associated with that team. However, practices typically require ten to fifteen hours a week, so students are unlikely to join if they do not enjoy the sport. If the student is not good at the sport, he or she may not be accepted into the crowd and become the butt of jokes. At large high schools, he or she may get little playing time. In effect the kid may be exchanging a respected position in a low-status crowd (for example, the Brains) for a disrespected role in a high-status crowd (the Jocks or the Preps). Many students probably doubt that such an exchange would make them better off.

Admission to high-status crowds with a fun ideology, such as the Populars, is typically by invitation. Even during the wanna-be phase when the aspirant is trying to become friends with members of the crowd, the hangout time commitment can be substantial and there is no certainty of success. In addition, aspirants must demonstrate to the crowd that they buy into the crowd's view of what is cool, who is cool, and who is not cool. An aspirant may have to abandon some of his or her friends.

These last two items—buying into the norms of the crowd and ending other friendships—are a price that everyone seeking to change crowd affiliation must pay. Deviant low-status crowds, we were told, are more accepting of new recruits than high-status crowds. However, they expect new members to honor the values and norms held by the other members of the crowd and to engage in the behaviors and wear the clothes that are characteristic of the crowd. Yes, changing crowds can be costly and uncertain. But staying in a denigrated identity is even more costly.

Harassment and Bullying

In our 1998–99 surveys, 13.1 percent of boys and 6.7 percent of girls said they were "teased, insulted or made fun of to [their] face . . . almost every day." Another 19.5 percent of boys and 13.3 percent of girls said they were insulted to their face "about once a week." Sixteen percent of boys and 12.7 percent of girls said that "almost every day" they were "insulted or made fun of behind [their] back." If these rates of peer harassment in EEA schools are representative of the rest of the nation's schools, 2.3 million secondary school students were insulted to their face just about every day they came to school. Another 3.9 million students had about a one in five chance of being insulted to their face on any given day.

Physical confrontations are less common. Almost 4 percent of students (an estimated 890,000 students) report being "pushed, tripped, or hurt by other students" almost every day. Another 4.3 percent say it happens about once a week. What is causing this epidemic of peer harassment?

BULLIES. Some students believe they can gain prestige in the eyes of other students by harassing and humiliating weaker, less popular students. They sucker victims over to their clique and then surprise them with a blast of insults. Trying to make sense of this behavior one middle school student said, "Maybe they like to prove to their friends that they're cool, that they can put someone else down without [being put down themselves]." While other qualities—being good in sports, being outgoing, funny, or attractive— are more important, playing and winning the dominance game is, for some boys, a way of trying to gain respect and prestige. The kids who do this tend to be wanna-bes who are on the fringe of one of the popular crowds. Mertens's ethnography of the Mels describes this phenomenon: "Some individuals sought out and denigrated boys who were reputed to be Mels in order to set themselves apart from the categorical identity."[31] Bullies seldom go after the school's popular students because they are better able to handle harassment and have ways of retaliating not available to others.[32]

PARIAHS. A student at Boynton Middle School said: "If a 'nerd' goes over and sits next to a jock or somebody who's really popular . . . —it doesn't happen very often—they would probably tell him to leave." Being a nerd is like having a communicable disease. Everyone tries to avoid a nerd because hanging out with one sends a signal that that person is a nerd as well. "If you hang out with people who are unpopular, most of the time you are unpopular." Thus, those who have an outcast label placed on them find it hard to make new friends and often lose old friends. This limits their ability to develop social skills that can help them get out of their predicament.[33]

SUBMISSIVE OUTCASTS. To maximize the humiliation, submissive male outcasts are typically harassed in the presence of other students.[34] The humiliation comes not so much from the harassment (almost everyone gets harassed some) but from their lack of an aggressive response to it. Friends of the victim seldom intervene in defense of the victim and sometimes join in the harassment in a joking manner. The victim's friends are trying to escape from their own outcast identity and fear that sticking up for their friend will prevent their escape. What they fail to realize is that not sticking up for their friend simply stigmatizes them as cowards. Nonaggressive outcasts are generally smaller and weaker than the kids who harass them, so a "You wanna fight?" response is seldom chosen. Another reason that they do not respond by starting a fight is that they have been told not to by parents and teachers. They do not want to lose the favorable opinion of teachers, the only people in the school who they feel are on their side.[35]

LOOKING DIFFERENT. A student who is odd looking can become a target of bullying. As one high schooler said, "This kid in our grade [tenth grade] is really weird looking. He has really big ears and is really tall, really awkward looking. One of the seniors called him 'dumbo' and really hurt his feelings. He was crying. I laughed, only because it was funny. But that kid [the senior] got [the same treatment] back . . . when he was a freshman. They made him stand up on the table in his boxers and sing 'I'm a little teapot.'"[36]

BEING SMALL. At Newport Junction High School, Paula spent a great deal of time playing sports (fifteen to nineteen hours a week) and hanging out (ten to fourteen hours a week). Nevertheless, she said, "I'm picked on all the time because of my size. I guess it's supposed to be a joke, although sometimes I care. . . . Just because I'm smaller, they know they can make fun of me. I'm not really upset—just angry." When asked where she sits at lunch, she laughed nervously and admitted, "I mostly eat my lunch in the bathroom. There are groups in the cafeteria and I don't really feel comfortable there." Asked what would happen if she sat down at a table with a different crowd than the one to which she was accustomed, Paula guessed, "They would probably say something about me after I left, like they didn't want me there."[37]

The consequences of harassment and bullying are severalfold. Harassment induces some victims to withdraw from social interaction. Students who are harassed naturally respond by trying to avoid the people and the situations that occasion the harassment. Classmates laugh at something they say in class, so they fall silent during class discussions. Like Morton of the Mels, some try to become invisible, walking quickly from class to class, avoiding opportunities to socialize. Often they do not participate in after-school activities and head for the safety of home as soon as school lets out. This response, however, makes things worse. When we asked sixty thousand students at EEA schools whether "studying a lot tends to make you less popular," only 18 percent agreed. But 60 percent agreed that "not spending time to socialize and hang out tends to make you less popular."

The mere climate of intimidation and threat of harassment can also induce withdrawal. We talked with two students, close friends in high school, who had the following exchange:

> Kim: "Neither of us had a real hard time. We weren't one of those kids who got ridiculed every single day. But we were sort of . . ."
> David: "Not really there."
> Kim: "We overreacted."
> David: "People would make fun of you once and you'd close up. If I ignore everybody then they won't make fun of me. They don't make fun of you but you don't get to know people very well doing that. It's socially isolating and if you are socially isolated, people don't interact with you so they can't make fun of you or make friends with you."

In severe cases, victims of peer abuse can be scarred for a lifetime. As one college student said:

"Up to that age [eleven years old] I had been quite happy at school but then something happened to me, I stopped growing and I became in no time the shortest and skinniest and soon the pimpliest little runt at my grade level. The other boys used to pick on me, hide my coat, steal my lunches and would never include me in their games. They'd laugh at me openly and the girls started avoiding me too because it wasn't cool being seen with the most unpopular boy. . . . You can't imagine how many times my mother had to keep me home because I'd start throwing up. I became scared shitless . . . and to this day I feel insecure around other guys."[38]

Powerful support for the proposition that social status during high school influences later success in the labor market comes from an excellent paper by Nicola Persico, Andrew Postlewaite, and Dan Silverman. Their study demonstrates conclusively that in both Great Britain and the United States height as a teenager has large effects on earnings. When adolescent height was controlled, adult height and height at age seven and eleven had no effect. Almost half of the effect of adolescent height on adult earnings was due to its impact on adolescent self-esteem and participation in extracurricular activities.[39]

The Outcasts

At the large suburban secondary schools we studied, three distinct types of students achieved outcast status.[40]

First, overly aggressive boys who are poor at reading social cues, bully others, and often get into fights are unpopular for seemingly good reasons. They make many enemies. Their antisocial behavior makes others feel insecure. Naturally, kids avoid them. They are sanctioned by being sent to Coventry. However, bullying does not always make the bully an outcast. Verbal bullying of outcast students—Mels, Freaks, Nerds, and so on—in the service of the norms and identity of a popular crowd is generally OK, at least in the eyes of the leaders of the popular crowd. Some kids do it in hopes of being accepted into a high-status crowd. It is the wanna-be's way of trying to prove that he or she buys into the norms and values of the crowd.

Second, groups that publicly challenge the norms and mock the identity of the school's popular crowds also achieve outcast status. Groups such as the Goths, Freaks, and Punks fall into this category. The other students, we believe, think the members of these groups choose to be outcasts. Our interviews encountered a number of cases in which Freaks were being harassed. At Harbor Edge, one student confessed: "I'm usually the one picked on . . .

mostly because of my [pink dyed] hair." At Longview High School, we learned of a couple of incidents of serious physical harassment. One student told us: "We were all hanging out . . . and then a couple of freaks walked by and everybody started throwing things at them, like rocks and stuff. . . . They just kept on walking. They just try to ignore it." Another incident was described thirdhand, "They threw them down Suicide Stairs—the big stairs over by the music wing. I think the freaks avoided that area just so that they wouldn't get thrown down the stairs. They would yell 'Oh it's a freak,' and start beating them up."[41]

Third, Nerds, Geeks, Dorks, Mels, and other studious, nonaggressive, socially unskilled students are also frequently outcasts, particularly in middle school. Robyn, a Harbor Edge student who eats lunch with the popular crowd, described Nerds as "being very involved with school, asking a million questions in class, and not having much fun in their spare time. . . . If someone asks a question and you're considered a nerd, then people will be like, 'Oh, shut up!' But if you're not [a nerd], then no one says anything. It's a double standard." Despite her sympathy for the nerds, Robyn, at another point in the interview, said, "Well my friends and I always makes fun of this one girl; all she does is study. It's like she studies for college already [tenth grade]—that's so stupid."[42]

At Newport Junction, a school with a strong International Baccalaureate program and a 94 percent college attendance rate, Eliza characterizes dorks as "constantly asking questions in class." This seems to annoy other students. She recounted what happened in her English class. "Nobody likes this girl. She talks and says the stupidest things which makes everyone want to cringe. It gets out of hand, so these boys stood up in the middle of class and shouted, 'You're a loser, just shut up and get out of this class.' The teacher had no control." [43] However, the Newport Junction students we talked to all agreed that getting good grades did not make you a nerd. "If you're smart you're lucky; no one considers you a nerd as a result. Everyone wants to get good grades now because of college, so you kind of envy those who do well."[44]

At small, intimate Lakeside High School, from which 89 percent of graduates go on to college, we were told the same thing: "If you study too hard, it will reflect in a good grade, and nobody makes fun of a good grade. . . . People who don't care about [grades], they don't say anything because probably they wish they could have gotten the same grade. So if you study hard and you get a good grade, people may envy you . . . but you wouldn't get ridiculed for it."[45] A direct question about nerd harassment elicits this kind of response, but the class also appears to have a norm against working hard.

> "In our grade in general, nobody wants to work hard at all. I'm friends with people who are juniors . . . and they are pushing. . . . I think it's a little too competitive, so I'm glad I am not in that grade. . . . [In our grade] everybody is smart enough to do the work, but everybody is too lazy to actually do it."[46]

There was one exception to this generalization: Rebecca, a recent transfer from a competitive private school. Her goal was to be the valedictorian. How did people react to her? "Rebecca is really, really smart. But I think [schoolwork] is all she does. She only cares about school and she stresses on school way too much. And it gets annoying to people." Another student commented: "She is taking two classes just to experiment with one, because she is getting an eighty-five in the advanced class and wants to know if she can get a one hundred in the basic class. And that really annoys us. That really annoys us." Rebecca realized she was unpopular but gave her situation a positive spin. "I don't like it here, but the only good thing is that since [Lakeside] is so small, you have a better chance at being higher in the class. So maybe, hopefully I'll be valedictorian, and be at the top." [47] Lakeside students saw themselves as reacting to Rebecca's obsessive personality, not to her academic work ethic. But if Rebecca had been obsessed about being the best basketball player, would they have reacted negatively? Probably not. Success in becoming a better basketball player helps Lakeside defeat rival schools. Becoming the valedictorian, by contrast, means someone else in the class does not.

For certain types of achievement—being athletic, funny, friendly, outgoing, popular, and attractive—more is better in the eyes of one's peers. When, however, it comes to academics, a norm, an optimal level of academic effort and achievement, is established. One is sanctioned for deviating from it, particularly on the up side. Lakeside's tenth grade set that work norm low. The eleventh grade set it higher. Above a certain point, trying harder in the academic arena gets one in trouble with one's peers. B. Bradford Brown and Laurence Steinberg point out that, as a result, "Many of the most intellectually capable high school students strive to be *less* than they can be in order to avoid rejection by peers."[48]

Who sets the norms?[49] In our judgment, for middle school and in some small high schools, the norms are set by the cool or popular crowd. Large high schools have many crowds. The norms the leading crowd imposed in middle school continue to be influential because they affect the sorting of students into crowds. Each crowd has its own distinct package of norms, and these influence the behavior of its members.

Norms are partially inherited from earlier generations of the crowd and partially established by the crowd's current leaders and core members. The cool or popular crowds define schoolwide norms in such a way that it reinforces the popularity and authority of the members of the crowd. If the insecure students are afraid of asserting their individuality, they will evaluate themselves by what the secure, confident students consider cool. High school crowds tend to value highly the abilities, resources, and personality traits that the crowd's leadership have in common. Because the leaders of the crowd exemplify the crowd's norms, self-serving bias of the leadership works to reinforce the popularity and authority of the crowd's leadership. Individuals tend to join crowds and cliques that have similar value systems to their own, so a crowd's size depends on the popularity of the normative system and identity that it exemplifies.

The views, values, and actions of the popular crowd and its leadership are particularly powerful influences on the peer pressures that all students face. Given that each member of the Populars is essentially encouraging the rest of the students to "be like me," it matters a great deal who the Populars are and what their norms are.

Being Popular

Nearly 100,000 students at Educational Excellence Alliance schools were given a list of twelve traits and asked to describe the qualities of the members of the "most popular crowd (your gender) . . . during the first year of middle or junior high school." In order from the top, the tally was: cool clothes—64 percent, attractive—61 percent, funny—60 percent, good in sports—55 percent, outgoing—53 percent, self-confident—48 percent, tough—31 percent, not attentive in class—24 percent, worked hard for grades—22 percent, attentive in class—21 percent, smart—19 percent, and made fun of those who study—18 percent. The traits that are most often associated with being popular reflect services—telling jokes, being entertaining, going out for sports—that the popular students are providing for their classmates. Jackie, an "A" student who was also a member of the Soccer Girls, one of popular cliques at Harbor Edge High School, put it this way: "The group I'm thinking of probably considers themselves to be the popular crowd. I don't know. I do sports, but maybe other people—those involved in Model Congress or World Interest club—consider themselves the popular ones." When asked what makes the popular crowd popular, Jackie points out, "Everyone wants to have a good time, no matter who your friends are. Sports are fun. . . . Battle of the Classes, Sports Night, parties, hanging out . . . they're all good time. The actual individuals are good people too; they're interesting, they have different talents and abilities and attractable [*sic*] themselves. [Their popularity is] not just based on what they do."[50]

Membership in a popular crowd confers power and influence in a variety of ways.

BEING A ROLE MODEL. Popular students are role models and exemplars of cool. Many of their peers respect them, so their opinions about who and what is cool and who and what is uncool are influential. Their example influences the dress, attitudes, and behavior of other students much more than the wishes and example of parents, teachers, and school administrators. New entrants into middle school are particularly susceptible to these influences. These new entrants are especially insecure and often hope to eventually join one of the high-status crowds in the school.

BECOMING BETTER AT SOCIALIZING. Membership in a popular crowd confers opportunities to learn from the acknowledged local masters of adolescent social interaction and to practice these social skills. Members become better performers in a middle school status and dominance game with very different rules than its elementary school counterpart. Because the popular students have already been sorted into the high-status crowds, students outside these crowds are less likely to have someone in their group who can teach and model the behavior needed to become popular.

VALIDATING THE POPULARITY OF OTHERS. Given that the primary signal of a person's popularity is who one hangs out with, reputation as a popular person depends on "being allowed to hang out with them [one of the popular crowds]." As one of our respondents said, "If you're friends with popular people, you're considered more popular." Inviting someone from outside the crowd to a party or including them in lunchtime conversation may be small matter to a popular student, but it sometimes has an important positive demonstration effect on that kid's reputation. This works for groups as well as individuals. If your clique interacts with a group that is seen as popular, your clique's reputation will improve.

SETTING ADMISSION RULES. Around most popular crowds are wanna-bes actively trying to join the crowd and potential wanna-bes who would try if they thought they had a reasonable chance of success. Members of a popular crowd control and limit entry into the crowd. Often, core members of a clique have the additional power of blackballing potential entrants. Rosalind Wiseman, author of *Queenbees and Wannabes*, describes how it worked in one clique:

> Each member of Jessica's group is allowed to invite an outside person to sit at their table in the lunch room several times a month, but they have to meet at the lockers to O.K. it with other members first, and then they cannot exceed their limit. "We don't want other people at our table more than a couple of times a week because we want to bond and bonding is endless," Jessica says.[51]

ATTRACTING THE OPPOSITE SEX. Because cross-gender socializing often occurs in reasonably stable groups, male and female cliques frequently pair up. This means that a new romantic relationship can help a student gain entry into a more popular clique. Popular students are thus given a further edge in the competition for attention from the opposite sex.

CREATING POSERS. Posers are individuals or groups who copy the dress and behavior of a high-status crowd, without being a part of that crowd. By adopting the norms and behaviors of a popular crowd as their own, Posers assist in the transmission of the norms and values of the popular crowd to the wider school community.

PLAYING THE DOMINANCE-BY-INSULT GAME. Insults from high-status peers are more damaging to one's self-esteem and reputation than insults hurled by low-status peers. Insults from unpopular students can be deflected by calling them names, such as "dirt bag" or "low life," that give life to the way others at the school view them. Finding cutting responses to taunts from popular students is more difficult. Insults are more effective when they target a vulnerability of one's opponent.[52] What aspect of the popular student's persona can the victim counterattack? The popular person exemplifies what most of the victim's classmates respect.

SIGNALING WHO HAS PARIAH STATUS. When an unpopular kid is harassed by someone from a popular crowd, wanna-bes and posers may take the incident as a signal that their own status can be improved by going after that victim. Individual popular students can wittingly or unwittingly single out specific students for harassment by others.

ESTABLISHING NORMATIVE HEGEMONY. The quickest way to change a school's peer norms is to persuade the leaders of the popular crowds that such a change is desirable. The student body is used to following their lead so if they advocate the change and adjust their own behavior to the new requirements others are likely to follow.[53]

A distinction must be drawn between membership in a popular crowd and the power of this crowd to set the normative environment of the school and personal popularity with the classmates one interacts with. In small schools, students interact with all the members of their class, so personal popularity tends to be based on a particular student's history of interactions with his or her classmates.

In large schools, however, students have only superficial contact with a significant portion of their grade and even less contact with older and younger students. This is particularly true in large middle schools that combine students from many different elementary schools. Inside the group one interacts with daily, status and popularity depend on the history of interactions between group members. One's social status and popularity in the eyes of students outside this group, however, is largely defined by the stereotype that is assigned to one's crowd and the outsider's valuation of that stereotype. Assignment to crowd occurs in the first weeks of middle school and is difficult to change.

Given the great benefits of membership in a popular crowd, many students not surprisingly try to wangle their way into one of them. However, many high school students get tired of the dominance-by-insult game that was so important in middle school. A student at Longview High School told us: "The people who used to make fun of other people don't anymore because it doesn't really matter. It's not important anymore . . . because everyone's kind of grown up and everyone's beyond that now."[54]

Furthermore, the power of the popular crowd can be corrupting. We found that many of the students outside the popular crowds disliked the Populars. When asked if there is a cool crowd at Harbor Edge, Susan said, "They seem to think they are. They're usually into sports and because they have so many friends, they just think of themselves as popular. . . . They are so obnoxious; they just make fun of others for who they are and I don't think that's right." Even though she ate lunch with them, Robyn described Harbor Edge's popular crowd as "the loud ones. Some of them make fun of the dorks and the nerds, and then the rest of them hang out with the meaner people. They're known to act like this; no one will make fun of them, because [they] are afraid they'll be totally abused."[55] Robyn seems to be suggesting that the Populars maintained their preeminent status by admitting into their ranks a group of enforcers who intimidated the rest of the students.

Over at Newport Junction, the dynamic was the same. Kate remarked, "Everyone looks up to [the Populars], but I don't really know why. There's nothing really different about them except that they hang out with upper-classmen and play sports." Judie described them as "a big group of blond snots." Eliza, a member of the Populars, boasted about her snobby reputation, proudly confiding, "When [all my friends] are together, everybody hates us."[56] Students at Ithaca High School said similar things about the popular students there: "I'm friends with many of them. . . . Individually, they are not elitist. But [when they are] together, they are all worried about associating with people of lesser status." Jackie argued that her friends in the popular crowd were good, interesting, and talented people. We do not disagree. But good people can behave badly when submerged in a crowd. Reinhold Niebuhr said it well in 1933.

> In every human group there is less reason to guide and check impulse, less capacity for self-transcendence, less ability to comprehend the needs of others and therefore more unrestrained egoism than the individuals who compose the group reveal in their personal relationships.[57]

Student Culture and the Learning Environment

The social norms and values of students are contested territory in most high schools. Teachers and administrators presumably stand for the proposition that school is first and foremost for learning. Students told us, however, that learning was only one of their reasons for coming to school. Socializing, sports, and extracurricular activities were at least as important for many students. Some students said they come to school primarily because they are required to by their parents and the law.

Teachers often express discontent with students' commitment to learning. In their view, "lack of student interest" is the single most important reason for poor achievement. Many principals feel helpless in the face of a student culture that they sense is more powerful than even the threat of failing courses or being prevented from graduating. The principal at Longview High School, for example, complained:

> "We have mandated extra help right now. . . . Any child who fails one of the four major subject areas is scheduled for mandated extra help. I will tell you—they didn't go. . . . I have to think that a kid who does go has to get something out of it.

Table 2. Ed-Excel Questionnaire Results, 1998–99
Percent

Statement	Agree	Disagree
"It's not cool to frequently volunteer answers or comments in class."	19	81
"It's not cool to study real hard for tests and quizzes."	15	85
"It's not cool to be enthusiastic about what you are learning in school."	27	73
"It's not cool to be competitive about grades."	51	49
"It's annoying when other students talk or joke around in class."	40	60
"It's annoying when students try to get teachers off track."	42	58

Source: Authors' analysis of Educational Excellence Alliance survey.

But, they don't go. And why don't they go? Well, someone said, what do you do when they don't go? We notify the parents. How much more discipline, how much more can we do? It would be an impossible task. What discipline is there if you don't go to mandated extra help? Well, that you'll keep failing."[58]

Most high school teachers love the subject they teach and hope that students will find it as intrinsically interesting as they do. Some students fit the "learning for its own sake" ideal: Forty-two percent of students in EEA high schools said they "enjoy doing math problems," 52 percent said they "like the books and plays we read in English," and 37 percent said they "find the history and science textbooks interesting." However, 48 percent agreed with the statement: "If I didn't need good grades, I'd put little effort into my studies." When all EEA students were asked why they worked hard in school, extrinsic reasons were most commonly cited. Seventy-seven percent said, "I need the grades to get into college," 58 percent said to "help me get a better job," and 56 percent said to "prepare myself for tough college courses."

Students are not of one mind on these matters. Different crowds and cliques have distinct views about the priority to be given to learning and the reasons for wanting to learn. The norms of these peer groups matter because "subgroups of youths tend to be granted increasing levels of hegemony in the establishment of social norms and values."[59]

What are these norms? We asked the thirty-five thousand students who completed the Ed-Excel questionnaire during 1998–99 a set of questions about what is uncool or annoying regarding student behavior (see table 2). We also asked about the behavior of their friends. Twenty-four percent agreed with the statement: "My friends make fun of people who try to do real well in school." Fifty-six percent agreed with the statement: "My friends joke around and annoy the teacher."

A Brief Exposition of the Theory

We assume that students allocate their free time among four activities: studying or learning (T^L), extracurricular activities including sports (T^S), hanging out with peers (T^P), and solitary leisure activities such as reading, playing video games, and watching television (T^V) subject to a time budget constraint.

$$\text{Time constraint} = 1 = T^L + T^S + T^P + T^V. \tag{1}$$

Learning depends on academic ability and previous learning (A^A), the quality of instruction (Q^i), and free time devoted to learning (T^L).

$$\text{Learning} = L_i = L(A^A, Q^i, T^L), \tag{2}$$

where $L_T > 0$ and $L_{TT} < 0$.

Learning generates three kinds of rewards.

1. Intrinsic rewards, $J(L^i)$, reflect the joy of learning for its own sake.

2. Direct extrinsic rewards, $\$(L^i)$, depend directly on how much the individual learns during high school. They include effects that operate through admission to preferred colleges, years of schooling completed, and higher wages holding schooling constant. They also include the benefits that parents derive from the economic success of their children and the honor and prestige given to those seen as high achievers. These benefits are larger if the skills developed in school are signaled to universities, employers, and parents.

3. Rank rewards, $R^j(L^i - L^m)$, depend on the extent to which the student learns more than the rest of the students in the school. These would include the effect of class rank and GPA relative to the school mean (L^m) on the present discounted value of lifetime earnings and self-esteem derived from comparisons with other students at the school.

$$U^L = I(L^i) + \$(L^i) + R^j(L^i - L^m), \tag{3}$$

$U^S(A^S, T^S) =$ Utility from extracurricular activities depends on time and ability (A^S) at it, (4)

$U^P(A^P, T^P) =$ Utility from socializing depends on time devoted and ability (A^P) at it, and (5)

$U^V(T^V) =$ Utility from solitary leisure that depends solely on time devoted to it. (6)

Students seek to avoid being harassed, insulted, teased, and ostracized by peers. In many secondary schools, a small number of students who exemplify denigrated traits and behaviors are targeted for harassment and ostracism. The theory treats this kind of peer harassment as punishment, the social purpose of which is to deter certain types of antisocial behavior (for example, squealing on peers, competing for grades, sucking up to teachers, deviating from the group's dress code) and encourage prosocial behavior (for example, letting friends copy homework). Besides avoiding harassment, students desire to be popular—that is, have many friends, be able to hang out with students in the leading crowd, and so on.

The concern here is with how popularity and harassment depend on the allocation of time between learning and studying, socializing, extracurricular activities, and solitary leisure and on success in learning. We hypothesize that popularity and harassment depend on four things.

1. Accomplishment in respected extracurricular activities, $\kappa A^S T^S$, where κ is the valuation that peers place on sports and extracurricular achievements when they judge another student's popularity and decide whether to harass him or her.

2. Socializing with friends, $\eta A^P T^P$, where η is the impact of socializing on peer judgments of popularity and the student's likelihood of avoiding harassment.

3. Conforming to peer group norms about academic commitment and achievement, $\delta(L^i - L^N)^2$, where L^N is the school norm specifying the optimal level of academic achievement (chosen by the leading crowd for the whole school or by the leaders of the crowd to which the student belongs) and $\delta < 0$ measures how strong conformity pressures are to be similar to peers in one's commitment to academic learning ($\delta < 0$).

4. Costs that studious individuals impose on others by pushing ahead of them in a competitive ranking system.[60] This effect is captured by $\Theta R_j(L^i - L^m)$, where L^m is the mean achievement level at the school and Θ is less than zero when peers harass or ostracize the studious as "nerds[,] . . . teachers pets[,] . . . or acting white." When $\Theta = -1$, the antinerd pressure against academic effort exactly offsets the losses that trying harder imposes on others, $R(L^i - L^m)$, because greater achievement for person i increases school mean achievement, L^m, and lowers everyone else's position relative to the mean (that is, rank in class). If $\Theta < -1$, antinerd peer pressure imposes larger costs on the studious than they impose on their classmates. If students honor those who win academic competitions, Θ would be positive. Schools with

competitive admissions and nearly universal participation in Advanced Placement (AP) courses, such as Stuyvesant High School in New York City, appear to have a positive Θ.

Putting it all together, equation 7 describes the determinants of harassment and popularity.

$$H_i = [\text{Popularity} - \text{Harassment}]$$
$$= \kappa A^S T^S + \eta A^P T^P + \delta(L^i - L^N)^2 + \Theta R_j(L^i - L^m) + u^i. \tag{7}$$

Most students care a great deal about their popularity with peers. The weight, ϕ_i, they attach to their popularity with other students will, however, vary across individuals.

$$U_i = J(L_i) + \$(L_i) + R_j(L^i - L^m) + U^S(A^S, T^S) + U^P(A^P, T^P)$$
$$+ U^V(T^V) + \phi^i H_i, \text{ and} \tag{8}$$

$$U_i = J(L_i) + \$(L_i) + R_j(L^i - L^m) + U^S(A^S, T^S) + U^P(A^P, T^P)$$
$$+ U^V(T^V) + \phi^i [\kappa A^S T^S + \eta A^P T^P + \delta(L^I - L^N)^2 + \Theta R_j(L^i - L^m)]. \tag{9}$$

We then maximize equation 8 with respect to the time budget constraint (equation 1). We obtain the following first-order conditions for learning time, for extracurricular time, for socializing time, and for solitary leisure time:

$$(J_T + \$_T + R)L_T + 2_i\phi^i \delta(L^i - L^N)L_T + \phi^i \Theta R_i L_T = \lambda, \tag{10}$$

$$U^S_T + \phi^i \kappa A^S T^S_T = \lambda, \tag{11}$$

$$U^P_T + \phi^i \eta A^P T^P_T = \lambda, \text{ and} \tag{12}$$

$$U^V_T = \lambda, \tag{13}$$

where $U^S_T > 0$, $U^S_{TT} < 0$, $U^P_T > 0$, $U^P_{TT} < 0$, $U^V_T > 0$, and $U^V_{TT} < 0$.

This set of first-order conditions will look familiar to economists. Students will allocate their time among activities in a way that equalizes the marginal utility of the last hour devoted to each activity. The Lagrangian multiplier, λ, is conventionally interpreted as the marginal utility of time. Consider equation 12, the first-order condition for time devoted to socializing. It says individual students increase time devoted to socializing if the utility they personally derive from it goes up (first term) or if the popularity or prestige they get from socializing goes up (second term). The popularity benefits of socializing are higher for people who are good at it (high on A^P), when the peer group greatly values it (η increases), and when the individual is particularly sensitive to what his or her peers think of him or her (ϕ_I is large). We know that η is positive in most schools. Sixty percent of the respondents in the EEA survey said that "not spending time to socialize and hangout tends to make you less popular." Thus $\phi_I\eta$ measures the intensity of peer pressure to socialize and $\phi_I\kappa$ measures peer pressure to participate in extracurricular activities. The stronger this pressure, the more time will be spent socializing or participating in extracurricular activities and the less time will be available to study and watch TV. This is the first mechanism by which peer pressure discourages learning. Peers encourage each other to hang out and reward those who do with popularity. Unless studying can be done simultaneously with hanging out, the inevitable result is less study time and less learning. This suggests that schools might counter this kind of peer pressure by promoting extracurricular activities with an academic focus such as debate club and interscholastic academic competitions. A portion of the time during athletic practice, chess club, and debate club meetings is social. Another approach is to encourage students to form study groups or to assign group projects that require face-to-face substantive discussions outside of school hours. The risk with this second approach, however, is that some students will free ride on the efforts of others. When close friends form a team, the social structure and norms of the group may prevent them from seriously engaging with the assignment. Some teams or study groups are likely to have members who joke around so much they subvert the effort of other members of the group to do a good job on the project.[61]

The second type of peer pressure comes from the "be like me" conformity pressure from the school's leading crowd(s) captured by $2\phi^i\delta(L^i - L^N)$ in equation 10. Remembering that δ is negative, this expression is positive when $(L^i - L^N)$ is negative (that is, the student has below average grades). Thus students with low grades are encouraged to try harder and students with grades that are higher than those of the leading crowd are discouraged from studying. This implies that the least popular students and, therefore, the ones most likely to be harassed by peers are the students whose commitment to school is either way above the norm set by the leading crowd or way below that norm. We will test this hypothesis in the empirical work to come. In the empirical work we will assume that L^N is the average achievement level of students in the school. However, our interviews and Reinhold Niebuhr's dictum that groups always act in their own self-interest suggest that a powerful leading crowd will impose on the school a system of normative evaluations (for example, the values for L^N, δ, κ, η, and Θ in our model) that place it at the top of the school's prestige hierarchy. This implies that if the leaders of the popular crowd set very challenging academic goals for themselves, their commitment to academic achievement will legitimate a "study hard" norm for their entire student cohort (as occurred with Lakeside's eleventh grade and the class of 1998 in Ithaca High School). Alternatively, a few charismatic leaders promoting a fun ideology might have the opposite effect.

The final reason for peer pressure against studying is the zero-sum nature of the competition for good grades caused by grading on a curve and the use of class rank as a criterion for awarding a fixed number of prizes and for admission to competitive colleges. The term $\phi^i \Theta R_L L_T$ captures this effect. Fifty-one percent of students in the EEA survey said, "It's not cool to be competitive about grades." Another question in the EEA survey evaluates whether students believe that hard work by other students makes it harder for them to get good grades. Our theory predicts that this belief should undermine incentives to study, and we will test that hypothesis. The theory implies that antilearning peer norms are more likely to develop among students when they perceive academic classrooms to be zero-sum games that pick winners and losers but cannot make everyone better off. To avoid this outcome, the academic enterprise should be and should be perceived to be a positive-sum game in which everyone can be successful. Teachers should not grade on a curve. Grades should be based on student effort (for example, completing homework assignments) and absolute achievement (results of quizzes and tests). The school should not publish or call attention to class rank. Having course content assessed externally by examinations set by the state department of education or Advanced Placement program also helps.

Another implication of the theory is that because student achievement is measured with error and imperfectly signaled to the labor market, the private rewards for learning will be smaller than the social returns to learning and this will lead to underinvestment in studying during school. This also implies that better signaling of student achievement to the labor market will increase $\$_L$, and this in turn should increase student effort levels.

Testing the Theory

To conduct some preliminary tests of the theory presented, we estimate ordinary least squares models in six areas.

1. Harassment—the incidence and extent of teasing and verbal harassment by peers.

2. Did not try hard—the incidence and frequency of students saying they did not try hard on a test or project because they were afraid of what their friends might think.

3. Study together—the incidence and frequency of students studying together outside of school or talking with friends about what was learned in school or both.

4. Classroom engagement—an index composed of questions about paying attention in class, contributing to classroom discussion, and not letting one's mind wander.

5. Homework completion—the proportion of homework assignments the student completes on average across four core subjects.

6. Grade point average—grade determined on a 4.0 scale.

Our purpose is to assess how much of the variance of peer harassment and student study effort and engagement (the first five variables) can be predicted by the racial and socioeconomic character of the school and the background characteristics of the student and how much of the variance can be predicted by the attitudes and culture of the school and of the student's clique. The final model uses the peer harassment variable and the study effort and engagement variables to predict grade point average. The peer culture and attitudes toward learning will be assumed to influence this final outcome, student GPA, only through their effects on peer harassment, study effort, and engagement.

Control Variables

The controls for student background are gender, grade in school, a dummy variable for seventh or eighth grade, parents' education, number of siblings, living in a single-parent family, self-reported ability, dummy variables for being African American, Hispanic, Asian, Native American, mixed ethnicity, and did not answer questions about race. The controls for the characteristics of the school were the school mean for parents' education, the proportion of the students at the school living in single-parent families, the proportion of students African American, the proportion Hispanic, the proportion Asian, the mean self-reported ability of the students at the school, the school mean for the school on the "teachers are demanding" index, and the school mean on the "teachers are interesting and motivating" index.

School means on the "parents motivate me" index and "future extrinsic motivation" index were included in the models predicting study effort and engagement. Appendix C provides a list of the items included in each of the attitude indexes. The curriculum track pursued by the student was controlled by including the number of accelerated courses taken in middle school, the share of this semester's courses that were honors or AP courses, the share of courses that were "basic" (or "local" in New York State parlance), the share of courses that were heterogeneous or mixed (the share of college prep courses was the excluded category), and the number of study halls taken. To prevent overestimation of the effects of clique norms and attitudes, we put in controls for the student's self-reported motivation: "intrinsic motivation," "future extrinsic motivation," and "parents motivate me" index.[62]

Hypotheses

Our primary focus is the effect of student culture. Students are exposed both to a school culture that is specific to their grade and their gender and to the attitudes and norms of their clique of close friends. We attempted to measure both. An overall prolearning school environment index was constructed by taking an average of the intrinsic motivation scale, the positive peer pressure scale, and the "it's annoying when students joke around" scale for the student's grade, gender, and school. We expect a prolearning environment to be associated with less harassment, fewer students saying they do not try, more studying together, and greater engagement in school. We also calculated a grade, gender, and school average of answers to "if others study hard, it is harder for me to get good grades." This variable measures the belief within the student body that they are engaged in a zero-sum competition with their classmates. We expect it to have a negative relationship with engagement and homework completion and a positive relationship with harassment, did not try hard, and study together. We expect a positive effect on studying together because students will want to learn from the smartest student in their friendship circle and to monitor how hard others are studying when they perceive their school to have a competitive grading system. The rest of the student culture variables are measured at the clique level. These variables are scales constructed by averaging normalized answers to two to six questions about the attitudes and norms of friends. Scales were developed for negative peer pressure, positive peer pressure, annoyed when others joke around in class, the leading crowd in middle school was antilearning, and the leading crowd was prolearning. Our theory predicts that negative peer pressure and antilearning leading crowd will have a positive relationship with harassment and did not try hard and a negative relationship with engagement and homework completion. We also predict that positive peer pressure, the annoyed when others joke around scale, and prolearning leading crowd will have a positive relationship with studying together, engagement, and completing homework. The final peer pressure variable assesses the student's belief about whether it is harder for them to get good grades when others study hard. We expect this to have a positive relationship with harassment, did not try hard, and studying together and a negative relationship with engagement and homework completion.

The final set of peer culture variables measures the deviation from the schoolwide norm of the student's GPA and his or her clique's academic commitment—positive peer pressure, annoyed when others joke around scale, and negative peer pressure (reflected; that is, times minus one). We expect that students who significantly deviate from school norms on these variables will experience more harassment. We have no reason to expect clique academic commitment variables to have a curvilinear effect on the other outcomes studied, so squared deviations from school norms were not entered in any of the other models.[63]

Table 3 presents the standardized regression coefficients from the models predicting outcomes in all six areas. A "+" to the right of a coefficient implies that the effect is not statistically significant (at the 5 percent level on a two-tail test). Coefficients without a "+" are statistically significant. The last column of the table gives the standard deviations (SDs) of independent and dependent variables. Unstandardized coefficients can be calculated by multiplying by the SD of the dependent variable and dividing by the SD of the independent variable.

Results

An examination of the results follows.

PEER HARASSMENT. We calculated that the average annual number of incidents of verbal harassment "to your face" was about twenty-three per student. Behind-your-back insults were more common: thirty-four per year per student. Boys experienced more harassment than girls. Hispanics and Asians experienced less than whites and African Americans. Children of

Table 3. Harassment, Study Effort, and Grades in School

Beta coefficients

Independent variable	Verbal harassment	Did not try hard because of friends	Study with friends	Engagement in class	Percent of homework done	Grade point average	Standard deviation of variable
Study behavior (endogenous)							
Verbal harassment (square root of the number of times per year)	***	**.089**	—	**-.051**	**-.055**	-.007+	3.51
Did not try hard because of friends (square root of the number of times per year)	—	***	—	—	—	-.013	2.46
Study with friends (square root of the number of times per year)	—	—	***	***	**.076**	.018	3.01
Engagement in class	—	—	***	***	—	.048	1.00
Percent of homework done	—	—	—	—	***	.269	0.224
Peer pressure (exogenous)							
"A" hard to get if others study	.043	**.070**	.025	-.047	-.041	—	0.681
Hard if others study (school average)	—	.022	.029	-.001+	-.001+	—	0.118
Good student leading crowd	—	—	**.054**	.003+	.016	—	
Bad students leading crowd	**.071**	**.160**	**-.046**	-.021	-.009+	—	0.99
Negative peer pressure	**.100**	**.081**	**.201**	**-.065**	-.002+	—	1.00
Positive peer pressure	.012+	.015	**.094**	**.069**	**.051**	—	1.00
Annoyed when others disrupt	.008+			**.188**	**.083**	—	1.00
(Negative peer pressure for person *i*—school mean for negative peer pressure) squared	.021	—	—	—	—	—	1.51
(Positive peer pressure for person *i*—school mean for positive peer pressure) squared	.024	—	—	—	—	—	1.79
(Annoyed by disruption index for person *i*—school mean for annoyed by disruption index) squared	**.055**	—	—	—	—	—	1.32

(GPA—3.0) squared (deviation of student's GPA from 3.0)	.027	—	—	—	—	—	1.28
Prolearning norm (school mean)	-.014+	.027	.021	.013+	-.008+	—	0.665
Student choice and time use							
Hours of homework per day	—	—	—	—	—	.040	1.44
Hours of TV per day	—	—	-.056	—	—	-.022	2.13
Number of accelerated courses	.025	.001+	.047	-.023	.015	.057	1.69
Percent honors courses	.017	-.025	.089	.013+	.049	.223	0.341
Percent basic courses	-.002+	.021	-.034	-.025	-.035	-.054	0.369
Percent heterogeneous classes	.006+	.001+	-.009+	.003+	-.004+	.004+	0.307
Number of study halls	.023	-.017	.011	—	-.033	-.011	3.42
School characteristic							
Middle school	.024	.026	.032	.017+	-.013+	.078	0.320
Grade in school	.000+	-.016+	.020	-.067	-.106	-.003+	0.980
Teachers are good index (school mean)	-.023	-.002+	.026	.044	.018	-.001+	0.251
Teachers are demanding index (school mean)	-.022	.008+	.029	.050	.028	-.039	0.192
Parents motivate me index (school mean)	—	-.022	—	—	—	—	
Future extrinsic motivation index (school mean)	—	.000+	.00	-.004+	.021	—	0.218
Student's attitude							
Intrinsic motivation index	-.014	.001+	.151	.292	.199	—	1.00
Future extrinsic motivation	-.011	-.031	.017	.090	.135	—	1.02
Parents motivate student	.055	.007+	.017	-.004	.000+	—	1.00
Characteristic of student							
Self-reported ability	-.002+	-.081	.045	.114	.077	.213	1.97
Reported ability (school mean)	.018+	.008+	.006	.003+	-.013+	-.036	0.419
Male	.075	.063	-.034	-.004+	-.043	-.076	0.498
Parents' schooling	.010+	.002+	.043	.040	.072	.070	2.89

(continued on next page)

Table 3. Harassment, Study Effort, and Grades in School (continued)
Beta coefficients

Independent variable	Verbal harassment	Did not try hard because of friends	Study with friends	Engagement in class	Percent of homework done	Grade point average	Standard deviation of variable
Parent schooling (school mean)	.018+	-.023	**.066**	-.002+	.000+	-.009+	1.19
Single-parent family	.019	.020	-.009+	-.025	**-.056**	**-.057**	0.408
Percent single-parent (school mean)	-.023+	.013+	-.011+	-.002+	**-.069**	-.007+	0.122
Number of siblings	.001+	.033	.005+	-.025	**-.062**	-.045	1.50
Black	.007+	.044	.001+	-.027	-.026	**-.097**	0.316
Hispanic	-.021	.011+	-.006+	-.017	-.037	-.024	0.192
Asian	-.030	.029	-.004+	-.011	.006+	.009	0.210
Native American	.015	.023	.010+	-.020	-.020	-.002+	0.075
Percent black (school mean)	.011+	-.047	-.035	-.039	.000+	.019+	0.172
Percent Hispanic (school mean)	.000+	.007+	-.002+	-.003+	-.002+	**-.052**	0.073
Percent Asian (school mean)	-.022	-.011+	-.005+	.037	.001+	-.016	0.061
Mean dependent variable	3.425	.849	4.283	.017	.818	2.97	
Standard deviation of dependent variable	3.513	2.461	3.014	1.01	.224	.84	
Root mean-squared error	3.374	2.21	2.64	.817	.190	.593	
R^2	.0624	.0874	.2215	.3031	.2312	.465	
Number of observations	24,772	27,190	26,917	26,313	27,443	25,677	

Note: Analysis of data on 35,604 students from 134 schools located in the Northeast that are members of the Educational Excellence Alliance. All of the models included three variables that were not shown: individual is of mixed race, data on race are missing, data on family status are missing. The model predicting harassment also included an interaction of middle school with antilearning leading crowd and with accelerated courses. The bold type signifies that the beta coefficient (or standardized regression coefficient) is greater than .05. A "+" to the right of a coefficient indicates it is not significant at the 5 percent level on a two-tail test. — = Variable not included in the model. GPA = grade point average.

Figure 1. Predictors of Verbal Harassment

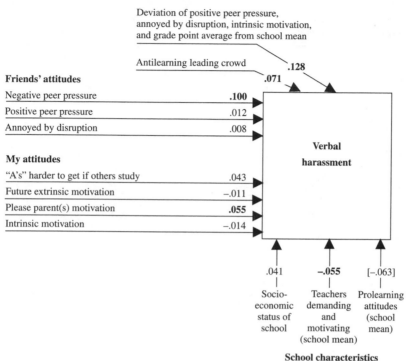

Deviation of positive peer pressure, annoyed by disruption, intrinsic motivation, and grade point average from school mean

Antilearning leading crowd   **.128**
                              .071

Friends' attitudes

Negative peer pressure   **.100**
Positive peer pressure   .012
Annoyed by disruption   .008

Verbal harassment

My attitudes

"A's" harder to get if others study   .043
Future extrinsic motivation   −.011
Please parent(s) motivation   **.055**
Intrinsic motivation   −.014

.041   **−.055**   [−.063]

Socio-   Teachers   Prolearning
economic   demanding   attitudes
status of   and   (school
school   motivating   mean)
                (school mean)

School characteristics

well-educated parents, students in high SES schools, and students in middle schools were more likely to be insulted and teased. These demographic characteristics, however, explained only 2.1 percent of the variance.

When we added student attitude and peer pressure variables, the variance explained by the model tripled but remained low at 6.2 percent. Figure 1 presents the main findings from our analysis of the attitudinal and cultural predictors of peer harassment. Standardized regression coefficients greater than 0.05 are in bold print. Attitudes and beliefs of the students are arrayed on the left underneath the norms of the student's clique. School characteristics are arrayed along the bottom. The school SES effect is the sum of the beta coefficient on the parents' schooling and the beta coefficient for the proportion of students living with both parents. The effect reported for teachers is the sum of the beta coefficients on the teachers are demanding and the teachers are motivating index. When we report the effect of a school average of student attitude scales, the effect reported (in brackets) is what

Figure 2. Peer Harassment's Association with the Prolearning Attitudes of One's Clique

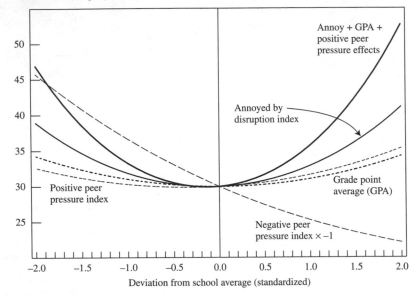

Number of incidents of
verbal harassment per year

would happen to the dependent variable in standard deviation units if student attitudes in the school, gender, and grade went up by 1 student standard deviation.[64]

Most of our hypotheses are supported. The incidence of harassment was lower in schools with demanding and motivating teachers. It was greater for honors students, for students with many study halls, and for students that took accelerated courses in middle school. Rates of peer harassment were greater for students who reported an antilearning leading crowd in middle school and for students who believed they were being graded on a curve. Students high on the negative peer pressure index (one of whose items is "my friends make fun of those who try to do real well in school") were also harassed much more frequently (see figure 2). Compared with the baseline of incidence of thirty per year, students who were 1.5 SDs above the mean (93d percentile) on the negative peer pressure index were harassed forty-one times a year. Those hanging out in cliques that were 1.5 SDs below the mean on this scale were harassed only twenty-four times a year on average.

A GPA that was significantly above or below the school norm led to increased harassment. When a clique's commitment to academic achievement (positive peer pressure and annoyed when others joke around scales) deviates significantly from the school norm, its members also experience more harassment. How strong is the pressure for conformity to school norms? Figure 2 presents a calculation of how much harassment increases as a student deviates from school norms on these four indexes. We picked thirty insults a year of each kind as the baseline level of harassment received by students who were at the school mean on GPA, positive peer pressure, and annoyed when others joke around. Holding negative peer pressure constant, students who were 1.5 SDs above the mean (93d percentile) on GPA and the commitment indexes were harassed forty-three times a year, a 42 percent increase from the baseline student. Those hanging out in cliques that were 1.5 SDs below the school mean on GPA and academic commitment were harassed about thirty-nine times a year, a 30 percent increase over the baseline level.

NOT TRYING BECAUSE OF WHAT FRIENDS MIGHT THINK. In responding to the statement "I didn't try as hard as I could in school because I worried about what my friends might think," 80 percent of students said it "never" happened. For those who said it had happened at least once, the number of instances was twenty-eight per year on average. What are the characteristics of the students who report consciously reducing effort because of a fear of how friends might react? They are more likely to be middle school students, male, Native American, Asian, Hispanic, or African American. They also tend to live with only one parent, to have many siblings, and to have parents with less schooling. The incidence of not trying hard is also lower in high SES schools and schools with larger numbers of African American students. These variables, however, explain only 2.3 percent of the variance of the square root of the frequency of not trying.

What are the effects of peer pressure and norms on not trying? When peer pressure variables are added to the model, 8.8 percent of the variance is explained. Figure 3 presents the main findings from our analysis of the determinants of not trying hard because of a fear of a negative reaction by friends. The most powerful determinant of not trying was being in a clique in which negative peer pressure was strong. Not trying because of fear about how friends would react was higher for students who were frequently harassed and for students who believed that "if others study hard, it's harder for me to get good grades." Surprisingly, students in cliques with strong

Figure 3. Predictors of Not Trying Because of Fear about Friends' Reaction

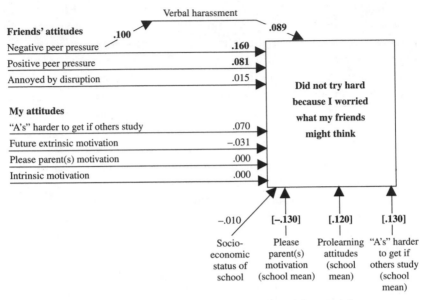

positive peer pressure were also more likely to report not trying as were students in schools with a strong prolearning norms. Schools where many of the students reported working to please and impress their parents had fewer instances of not trying. In addition, schools where many students believed they were being graded on a curve had significantly higher incidence of not trying.

STUDYING TOGETHER AND TALKING ABOUT CLASS WITH FRIENDS. Studying with friends and talking about what was learned in school outside of class is more common for girls, for those living with two well-educated parents, for middle school students, and for those in high SES communities. Studying together is also positively correlated with self-reported ability. These variables, however, explain only 7 percent of the variance of square root of the frequency of studying together variable.

When peer culture scales and the student course-taking patterns and attitudes are added to the regression, variance explained rises to 22 percent. Studying together was more common for students in honors courses and for students who had taken accelerated courses in middle school. Figure 4 pre-

Figure 4. Predictors of Studying Together

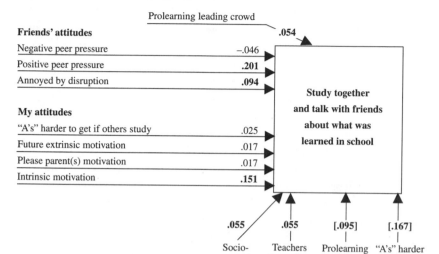

Prolearning leading crowd

Friends' attitudes

Negative peer pressure	−.046
Positive peer pressure	**.201**
Annoyed by disruption	**.094**

.054

My attitudes

"A's" harder to get if others study	.025
Future extrinsic motivation	.017
Please parent(s) motivation	.017
Intrinsic motivation	**.151**

**Study together
and talk with friends
about what was
learned in school**

.055   .055   [.095]   [.167]

| Socio-economic status of school | Teachers demanding and motivating (school mean) | Prolearning attitudes (school mean) | "A's" harder to get if others study (school mean) |

School characteristics

sents the main findings from our analysis of the effects of student motivation and peer pressure. The incidence of studying together after school is higher in schools with demanding and motivating teachers, schools with a prolearning student culture, and schools that had a prolearning leading crowd in seventh grade. As hypothesized, studying together with friends was more common in schools where students thought they were graded on a curve.

Students with high levels of intrinsic motivation were much more likely to study with friends. Students whose motivation was impressing their parents or getting into college and obtaining a good job were only slightly more likely to study with friends. As hypothesized, students who believed they were graded on a curve were more likely to study together. As one might suspect, the norms and attitudes of one's clique had a very large effect on studying together. Positive peer pressure and annoyed when others joke around had a strong positive relationship with studying together. Negative peer pressure had a negative relationship.

CLASSROOM ENGAGEMENT. Classroom engagement is lower for students who are male, for students from single-parent families, for students whose parents have limited amounts of schooling, and for students with many brothers and sisters. Holding school characteristics constant, African Americans, Hispanics, and Asians have the same level of engagement as whites. Only Native American and mixed ethnicity students were significantly less engaged. The schools with the highest levels of engagement were schools that had large Asian, African American, and Hispanic minorities and schools serving the children of poorly educated parents. These findings suggest that disengagement from school is not a problem that is confined to minority communities and low-income neighborhoods. Upscale suburban schools have just as bad a case, and probably worse, of the disease than other schools. These variables, however, explain only 7 percent of the variance of the engagement index.

When peer culture scales, attitudes, and self-reported ability are added to the regression, variance explained rises to 30.3 percent. Engagement is higher for more able students and lower for students in basic classes. It is higher in middle school and in the early grades of high school and in schools with motivating and demanding teachers. Figure 5 presents the main findings from our analysis of the effects of student motivation and peer pressure. Intrinsic motivation has a powerful positive effect on engagement. Future extrinsic motivation has a positive but smaller positive effect on engagement. Students who reported being motivated by the desire to impress their parents were not more engaged in class.

Peer pressure effects were also substantial. Students in cliques that were annoyed when others joked around in class were much more engaged. Positive peer pressure had the expected positive effect and negative peer pressure a negative effect. Engagement was lower for those who believed they were graded on a curve and for students who were frequently verbally harassed by peers. An antilearning leading crowd in seventh grade was also associated with lower engagement.

COMPLETING HOMEWORK ASSIGNMENTS. The proportion of homework assignments completed is lower for students who are male, for students from single-parent families, for students whose parents have limited amounts of schooling, and for students with many brothers and sisters. Hispanics and Native Americans completed less of their homework, and Asians completed more. Homework completion is higher for more able students and for students in honors classes. Students with many scheduled study halls complete less of their homework. Completion rates are higher in schools with only a few single-parent families and in schools with interest-

Figure 5. Predictors of Classroom Engagement

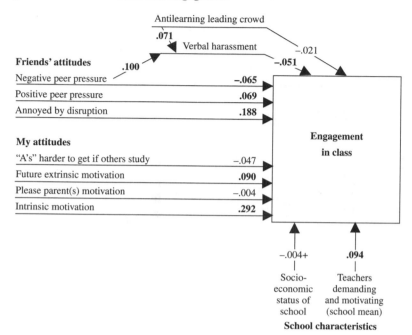

ing and demanding teachers but decline as the student progresses through high school. These demographic variables explain by themselves 8.3 percent of the variance of the homework completion.

When peer culture scales, attitudes, self-reported ability, and course-taking patterns are added to the regression, variance explained rises to 23.1 percent. Figure 6 presents the main findings from our analysis of the effects of student motivation and peer pressure. Intrinsic motivation and future extrinsic motivation both have powerful positive effects on homework completion. Students who reported being motivated by the desire to impress their parents did not complete more of their homework.

Peer pressure effects were also substantial. Students in cliques that were annoyed when others joked around in class and that encouraged each other's learning were more likely to complete their homework. Negative peer pressure had no effect, suggesting that when a school activity is done in private, the negative peer pressure attitudes of one's clique have little effect. Students who studied with friends completed a larger share of their home-

Figure 6. Predictors of Homework Completion

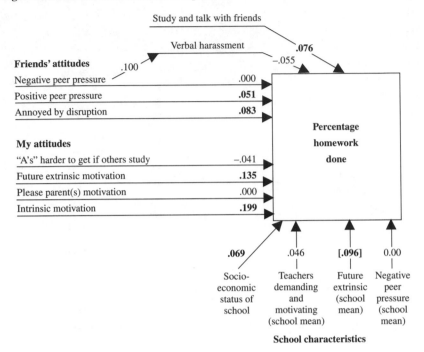

work. Homework completion was lower for those who believed they were graded on a curve and for students who were frequently verbally harassed by peers. A prolearning leading crowd in seventh grade was associated with higher rates of homework completion.

GRADE POINT AVERAGE. Parents' schooling and living with both parents both have positive effects on GPA. African Americans, Hispanics, and students with many siblings have lower GPAs. Asian American students have higher GPAs. Mean GPAs were higher in middle schools and in schools with large shares of Asian American or African American students. Schools serving communities with well-educated parents did not have a tendency to hand out better grades. On their own, these demographic variables explained 16.4 percent of the variance of GPAs. When self-reported ability and course-taking patterns were added to the regression, variance explained rose to 35.2 percent. Students who took accelerated classes in middle school and who were currently in honors classes had higher GPAs.

The final regression predicting GPA reveals how the five indicators of student behavior combine to generate the teacher's overall judgment of the student's performance. Attitudes and peer norms were assumed to influence GPA only through their effects on study behavior, so they were left out of the regression. Adding study behavior indicators to the regression increases the explained variance to 46.5 percent. The proportion of homework done had a much larger effect on GPA than any other effort indicator. Increasing the proportion of homework done by 1 standard deviation (0.224) increased GPA by 0.23, or by more than one-third of the within-school standard deviation of GPA. The second most important effort-related determinant of GPA was classroom engagement. Harassment by peers had no direct negative effect on GPA. However, because harassment influenced engagement and homework completion, it has indirect negative effects on GPA. Studying together has both direct and indirect effects (through homework completion) on GPA.

Policy Speculations

This paper addresses two of secondary education's most serious problems—peer abuse of weaker socially unskilled students and a peer culture that in most schools discourages many students from trying to be all that they can be academically. We have documented the two problems by reviewing ethnographies of secondary schools, by interviewing students in eight New York State suburban high schools, and by analyzing data from questionnaires completed by thirty-five thousand students in 134 schools. Grounded in these observations, we built a simple mathematical model of peer harassment and popularity and of the pressures for conformity that are created by the struggle for popularity. The theory and our data analysis suggest that while the two problems are related, solving one will not necessarily solve the other. Nerds or Geeks are just one of the many groups of outcasts in most secondary schools. If all of a sudden being a geek were cool, other groups would still be targeted for harassment, and the geeks would probably participate in the harassment along with everyone else. Nevertheless, the oppression that nerds experience sends powerful normative signals to other students in the school to withdraw from alliances with teachers and get with the program of becoming popular with peers. "Be like us," the Populars say. Spend your time socializing, do not "study too hard." Value classmates for their athletic prowess and their attractiveness, not their interest in history or their accomplishments in science.

At Newport Junction the popular students wanted an unpopular girl to stop "constantly asking questions in class." So they humiliated her by shouting, "You're a loser, just shut up and get out of this class." The story of that incident must have traveled quickly around the school and deterred many others from speaking up in class. Populars get to talk in class, not geeks.

What is it that the rest of the students so dislike about the students they cast out as nerds and geeks? They tell us the nerds are to blame. They do not socialize much, "they say stupid things," they have geeky interests, they wear unstylish clothes, they are competitive about grades, they talk too much in class, and they lack self-confidence. These are the stereotypes. There is, however, a chicken and egg problem. Nerds are identified in the first weeks of middle school. Once singled out, they are subjected to harassment intended "to wear down your self-esteem." Is it any wonder that they lack self-esteem, that they leave school at 3:00 p.m., or that they hang out with other geeks? Maybe they started out being just a little different and then the harassment and ostracism turned them into the stereotypical nerds.

This phenomenon should not be ignored. Requiring youngsters to attend an institution where they are regularly bullied by their classmates is clearly unjust. While some parents respond by moving to another town or enrolling their child in a private school, most cannot afford such a response. It is only a matter of time before parents successfully sue school districts over the issue. The second reason that schools cannot ignore nerd harassment is that it poisons the prolearning environment that educators are trying to establish. In the eyes of most students the nerds exemplify the "I trust my teacher to help me learn" attitude that prevails in most elementary school classrooms. The dominant middle school crowd is telling them that trusting teachers is baby stuff. It is "us" versus "them." Friendships with teachers make you a target for harassment by peers. The crowd enforces the norm by harassing those who try to become a teacher's friend. The norms prevailing in Cronkite Junior High School are not an aberration. At Boynton Middle School, a school where children of college faculty account for nearly a third of the students, boys were not supposed to suck up to teachers. A middle school student told us, you avoid being perceived as a suck-up by "avoiding eye contact with teachers," "not handing in homework early for extra credit," "not raising one's hand in class too frequently," and "talking or passing notes to friends during class" (this demonstrates that you value relationships with friends more than your reputation with the teacher).

How can schools and teachers meet this challenge? Schools must vigorously defend the position that school is first and foremost about learning and students are expected to work hard. The EEA schools with the most demanding teachers had significantly lower levels of peer harassment and students studied together more frequently, were more engaged in class, and did their homework more regularly. Schools high on the teachers are motivating index also had lower levels of harassment and higher levels of engagement and homework completion.

KIPP Academies

The first best solution to the problem is for teachers to take over normative leadership of the school and make working hard the norm. This is what they do at KIPP (Knowledge Is Power Program) Academy middle schools. According to the dean of students at the KIPP Academy in Washington, D.C.,

> the cool kids in our school are kids who work hard, because we as adults have made sure that to be "in" you have to work hard. We have an extensive system of rewards and consequences that every teacher in every grade administers the exact same way. The consistency from classroom to classroom and across grade levels is the key, and it has helped us to establish that culture of hard work. We are all working together and have been successful because, to be frank, we haven't allowed kids, who in the past may have gotten away with not doing any work or who may have put other kids down for being nerdy or too studious, the opportunities to become "cool" or "in." Our discipline is firm; if you don't work hard you don't get to sit with your friends at lunch, go on field trips, participate in gym class, attend special events, etc., and we, the adults, are all on the same page with this. It's hard to set the norms when you are not the one participating. On the flip side, if you do work hard, then you will be rewarded in fun ways—pizza parties, skating trips, things like that. So, to have fun and fit in, kids must adapt, they must work hard. You're probably saying to yourself that this doesn't sound like your traditional middle school and why would any kid want to put in such hard work. But the kids love it here, because they are discovering that great things happen to people who work hard. And they want to be included.

KIPP academies are nonselective choice schools that run from 8:00 a.m. to 5:00 p.m. during the normal 180-day school year, have compulsory Saturday enrichment programs three times a month, and a three-week summer school. Kids commute from all over the city. During the summer before entering the school for the first time, new students spend a couple of weeks in skills-building exercises, learning the KIPP culture and bonding with their future classmates and teachers. The goal is to develop the skills and knowledge necessary to gain admission to and succeed in a private or charter high school. Students are not competing against each other for a limited number of opportunities to go to a private or charter high school. If they achieve at the required level, they will all make it into good high schools. KIPP academies are islands of discipline with caring and demanding teachers, in a sea of chaotic schools led by dispirited adults. Parents queue for a chance to enroll their child in a KIPP school.

Regular Public Schools

However, when students and parents are not choosing the middle school, establishing a strong adult-dominated, academically focused student culture is more difficult. For certain types of achievement—being athletic, funny, friendly, outgoing, popular, and attractive—more will always be better in the eyes of peers. When, however, it comes to academics, peer pressure sets a norm—an optimal level of academic effort—that seeks to prevent many students from achieving all they are capable of academically. How do state policymakers get serious engagement with learning to be normative among students? Niebuhr's dictum provides a number of avenues. Leading crowds (and other crowds as well) can be counted on to promote norms that reflect their own interests. If the leading crowd is taking learning seriously, peer norms about the optimal level of academic effort will shift up and the whole school will be pulled to a higher level. Thus all of the instruments for persuading individuals to take on academic challenges and study harder—hiring competent and demanding teachers, state or departmental end-of-course exams, minimum competency exam graduation requirements, higher college admissions standards, increases in payoffs to schooling and learning, and so on—will have the same effects on peer norms that they have on the incentives faced by individuals.

College Completion as a Common Goal

Almost all middle school students aspire to go to college—even those with very poor basic skills.[65] Middle schools should encourage this universal aspiration by taking their students on trips to local colleges, briefing parents on financial aid options, and inviting former students to talk about the enjoyable aspects of college life and the importance of studying in secondary school so that they are well prepared. Everyone should be presumed to have college as their goal, including children from very disadvantaged families. Many students do not realize that the academic foundation they are developing in high school is critical to success in college.[66] Once this mistaken belief is corrected, students will be more motivated to take demanding courses and study hard.[67]

Teachers should make a special effort to persuade the leaders of influential student crowds to set particularly demanding personal goals (for example, attending the state's top public university or a competitive private college). If the leadership and core members of the leading crowd are trying to get into competitive colleges, they will need to take honors classes and work hard in them. This will tend to make studying and contributing in class normative and will encourage other students to raise their aspirations and commitment to academics.

Success for All with Cooperation and Hard Work

An antilearning peer culture is likely to develop if students perceive academic classrooms to be zero-sum games that pick winners and losers but cannot make everyone better off. To avoid this, the academic enterprise needs to be and need to be perceived to be a positive-sum game in which everyone can be successful. Teachers should not grade on a curve. Grades should be based on student effort (for example, completing homework assignments), good discipline (not disrupting the learning of others), and absolute achievement (results of quizzes and tests). The school should not publish or call attention to class rank. Having course content assessed externally by examinations set by the state department of education or Advanced Placement program is also desirable.

Competition between Schools in the Academic Arena

Band, choir, theater, cheerleading, and athletic programs receive enthusiastic support from the community because they represent the school to neighboring communities and student achievements in these arenas are visible to the community and rest of the student body. Academic extracurricular activities need to harness the energy and school spirit that interschool rivalry and public performances generate. Individual states and foundations should establish interscholastic team competitions in academic subjects and for activities such as debate, constructing robots, and the stock market game. As many students as possible should participate, and all students who practice regularly should be given a valued role. This can be accomplished by arranging separate competitions for each grade, increasing the minimum size of teams, and allowing schools to field larger teams or more than one team.[68] Academic teams should be celebrated in pep rallies, awards ceremonies, homecoming parades, trophy displays, and local newspapers, along with the school's sports teams. A sixth-grade team should begin training in the first week of middle school. The purpose of starting early is to encourage the creation of large academically oriented friendship networks (where students such as William and Les would find support), to give those groups a positive identity and accomplish this while the social order is still fluid.

Normative Pluralism versus Normative Hegemony

In some of the schools studied a tight-knit group of Populars wielded normative hegemony over the students in their grade. This centralization of normative hegemony in a student group that is typically dominated by athletes, cheerleaders, and students with a fun ideology undermines teacher efforts to develop a prolearning culture. Students who devote their time to academic learning instead of sports and socializing are viewed as antisocial rate busters by the leading crowd and are often harassed and ostracized. A leading crowd that holds normative sway over the entire student body and has the power to marginalize students who study too hard will be able to set a lower target L^N, pulling down effort levels of all students. This is what happened in tenth grade at Lakeside High School.

If, by contrast, a school has several leading crowds and those excluded from the leading crowds have formed groups of their own, leading crowds are less able to impose their norms on everyone else. In this pluralistic normative environment, students who like science or who aspire to get into competitive colleges can find a group of like-minded friends and insulate themselves to some degree from peer pressures against studiousness. Target learning levels, L^N, will be set by each crowd, but the average of these levels will be higher than when one leading crowd sets norms for everyone.[69] When establishing a schoolwide prolearning normative environment (as the

KIPP Academies have done) is not feasible, a pluralistic student culture is the next best outcome.

No Pass–No Play

Eighty-five percent of high schools have a minimum GPA requirement for participation in interscholastic sports. A clean disciplinary record—no drugs, alcohol, or fights and so on—is also typically required. These policies have both practical and symbolic effects. Academic support is offered to athletes who are struggling. Some athletes are induced to study harder. Others either avoid parties where drugs and alcohol will be consumed or attend without imbibing. Because athletes are the nucleus of the popular crowds of most schools, their behavior influences the behavior of everyone else. A third effect of these policies is on the makeup of the team. Students who are unable or unwilling to keep their average above the required minimum are either benched or cut from the team. The composition of the popular crowds changes, and, as a result, the norms promoted by the leading crowds become more favorable to academic learning. Our final suggestion for school administrators, therefore, is to reinvigorate their no pass–no play policy and extend it to cheerleading and possibly to other high prestige extracurricular activities in which students represent the school to surrounding communities.

The policy ideas presented here are a sample of the initiatives educators described to us when we asked them about their successful efforts to promote a prolearning environment. The list is certainly not exhaustive and is intended to stimulate thinking about new initiatives. The research of Educational Excellence Alliance on how school policies influence peer culture is just beginning. There is a great deal to be learned.

Appendix A

Table A-1. Characteristics of High Schools Studied

School	Sex of respondent	Percent to college	Percent poor	Income to wealth ratio	Percent Hispanic	Percent black	Funding per student (dollars)	Median teacher salary (dollars)	Number of students per grade	Percent Regents diploma
Boynton Middle School and Ithaca High School	M	88	14	1.21	3	10	10,400	42,000	450	74
Harbor Edge High School	F	96	4	1.59	6	1	12,100	70,000	430	64
Newport Junction High School	F	94	2	1.87	10	7	13,400	65,000	260	80
Longview High School	F	88	5	0.88	4	1	11,500	80,000	1,000	55
Madison High School	F	83	4	0.79	6	3	10,700	n.a.	330	53
Lakeside High School	F, M	89	1	2.54	10	3	11,600	59,000	70	65
Wittison High School	F	90	6	2.10	3	1	14,100	71,000	80	67
Coso High School	F	83	4	1.28	1	5	9,000	45,000	420	69
New York State low-need districts	. . .	92	3	1.86	5	3	12,500	64,700	n.a.	92
New York State public school average	. . .	78	18	1.00	18	20	9,800	49,500	n.a.	78

n.a. = Not available.

Appendix B

Cornell Assessment of Secondary School Student Culture

- Use a No. 2 pencil only.
- Do not use ink, ballpoint, or felt tip pens.
- Make solid marks that fill the oval completely.
- Erase cleanly any marks you wish to change.
- Make no stray marks on this form.
- Do not fold, tear, or mutilate this form.

INCORRECT MARKS   CORRECT MARK

1. Which courses are you taking this semester? At what level?

	Advanced Placement/ Honors	College Prep/ Regents	Basic/ Local	Heterogeneous or Mixed	Does class meet more than 5 periods a week?
English	○	○	○	○	○
Social Studies	○	○	○	○	○
Foreign Language	○	○	○	○	○
Science	○	○	○	○	○
Mathematics	○	○	○	○	○

2. Which elementary school did you graduate from? (consult key with list of schools)
   - ○ School outside current district
   - ○ Catholic school
   - ○ Other private school
   - ○ #1 public school
   - ○ #2 public school
   - ○ #3 public school
   - ○ #4 public school
   - ○ #5 public school
   - ○ #6 public school
   - ○ #7 public school
   - ○ #8 public school
   - ○ Other public school

3. What grade are you in?
   - ○ 7
   - ○ 8
   - ○ 9
   - ○ 10
   - ○ 11
   - ○ 12

4. Are you male or female?
   - ○ Female ○ Male

5. If you are in high school, which junior high/middle school did you graduate from?
   - ○ School outside current district
   - ○ Catholic school
   - ○ Other private school
   - ○ #1 public school
   - ○ #2 public school
   - ○ #3 public school
   - ○ #4 public school
   - ○ Other public school

6. How many free or study hall periods including lunch do you have per week?
   - ○ 0-2
   - ○ 3-4
   - ○ 5
   - ○ 6-7
   - ○ 8-9
   - ○ 10
   - ○ 11-13
   - ○ 14-15
   - ○ 16+

7. In middle school, were you put in accelerated or advanced classes in any subject? (Mark all that apply)
   - ○ No
   - ○ Yes, in *all classes*
   - ○ Yes, in *math*
   - ○ Yes, in *science*
   - ○ Yes, in *English*
   - ○ Yes, in *other subjects*

8. Everyone gets a poor grade sometimes. When you get a poor grade, which reason usually causes the poor grade? (Darken the most important ONE OR TWO choices)
   - ○ I had bad luck.
   - ○ The class was hard.
   - ○ I didn't work hard.
   - ○ I'm not good at this subject.
   - ○ The teacher was unfair.

9. How often . . .

	Never	Seldom	Fairly	Often	Usually	Always
do you really pay attention during class?	○	○	○	○	○	○
does your mind wander?	○	○	○	○	○	○
do you joke around during class?	○	○	○	○	○	○
do you contribute to class discussion?	○	○	○	○	○	○
do you do homework for one class in another?	○	○	○	○	○	○
is what you are studying intrinsically interesting?	○	○	○	○	○	○
are students whose hands are not up called on?	○	○	○	○	○	○
are the slower students in the class called on?	○	○	○	○	○	○

10. When your teacher assigns homework, how much of the homework do you usually do? (Darken one choice for each class)

	Homework is never assigned	None of it	Some of it	Most of it	All of it	I do more than is required
Math	○	○	○	○	○	○
English	○	○	○	○	○	○
Social Studies	○	○	○	○	○	○
Science	○	○	○	○	○	○

Mark Reflex® by NCS EM-219115-1:654321   ED06   Printed in U.S.A.   © Copyright 1996 by National Computer Systems, Inc. and John H. Bishop All rights reserved.

PLEASE DO NOT WRITE IN THIS AREA

23057

• 1 •

11. On week days after school, how many HOURS PER DAY:

	No time	Half an hour	1 hour	2 hours	3-4 hours	5-7 hours	8 or more hours
are you studying and doing homework?	○	○	○	○	○	○	○
are you watching TV or playing video games?	○	○	○	○	○	○	○

12. How many hours do you typically study for an end of marking period exam in History? ○   ○   ○   ○   ○   ○   ○

13. How many hours a WEEK do you get tutoring or extra academic help from teachers or older students during free periods or outside of school hours? ○   ○   ○   ○   ○   ○   ○

14. Have you attended summer school at any time since 5th grade?

○ No
○ Yes, once
○ Yes, 2+ times
If Yes, why?
  ○ Failed a course   ○ For fun
  ○ Get requirement   ○ To catch up
    out of the way

15. What was your grade point average last semester?

○ A   ○ B   ○ C   ○ F
○ A-   ○ B-   ○ C-/D+
○ B+   ○ C+   ○ D/D-

16. How quickly do you learn things? (Mark one)

Slower than most			Average				Faster than anybody else
○	○	○	○	○	○	○	○

17. When you work real hard in school, which of the following reasons are most important for you? (ANSWER AS MANY AS APPLY TO YOU)

○ My parents put pressure on me.
○ My friends put pressure on me.
○ I don't want to embarrass my family.
○ I want to learn the material.
○ I want to keep up with my friends.
○ The teacher demands it.

○ Help me get a better job.
○ To please or impress my parents.
○ To please or impress my teacher.
○ I need the grades to get into college.
○ My teachers encourage me to work hard.
○ The subject is interesting.

18. Think of the times you did not study for a test or did not complete homework during the last year. Which of the following reasons were most important? (ANSWER AS MANY AS APPLY TO YOU)

○ I could get a good grade without studying.
○ The assignment was boring or pointless.
○ I preferred to party or hang out with friends.
○ I didn't understand the material.
○ The assignment was too long and difficult.
○ I didn't care about the grade in that course.
○ No one to help me at home.
○ The teacher didn't care.

○ Not enough time because of work and/or school activities.
○ Teacher did not collect and grade homework.
○ My friends wanted me to do something else.
○ Started too late, poor planning.
○ I disliked the teacher.
○ I got distracted at home.
○ I forgot the assignment.
○ The teacher was very disorganized.

19. What is the highest level that you would like to go to in school? I would like to:

○ leave before graduating.
○ finish high school.
○ 2-year college degree.

○ 4-year college degree.
○ 4-year college degree plus some further training.
○ post graduate degree (medical, law, PhD., MBA).

20. Indicate the HIGHEST level of education completed by each person. (Mark one answer for each column.)

	Mother/ Stepmother	Father/ Stepfather		Mother/ Stepmother	Father/ Stepfather
Some or finished grade school	○	○	4-year college graduate	○	○
Some high school	○	○	Some school beyond college	○	○
Finished high school	○	○	Professional or graduate degree	○	○
Some college or 2-year degree	○	○	Don't know or not applicable	○	○

21. Do you agree or disagree with the following statements:

	Strongly agree	Agree	Disagree	Strongly disagree
My friends make fun of people who try to do real well in school.	○	○	○	○
My friends joke around and annoy the teacher.	○	○	○	○
To keep up with my friends, I have to work hard at my school work.	○	○	○	○
Kids who study a lot, tend to be less popular.	○	○	○	○
Studying a lot tends to make you less popular.	○	○	○	○
My teachers maintain good discipline in the classroom.	○	○	○	○
My teachers grade me fairly.	○	○	○	○
Many of my courses are not challenging.	○	○	○	○
The stuff we learn in classes is interesting.	○	○	○	○
If I didn't need good grades, I'd put little effort into most classes.	○	○	○	○
Too many students get away with being late and not doing their work.	○	○	○	○
If others study hard, it is harder for me to get good grades.	○	○	○	○
If most of the class did not understand a concept, some of my teachers do not put it on the test.	○	○	○	○

We would like to ask about what your closest friends think and do. To help you answer these questions, create a list in your head of your six closest friends.

22. How many attended the same elementary school you did?

○ All   ○ A few
○ Most   ○ None
○ Half

23. My friends think it is important for me to:

	Strongly agree	Agree	Disagree	Strongly disagree
do well in science at school.	○	○	○	○
do well in mathematics at school.	○	○	○	○
do well in English at school.	○	○	○	○
have time to have fun.	○	○	○	○
be good at sports.	○	○	○	○
be placed in the high achieving class.	○	○	○	○

24. Do you think your friends would agree or disagree with the following statements:

	Strongly agree	Agree	Disagree	Strongly disagree
It's not cool to be competitive about grades.	○	○	○	○
It's not cool to frequently volunteer answers or comments in class.	○	○	○	○
It's not cool to study real hard for tests and quizzes.	○	○	○	○
It's not cool to be enthusiastic about what you are learning in school.	○	○	○	○
It's annoying when other students talk or joke around in class.	○	○	○	○
It's annoying when students try to get teachers off track.	○	○	○	○

25. How important do your FRIENDS THINK IT IS TO:

	Very important	Somewhat important	Not too important	Not at all important
study hard to get good grades.	○	○	○	○
talk/hang out with friends.	○	○	○	○
to participate actively in class.	○	○	○	○
go to parties.	○	○	○	○
continue your education past high school.	○	○	○	○
go to one of the best colleges in the U.S.	○	○	○	○

26. How often have each of these things happened so far in this school year?

	Almost every day	About once a week	Up to once a month	Never
My friends and I talked outside of class about things we learned in school.	○	○	○	○
I didn't try as hard as I could at school because I worried about what my friends might think.	○	○	○	○
My friends and I studied together (outside of class).	○	○	○	○
One of my friends was insulted or made fun of behind their back.	○	○	○	○
I was insulted, teased or made fun of to my face.	○	○	○	○
Do you think you were insulted or made fun of behind your back.	○	○	○	○
My friends cut classes or skipped school.	○	○	○	○
I copied homework from one of my friends.	○	○	○	○

27. During the 1st year of middle or junior high school, the members of the most popular crowd (your gender) were: (Mark all that apply)

- ○ real smart.
- ○ attractive.
- ○ funny.
- ○ self-confident.
- ○ outgoing.
- ○ tough.
- ○ cool clothes.

- ○ very good in sports.
- ○ attentive in class.
- ○ not attentive in class.
- ○ worked hard to get good grades.
- ○ made fun of those who studied a lot.
- ○ mostly from my elementary school.
- ○ not from my elementary school.

28. Which parent(s) or guardians do you live with during the school year? (Mark all that apply)

- ○ My Mother
- ○ Stepmother
- ○ My Father
- ○ Stepfather

- ○ Other relative/guardian or foster parent
- ○ Alone or with friends

29. What is your Race/Ethnicity? (Mark all that apply)

- ○ White
- ○ Black
- ○ Hispanic

- ○ Asian
- ○ Native American

30. Are any of your six closest friends of a different race/ethnicity than yourself?

- ○ Most
- ○ Some
- ○ None

31. How many brothers and sisters do you have?

- ○ None
- ○ 1
- ○ 2

- ○ 3
- ○ 4
- ○ 5 or more

32. When you apply for jobs after leaving high school, do you expect employers to ask about your high school grades or ask to see a transcript?

- ○ Never
- ○ Seldom
- ○ Sometimes

- ○ Usually
- ○ Always

(Students from New York, Massachusetts, New Jersey and Ohio should complete 33-36)

33. When did you first learn that graduating from high school depends on passing statewide exams/tests: (i.e., NY Regents exams, Massachusetts 10th grade Comprehensive Assessment Tests, New Jersey's Grade 11 Proficiency tests, or Ohio's 9th grade Proficiency Tests?)

- ○ Just now
- ○ 12th grade
- ○ 11th grade
- ○ 10th grade
- ○ 9th grade

- ○ 8th grade
- ○ 7th grade
- ○ 6th grade
- ○ Before 6th grade
- ○ Not true for me

34. Did your knowing this change anything? (Mark all that apply)

- ○ Changed nothing
- ○ I study harder
- ○ I took a tougher course(s)

- ○ I took an easier course(s)
- ○ I was tutored
- ○ I took extra course(s)

35. Which, if any, of these exams/tests have you failed? (Mark all that apply)

- ○ None taken
- ○ None failed
- ○ Math
- ○ English
- ○ Science

- ○ History
- ○ Civics
- ○ Writing
- ○ Foreign Lang.

36. Which of the following happened as a result of failing the test(s)? (Mark all that apply)

- ○ I repeated the same course the next year.
- ○ I took a special course the next year.
- ○ I went to summer school.
- ○ I retook the test at the end of the summer.
- ○ I passed the test on one of the retakes.
- ○ I do not think I will graduate.

- ○ I got extra help or tutoring after school or on weeke
- ○ I got extra help or tutoring during school hours.
- ○ I studied harder the next year.
- ○ I retook the test the next year.
- ○ I haven't passed it yet.
- ○ None of the above.

Appendix C

Scales Describing Student Motivation to Do Well in School

A number of summary indicators combining similar questions were defined to capture various aspects of student motivation to do well or try hard in school and to summarize student behavior and family background. Each of these variables is an average of the student's responses to related questions. Items from different questions with different response formats were often combined. The z-scores were created by subtracting the mean tenth-grade response of each component question from the student's individual response and then dividing by the tenth-grade standard deviation for that question. A z-score measures the distance of the student's response from the mean tenth-grade response in standard deviation units. The Statistical Analysis System mean command was used to average the z scores from related questions creating an index variable for each type of motivation. Thus if an individual item was not available, we used the other standardized variables to create the average. To make the variables easier to understand, each index was divided by its standard deviation to create a standardized variable with a mean of zero and a standard deviation of 1. A one-unit change in the motivation indexes, therefore, is equivalent to a 1 standard deviation change in the scale. A movement of 1 standard deviation means a student has moved from, say, the 50th percentile of a normal distribution to about the 84th percentile or from the 84th percentile to the 97.7th percentile.

Intrinsic Motivation

The variable *INTRINM2* is a standardized index obtained by combining several of the student attitude questions ["I find what I learn in school intrinsically interesting" (*_9intere;* question 9), "I work hard because I want to learn the material" (*wkhdd;* question 17), and "I work hard because the subject is interesting"(*wkhdl*; question 17)] and (−1) times "If I didn't need good grades, I'd put little effort into my classes" (question 21).

The average value of *_9intere* is 3.199 (standard deviation = 1.237), meaning that most students claim that what they study is intrinsically interesting a "fair" amount of the time. The average response is closer to "fair" but lies in between "fair" and "often."

The average value of *wkhdd* is .457; therefore 46 percent of students say they work hard because they want to learn the material.

The average value of *wkhdl* is .414; therefore 41 percent of students say they work hard because the subject is interesting.

The average value of *gni21j* is 1.50. About half of students say they would study less if they did not need the grades.

Parental Motivation

Another motivation for students to do well in school is their parents. The variable *PARENTMV* indicates whether students are motivated by their parents ["I work hard to please or impress my parents" (*whhdh*); "I work hard because my parents put pressure on me" (*wkhda*)].

The average value of *wkhdh* is .554; therefore 55 percent of students claim they work hard to please their parents.

The average value of *wkhda* is .435; therefore 43 percent of students claim they work hard because their parents put pressure on them.

Parental motivation variables are negatively correlated with intrinsic motivation variables and positively correlated with future motivation variables and positive peer motivation variables. Parental pressure to work hard is not related to friends' thinking it is important to do well in math, science, and English and is negatively correlated with friends' thinking it is important to study and get good grades. This suggests that parents may increase their pressure to work hard in school when they perceive their children to have poor study habits or friends who are bad role models.

Positive Peer Motivation

Positive peer motivation to do well *(PPEERMV)* is indicated by responses to the following:

wkhdb— "I work hard because my friends put pressure on me" (question 17)

wkhde— "I work hard because I want to keep up with my friends" (question 17)

dwsci23a— "My friends think it is important for me to do well in science at school" (on a one-to-three scale) (question 23)

dwmat23b— "My friends think it is important for me to do well in mathematics at school" (on a one-to-three scale) (question 23) *dweng23c*— "My friends think it is important for me to do well in English at school" (on a one-to-three scale) (question 23)

hitrk23— "My friends think it is important for me to be placed in the high achieving class" (on a one-to-three scale) (question 23)

frstu25a— "My friends think it is important to study hard to get good grades" (on a one-to-three scale) (question 25)

The average value of *wkhdb* is .051; only 5 percent of students claim they work hard because their friends put pressure on them.

The average value of *wkhde* is .204; only 20 percent of students claim they work hard to keep up with their friends.

The mean of *frstu25a* is 2.26, indicating that their friends think studying is somewhere between "somewhat important" and "very important" in the given range of responses. The mean is closer to "somewhat important" ($s = .725$).

Annoyed by Disruptions

ANNOYDV is a normalized variable averaging normalized answers to the two questions about how annoying it is when other students sidetrack the teacher or joke around in class:

Anjok24e—"It's annoying when other students talk or joke around in class" (agree or disagree, on a one-to-three scale) (question 24)

Anoft24f—"It's annoying when students try to get teachers off track" (agree or disagree, on a one-to-three scale) (question 24)

Negative Peer Motivation

NPEERMV3 is the normalized index indicating peer influence to not do well in school. It is constructed from the following:

funof21a—"My friends make fun of people who try to do real well in school" (on a one-to-three scale) (question 21)

lespo21d—"Kids who study a lot tend to be less popular" (on a one-to-three scale) (question 21)

mkpop21e—"Studying a lot tends to make you less popular" (on a one-to-three scale) (question 21)

ncvol24b—"It's not cool to frequently volunteer answers or comments in class" (on a one-to-three scale) (question 24)

ncstu24c—"It's not cool to study real hard for tests and quizzes" (on a one-to-three scale) (question 24) *ncint24d*—"It's not cool to be enthusiastic about what you are learning in school" (on a one-to-three scale) (question 24)

The negative peer motivation variables are all positively correlated with each other. The strongest relationships are between "studying makes you less popular" and "kids who study tend to be less popular" ($r = .667$). Negative peer motivation variables are negatively related to intrinsic motivation and positive peer motivation variables, and they are unrelated to parent motivation variables. Negative peer motivation variables are also negatively related to all the parent motivation variables (although the negative relationship between "studying tends to make you less popular" and "working hard to help me get a better job" is insignificant).

Future Motivation

Some students are motivated to do well in school by the desire for a good job or college admission. This type of motivation is measured by the variable *FUTUREMV*, which averages the responses to two questions:

wkhdg—"I work hard to help me get a better job" (question 17)

wkhdj—"I work hard because I need the grades to get into college" (question 17)

On average, 58 percent of students say they work hard to get a better job in the future. On average, 79 percent of students say they work hard because they need good grades to get into college.

Peer Culture

Two indexes were created from question 27 about the characteristics of the students in the most popular crowd in the first year of middle school. The standardized variables referred to have a mean of zero and a standard deviation of 1.

gdstd7dv—standardized variable measuring the proportion of the three positive study orientation traits that were selected as characteristic of the most popular students at the beginning of middle school. The three items in the index were "real smart," "attentive in class," and "worked hard to get good grades."

bdstd7dv—standardized variable measuring the proportion of the two antistudy traits that were selected as characteristic of the most popular students at the beginning of middle school. The two items in the index were "not attentive in class" and "made fun of those who studied a lot."

Engagement

The variable *ENGAGEMT* captures a student's attitude and behavior while in school. A high value for this variable indicates that a student often pays attention in class (*_9attend*), rarely or never has a wandering mind (*_9wander* multiplied by –1 in the averaging process to change the direction of the response), rarely or never jokes around in class (*_9joke* multiplied by –1 to change the direction), often contributes to class discussion (*_9discuss*), and rarely or never does homework for one class in another (*_9otherhw* multiplied by –1 to change the direction of response). This variable was created in the same way as the motivation variables, so its mean is zero and its standard deviation is 1.

The average response for *_9attend* is 4.617; kids are somewhere between "often" and "usually" with respect to how they pay attention in class ($s = 1.01$).

The average response for *_9wander* is 3.193; kids' minds "fairly" often wander in class ($s = 1.279$).

The average response for *_9joke* is 2.839; students "fairly" often joke around in class ($s = 1.321$).

The average response for *_9discuss* is 4.184; students "often" contribute to class discussion ($s = 1.334$).

The average response for *_9otherhw* is 3.199; students "fairly" often do homework for one class in another ($s = 1.237$).

All of the items in the engagement scale are correlated in the expected directions.

Question 26

We dealt with students' not responding to question 26 by giving the same frequency for all items and by treating answers as missing if the same response was given for all eight items. This eliminated 781 responses to these questions.

NOTRYSQR is the square root of the number of times in the last year the respondent did not try because of what his or her friends might think. It is based on the response to:

Notry26b—"I didn't try as hard as I could at school because of what my friends might think."

The response is scored 0 for "never," 5 for "up to once a month," 40 for "about once a week," and up to 160 for "almost every day." Then the square root is taken.

INSSQR is the square root of the number of insults the student experienced in the last year. It is based on two questions scored from 0 for "never," 5 for "up to once a month," 40 for "about once a week," and up to 160 for "almost every day":

Insuf26e—"How often . . . I was insulted, teased, or made fun of to my face?"

Insub26f—"How often . . . did I think I was insulted or made fun of behind my back?"

First the square root was taken of each variable. Then a weighted average was calculated with a .6 weight assigned to insults to your face and a .4 weight for insults behind your back.

STUTLKQR measures the frequency of students studying together (outside of school) or talking with friends about what was learned in school. It is based on two questions scored 0 for "never," 5 for "up to once a month," 40 for "about once a week," and up to 160 for "almost every day":

Talkc26a—"My friends and I talked outside of school about what we learned at school"

Studt26c—"My friends and I studied together (outside of class)"

The square root was taken of each variable first and then they were averaged.

Student Time Use

Indicators of student time use are:

Hwkavg—an index of the average share of assigned homework in four core subjects that students are taking. "None of it" was assigned a value of 0; "all of it," 1; "some of it," 0.333; "most of it," 0.67; and "more than required," 1.33. On this scale, the index had a mean of 0.81 for all Educational Excellence Alliance schools (*HWKMATH, HWKENG, HWKSOSC, HWKSCI, HWKAVG*).

Hmwkhr—average number of hours per day students report doing homework

tvhrday—average number of hours per day that students report watching TV

Family Background Indicators

The family background indicators are:
edpar—average number of years of schooling of the student's two parents (15.16 years)
MEDPAR— mean of *edpar* for the grade, gender, and school
afamidx—mean proportion single parents for the grade, gender, and school

---

Comment by Amy Ellen Schwartz

Why do schoolchildren harass nerds and freaks? John H. Bishop, Matthew Bishop, Lara Gelbwasser, Shanna Green, and Andrew Zuckerman have made an impressive effort to provide some answers to this interesting and important question. In addition to gathering and analyzing new data, Bishop and his colleagues develop and explore an economic model that explains why some students choose to become nerds and others choose to become athletes. This economic approach is consistent with much previous work on individual and family decisionmaking about a wide range of subjects including employment, education, marriage, and fertility but has not, to my knowledge, been employed to this particular situation. The essence of the model is to characterize the objectives, opportunities, abilities, and constraints faced by students to derive explanations for why some students become nerds or freaks and others become athletes, for example.

Focusing on the Economic Model

Students face a binding time constraint. Put simply, kids have a fixed amount of time to allocate among the alternative activities available to them. They can spend their time on learning and studying, on sports or other extracurricular activities, or on hanging out with their peers (socialization), or they can spend their time in solitary leisure. Because time is fixed, they cannot do it all and must choose how much time they spend on each activity.

How do students make these choices? Essentially, they choose based upon the impact that time spent has, ultimately, on their happiness. For extracurricular activities and socializing, happiness depends upon the time they spend on these activities and also on their individual ability to turn time spent on an activity into utility, or happiness. The reward of solitary leisure depends only upon time spent; it is assumed that everyone is equally able to derive happiness from solitary leisure.

Thus students' allocation of time determines their accomplishments in various areas, in the amount of learning they garner, and in the extent to which they are harassed by other students. An important contribution of this model is to explicitly specify the rewards to learning and the ways in which individual and peer learning and accomplishment interact to determine each student's success and his or her treatment by peers.

According to the model in this paper, learning yields three kinds of rewards. Intrinsic rewards accrue simply because a student enjoys learning. Extrinsic rewards accrue based upon the level of learning or increase in human capital resulting from, say, the value in the job market of knowing Java or speaking French. Rank rewards accrue based upon the rank of the student relative to the other students in the school, regardless of any learning or human capital accumulation stemming from, for example, becoming valedictorian.

A critical feature of the economic model is that each student's utility (or happiness) also depends upon popularity. As with learning, a number of factors determine a student's popularity, including the student's accomplishment in sports and at socializing, how successful a student is at conforming with peers, and on the extent and causes of competition in the school. Specific functions capture the relationship between popularity (or harassment) and students' accomplishment in extracurricular activities, socialization, conformity with peer group norms about academic commitment and achievement, and the "costs that studious individuals impose on others by pushing ahead of them in a competitive ranking system."

The result is a set of equations (the economic model) that captures the problem facing the student. Given his or her own abilities and preferences, and constrained by time and the behavior and characteristics of the school and peers, the student is viewed as solving the problem of determining how to balance time spent on different activities to be as happy as possible. The model is intuitively appealing and internally consistent, and it yields interesting insight about phenomena that have attracted little attention from economics.

The model is then used to motivate subsequent empirical work, although the links between the model and the statistical analyses are weak. Given the specificity of the model, the functional forms of the relationships, and the definitions of the variables, additional effort might be well spent tying these together, testing the predictions of the model, and attempting to identify the underlying parameters. In particular, alternative versions of these models could hold similar intuitive appeal, and disentangling this model from one, say, that includes a financial constraint would be useful.

Insights

What, then, can be learned from the model? First, the analysis suggests that being a geek or a nerd reflects, in part, the choices that a student has made. Harassment does not happen by itself to some randomly selected student. Instead, students who are harassed for being nerds have chosen behavior that has led them to be harassed (or increased the probability of being harassed). At the same time, because each student is endowed with different abilities or aptitudes in pursuing activities important to his or her school experience (sports, extracurriculars, learning, socialization, and so on), the likelihood of becoming a nerd, or being harassed, differs across students. And, because school policies may affect the relationship between student behavior and the responses of their peers, the extent of harassment may differ across different school settings and different policy regimes for a particular type of student.

This is, in some sense, an empowering story about geeks and nerds. Instead of seeing nerds as merely victims of phenomena outside their control, or the control of their schools, this view of nerds and harassment suggests that there are strategies and policies that might be employed to reduce or control the harassment of nerds. However, it is important to acknowledge the rigidities and constraints that prevent students from freely choosing their social treatment and to avoid going too far toward blaming the victim.

A second insight from the model and discussion is that heterogeneity in student behavior and accomplishments may imply costs to the individual student who deviates from the mean behavior. The more heterogeneity the greater is the likelihood that there will be geeks and nerds who get harassed; the less heterogeneity, the less harassment. Thus this analysis provides some justification for creating schools in which the student body is more homogeneous—including both magnet schools for the academically gifted and theme schools that focus on particular subject areas such as the arts or the environment and, perhaps, vocational schools, among others.

The model (and the empirical work) also highlights the possibility that school quality and the time students spend on learning may be substitutes.

Improving school quality will not necessarily translate into concomitant (or proportionate) improvements in learning because, at least to some extent, students may respond to improvements in instruction, for example, by spending more time on other activities and less time on learning. This is an important phenomenon that deserves additional investigation.

The paper begins with a quote from parents saying that, if forced to choose, they would prefer that their children get "C's" in school but participate in extracurricular activities than that they get "A's" and do not participate in extracurricular activities. What is interesting to me, and also worthy of additional exploration, is the possibility that, despite the experience and preferences of academics, researchers, and policy wonks, parents may, in fact, be right about what is most likely to lead to success and happiness for their children. A combination of mediocre grades and success in extracurriculars may, for some children or even many children, be a surer path to success in employment and beyond than academic excellence without the social success.

While a substantial body of existing literature and research seeks to identify the impact of academic success and school quality, either at the high school or college level, on employment and earnings, among other economic outcomes, the literature investigating the impact of extracurricular activities and popularity on these outcomes is far thinner. How much is popularity worth in the job market? Casual observation suggests that popularity, or success in extracurricular activities including, but not limited to, sports, may be important determinants of success in the job market. Understanding these impacts will shed light on why students (and parents) make the choices they do and could lead to the designing of schools and policies to better serve both the nerds and the jocks.

Caveats and Extensions

While the model is, in some dimensions, quite rich and flexible, some extensions and generalizations seem worth developing. First, while students are viewed as differing in their abilities to benefit from extracurricular activities, learning times, and socialization, they are treated as if no differences exist in ability with respect to solitary time. The notion that students may differ in their ability to use solitary time productively seems intuitively appealing to me and worth exploring.

Second, and far more important, this analysis makes no provision for any financial constraint, which binds students and determines their behavior and success, broadly defined. In the real world, some students need to engage in paid employment, while others are free to devote themselves to the activities described and investigated in this paper. Further, students with greater financial resources will be better able to buy clothing, cars, and accessories, for example, that may influence their treatment by their peers. And, richer students may be able to take advantage of tutors or coaches or computers to assist them in their academic work. In the end, a preponderance of evidence seems to suggest that financial resources matter and a fully satisfying explanation of nerds and harassment will have to incorporate this sort of constraint.

Third, the authors treat student abilities in the various activities as exogenous, and it seems to me worth thinking about which of these parameters, if any, is malleable. Why are some kids good at socializing and others not? Can schools (or parents) teach kids how to handle themselves in social situations and thereby affect their treatment by their peers? Is there a difference between good students and geeks? Not all good students are teased and harassed. A distinction needs to be made between harassment as a result of poor social skills and harassment as a reaction to high academic performance. Given their data and model, the authors may be able to shed light on this in future work.

This work offers an intriguing way of thinking about school choice, small schools, and schools within schools. Would children fare better in schools in which students share common abilities and interests? This work seems to suggest the answer is yes and is consistent with the anecdotally reported experience of nerds who left heterogeneous schools for selective academic schools. Moving from a school in which football players and jocks dominate social standing to a school in which academic aspirations and abilities are shared and academic accomplishments are lauded has meant, for some nerds, rebirth as one of the cool kids or, at least, as a member of the wide middle range.

At the same time, would smaller schools be better? School size clearly plays a role in determining heterogeneity and social interactions, and this work offers some support for the creation of small schools because of the potentially better social environment for learning.

Comment by David F. Labaree

John H. Bishop, Matthew Bishop, Lara Gelbwasser, Shanna Green, and Andrew Zuckerman present a chilling analysis of the way student culture punishes the nerds in American high schools. The interviews and other data in the paper make a powerful case that this culture undermines learning by making students pay a high social price for becoming visibly engaged and successful in academic pursuits. The pattern they describe is particularly frightening, both because it depicts a kind of antischool, where learning is for losers, and because it is too familiar to dismiss as an empirical fluke. In an effort to explain this pattern, the authors view the antinerd culture as a rational response to the incentives and disincentives that students encounter in school. The popular students set the norms for student culture. Given that academic achievement costs time and effort, all else being equal, they have an incentive to lower the overall level of academic work required of students. When students are graded on a curve—that is, relative to each other's performance instead of to a fixed performance criterion—punishing students, such as the nerds, who perform at a high level makes sense. In such a system, nerds are rate busters, so the culture punishes them to lower the curve for the collective benefit of the other students.

In some ways, the analysis may overstate the seriousness of the nerd problem. As Laurence Steinberg and several others pointed out during the discussion of this paper, nerds are targets because of their weak social skills as much as for their academic prowess. A student can be both popular and smart as long as he or she is good at playing the social game with peers. But this does not eliminate the depressing picture Bishop and his colleagues paint of schools as places where being a good scholar carries negative weight and needs to be counterbalanced by athletic ability or good looks. Another point that came up in the discussion is that one simple and obvious answer to the problems in student culture is for teachers to assert stronger control. But evidence suggests that this is possible only within narrow limits. As Willard Waller and many others have long shown, students are in a powerful position to resist the impositions of teachers. This is particularly true in ordinary nonselective public schools, where teachers do not enjoy the advantage of having a student body made up of individuals who selected themselves and were selected by the school on the basis of their agreement with the school culture.[70]

The response to the nerd problem that the paper raises (and Bishop and others develop more fully in a paper presented at the 2001 Brookings education forum) focuses on the mechanism for school reform that was also brought up by most participants at this conference: setting firm standards for student performance.[71] Bishop argues that, especially when standards are enforced by curriculum-based external exit exam systems (CBEEES), they can change the incentives for the student players in the game. CBEEES shift the basis of student evaluation from relative norms to fixed criteria, move control of assessment outside the classroom and school system, and assess the full range of knowledge gained instead of just minimum competency. This forces the leading crowd to raise its level of academic effort to avoid failing, and it removes the zero-sum quality of academic achievement, providing incentives to study for all students and not just those near the cut score. Add to this exam system other elements of the standards movement, such as restricting course taking to core academic subjects and pushing students toward more advanced levels in these subjects, and a formula may emerge that begins to reverse the antinerd culture in schools.

I focus here on some of the deep-seated characteristics of American school and society that support the student culture of punishing the nerds and on the ways in which a standards approach might and might not succeed in undermining elements of this support framework.

Raising and enforcing academic standards in schools can potentially exert a strong impact on two components of the social structure of the school that currently reinforce the antinerd culture. One is the loose coupling of school systems. The links between the elements of the American school system are unusually weak. Buffers separate classrooms from schools, schools from school systems, school systems from states, and K–12 education from higher education. These buffers reinforce the isolation of teachers and make it hard to effect change from above on the teaching and learning that takes place in the classroom. Exam-enforced standards regimes, such as CBEEES, are a strong intervention aimed at tightening the links in the systems through chains of accountability.

The second feature of American schooling that enables the culture of victimizing the nerds is the weak position of the teacher to press for student engagement in learning the curriculum. Teaching is a form of work governed by weak extrinsic rewards arising from pay and promotion and strong psychic rewards arising from interaction with students. The result is that administrators have little leverage over how teachers teach, whereas students have a considerable amount. Teachers' sense of competence and satisfaction depends on the cooperation of the students, which leads to bargaining over effort and grades, dumbing down the curriculum, and settling for form over substance in learning outcomes.[72] Exam-based standards can change this relationship between teacher and student. Instead of being in the vulnerable position of both designing the assessment and setting the standard for judging its results, the teacher is now the coach and ally of the students, who is helping them to conquer a common enemy in the form of the external test.

However, some key elements in American culture and society that support the victimization of the nerds are more likely to block efforts to impose academic standards than to yield to these efforts. One such element is the long history of anti-intellectualism in American life. A strong tradition exists of stressing doing over thinking, considering the practical over the theoretical, and having street smarts over being book smart, so student culture naturally reflects this orientation. The paper by Arthur G. Powell and the comment by Richard J. Murnane both support this point. The problem is reflected in the traditional caricatures of the teacher, Ichabod Crane and the dotty spinster, as hapless nerds. And it all too often is reproduced within an anti-intellectual culture of teaching and teacher education. Standards and tests can have an impact only if the learning they represent is taken seriously and the intellectually able are viewed as models worthy of emulation.

A second factor that is likely to block the impact of standards on student culture is the strong libertarian strain that runs through the American psyche. This takes a number of different forms. One is a strong devotion to local control in politics and in education. Communities have a substantial loyalty to the local school and school district, and this creates a potential for resistance to any efforts to impose standards, which are necessarily centralizing in character and thus, as an infringement on local liberty, provoke resistance. Another form this takes is a dedication to the principle of choice in education at all levels and in all forms, which is threatened by any effort to impose standardized curriculum and assessment on schools. Americans value the ability to choose curriculum through the elective principle. They also value the ability to choose how to spend their time and effort, including a student's right to focus on sports, social life, or TV instead of studies. Still another form of libertarianism is embodied in the school choice movement. Its primary focus is on maintaining the right of groups of like-minded people to construct schools that match their own values and goals, and this right is severely constrained by requirements that they meet state-set standards for curriculum content and student achievement.

A third element in American life that supports a student culture hostile to learning is the emphasis given to social mobility as the primary goal of education. Pushing into the background alternative goals such as the preparation of productive workers and competent citizens, the focus instead is on education as the way that a person and his or her children can socially get ahead and keep ahead of the pack. To the extent that this is the case, then education is seen as a private good to be acquired in a competition with others. The results of this emphasis on educational opportunity over learning outcomes are educationally devastating. It produces a focus on making education enrollment at all levels as accessible as possible and on keeping education easy enough to make graduation at all levels just as accessible. Standards, by nature, make enrollment (at upper levels) and graduation (at all levels) more difficult by making both of them dependent on performance.

The result of the mobility orientation is a stress on quantity over quality of education, on completing the course over learning the subject. In this educational formalism, form outweighs substance, and schooling trumps learning. It is a milieu that directly supports the student culture that demeans academic accomplishment. What else could be expected in the country that invented the Carnegie unit? An entire system of education was constructed on the credit hour, which measures not what people have learned in school but the amount of time they spent at risk of learning. Thus, like the student culture Bishop and his colleagues describe, the emphasis is on the acquisition of grades, credits, and degrees over getting an education, a position that makes the attack on the nerds only reasonable. A related issue is the fungibility of educational attainments that arises from the social mobility approach to schooling. In the currency of credits, all courses are interchangeable, which means that issues of subject, quality, level, and depth make little difference as long as the student accumulates the necessary hours.

All this adds up to a culture of credentialism and consumerism, grounded in a market-based view of education that stresses exchange value over use value, where the point is to cash in credentials for position, wealth, and security.[73] In short, it is a zero-sum game, much like the one that Bishop and his colleagues show playing out in the student culture of American high schools—where punishing the nerds makes sense, where lowering the curve is a reasonable collective goal, and where the ideal is to do well enough in school but not too well.

Under these conditions, it is not clear that the standards movement has much chance to roll back the tide of American culture by trying to create an educational system that makes nerds not the target but the ideal.

Notes

1. Lowell Rose, Alec Gallup, and Stanley Elam, "The 29th Annual Phi Delta Kappa/Gallup Poll of the Public's Attitudes toward the Public Schools," *Phi Delta Kappan* (September 1997), pp. 41–56.

2. Participation in interscholastic sports is positively associated with school success partly because 85 percent of schools have a minimum grade point average (GPA) requirement for participation. Deborah Anderson, "If You Let Me Play: The Effects of Participation in High School Athletics on Students' Educational and Labor Market Success," University of New Mexico, January 2001, pp. 1–39. See also John M. Barron, Bradley T. Ewing, and Glen R. Waddell, "The Effects of High School Athletic Participation on Education and Labor Market Outcomes," *Review of Economics and Statistics*, vol. 83, no. 3 (2000), pp. 409–21.

3. Analysis of National Education Longitudinal Study of 1988 data. Completion was defined as obtaining a regular high school diploma or general equivalency diploma (GED) before the 1994 interview. The probabilities reported are predictions from a model controlling for self-esteem and locus of control in eighth grade and demographic and socioeconomic characteristics of the student's family. John Bishop and others, "The Role of End-of-Course Exams and Minimum Competency Exams in Standards-Based Reforms," in Diane Ravitch, ed., *Brookings Papers on Education Policy 2001* (Brookings, 2001), pp. 267–345 and figure 2.

4. Analysis of High School and Beyond data. James Rosenbaum, *Beyond College for All* (New York: Russell Sage Foundation, 2001), p. 67.

5. Norton Grubb, "The Varied Economic Returns to Postsecondary Education: New Evidence from the National Longitudinal Study of the Class of 1972," *Journal of Human Resources,* vol. 28, no. 2 (Spring 1993), pp. 365–82.

6. James Coleman, *The Adolescent Society* (Free Press, 1961).

7. Abraham J. Tannenbaum, "Adolescents' Attitudes toward Academic Brilliance," Ph.D. dissertation, New York University, 1960.

8. D. S. Eitzen, "Athletics in the Status System of Male Adolescents: A Replication of Coleman's *The Adolescent Society,*" *Adolescence*, vol. 10 (1975), pp. 267–76.

9. Laurence Steinberg, Bradford Brown, and Sanford Dornbusch, *Beyond the Classroom* (Simon and Schuster, 1966), pp. 145–46.

10. Don E. Mertens, "Visibility and Vulnerability: Responses to Rejection by Nonaggressive Junior High Boys," *Journal of Early Adolescence,* vol. 16, no. 1 (February 1996), p. 12.

11. Mertens, "Visibility and Vulnerability," p. 19.

12. Mertens, "Visibility and Vulnerability," p. 14.

13. Mertens, "Visibility and Vulnerability," p. 16.

14. Mertens, "Visibility and Vulnerability," p. 19.

15. Mertens, "Visibility and Vulnerability," p. 19.

16. Mertens, "Visibility and Vulnerability," p. 18.

17. The studies and ethnographies that were particularly useful (but not quoted) were Philip Cusick, *Inside High School* (Holt, Rinehart, and Winston, 1973); Donna Eder and oth-

ers, *School Talk* (Rutgers University Press, 1995); Rosalind Wiseman, *Queenbees and Wannabes* (Crown Publishers, 2002); Rachel Simmons, *Odd Girl Out* (Harcourt, 2002); Patricia Hersch, *A Tribe Apart* (Ballantine Books, 1999); Mary Haywood Metz, *Classrooms and Corridors* (Berkeley: University of California Press, 1978); Theodore Sizer, *Horace's Compromise* (Houghton, 1984), pp. 1–299; Arthur G. Powell, Eleanor Farrar, and David K. Cohen, *The Shopping Mall High School: Winners and Losers in the Educational Marketplace* (Houghton Mifflin, 1985); and Thomas French, *South of Heaven* (Simon and Schuster, 1993).

18. During the fall of 1997 John H. Bishop, the lead author of this paper, hired seven student interviewers to collect data for a study of peer cultures in eight high-performing suburban New York State high schools. The team met frequently during the fall to develop a protocol for the open-ended interviews and a paper-and-pencil questionnaire that respondents completed just before their personal interview. The interviewers were trained in interviewing techniques and given a tape recorder to use during the interview. The high schools that were approached had published data indicating that they were high performing. Furthermore, they were a short drive from the suburban residences of the Cornell University students conducting the interviews during the winter break. Respondents were selected and parental permissions were handled by the cooperating high school. One hundred and thirty-five tenth graders were interviewed (most of them female) during January 1998. The following semester all but one of the interviewers took a seminar taught by the lead author that explored qualitative research methodologies more deeply and read articles and books discussing student peer culture. The students listened to the tapes of the interviews they had conducted, analyzed the questionnaire responses, and then wrote an ethnography of the school they had studied. Student ethnographies were shared with the principal of the high school studied. A second wave of personal interviewing was undertaken by Matthew Bishop and John Bishop using a convenience sample of male students attending Ithaca-area middle schools and high schools.

19. The Educational Excellence Alliance offers its members a convenient means of assessing and diagnosing their student peer cultures in a way that allows them to compare themselves with other similar schools and to track changes over time. During the 1998–99 school year, 134 schools in Connecticut, Massachusetts, New Jersey, New York, and Pennsylvania undertook a standardized assessment of the culture of their tenth graders and were sent reports comparing their students responses with the responses of students at comparable schools. The questionnaire was revised in January 2000 and another 270+ schools (nearly half of them middle schools) have participated since then. Many of the schools participating in this second wave of data collection are located outside of the Northeast. The reports sent back to each school point out areas of concern and have suggested reading materials that might be helpful in planning interventions designed to build a student culture that honors academic achievement and respects individual differences.

20. A mathematical version of the theory is being developed for another paper.

21. B. Bradford Brown, "Peer Groups and Peer Cultures," in S. S. Feldman and G.R. Elliot, eds., *At the Threshold: The Developing Adolescent* (Harvard University Press, 1990), pp. 171–96.

22. Denise Kandel, "Homophily, Selection, and Socialization in Adolescent Friendships," *American Journal of Sociology*, vol. 84, no. 2 (1978), pp. 427–36; and Jere M. Cohen, "Sources of Peer Group Homogeneity," *Sociology of Education*, vol. 50 (October 1977), pp. 227–41.

23. Margaret Talbot, "Girls Just Want to Be Mean," *New York Times*, magazine section, February 24, 2002.

24. David A. Kinney, "From Nerds to Normals: The Recovery of Identity among Adolescents from Middle School to High School," *Sociology of Education*, vol. 66 (January 1993), p. 27.

25. Sandra B. Damico, "The Effects of Clique Membership upon Academic Achievement," *Adolescence*, vol. 10, no. 37 (Spring 1975), p. 93–100.

26. Vernon D. Gifford and Douglas H. Colston, "Group Influences on the Decisions of Selected Secondary School Students," *Adolescence*, vol. 10 (Fall 1975), p. 371.

27. David Zimmerman, *Peer Effects on Academic Outcomes: Evidence from a Natural Experiment* (Cambridge, Mass.: National Bureau of Economic Research, 1999); Caroline Hoxby, "Peer Effects in the Classroom: Learning from Gender and Race Variation," Working Paper 7867 (Cambridge, Mass.: National Bureau of Economic Research, 2000), pp. 1–62; and Bruce Sacerdote, "Peer Effects with Random Assignment: Results for Dartmouth Roommates," Dartmouth College, 2000.

28. An excellent description of the stereotypes associated with each of the major crowd types is available in Bradford Brown, Mary Jane Lohr, and Carla Trujillo, "Multiple Crowds and Multiple Life Styles: Adolescents' Perceptions of Peer-Group Stereotypes," in R. E. Muuss, ed., *Adolescent Behavior and Society: A Book of Readings* (Random House, 1990), pp. 30–36.

29. Interview conducted by Erica Peterson, in Wittison High School, January 1998.

30. Brown, "Peer Groups and Peer Cultures."

31. Don E. Mertens, "Information versus Meaning: Toward a Further Understanding of Early Adolescent Rejection," *Journal of Early Adolescence*, vol. 16, no. 1 (February 1996), p. 41.

32. D. Olweus's study of sixth graders found popularity was negatively correlated with "being a target of other boys' aggression" and uncorrelated with "starts fights." D. Olweus, "Aggression and Peer Acceptance in Adolescent Boys: Two Short-Term Longitudinal Studies of Ratings," *Child Development*, vol. 48 (1977), pp. 1301–13.

33. Marlene Jacobs Sandstrom and John D. Coie, "A Developmental Perspective on Peer Rejection: Mechanisms of Stability and Change," *Child Development*, vol. 70, no. 4 (July/August 1999), p. 956.

34. Studies of younger children also find that submissive students tend to be victimized. A study of kindergarten-age students, for example, found that "children who eventually emerged as victims were pervasively submissive." David Schwartz, Kenneth A. Dodge, and John D. Coie, "The Emergence of Chronic Peer Victimization in Boys' Play Groups," *Child Development*, vol. 64 (1993), p. 1755.

35. For a more complete analysis of the dominance-by-insult game, see John H. Bishop, "Nerd Harassment, Incentives, School Priorities, and Learning," in Susan Mayer and Paul Peterson, eds., *Earning and Learning: How Schools Matter* (Brookings, 1999), pp. 231–80, especially pp. 231–41.

36. Interview conducted by Erica Peterson, in Wittison High School, January 1998.

37. Student at Newport Junction High School, quoted from Lara Gelbwasser, "Organizational Culture and the Power of Peers," Cornell University, School of Industrial and Labor Relations, 1998.

38. Anne-Marie Ambert, "A Qualitative Study of Peer Abuse and Its Effects: Theoretical and Empirical Implications," *Journal of Marriage and the Family*, vol. 56 (February 1994), p. 125.

39. Nicola Persico, Andrew Postlewaite, and Dan Silverman, "The Effect of Adolescent Experience on Labor Market Outcomes: The Case of Height," University of Pennsylvania, 2001, pp. 1–37.

40. Because our interviews focused on peer support for or discouragement of studiousness, we might not have learned about all the groups that were being victimized by peers. Physically unattractive special education students were the victimized outcasts in the Indiana middle school Donna Eder studied. This school had a very sharp split between rural working class students (the "grits") and more stylishly dressed students from a middle-class suburb. There were important divisions along social class lines in at least two of our schools. Donna Eder with Catherine Evans and Stephen Parker, *School Talk* (Rutgers University Press, 1995).

41. Student at Longview High School, quoted from Shanna Green, "The Door Opens Once You Get Here," Cornell University, School of Industrial and Labor Relations, May 22, 1998, pp. 14, 15.

42. Student at Harbor Edge High School, quoted in Gelbwasser, "Organizational Culture and the Power of Peers."

43. Student at Newport Junction High School, quoted in Gelbwasser, "Organizational Culture and the Power of Peers."

44. Student at Newport Junction High School, quoted in Gelbwasser, "Organizational Culture and the Power of Peers."

45. Andy Zuckerman, "Working Hard or Hardly Working? A High School Ethnography," Cornell University, School of Industrial and Labor Relations, 1998, p. 23.

46. Zuckerman, "Working Hard or Hardly Working?" p. 23.

47. Zuckerman, "Working Hard or Hardly Working?" p. 23.

48. B. Bradford Brown and Laurence Steinberg, "Academic Achievement and Social Acceptance," *Education Digest* (March 1990), pp. 57–60.

49. The norms at issue here cover both the desired level of academic effort and engagement and the relative priority attached to different ways of using time and to different types of achievements.

50. Student at Harbor Edge High School, quoted in Gelbwasser, "Organizational Culture and the Power of Peers."

51. Rosalind Wiseman quoted in Talbot, "Girls Just Want to Be Mean."

52. Bishop, "Nerd Harassment."

53. In schools with major racial or socioeconomic divisions, separate leading crowds often exert normative leadership in their race and socioeconomic group. In these schools it will be necessary to change the views of all of the leading crowds, not just the one that dominates school elections or sports teams.

54. Quoted from Green, "The Door Opens Once You Get Here," p. 16.

55. Student at Harbor Edge High School, quoted from Gelbwasser, "Organizational Culture and the Power of Peers."

56. Student at Newport Junction High School, quoted from Gelbwasser, "Organizational Culture and the Power of Peers."

57. Reinhold Niebuhr, *Moral Man and Immoral Society* (New York: Charles Scribner's Sons, 1933), p. xii.

58. Principal of Longview High School, quoted from Green, "The Door Opens Once You Get Here," p. 9.

59. Robert B. Cairns and Beverly D. Cairns, *Lifelines and Risks: Pathways of Youth in Our Time* (Cambridge University Press, 1994), p. 91.

60. Studying by one student imposes costs on other students. Greater achievement for person i increases school mean achievement, L_j, and lowers everyone else's position relative to the mean (for example, rank in class). The loss that others experience when person i tries harder is exactly equal to $R_j(L_I - L_J)$, the gain person i experiences from raising his or her

achievement relative to the school mean. If, for example, the graduating class has two hundred students, a one-unit increase in L_i for person i raises L_m by .005. This lowers the benefits that each of the 199 other students gets from the second term of equation 3 by .005*R_j.

61. Philip Cusick, *Inside High School* (Holt, Rinehart, and Winston, 1973), pp. 175–203.

62. Even with all the efforts to control for personal attitudes and environmental factors, these regressions do not provide unbiased estimates of the causal impact of peer norms on behavior. Bias comes from measurement error in the attitude and peer pressure variables and from possible feedback effects of behavior on our indicators of attitudes and peer pressure (respondents might be justifying their behavior by describing their friends as advocating it). Another problem is that students have chosen their clique and were probably aware of the peer pressures they would be subjected to when they joined it. The school, gender, and grade means of attitude and peer pressure scales should be less subject to measurement error and close to exogenous. Students do not choose the grade they are in and seldom influence the school they are sent to.

63. At one reviewer's suggestion we entered the squared deviation variables to models predicting other outcomes to test for curvilinear effects. Despite the large sample size, few of these variables were statistically significant.

64. This parameter is calculated by multiplying the standardized regression coefficient on the school characteristic by the ratio of the student standard deviation (SD) for this attitude scale to the school standard deviation for the variable. In most cases this ratio is about 6. This means that the unstandardized coefficients on school mean attitude scales are being standardized by the same SD that the clique attitude scales are being standardized by. This makes the coefficients directly comparable in much the same way that unstandardized coefficients would be comparable.

65. Seventy-five percent of the tenth graders in the bottom quartile on achievement tests in 1980 said they planned to attend college. National Center for Education Statistics, *Digest of Education Statistics* (Washington: 1993), p. 137.

66. Twelve years later, in 1992, only 3.3 percent of students in the bottom quartile on a battery of achievement tests taken in the twelfth grade had obtained a bachelor's degree and only 4.1 percent had gotten an associate's degree. Students in the top quartile were twenty times more likely to get a bachelor's degree. National Center for Education Statistics, *Digest of Education Statistics* (Washington: 1998), p. 329. When this information is presented to students, it should be stressed that college completion rates are influenced by absolute achievement levels, not one's class rank, and that poor achievement in the early years of secondary school can be overcome by hard work in the upper grades.

67. Making college attendance and completion a part of a school's ethos need not marginalize applied technical education. Many of the jobs that used to be filled by young high school graduates now require a strong background in writing, math, and science and a longer period of occupationally specific training. This training is now being done partly in high school and partly in community college. Consequently, vocational teachers should present their program as the occupational equivalent of Advanced Placement courses in academic subjects. Those who graduate with three or four occupational courses earn substantially more and are better able to support themselves while attending college. At the end of tenth grade, students with low academic achievement levels should be required to develop a backup plan that involves training for immediate employment after high school.

68. Other ways of broadening participation would be to include scores on subject matter tests taken by students in a particular course (for example, third-year French) or in the whole school (for example, the state's seventh-grade science test). As in sports, fair competition can be ensured by placing small schools and schools serving disadvantaged populations in sepa-

rate leagues. While cable TV broadcasts of High School Bowl-like contests can be a component of the program, most of the points obtained by a school's team should come from assessments of the performance of the entire team on authentic tasks such as writing an essay, giving a speech, determining the chemical composition of a compound, working out long mathematics problems, writing a computer program, or fixing a car.

69. In a pluralistic environment, crowds must take into account that members are competing for grades mainly with students outside their group and that the members of a particular crowd lack the power to enforce norms against studying hard outside their group. Consequently, having a crowd norm against studying will simply result in everyone in the crowd getting lower grades. If an antistudying norm is to be effective, many crowds have to agree on the norm and cooperate in punishing norm violators from other crowds. These problems had been solved at many of the schools we studied, but the norm against studying appeared to have resulted in sanctions only for those who had all three of the following characteristics: socially awkward, athletically incompetent, and competitive about grades.

70. Willard Waller, *The Sociology of Teaching* (Wiley, 1932, 1965); Dan C. Lortie, *Schoolteacher: A Sociological Study* (University of Chicago, 1975); and Philip A. Cusick, *The Educational System: Its Nature and Logic* (McGraw-Hill, 1992).

71. John H. Bishop and others, "The Role of End-of-Course Exams and Minimum Competency Exams in Standards-Based Reforms," in Diane Ravitch, ed., *Brookings Papers on Education Policy 2001* (Brookings, 2001), pp. 267–345.

72. Lortie, *Schoolteacher*; Michael W. Sedlak and others, *Selling Students Short: Classroom Bargains and Academic Reform in the American High School* (New York: Teachers College Press, 1986); and Powell, Farrar, and Cohen, *The Shopping Mall High School.*

73. David F. Labaree, *How to Succeed in School without Really Learning: The Credentials Race in American Education* (Yale University Press, 1997).

Attacking the
African American–White
Achievement Gap on
College Admissions Tests

MICHAEL T. NETTLES,
CATHERINE M. MILLETT, *and*
DOUGLAS D. READY

For decades researchers have discussed the lower levels of educational achievement of African American compared with white students.[1] This achievement gap exists even among the youngest children; African American students arrive at kindergarten considerably behind their white peers in measurable cognitive skills.[2] Although the gap has narrowed somewhat over the past several decades, the average African American still scores below 75 percent of white students on standardized tests.[3]

Alarming racial gaps are consistently found on the SAT, which plays an important role in the quality of access to higher education and, in turn, to social and economic mobility. Between 1976 and 1988 substantial progress was made in closing the gap, and the advantage for whites was reduced by 25 percent.[4] In subsequent years, however, the gap has remained steady or even increased slightly. In 1999 the African American–white SAT gap was between 0.75 and 1 full standard deviation (SD).[5]

A seemingly endless array of theories has been advanced to explain the consistently lower academic performance of African American students: linguistic and social incongruities between home and school culture; historic immigrant status; differing levels and types of parental involvement; contrasting forms of cultural and social capital; the generally lower socio-

215

economic status (SES) of African American children; divergent study habits and motivational levels; racist and classist school practices; African American adolescents' fear of "acting white"; the quantity and quality of academic material to which minority students are exposed; and lower teacher expectations of African American students. Although these theories come in and out of favor, one that has remained relatively constant is the lower quality of schools attended by African American students. This paper investigates the African American–white achievement gap on the SAT at both the student and school level. Even though the achievement gap has been a long-term concern to educational policymakers and researchers, research that applies the appropriate methodology to investigate the influence of both student and school characteristics upon the gap is sparse.

Background

The following brief overview of research that examines racial disparities in academic achievement reflects our analytical approach, in that it explores both student- and school-level influences on achievement.

Student-Level Relationships: Social Class and SAT Performance

Researchers consistently report a strong relationship between social class and performance on the SAT, with students from more affluent, more educated families scoring higher.[6] On average, students whose parents have some graduate school experience score over 0.4 standard deviations above the SAT mean, while students from families with yearly incomes above $100,000 score one-half standard deviation above the mean.[7] The relationship between family income and SAT scores appears to be stronger among African American than white students. An almost 130-point gap on combined SAT scores separates African American students whose parents earn less than $10,000 from those whose parents earn more than $100,000. Among white students the gap between these same income ranges is only 50 points.[8] Although disparities in social class among African Americans and whites remain stark, these differences generally explain less than one-third of the achievement gap in standardized test scores.[9]

Many researchers have concluded that one path through which SES influences achievement in high school is the academic courses in which students enroll. Over the past two decades, researchers have placed increasing emphasis upon the relationship between course taking and achievement. Historically, high schools organized their curricula into tracks, wherein students followed prescribed courses of study based on their measured (or perceived) attributes, abilities, and future occupational and educational plans. Contemporary comprehensive high schools have largely moved away from formal tracking and permit students to select their own courses and programs of study. Hence curricular choice assures that students in the same comprehensive high school will experience the curriculum differently. The desire of most comprehensive high schools to match students' interests to the curricular offerings and to please their "customers" has led researchers to characterize the modern public high school as a "shopping mall" where the "customer is always right."[10]

The faculty and staff in most high schools see this laissez-faire approach to students' curricular choices as an appropriate way to actualize one of their major goals—accommodating student diversity. Teachers and administrators recognize the relationship between students' backgrounds and the choices they make in high school. However, "there is an implicit understanding that the school itself provides individuals with the means to make choices, and that the maturity of adolescence entails the responsibility to make the 'right' choice regardless of childhood experience."[11] Unfortunately, the knowledge and skills not gained by many African American students as a result limit their educational, social, and economic futures.

Although many public high schools have replaced formal tracking with student choice as the means to match students to courses, the relationship between students' choices and their personal backgrounds resembles that found within traditional tracked curricula. Students now often determine the track that they take through the curriculum, resulting in their physical and social separation from those with different racial and social backgrounds.[12] Many schools that boast of their diversity rarely mention the extent to which their schools are internally segregated. Diverse high schools that sort students or allow students to sort themselves often create pockets containing disproportionate numbers of white students. Through tracking and assigning students to special educational and bilingual programs, desegregated schools often become resegregated.[13] White parents of students enrolled in an integrated suburban school stated that they were relatively unconcerned about the influx of nonwhite students because their children were in upper-level courses that enrolled very few African Americans.[14]

Another negative outcome associated with the diversity in course taking is that it generally increases diversity in student learning. High school students' academic achievement is related to the level and quantity of courses they take: Higher-level courses and further advancement through the curriculum results in increased learning.[15] The degree to which students advance through the mathematics curriculum is more strongly associated with early math achievement than with their social or academic backgrounds.[16] The effects of curricular choice on student learning are exacerbated by the fact that lower-level courses are generally less demanding, centered more around behavior than content, and taught by less-motivated teachers than are higher-level courses.[17] Even after prior achievement is taken into account, students in lower-level classes learn less than their upper-level peers, and they are less likely to use higher-order thinking skills.[18]

In addition to the numerous relationships that exist between student characteristics and achievement, the characteristics of schools that students attend also influence student academic performance. This is especially important considering the substantial differences in the nature and quality of high schools attended by African American and white students.

School-Level Relationships: Minority Concentration

A half-century after the 1954 U.S. Supreme Court decision in *Brown* v. *Board of Education*, continued residential segregation combined with the tradition of neighborhood school assignment ensures that the majority of African American children attend segregated schools.[19] Over two-thirds of African American public school students attend majority minority schools, while one-third attend schools with more than 90 percent minority enrollment.[20] Most African American public school students attend school in districts that are less than half white, and over one quarter are enrolled in majority African American districts. Conversely, over 90 percent of white students attend school in majority white districts.[21]

This continued educational and residential segregation has serious negative ramifications for the education of African American children. Majority minority schools and districts often have difficulty attracting qualified teachers. For example, half of New York City's teachers failed teacher certification tests compared with less than one quarter statewide and fewer than one-fifth in the surrounding suburbs.[22] Students enrolled in high-minority schools are also more likely to be taught English, math, science, and social studies by teachers who have neither a college major nor minor in the subject they are teaching.[23]

Schools' demographic characteristics also affect the overall educational experiences of their students. African American students learn less in schools with high concentrations of African American students, even after taking into account the socioeconomic backgrounds of the students in the school.[24] Students attending majority African American high schools are also less likely to have access to advanced coursework and information about college entrance requirements.[25]

SCHOOL SIZE. Researchers generally focus on two paths through which school size influences student achievement: (1) the nature of social relations among school members and (2) the curricula schools offer, and hence the courses students are able to take. Sociologists of education have concluded that as schools grow larger, their social relations become more hierarchical, inhibiting the development of personal relations among their members.[26] Because smaller schools have fewer members, their social organizations are generally more communal than bureaucratic, and their members more likely to report feelings of belonging.[27] This may be most evident through the lower dropout rates found in smaller high schools.[28] Teachers also tend to take more personal responsibility for student learning in smaller schools and are more likely to feel they are able to increase student learning, regardless of their students' social or academic backgrounds.[29]

As high schools grow larger they also tend to offer a more diversified curriculum, which schools often see as a logical response to increased student diversity.[30] This practice generally may widen even further the already existing racial and socioeconomic achievement gaps. In schools with broad curricula and course offerings that vary in academic rigor, the relationship between student social background and achievement is stronger.[31] High schools that are organized to teach different students different material usually accomplish just that.

Although proponents argue that only large high schools can provide the wide array of curricular offerings student diversity requires, large high schools often use their size to simply add introductory and other low-level courses instead of offering more advanced courses. A broad curriculum can likely be offered in schools enrolling as few as four hundred students.[32] However, most researchers agree that there may be a fine line in determining the most productive and equitable high school size. Schools must be large enough to offer a suitable curriculum and appropriate facilities, but not so large as to inhibit a sense of shared community.[33] In terms of a specific size, recent research suggests that students learn the most (and that learning is most equitable) in medium-size high schools enrolling between six hundred and nine hundred students.[34]

SECTOR DIFFERENCES. Not all high schools have adopted the diversified curriculum. Although Catholic schools have experienced shifts in student demographics similar to those in public schools over the last century (increased numbers of immigrant and minority students), they responded to these changes differently.[35] Catholic schools maintained a belief that a rigorous, narrow academic program should be followed by all students.[36] This more focused or constrained curriculum lessens the relationship between race and academic achievement, because minority students are generally assigned to challenging courses regardless of their social or economic backgrounds.[37]

Although elite independent schools now also serve a somewhat more diverse clientele, their mission of training students for future leadership positions remains virtually unchanged.[38] Parents who enroll their children in such schools generally have common expectations, chief among them that their children will be well prepared for college. In keeping with both tradition and expectations, curricula in elite private schools stress academically oriented coursework and have as their goal the preparation of students for college.[39] However, recent studies indicate that after accounting for the greater selectivity of private schools, private school students follow a similar curriculum (at least in mathematics) to their public school peers.[40] Conversely, even after accounting for these differences, Catholic school students follow a more academic mathematics curriculum than their public school peers.

Method, Data, and Sample

The College Board/Educational Testing Service (CB/ETS) provided a database containing all 1999 high school graduates who took the SAT. In addition to students' test scores, the database includes students' responses to the Student Descriptive Questionnaire (SDQ), which they completed when registering to take the test. From the SDQ we obtained information about students' social and academic backgrounds (race, gender, citizenship, family income, and parental education) and their high school experiences (courses taken and grades received, extracurricular activities, and college aspirations).

As valuable as the CB/ETS data are, we also sought information about the high schools that students attended. We used two National Center for Education Statistics (NCES) databases to augment the student-level databases with school-level information: the Common Core of Data (CCD) and Private School Universe Survey (PSS). The CCD is a national database of all public elementary and secondary schools and school districts collected annually by the Department of Education. Information collected on high schools includes school location and type, the number of teachers, and enrollment by grade, gender, and race. We used the 1998–99 school-year CCD file. The target population of the PSS, which contains data similar to the CCD, is all nonpublic schools in the United States. We were forced to use the 1997–98 PSS file—when these students were in eleventh grade—because the PSS is only collected every two years.

The CB/ETS student-level SAT file uses a common code to identify the high school attended by each test taker (referred to as the attending institution, or AI, code). The College Board provided a file that linked AI codes to NCES codes. However, this file consisted of only a sample of public high schools and included no nonpublic high schools. Several steps were taken to increase the proportion of AI codes that could be linked with NCES school codes. To begin this process, we created a composite file by merging variables from several data files: AI codes, school names and addresses, and related NCES identification codes from the crosswalk file provided by the College Board; AI codes and school names from another file provided by the College Board; and NCES school identification codes, names, and addresses from the CCD and PSS data files. Duplicate entries [AI codes that appeared in both the College Board and American College Test (ACT) data files] were eliminated. Schools that did not enroll eleventh or twelfth graders were also eliminated from the file, as were foreign and Department of Defense high schools.

School names and addresses were used to match AI codes with NCES codes. Matching was first done using a computer algorithm. The remaining schools were then matched manually. To begin, a complete list of schools with AI codes and those from the NCES databases were sorted by state and then by school name. Schools on both lists with the same state, name, and zip code were considered an acceptable match. In cases in which schools matched in name but not by zip codes, we consulted the Internet to determine if the schools were a likely match. The work involved in this process was considerable, as we began with more than 1.1 million students and fifteen thousand high schools.

ANALYTIC SAMPLE. We began constructing our analytic sample by selecting students with scores on both the math (SAT-Math, or SAT-M) and verbal (SAT-Verbal, or SAT-V) sections of the SAT and by gathering information on race and gender and identifying those who were in eleventh or twelfth grade when they took the test. We then selected schools we could match to the CCD or PSS that enrolled at least five SAT takers, and schools with full information on student racial composition, sector, enrollment size, location, the number of Advanced Placement (AP) courses offered, and the percent of students taking calculus. Our final analytic sample contains 878,695 students, 87,795 of whom are African American, 52,489 Asian, 65,391 Hispanic, 6,373 Native American, 589,548 white, 24,787 other race/ethnicity, and 52,312 non–U.S. citizens. These students are located in 9,061 schools: 7,551 public, 391 private nonreligious, 679 Catholic, and 440 private other-religious.

Measures: Outcomes

Our dependent measures are 1999 high school graduates' scores on the SAT-M and SAT-V. Initial analyses revealed that significantly different relationships exist between student and school characteristics and scores on the SAT-M and SAT-V. As such, we perform all analyses separately, and not on students' combined SAT scores. Because SAT scores are in a commonly recognized metric (200–800 possible points on each test) and are normally distributed, we use students' raw SAT-M and SAT-V scores as outcomes.

STUDENT CHARACTERISTICS. Our race/ethnicity measures include a series of dummy variables indicating whether a student is African American, Hispanic American, Asian American, Native American, other race/ethnicity, or non–U.S. citizen (using white U.S. citizens as the uncoded comparison group in all multivariate analyses). We also use an array of items measuring students' social and academic characteristics. Social characteristics include gender (female = 1, male = 0), whether English is a student's second language (ESL = 1, non–ESL = 0), and a composite measure of SES that incorporates parents' education and income [a z-score, mean (M) = 0, SD = 1].

To capture students' academic preparation in high school we created a measure that indicates whether they took honors English courses and two variables indicating their coursework in mathematics. The first of these math course-taking variables (*TRIG*) indicates whether a student completed trigonometry (yes = 1, no = 0), and the second (*CALC*) indicates whether the student completed calculus (yes = 1, no = 0). We constructed these measures so that students who completed calculus generally have a value of 1 for both *TRIG* and *CALC*. Thus, in our multivariate analyses we can interpret the *TRIG* coefficient as the additive effect of taking trigonometry compared with not taking trigonometry and *CALC* as the effect of taking calculus over completing only trigonometry (sometimes referred to as "ladder" measures). We also include a measure indicating whether the student took the pre-SAT, the PSAT (yes = 1, no = 0).

SCHOOL CHARACTERISTICS. We used several measures to capture high schools' academic climates, including one indicating the number of AP courses the school offers. We are fortunate to have also obtained full information on 1999 high school graduates' ACT scores from ACT Inc.[41] By combining these data with those provided by the CB/ETS, we were able to develop a more accurate picture of schools' academic climates. We created a measure indicating the percent of college admissions test takers who completed calculus, and we use the percent of each school's twelfth graders who took either the SAT or ACT as an indicator of college attendance rates.[42]

School organizational characteristics include a series of dummy variables measuring school size (< 500, 501–800, 1,151–1,700, and > 1,701 students), all compared with schools enrolling 801–1,150 students. To indicate school sector, we created dummy variables indicating whether the school is private nonreligious, Catholic, or private other-religious (all compared with public schools). We employ another series of dummy variables to indicate school location: *URBAN*, *TOWN*, and *RURAL*, compared with *SUBURBAN* schools.[43] We also use a dummy variable indicating whether the school enrolls a large proportion (over 40 percent) of African American students. Finally, we use a *z*-scored measure indicating school-average student SES.[44]

Analytic Approach: Multilevel Questions and Methods

We begin our analysis with simple multivariate regressions that explore the African American–white SAT gap. However, given the multilevel nature of our data, our primary analyses involve a multilevel method, HLM (Hierarchical Linear Modeling).[45] HLM used in school-effects studies such as this usually involves three steps. The first step is generally called the unconditional model because it includes no student- or school-level measures. In this step, we partition the variance in the outcome into its within- and between-school components. The proportion of variance in the outcome that exists between schools (the intraclass correlation, or ICC) is crucial. A low ICC (meaning little variation exists in the outcome between schools) indicates that finding school effects is unlikely for the simple reason that there is little variation to explain; only the between-school proportion of the variance can be modeled as a function of school characteristics.

A TWO-LEVEL MODEL. Once the variance in the outcome has been partitioned, the analysis continues with two additional steps. In an HLM model such as we use here—students nested within schools—analyses are at two levels. At the student level (Level 1), we estimate relationships between students' academic and social backgrounds and their SAT scores. Although HLM uses maximum likelihood statistical estimation, this procedure is analogous to a series of small within-school regressions (one in each school). At this point researchers decide whether the independent variables are estimated as fixed or random effects. In our analyses, the African American indicator is allowed to vary between schools. All other student-level variables are estimated as fixed effects. Thus the between-school variances in their relationships to the outcomes are constrained (or fixed) to zero. At the school level (Level 2), we estimate school effects on the intercept (which we allowed to vary) and on the African American slope. By modeling the African American slope we can investigate school characteristics that influence the relationship between African Americans and their performance on the SAT.

PRESENTATION OF RESULTS. We present both analytic and descriptive results. Descriptive results are of two types. The first type, which includes information about students, focuses on racial differences in SAT scores and social and academic backgrounds. We tested group mean differences for statistical significance using one-way ANOVA (analysis of variance) for continuous variables and cross-tabulation for categorical variables. The second type of descriptives includes information about schools, which is organized around the proportion of African American enrollment. Again, we tested group differences using ANOVAs and cross-tabulations.

After presenting the results of our exploratory regressions, we present multilevel (HLM) results in three steps. Step 1 provides information about the proportion of variance in both SAT-M and SAT-V that is within and between schools. Step 2, our within-school (or Level 1) HLM models, explores relationships between students' social and academic background and their SAT scores. In Step 3, our Level 2 models report how school characteristics influence students' performances on the SAT or, more specifically, how school characteristics influence the African American–white SAT gap.

Because of the large size of the data set, we are careful to distinguish between statistically significant and substantially important results. The statistical power these data provide often produces results that are statistically significant, but practically immaterial. To keep this distinction clear, we report our multivariate results in both the raw SAT metric and in effect size (standard deviation) units. Effects of 0.5 SD or above are generally considered large; effects 0.3–0.5 SD, medium; effects 0.1–0.3 SD, small; and effects below 0.1 SD, trivial.[46]

A NOTE OF CAUTION REGARDING CAUSAL CLAIMS. An important limitation of these data is the absence of a measure of students' achievement before high school. As such, we are careful not to make the causal claims common to many school-effects studies. For example, we describe how the African American–white SAT gap varies by school sector. However, our data do not permit us to identify the nature of this relationship before students entered high school. Hence the relationships we report here may have been established before high school, meaning our results are more descriptive than causal in nature.

Descriptive Results

Table 1 presents racial/ethnic subgroup means for students who graduated from high school in 1999. Approximately 10 percent were African American, the largest racial/ethnic group after whites, who make up 68 percent of the sample. Despite decades of progress by African Americans, the black-white achievement gap clearly persists. Almost 200 points—1 full standard deviation—separate African Americans and whites on their combined SAT scores [effect size (ES) = 0.96]. When SAT-M and SAT-V are examined separately, we find that the gap is slightly larger on SAT-M (104 points, ES = 0.93) than on SAT-V (91 points, ES = 0.84). The widest gap is not between African Americans and whites, but between African Americans and Asians (combined SAT ES = 1.09). Non–U.S. citizens' SAT-V scores

Table 1. Racial Differences in 1999 SAT Scores and Student Social and Academic Backgrounds

Variable	African American (N = 87,795)	Asian (N = 52,489)	Hispanic (N = 65,391)	Native American (N = 6,373)	White (N = 589,548)	Other race/ ethnicity (N = 24,787)	Non–U.S. citizen (N = 52,312)
SAT score							
SAT-Math[a]	425	559	462	486	529	519	504
Standard deviation	97	120	103	104	103	113	127
SAT-Verbal[b]	437	524	463	489	528	527	443
Standard deviation	99	116	103	103	100	114	121
SAT-Composite[a]	861	1083	926	975	1058	1046	946
Standard deviation	180	221	191	192	188	212	224
Social background							
Socioeconomic status (z-score)[a]	-0.44	0.02	-0.69	-0.16	0.18	0.03	-0.54
Standard deviation	0.90	1.09	1.04	0.94	0.92	1.00	1.13
Female (percent)[c]	59.0	53.0	57.6	54.0	54.4	57.8	54.8
Academic background (percent)							
Took honors English[a]	27.7	46.2	35.8	32.6	39.6	41.7	28.6
Took calculus[b]	12.5	39.6	16.9	16.9	25.1	24.5	29.1
English is second language[a]	1.1	24.1	21.8	1.1	0.7	8.6	66.5
Took PSAT[a]	71.8	86.0	71.8	74.1	83.0	80.5	67.9

Source: Authors' calculations.
a. All race/ethnic group means differ statistically from whites ($p < 0.001$).
b. All race/ethnic group means except other race/ethnicity differ statistically from whites ($p < 0.001$).
c. All race/ethnic group means except Native Americans and non–U.S. citizens differ from whites ($p < 0.001$).

are comparable to those of African Americans' even though English is a second language for two-thirds of noncitizen test takers.

Racial gaps in social class are also evident among SAT takers. A 0.62 SD gap in SES separates African American (SES = –0.44 SD) from white students (SES = 0.18 SD). Although females are overrepresented in each racial/ethnic category, the gender gap in SAT taking is the widest among African Americans. Among all racial/ethnic groups, African American males are the least likely to take the SAT. African American and white students' academic experiences in high school also differ. More whites (39.6 percent) than African Americans (27.7 percent) took honors English. Whites were also twice as likely (and Asian students three times as likely) as African Americans to complete calculus. African Americans are slightly (though statistically) more likely than whites to have English as their second language and less likely to take the PSAT.

SCHOOL-LEVEL DESCRIPTIVES. Table 2 presents school-level information organized around the proportion of schools' African American enrollment. The largest group of schools (*N* = 5,657) enrolls between 1 and 40 percent African Americans (M = 10 percent), followed by schools enrolling less than 1 percent African Americans (*N* = 2,612, M = 0.4 percent). High-enrollment African American schools—schools with greater than 40 percent African American enrollment—constitute roughly 9 percent of the sample (*N* = 792, M = 65 percent).

Reflecting the overall performance of African American students, high African American enrollment schools have significantly lower average SAT-Composite scores (M = 901) than schools enrolling very few African Americans (M = 1047) or moderate numbers of African Americans (M = 1043). High African American enrollment schools offer roughly the same number of AP courses (6.1) as low African American enrollment schools (5.7), while medium African American enrollment schools offer an average of 8.6 AP courses.

We created the next two variables using data from both SAT and ACT takers, allowing us to paint a broader portrait of the students in each school. Over 28 percent of students in low and medium African American enrollment schools completed calculus compared with only 20 percent in high African American enrollment schools. A greater proportion of twelfth graders in low (43.6 percent) and medium (47.4 percent) schools also took either the SAT or ACT than in high African American enrollment schools (42.3 percent).

Brookings Papers on Education Policy: 2003

Table 2. School Characteristics by Proportion of African American Enrollment

School characteristic	Low African American enrollment (< 1 percent) (N = 2,612)	Medium African American enrollment (1–40 percent) (N = 5,657)	High African American enrollment (> 40 percent) (N = 792)
Social and academic organization			
Average SAT-Composite score[a]	1,047	1,043	901
Standard deviation	97	103	105
Number of Advanced Placement			
courses offered[b]	5.7	8.6	6.1
Standard deviation	4.5	5.6	4.6
SAT/ACT takers completing			
calculus (percent)[b]	28.7	28.4	20.2
Standard deviation	17.3	16.0	14.9
Twelfth graders taking SAT or			
ACT (percent)[b]	43.6	47.4	42.3
Standard deviation	26.2	25.6	22.1
Average socioeconomic status			
(z-score)[b]	–0.06	0.15	–0.85
Standard deviation	0.94	0.99	0.85
School size[c]	849	1,249	1,265
Standard deviation	551	761	626
School sector (percent)			
Public (N = 7,551)[b]	86.5	80.0	96.5
Private nonreligious (N = 391)[b]	2.5	5.7	0.3
Catholic (N = 679)[b]	6.6	8.6	2.3
Private other-religious (N = 440)[b]	4.3	5.6	1.0
School location (percent)			
Urban (N = 2,397)[a]	10.6	30.5	49.7
Suburban (N = 3,947)[a]	39.1	47.6	29.3
Small town (N = 1,138)[b]	19.9	9.4	11.1
Rural (N = 1,579)[c]	30.3	12.5	9.8

Source: Authors' calculations.
Note: ACT = American College Test.
a. Mean difference between medium and high black enrollment schools is statistically significant ($p < 0.001$).
b. Mean differences between low and medium, and medium and high, black enrollment schools are statistically significant ($p < 0.001$).
c. Mean difference between low and medium black enrollment schools is statistically significant ($p < 0.001$).

Again, reflecting the socioeconomic status of African American students, the school-average SES of high African American enrollment schools (0.85 SD below the school-average mean) is considerably below that of schools enrolling fewer African American students. This school-level difference is almost double the SES gap found at the student level. In schools enrolling large numbers of African Americans, non–African Americans also tend to come from more disadvantaged backgrounds. Unsurprisingly, the vast majority of high African American enrollment schools are public (96.5 percent) and located in urban centers (49.7 percent). The relatively large number of medium African American enrollment schools located in suburban areas is reflected in the socially advantaged backgrounds of their students (0.15 SD above the mean). The smaller size of low African American enrollment schools is related to the fact that over half are located in small towns and rural areas.

SUMMARY OF DESCRIPTIVE RESULTS. These results reaffirm the importance and saliency of research on the black-white achievement gap. On average, African American students score almost 1 standard deviation below their white counterparts. This is even more alarming considering African American SAT takers are commonly viewed as a more socially and academically advantaged group of African Americans. However, as table 1 indicates, compared with their white peers, even African American SAT takers come from relatively disadvantaged homes. A vast body of literature suggests that achievement in high school is strongly related to the courses students take. In this sense, African American SAT takers are again at a disadvantage compared with their white peers in that they are less likely to follow rigorous academic programs in high school.

Previous research suggests that schools' academic and social climates also influence student achievement. We find here that African American students are more likely to attend low SES high schools in which fewer students follow a college preparatory curriculum. These simple descriptive results confirm the complex associations between race and achievement, and between race and the qualities of schools students attend, even among the highest-achieving students. As such, a multivariate and multilevel analytic approach is required to sort out these tangled relationships.

Multivariate and Multilevel Results

We begin by presenting the results of our multivariate regressions exploring the African American–white SAT gap (see figures 1 and 2). Instead of the standard regression table, we present these results using simple bar charts to help readers visualize the relative effects. The zero line in each figure represents the average score for white students (SAT-M = 529, SAT-V = 489). Each column introduces an additional social or academic student characteristic while controlling for the previous predictors (a stepwise regression).

Figure 1. Student Characteristics Influencing the African American–White SAT-Math Gap

African American–white gap (raw points)

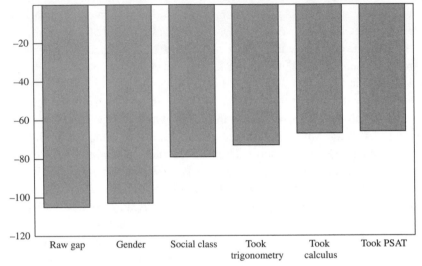

Raw gap   Gender   Social class   Took trigonometry   Took calculus   Took PSAT

Note: For African Americans, $N = 87,795$; whites, $N = 589,548$. Unstandardized regression coefficients; whites are comparison group. All coefficients significant ($p < 0.001$). Zero equals average score for whites (529).

In figure 1, the first column on the left represents the unadjusted black-white SAT-M gap, which is 105 points, or almost 1 full standard deviation. The gap narrows slightly when we control for gender. When we account for African American–white differences in SES, the gap narrows considerably to 79 points. This finding alone discredits the common public perception that the black-white achievement gap is due solely to the lower socioeconomic status of African American students.

The gap closes by 6 additional points when we account for the fact that white students are more likely to take trigonometry, and 6 points again when we control for racial differences in taking calculus (compared with taking only trigonometry). After adjusting for racial differences in taking the PSAT, the gap stands at 66 points; still a disturbing gap of over 0.5 SD.

The situation is similar with SAT-V (see figure 2), although the unadjusted gap (92 points) is considerably smaller than that on SAT-M. Adjusting for SES differences between African Americans and whites reduces the gap further by 24 points (as it did with SAT-M). Similar to the effects of advanced course taking in mathematics, when we account for the fact that

Figure 2. Student Characteristics Influencing the African American–White SAT-Verbal Gap

African American–white gap (raw points)

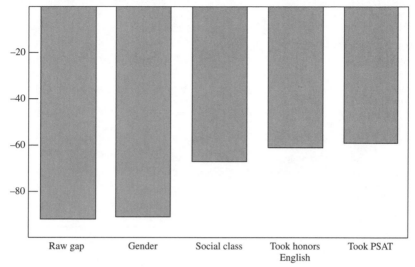

Note: For African Americans, $N = 87,795$; whites, $N = 589,548$. Unstandardized regression coefficients; whites are comparison group. All coefficients significant ($p < 0.001$). Zero equals average score for whites (528).

whites are more likely than African Americans to take honors English, the gap narrows to 61 points. As other researchers have noted, the courses students take matter, even after accounting for students' socioeconomic backgrounds. Finally, after controlling for whether students took the PSAT, the gap stands at 59 points (over two-thirds of a standard deviation).

As table 2 indicated, the schools African Americans and whites attend often differ dramatically. As such, the relationships we presented in figures 1 and 2 could potentially vary depending on the characteristics of the schools African Americans and whites attend. Hence, we turn to our multilevel (HLM) analyses.

WITHIN-SCHOOL HLM MODELS. The intraclass correlation indicates the proportion of variance in the outcome that lies systematically between schools. As with virtually all educational outcomes, a greater proportion of variance lies among students in the same school than between schools. In the case of SAT scores, over one-fifth of the variance lies between schools: 22.5 percent for SAT-Math, 21.2 percent for SAT-Verbal (see table A-1). Only variance that exists between schools can be explained by differences in the qualities of

Table 3. Within-School Models of SAT Performance

Predictor variable	SAT-Math	SAT-Verbal
Random effects		
Intercept	512.2	510.8
African American[a]	−55.7 (0.50)[b]	−44.9 (0.41)
Fixed effects		
Female	−29.4 (0.26)	−13.7 (0.13)
Asian	3.5 (0.03)	−6.0 (0.06)
Hispanic	−21.8 (0.20)	−16.0 (0.15)
Native American	−18.6 (0.17)	−16.5 (0.15)
Other race/ethnicity	−6.6 (0.06)	3.8 (0.03)
Non-U.S. citizen	−11.4 (0.10)	−37.3 (0.34)
Socioeconomic status (z-score)	17.2 (0.15)	18.7 (0.17)
Took trigonometry (over no trigonometry)	45.9 (0.41)	—
Took calculus (over trigonometry)	94.0 (0.84)	—
Took honors English	—	87.8 (0.81)
Took PSAT	29.8 (0.27)	25.6 (0.24)
English is second language	5.2 (0.05)	−13.4 (0.12)

Source: Authors' calculations.
Note: The intercepts and all random and fixed effects are statistically significant ($p < 0.001$ using robust standard errors). For students, $N = 878,695$; schools, $N = 9,061$.
a. All racial/ethnic groups are compared with whites.
b. Effect size units are in parentheses.

schools themselves. The considerable amount of variation in SAT scores between schools reaffirms our decision to employ hierarchical models.

Table 3 presents our within-school (or Level 1) HLM models, which explore the relationships between student characteristics and SAT performance. The intercepts represent average achievement on the respective tests adjusted for the student-level predictors. Similarly, the African American coefficients represent the black-white SAT gaps after adjusting for differences in students' social and academic backgrounds. Even after accounting for these differences, a 55.7-point gap (ES = 0.5) remains on SAT-Math, while a slightly smaller 44.9-point gap (ES = 0.41) persists on SAT-Verbal. These parameters are considered random effects because they have been permitted to vary between schools. Not being fixed, they allow us to investigate them as a function of school characteristics. These gaps are somewhat smaller than those reported in figures 1 and 2, because HLM within-school models adjust for the differing social and academic characteristics of students in each school.

Several other areas of social inequality exist on the SAT. For example, the gender gap on SAT-M (ES = 0.26) is double that found on SAT-V (ES =

0.13). Both Hispanic and Native American students continue to underperform their white peers. The influence of socioeconomic background on SAT scores also persists, with a 1 SD increase in SES associated with a 0.15 SD increase in SAT-M and a 0.17 SD increase in SAT-V, even after accounting for the other social and academic characteristics. It seems likely that the relationship between taking the PSAT and SAT scores (ES = 0.27 for SAT-M, ES = 0.24 for SAT-V) is not simply evidence of test preparation but is capturing other student characteristics, such as higher levels of motivation, parental involvement, or higher prior achievement among students taking the PSAT.

The associations between advanced course taking and SAT scores are also noteworthy. Compared with students who completed only algebra II or less, students who completed trigonometry scored an average of almost 46 points higher (ES = 0.41) on SAT-Math. Even more striking is the 94-point advantage (ES = 0.84) enjoyed by students who completed calculus over those who completed only trigonometry. Similar relationships are found with SAT-V. Adjusting for other student characteristics, students who took honors English in high school scored an average of 88 points higher (ES = 0.81) than students who did not. However, this within-school model does not contain controls for prior achievement. The effects of advanced course taking likely partly reflect the already higher achievement of students who take advanced courses.

BETWEEN-SCHOOL HLM MODELS: SCHOOL EFFECTS ON THE BLACK-WHITE SAT GAP. Although we modeled the effects of school characteristics on SAT performance, these results are not our focus (see instead table A-2). We focus here on school characteristics that influence the black-white SAT gap (see table 4). To begin, it is important to note that these coefficients do not indicate the effects of school characteristics on African Americans' SAT scores. They reflect how school characteristics influence the black-white SAT gap. Positive coefficients indicate the characteristics of schools in which the gap is narrower; negative coefficients indicate wider gaps. The challenge in interpreting dichotomous slopes in HLM is that it indicates equity, but a form of equity that may in some cases be undesirable. For example, a positive coefficient (meaning the gap is narrower) could indicate school characteristics associated with lower performance among white students, but average performance of black students. The goal is to narrow the achievement gap by raising minority student achievement, not reducing the achievement of nonminority students.

Table 4. Relationships between School Characteristics and the African American–White SAT Gap

Predictor variable	SAT-Math		SAT-Verbal	
Intercept	–57.5***		–46.0***	
School sector[a]				
Private nonreligious	24.6***	(0.22)[b]	27.1***	(0.25)
Catholic	14.5***	(0.13)	17.1***	(0.16)
Private other-religious	13.0***	(0.12)	11.4**	(0.10)
School location[c]				
Urban	–2.6**	(0.02)	–2.7**	(0.02)
Small town	–3.2	(0.03)	–1.5	(0.01)
Rural	–1.0	(0.01)	–5.1***	(0.05)
School size[d]				
Small school (< 500)	–.9	(0.00)	–2.1	(0.02)
Medium-small school (501–800)	1.4	(0.01)	.5	(0.00)
Medium-large school (1,151–1,700)	.8	(0.00)	.0	(0.00)
Large school (> 1,701)	4.5**	(0.04)	5.2**	(0.05)
Social and academic characteristics				
Average student socioeconomic status (z-score)	–9.3***	(0.08)	–5.6***	(0.05)
African American enrollment (> 40 percent)	2.5**	(0.02)	–4.2**	(0.04)
Number of Advanced Placement courses offered	–.6***	(0.00)	–.5***	(0.00)
Percent SAT/ACT takers completing calculus (z-score)	2.8***	(0.03)	–1.0	(0.01)
Percent twelfth graders taking SAT or ACT (z-score)	1.6**	(0.01)	3.5***	(0.03)

Source: Authors' calculations.
Note: For students, $N = 878,695$; schools, $N = 9,061$. ACT = American College Test.
a. Compared with public schools.
b. Effect size units are in parentheses.
c. Compared with suburban schools.
d. Compared with schools enrolling 801–1,150 students.
**$p < 0.01$; ***$p < 0.001$ (Hierarchical Linear Modeling robust standard errors).

The strongest school-level effects on the African American–white SAT gap are associated with school sector. Even after accounting for both student- and school-level characteristics, the gap is considerably narrower in nonpublic schools. The gap is almost half as large in private nonreligious schools as in public schools, and almost one-quarter as large in Catholic and private other-religious schools. This is the case even after adjusting for the characteristics commonly associated with nonpublic schools, such as smaller school size and a more academically focused curriculum.

After taking into account the other student- and school-level characteristics, few substantive effects are associated with school location or size. The black-white gap is wider in urban schools (compared with suburban schools) on both SAT-M and SAT-V, but the differences are trivial (ES = 0.02). A somewhat larger gap exists within rural schools on SAT-V, but, again, the effect is small (ES = 0.06). Conversely, the black-white gap is slightly smaller (ES = 0.04) in large compared with medium schools. This finding regarding the relationship between school size and the black-white achievement gap is not consistent with previous research on size. One reason is that our dependent variables and our population of students are different. We focus on more advanced, and likely more affluent, students than studies using data such as NELS:88, whose students are representative of the population of high school students. The results we present in table A-2—that student achievement is highest in medium-size schools—mirror those of V. E. Lee and J. B. Smith.[47]

One puzzling result is the opposite effect of high African American enrollment schools on the black-white gap. In schools enrolling large numbers of African Americans, the gap is smaller on SAT-M than on SAT-V (although the effects are small in both instances). The finding that the gap is wider in schools offering more AP courses makes sense considering the positive relationship between advanced course taking and achievement as well as the fact that African American students are less likely to take advanced courses. This is an instance in which overall achievement can be raised by a policy initiative or curricular decision, but achievement is more inequitable because certain types of students systematically do not receive the benefits of courses or programs.

Furthermore, the black-white gap is generally wider in schools enrolling more socially advantaged students. This does not indicate that African American students perform worse in higher SES schools. Instead, it indicates that although African American students in higher SES schools generally outperform African Americans in lower SES schools, in higher SES schools African American students' white peers score even higher. This phenomenon has brought together a consortium of school districts that enroll substantial numbers of affluent African American and white students (including Ann Arbor, Michigan; Cambridge, Massachusetts; Madison, Wisconsin; and Shaker Heights, Ohio). These districts are interested in closing a gap they have noticed is widest among their highest-achieving African American and white students.

Conclusion

These findings are simultaneously disheartening and hopeful. They are disheartening in that substantial achievement gaps continue to separate African American and white students; hopeful, because students, parents, and schools can take steps to help close the gap. The largest single factor explaining the black-white achievement gap is the socioeconomic backgrounds of students. Improvement in the socioeconomic backgrounds of African American students is likely to improve their admissions test performance and reduce the distance between themselves and whites. The public policy environment is such that improvements in the social and economic plight of African American families are likely to take place through private sector initiatives and through continuing emphasis by African Americans upon the attainment of high-quality education. One policy approach that enjoys support across a broad political spectrum is an increase in the academic rigor of high school for African American students. The analyses in this paper reaffirm those of others, that increased exposure to higher-level coursework is related to higher and more equitable achievement, even after controlling for student SES.

The HLM analyses presented in this paper reveal how the characteristics of high schools are also a culprit in the admissions test performance gap of African American and white students. Like the general population of African American high school students, African American SAT takers more often attend lower SES schools that are likely to offer less rigorous academic courses. Given that public school students are typically assigned to schools near their home residence, and school demographics mirror the communities in which they are located, it is very difficult for college-bound African American youngsters to attend better schools without policies that either give them greater choice or radically improve their schools. The findings in this paper indicate that, after controlling for SES, the SAT score gap is narrower between African Americans and whites who attend private high schools than public high schools. Despite this finding, regarding weaker relationships between race and achievement in nonpublic schools, further evidence is needed to support a policy recommendation that favors private school choice. In addition to analyses that make finer distinctions among types of public and private schools, perhaps most important are analyses that take into account student preparation before entering high school. Because the SAT database does not include student achievement before high school, it is not possible to distinguish the extent to which narrower gaps in nonpublic schools are related to selective admissions or choices of students of the nonpublic high schools or the qualities, policies, and practices of schools.

Perhaps the most puzzling question remaining is why the black-white gap is greatest among the most affluent students attending the most affluent schools. One potential explanation lies in the quality of instruction African American students receive in school. While this study identifies the level of courses that students are taking, the quality of instruction occurring within those courses remains unclear. Also important, but not available in the data for this study, is the quality of interactions African American students have with their instructors inside and outside of class.

Although the focus of this paper is on high school students and their schools, success requires a solid academic foundation that is built over many years. High schools have an important role to play in narrowing the admissions test score gap, but benefiting fully from courses such as calculus and trigonometry requires at least a modicum of basic skills in mathematics, which are obtained before high school. Similarly, for African American students to benefit from honors English, they need high-quality preparation in reading and writing in the early grades. Therefore, although examining high schools is clearly important, the academic experiences of the youngest African American students must remain in mind as investigations continue into the black-white achievement gap in college admissions tests.

Appendix

Table A-1. Fully Unconditional HLM Model: Psychometric Characteristics of SAT-Math and SAT-Verbal

	SAT-Math	*SAT-Verbal*
Within-school variance (σ^2)	9865.62	9630.98
Between-school variance (τ)	2865.54	2588.58
Between-school standard deviation ($\sqrt{\tau}$)	53.53	50.88
Reliability (λ)	0.92	0.91
Unadjusted intraclass correlation[a]	22.51	21.18

Source: Authors' calculations.
Note: HLM = Hierarchical Linear Modeling.
a. Intraclass correlation computed $\tau/(\tau+\sigma^2)$.

Table A-2. School Effects on SAT Scores

Predictor variable	SAT-Math		SAT-Verbal	
Intercept	516.0***		511.3***	
School sector[a]				
Private nonreligious	2.5	(0.02)[b]	11.9***	(0.11)
Catholic	−18.3***	(0.16)	−6.4	(0.06)
Private other-religious	−8.8***	(0.08)	1.8	(0.02)
School location[c]				
Urban	−0.8	(0.01)	1.2	(0.01)
Small town	2.8**	(0.03)	6.2***	(0.06)
Rural	−0.4	(0.00)	2.8**	(0.01)
School size[d]				
Small school (< 500)	1.5	(0.01)	0.6	(0.01)
Medium-small school (501–800)	3.1***	(0.03)	3.3***	(0.03)
Medium-large school (1,151–1,700)	−0.5	(0.00)	−2.3**	(0.02)
Large school (> 1,701)	−1.0	(0.01)	−5.9***	(0.05)
Social and academic characteristics				
Average student socioeconomic status (z-score)	22.8***	(0.20)	24.1***	(0.22)
African American enrollment (> 40 percent)	−33.7***	(0.30)	−26.3***	(0.24)
Number of Advanced Placement courses offered	1.2***	(0.01)	.3***	(0.00)
SAT/ACT takers completing calculus (z-score) (percent)	−6.4***	(0.06)	2.5***	(0.02)
Twelfth graders taking SAT or ACT (z-score) (percent)	0.3	(0.00)	0.4	(0.00)

Source: Authors' calculations.
Note: For students, $N = 878,695$; schools, $N = 9,061$. ACT = American College Test.
a. Compared with public schools.
b. Effect size units are in parentheses.
c. Compared with suburban schools.
d. Compared with schools enrolling 801–1,150 students.
**$p < 0.01$; ***$p < 0.001$ (Hierarchical Linear Modeling robust standard errors).

Comment by Jens Ludwig

The paper by Michael T. Nettles, Catherine M. Millett, and Douglas D. Ready addresses one of the most important issues in current education policy: reducing inequality in educational outcomes, particularly between African American and white students. The paper follows in the tradition of previous studies that try to identify those factors that have a causal effect on the black-white achievement gap, although Nettles and his colleagues appropriately note that their paper cannot identify causal relationships. I elaborate here on why causal inferences cannot be drawn from these findings. I also note that even if strong conclusions could be made about what drives the black-white gap from these findings, the implications for public policy are not obvious.

Causes of the Black-White Test Score Gap

Causal inference is complicated primarily for two reasons, both of which relate to the role of self-selection. First, SAT takers are not a random sample of American adolescents. Those students who are most likely to take the SAT are also disproportionately likely to have well-educated parents or good high school grades.[48] All else equal, when SAT-taking rates increase, the average level of socioeconomic and academic advantage of SAT-takers declines. The result is that average SAT scores and the proportion of students who take the SAT are negatively correlated, both across states at a particular time and within states over time.[49] This pattern poses a problem for Nettles and his colleagues, because the same factors that affect the academic achievement of black and white students may also affect the likelihood that students take the SAT. In this case, some policy lever may improve overall student achievement but not increase average SAT scores if the intervention also induces a substantial increase in the proportion of students who take the SAT.

To illustrate the problem, assume for simplicity that white students always take the SAT and always score a combined 900 on the math and verbal tests. Suppose further that some school characteristic (smaller class sizes) has little effect on how much white students learn in school but increases how much African American students learn and improves their odds of considering college and thus taking the SAT. In this example, the size of the black-white SAT gap may be no smaller—and may even be larger—in schools with small classes, even though the overall population of black students learns more with small classes both absolutely and relative to whites. In reality, school characteristics may affect the academic achievement and SAT-taking rates of both whites and blacks, so in practice the magnitude and even sign of bias that results from inadequately controlling for the nonrandom self-selection of SAT takers is difficult to predict.

One way to begin to address this problem is to adjust for the SAT-taking rates separately of white and black students within each school, with some care paid to the functional form of the relationship between average black (or white) SAT scores and the proportion of black (white) students taking the SAT.[50] This type of procedure has limitations but would at least be a step in the right direction.

A second problem, which is more fundamental to education research generally, is that students are not randomly assigned to schools with different characteristics such as class sizes. Many parents care a great deal about where their children go to school, as evidenced by the relationship between local school spending or quality and house prices.[51] The result is some systematic relationship between the family backgrounds of students and the schools that they attend. Parent and student characteristics may also be related to the child's school inputs because educational administrators assign additional resources to schools or classrooms that disproportionately serve low- (or high-) achieving students.

The paper by Nettles, Millett, and Ready attempts to address this version of the self-selection problem by regression adjusting for observed student and family characteristics. The standard regression-based approach breaks down in cases in which student and family attributes that affect both achievement and the child's school inputs are unmeasured or only partially measured. The magnitude of the bias that results may be nontrivial, as evidenced by studies that examine whether standard nonexperimental regression approaches can reproduce the results of randomized experiments.[52] Adequately controlling for this type of self-selection bias may require explicitly modeling the process through which students are sorted across different types of schools and classrooms. At the very least an explicit model for the sorting process can help policy analysts utilize available student and family control variables in a way that relies less crucially on strong functional form assumptions, as with propensity score matching methods.[53] Perhaps better still is the identification of natural experiments or other factors that drive the process through which students wind up in different types of classrooms and schools but have no other direct effect on student achievement.[54]

The problem is not that the technology for adequately addressing this type of self-selection problem is entirely unknown. The economics literature, for example, contains a growing number of studies that apply a variety of methods to nonexperimental data to overcome the self-selection problem in fairly convincing fashion. Many of these studies focus explicitly on education topics.[55] And within the evaluation of medical interventions and even many social policy programs, randomized experiments are common.

The problem instead seems to be one of a methodology gap between education research and many of the other social sciences. The traditional education literature does contain some excellent work that tries hard to address causal issues, and other disciplines are not free from research that is unrealistic, unhelpful, or otherwise problematic. But on average a marked difference appears across areas in the attention that is paid to problems of determining causality. This is not an original observation. For example, in his review of the state of nonexperimental (or quasi-experimental) research in education, Thomas Cook of Northwestern University laments that "many of the studies calling themselves quasi-experiments in educational evaluation are of types that theorists of quasi-experimentation reject as usually inadequate. To judge by the quality of the educational evaluation work I know best . . . the average quasi-experiment in these fields inspires little confidence in its conclusions about effectiveness. Recent advances in the design and analysis of quasi-experiments are not getting into research evaluating education."[56]

Randomized experiments could in principle overcome the limits of problematic nonexperimental analysis, but, as Cook notes, these are disappointingly rare within the area of education. University schools and departments of education would appear to bear some of the responsibility, but perhaps so also does the federal government. It is noteworthy that one of the most influential experiments in the education area—Tennessee's Project STAR (Student/Teacher Achievement Ratio) class-size experiment—was implemented by a state agency.[57] If society's limited understanding of what works in education is an impediment to reforming American public schools, then it follows that the problems with current education research are an important part of the nation's educational crisis.

Remedies

The paper focuses attention largely on four factors that influence the black-white gap in SAT scores: students' socioeconomic status (SES), school size, school curriculum, and school sector (that is, private versus public schools). Suppose that the paper persuasively made the argument that each of these factors exerts a causal effect on the black-white achievement gap. What actions should public policymakers take in response? The answer is, perhaps surprisingly, not entirely straightforward.

Changing the curricula offered by schools and the classes that individual students take is perhaps the easiest of these interventions to implement. If the existing set of teachers is able to teach higher-level material, then the financial costs of offering and teaching more demanding classes are low. However, a student's course-taking pattern in high school is perhaps the most likely of the policy levers mentioned by Nettles, Millett, and Ready to be confounded by self-selection. Student achievement is clearly both cause and effect of the high school courses in which a student is enrolled.

In comparison to changing course content, reducing school size is a more costly intervention. Even if it were convincingly demonstrated that school size affected student achievement, would reducing the size of schools be the best use of scarce resources? Would funds be better spent on reducing class sizes within existing schools, or expanding and intensifying remedial pre-school or after-school programs for at-risk children, or improving teacher training or increasing salaries? Put differently, just because an intervention is effective in improving student achievement does not imply that it is the most cost-effective use of scarce public funds. Some people may argue that the real solution to any resource constraints in schools is to spend even more on education. But school budgets, whatever their size, will always be finite, leaving policymakers with difficult decisions about how to allocate available resources among competing uses. Understanding how much students benefit from allocating an additional dollar to different uses seems like useful, if not decisive, information for the policy process.

The possible effects of school sector on student achievement highlights another policy lesson—the potential pitfalls of taking demonstration programs (in this case, school vouchers) to scale. Arguably the best available evidence to date comes from Milwaukee's school voucher experiment, which suggests some achievement advantage in math but not reading for private versus public school students.[58] But what would happen under a larger-scale program of school choice? Which private schools would expand, and what would happen to their effectiveness if they served more students? What types of new schools would enter the market? Which students would apply to private schools? Who would be admitted? Given the poor quality of many urban public school systems, it is not hard to believe that almost anything might be better. But a study of New Zealand's large-scale school choice program suggests that the system-level effects can be complicated.[59] Unfortunately, the effects of a large-scale school choice system in the United States are unknown because something like it has never been tried.

Finally, the most compelling finding reported by Nettles, Millett, and Ready is likely to be the role of black-white differences in SES in explaining the gap in achievement test scores. Given the country's history of slavery and racial discrimination and the substantial correlation across generations in SES, a number of good arguments can be made for reducing the black-white gap in income and wealth.[60] But would income redistribution toward African American families also serve to reduce the black-white test score gap? Not necessarily. Sociologist Susan Mayer has argued that once a family's basic needs are met, additional income from government programs may not improve how children perform in school.[61]

Efforts targeted at out-of-school factors do strike me as a potentially productive way to address the black-white test score gap, although the technology and politics of addressing those factors that might matter most are likely to be more difficult than simply sending low-income families larger earned-income tax credit checks. For example, changing how parents interact with their children may improve academic achievement, but some parents may be understandably resistant to government suggestions about how to raise their families.[62] Other research shows that living within a high-poverty neighborhood may depress children's educational outcomes.[63] Because African American families are more likely to live within high-poverty areas than whites, even after controlling for the family's own poverty status, efforts to further reduce economic and racial segregation across neighborhoods may help reduce the black-white test score gap.[64] While the United States has made some progress in reducing racial residential segregation, most American metropolitan areas remain quite segregated.[65]

In sum, future analyses of SAT and other education data by those within the education research community could be strengthened in a variety of ways to help identify the determinants of the black-white gap in academic achievement. However, even with such information in hand, a number of important unanswered questions remain about how to map the causes of the test score gap into effective policy interventions.

Comment by James Forman

The paper by Michael T. Nettles, Catherine M. Millett, and Douglas D. Ready makes an important contribution to the ongoing conversation about the racial gap in standardized test scores. Among other findings, the paper documents that blacks on average score lower on the SAT, American College Test (ACT), and National Assessment of Educational Progress (NAEP) than whites and that the disparities exist at all income and socioeconomic status (SES) levels. While I have no quarrel with the paper's findings, as a preliminary matter I do wonder whether a mistake is being made by focusing on income instead of wealth. Nettles, Millett, and Ready's research, like all the research in this field, is based on income comparisons. But as the work of Melvin Oliver, Thomas Shapiro, and Dalton Conley has made clear, income disparities can mask even greater wealth disparities. The real point may be that reductions in income disparities—as more African American families enter the middle class—mask large and continuing disparities in wealth. In other words, black families, on average, do not have the same household wealth as white families with comparable incomes (factoring in savings, home value, and so on). Because wealth, even more than income, allows families to purchase important educational goods at every stage of a child's development, research on racial gaps needs to begin to take account of differences in wealth.

Nettles, Millett, and Ready's research also raises a more fundamental question: Is it a mistake to speak of the racial gap in standardized test scores and to overlook the greater consequences of the gap when disadvantaged kids are the ones on the losing side?

I would suggest that more than one racial gap is at work and that the racial gap has more dire consequences for kids at the bottom end of the social class hierarchy. My position is based in part on personal experience, because I have been on the wrong side of the racial achievement gap in both contexts. In seventh grade, I went to Hunter College High School in New York City, which is a school for high achievers and is, at least in a relative sense, a high socioeconomic status school. The racial test score gap was obvious, and as a result of it, most of the black and Latino students were required to go to summer school before seventh grade started. Though I left Hunter after one year, I stayed in touch with some of the minority students I entered with. Upon graduation from Hunter, they went off en masse to college and university.

After leaving Hunter I moved to Atlanta and went to Franklin Roosevelt High School—a mostly black, low socioeconomic status public school. The differences between the educational opportunities available at Hunter and Roosevelt were stark. I loved my school, my classmates, and my teachers, but I am not proud of the reality that fewer than ten of the kids in my graduating class went on to finish college.

Though I have not seen the research, I would imagine, based on the work of Nettles and others, that the African American students at Hunter and Roosevelt both performed at a lower rate than white students of comparable socioeconomic status. And I guess that this reflects a black-white test score gap. But the consequences of the test score gap for the students at Hunter and the students at Roosevelt are dramatically different. And I personally believe that the more pressing issue today is the Roosevelts of the inner cities—the schools where only a few kids are going to college and more are dropping out, getting pregnant, or, in many cases, getting locked up.

The importance of the question of educating disadvantaged students is reflected in some of the papers presented at the Brookings conference. David P. Baker's excellent paper discusses how the achievement gap between advantaged students and disadvantaged students in this country is much greater than in many others around the world. Hilary Pennington's paper brilliantly points out the ways in which the one-size-fits-all model of the American high school is failing disadvantaged students. It also begins to move educators and policymakers in the direction they need to go: beyond identifying problems and toward discussing solutions. One proposal is to move low SES students into higher SES schools. Both the Nettles, Millett, and Ready paper and Richard Kahlenberg's work suggest that this might make a difference.

But, in most jurisdictions, no such reform is likely to be implemented anytime soon. It might happen more easily in districts that already have a mix of students, in terms of race and class. But it will not happen soon in urban districts such as Washington, D.C., where almost all of the schools are high-poverty schools. The concept of school for the population of students in these districts must be radically changed.

This is what David Domenici and I tried to do when we started the Maya Angelou Public Charter School in Washington, D.C. Maya Angelou students are in school ten and a half hours a day, studying mostly core subjects. When not in class, they work in student-run businesses, where they earn money and learn practical job skills. The results have been impressive. More than half of the students had stopped attending school on a regular basis before they came to Maya Angelou. Over one-third had been acquainted with the juvenile court system. Nonetheless, more than 80 percent of Maya Angelou graduates go on to college.

The first priority for high-poverty schools is to take responsibility for, and be equipped to respond to, the range of problems that have long been associated with poor academic and behavioral performance. The problems have been identified, but the society is not equipping schools to deal with them and educators are too often unwilling to change what they do to address these problems.

While no single prototype exists for a successful school, almost everyone agrees on some essential components: sustained relationships with caring adults, a peer culture that pushes students to excel academically, a rigorous and engaging curriculum, an administration dedicated to supporting its frontline staff, sustained parental involvement in learning, and meaningful connections to the workplace and to higher education. In addition, as Diane Ravitch has been saying, adults cannot retreat. My experience at Maya Angelou makes this clear. If you ask students at Maya Angelou why the school is working, they will tell you it is because "the teachers are always in our business." Now, they will complain about this all day long when they talk to teachers and counselors at the school. But when they take a step back and talk to outside evaluators, they will always point to this feature.

For schools serving this population, extended hours are also essential, both for academic enrichment purposes and to provide a safe and nurturing after-school environment, given that kids will otherwise spend a significant portion of their day in chaotic and violent neighborhoods.

Given the trauma that comes from growing up in these neighborhoods, another key is to build intensive counseling into the core school curriculum. I am not referring just to guidance counselors, although, as others at the Brookings conference mentioned, their role is important. I am talking about licensed clinical social workers. I am talking about psychologists. I am talking about people who are prepared to work with kids who are suffering from untreated trauma, from depression, and from a host of other mental health issues that predominate in these communities but are rarely addressed, admitted to, or even discussed.

Finally, schools must make a commitment to creating a culture or climate of mutual respect, trust, and high achievement. It has to be a whole school commitment, and it has to be relentless. Adults have to take responsibility for the little stuff that students do or say that can harm the school climate—the comments in the hallways, the teasing in the cafeteria, the touching and grabbing when kids think adults are not around. I do not suggest schools respond with zero tolerance and expulsions for idiotic reasons. Adults in schools need to respond with meaningful counseling and conversations, forging relationships with individual kids, so that students and teachers can work together to establish a school climate that promotes both discipline and academic achievement.

One final word—on funding. Having started a school in a high-poverty neighborhood that people point to as successful, I am not going to say that funding and resources do not make a difference. But it does seem to me, in some of these contexts, thinking about funding has to start to change. In some cases, money is already being spent on disadvantaged kids. But it is not being targeted intelligently. Cities are spending money on after-school programs through one agency, spending money on counseling and mental health through another, and funding youth employment through a third. The result is that cities have created these disconnected silos. Kids and families are treated as if they were a bizarre constellation of needs. The assumption is that if they can just go across town with a referral for mental health treatment, they can go over here for a job training program, and then go someplace else for after-school activities.

That is not how anything works. And it is certainly not how things work in a kid's life. Sometimes a little common sense must be applied. Someone must say, "Wait a minute—why does a kid come back to a place?" Well, he or she comes back because of the personal connections with the people there, not because a program, in name, does a specific thing. If those who care about schools can redefine school as a place that does all the things I have described, and redirect the funding so that kids and families can gain access to these services in one integrated program, they will have gone a long way toward making schools work for kids and families in high-poverty areas.

Notes

1. For example, J. S. Coleman and others, *Equality of Educational Opportunity* (Government Printing Office, 1966); M. T. Nettles and R. A. Thoeny, *Toward Black Undergraduate Student Equality in American Higher Education* (Westport, Conn.: Greenwood Press, 1988); L. V. Hedges and A. Nowell, "Changes in the Black-White Gap in Achievement Test Scores," *Sociology of Education,* vol. 72, no. 2 (1999), pp. 111–35; and C. Jencks and M. Phillips, "The Black-White Test Score Gap: An Introduction," in C. Jencks and M. Phillips, eds., *The Black-White Test Score Gap* (Brookings, 1998), pp. 1–51.

2. M. T. Nettles and L. W. Perna, *African American Education Data Book,* vol. 2: *Preschool through High School Education* (Fairfax, Va.: Frederick D. Patterson Research Institute of the College Fund/United Negro College Fund, 1997); and V. E. Lee and D. T. Burkam, "Inequality at the Starting Gate: Social Background and Achievement at Kindergarten Entry," paper presented at the annual meeting of the American Educational Research Association, New Orleans, Louisiana, April 2002.

3. Jencks and Phillips, "The Black-White Test Score Gap," pp. 1–51.

4. W. G. Bowen and D. Bok, *The Shape of the River: Long-Term Consequences of Considering Race in College and University Admissions* (Princeton University Press, 1998).

5. Wayne J. Camara and Amy E. Schmidt, *Group Differences in Standardized Testing and Stratification*, College Board Report 99–5 (New York: College Entrance Examination Board, 1999).

6. D. Chaplin and others, *African American High Scorers Project, Technical Report Three: Student Activities, Course Taking, School Performance, and SAT Performance* (Washington: Urban Institute, 1998); Camara and Schmidt, *Group Differences in Standardized Testing and Stratification*; and M. T. Nettles, C. M. Millett, and M. M. Einarson, "Improving Minority Students' Performance on College Admission Tests," *College Board Review,* vol. 192 (2001), pp. 32–41.

7. Camara and Schmidt, *Group Differences in Standardized Testing and Stratification.*

8. Chaplin and others, *African American High Scorers Project.*

9. Hedges and Nowell, "Changes in the Black-White Achievement Gap."

10. A. G. Powell, E. Farrar, and D. K. Cohen, *The Shopping Mall High School: Winners and Losers in the Educational Marketplace* (Houghton Mifflin, 1985).

11. P. Eckert, *Jocks and Burnouts: Social Categories and Identity in the High School* (New York: Teachers College Press, 1989), p. 7.

12. G. Grant, *The World We Created at Hamilton High* (Harvard University Press, 1988); J. Oakes, *Keeping Track: How Schools Structure Inequality* (Yale University Press, 1985); and J. E. Rosenbaum, *Making Inequality: The Hidden Curriculum of High School Tracking* (Wiley, 1976).

13. J. Eyler, V. J. Cook, and L. E. Ward, "Resegregation: Segregation within Desegregated Schools," in C. H. Rossell and W. D. Hawley, eds., *The Consequences of School Desegregation* (Temple University Press, 1983), pp. 126–62; and A. S. Wells and R. L. Crain, *Stepping Over the Color Line: African American Students in White Suburban Schools* (Yale University Press, 1997).

14. Wells and Crain, *Stepping Over the Color Line.*

15. A. Gamoran, "The Stratification of High School Learning Opportunities," *Sociology of Education,* vol. 60 (1987), pp. 135–55; and V. E. Lee and A. S. Bryk, "A Multilevel Model of the Social Distribution of High School Achievement," *Sociology of Education,* vol. 62 (1989), pp. 172–92.

16. V. E. Lee and A. S. Bryk, "Curriculum Tracking as Mediating the Social Distribution of High School Acievemement," *Sociology of Education,* vol. 61 (1988), pp. 78–94.

17. Oakes, *Keeping Track.*

18. Oakes, *Keeping Track*; and S. W. Raudenbush, R. P. Fotiu, and Y. F. Cheong, "Inequality of Access to Educational Resources: A National Report Card for Eighth-Grade Math," *Educational Evaluation and Policy Analysis,* vol. 20, no. 4 (1998), pp. 253–68.

19. See D. S. Massey and N. A. Denton, *American Apartheid: Segregation and the Making of the Underclass* (Harvard University Press, 1993).

20. G. Orfield and others, *Deepening Segregation in American Public Schools* (Harvard University, Harvard Project on School Desegregation, 1997).

21. Department of Education, *Profile of Children in U.S. School Districts,* NCES 96–831 (Washington, 1996).

22. R. C. Johnston and D. Viadero, "Unmet Promise: Raising Minority Achievement," *Education Week* (March 15, 2000), pp. 14–16.

23. Department of Education, *Out-of-Field Teaching and Educational Equality,* NCES 96–040 (Washington, 1996).

24. S. J. Caldas and C. Bankston, "The Inequality of Separation: Racial Composition of Schools and Academic Achievement," *Educational Administration Quarterly,* vol. 34, no. 4 (1998), pp. 533–77; and D. R. Entwisle and K. L. Alexander, "Summer Setback: Race, Poverty, School Composition, and Mathematics Achievement in the First Two Years of Schools," *American Sociological Review,* vol. 57 (1992), pp. 72–84.

25. Wells and Crain, *Stepping Over the Color Line.*

26. C. E. Bidwell. "The School as Formal Organization," in J.G. March, ed., *Handbook of Organizations* (Chicago: Rand McNally, 1965), pp. 972–1022; and A. S. Bryk and M. E. Driscoll, *The School as Community: Theoretical Foundations, Contextual Influences, and Consequences for Students and Teachers* (University of Wisconsin, Center on Effective Secondary Schools, 1988).

27. Bryk and Driscoll, *The School as Community.*

28. V. E. Lee and D. T. Burkam, "Dropping Out of High School: The Role of School Organization and Structure," paper presented at the Dropout Research: Accurate Counts and Positive Interventions conference, Cambridge, Massachusetts, January 2001; and R. B. Pittman and P. Haughwout, "Influence of High School Size on Dropout Rate," *Educational Evaluation and Policy Analysis,* vol. 9, no. 4 (1987), pp. 337–43.

29. V. E. Lee and S. Loeb, "School Size in Chicago Elementary Schools: Effects on Teachers' Attitudes and Student Achievement," *American Educational Research Journal,* vol. 36, no. 4 (2001), pp. 3–31.

30. Lee and Bryk, "A Multilevel Model of the Social Distribution of High School Achievement."

31. A. S. Bryk, V. E. Lee, and P. B. Holland, *Catholic Schools and the Common Good* (Harvard University Press, 1993); and Lee and Bryk, "A Multilevel Model of the Social Distribution of High School Achievement."

32. D. H. Monk, "Secondary School Size and Curriculum Comprehensiveness," *Economics of Education Review,* vol. 6, no. 2 (1987), pp. 137–50.

33. V. E. Lee, A. S. Bryk, and J. B. Smith, *The Organization of Effective Secondary Schools,* vol. 19: *Review of Research in Education* (Washington: American Educational Research Association, 1993).

34. V. E. Lee and J. B. Smith, "High School Size: Which Works Best, and for Whom?" *Educational Evaluation and Policy Analysis,* vol. 19, no. 3 (1997), pp. 205–27.

35. II. M. Kleibard, *The Struggle for the American Curriculum 1893–1958* (New York: Routledge, 1986).

36. Bryk, Lee, and Holland, *Catholic Schools and the Common Good.*

37. Bryk, Lee, and Holland, *Catholic Schools and the Common Good*; and J. S. Coleman, T. Hoffer, and S. Kilgore, *High School Achievement: Public, Catholic, and Private Schools Compared* (Basic Books, 1982).

38. B. L. Schneider and D. T. Slaughter, "Educational Choice for Blacks in Urban Private Secondary Schools," in L. Weiss, ed., *Class, Race, and Gender in American Education* (State Univeristy of New York Press, 1988), pp. 294–310; and L. S. Lewis and L. A. Wanner, "Private Schooling and the Status Attainment Process," *Sociology of Education,* vol. 52 (1979), pp. 99–112.

39. V. E. Lee and H. M. Marks, "Who Goes Where? Choice of Single-Sex and Coeducational Independent Secondary Schools," *Sociology of Education,* vol. 65 (1992), pp. 226–52.

40. V. E. Lee and others, "Sector Differences in High School Coursetaking: A Private or Catholic School Effect?" *Sociology of Education,* vol. 71, no. 4 (1998), pp. 314–35.

41. We are performing similar analyses with these data.

42. These data include more than 300,000 students who took both the SAT and American College Test (ACT). With both of these measures, dual test takers are counted only once.

43. School locations were determined using the following criteria: Urban = central city of a Consolidated Metropolitan Statistical Area (CMSA) or Metropolitan Statistical Area (MSA). Suburban = an incorporated area within a CMSA or MSA designated urban, but not a central city. Town = incorporated area with a population greater than twenty-five hundred located outside a CMSA or MSA. Rural = an incorporated place designated as rural by the Bureau of the Census.

44. One challenge we faced analyzing the SAT student files in combination with the Common Core Data (CCD) and Private School Universe Survey (PSS) was the lack of a school-average socioeconomic status (SES) measure. The only measure available on the CCD is the percent of students receiving free or reduced-price lunch—a rough measure of SES at best, especially at the high school level. Furthermore, the free or reduced-price lunch measure is available only on the CCD, meaning we would have the information only for public schools. Because HLM utilizes a listwise approach to missing data at the school level, we would have been forced to restrict our analyses to only public schools. However, a substantial body of literature suggests that the relationship between race and achievement varies by school sector. This led us to construct a school-level aggregate from the student-level SES variable. There are certainly problems with this decision. First, the SAT takers in each school are more likely to be nonminority and socially advantaged. Second, in some cases, school-average SES is represented by as few as five students. Nevertheless, the resulting measure is normally distributed and psychometrically sound (if not conceptually ideal).

45. A. S. Bryk and S. W. Raudenbush, *Hierarchical Linear Models: Applications and Data Analysis Methods* (Newbury Park, Calif.: Sage Publications, 1992); and S. W. Raudenbush and others, *HLM5: Hierarchial Linear and Nonlinear Modeling* (Chicago: Scientific Software International, 2000).

46. R. Rosenthal and R. Rosnow, *Essentials of Behavioral Research: Methods and Data Analysis* (McGraw-Hill, 1984).

47. Lee and Smith, "High School Size."

48. David Card and A. Abigail Payne, "School Finance Reform, the Distribution of School Spending, and the Distribution of SAT Scores," Working Paper 6766 (Cambridge, Mass.: National Bureau of Economic Research, 1998).

49. Card and Payne, "School Finance Reform."

50. See, for example, the discussion of the choice of control function in Card and Payne, "School Finance Reform."

51. Sandra Black, "Do Better Schools Matter? Parental Valuation of Elementary Education," *Quarterly Journal of Economics*, vol. 14, no. 2 (1999), pp. 577–99; Lisa Barrow and Cecilia E. Rouse, "Using Market Valuation to Assess Public School Spending," Working Paper 9054 (Cambridge, Mass.: National Bureau of Economic Research, 2002); and David N. Figlio and Maurice E. Lucas, "What's in a Grade? School Report Cards and House Price," Working Paper (University of Florida, Department of Economics, 2002).

52. The classic papers in this area focus on comparing nonexperimental and experimental regression estimates using data from job-training demonstrations. See Robert LaLonde, "Evaluating the Econometric Evaluations of Training Programs with Experimental Data," *American Economic Review*, vol. 76, no. 4 (1986), pp. 604–20; and James J. Heckman and V. Joseph Hotz, "Choosing among Alternative Nonexperimental Methods for Estimating the Impact of Social Programs: The Case of Manpower Training," *Journal of the American Statistical Association*, vol. 84, no. 408 (1989), pp. 862–74. However, work that draws on data from a housing voucher experiment also shows that even richly specified regression models

that control for past values of the outcome variable of interest, as in the value added approach that is common within education, may yield estimates that are severely biased. See Jens Ludwig, "Neighborhood Effects and Self-Selection," Working Paper (Georgetown University, Public Policy Institute, 2000).

53. Donald Rubin, "Using Multivariate Matched Sampling and Regression Adjustment to Control Bias in Observational Studies," *Journal of the American Statistical Association*, vol. 74 (1979), pp. 318–28; Paul Rosenbaum and Donald Rubin, "The Central Role of the Propensity Score in Observational Studies for Causal Effects," *Biometrika*, vol. 70 (1983), pp. 41–55; Rajeev H. Dehejia and Sadek Wahba, "Causal Effects in Nonexperimental Studies: Reevaluating the Evaluation of Training Programs," *Journal of the American Statistical Association*, vol. 94, no. 448 (1999), pp. 1053–62; and Jeffrey Smith and Petra Todd, "Does Matching Overcome LaLonde's Critique of Nonexperimental Methods?" *Journal of Econometrics* (forthcoming).

54. Joshua D. Angrist and Alan Krueger, "Empirical Strategies in Labor Economics," in Orley Ashenfelter and David Card, eds., *The Handbook of Labor Economics*, vol. 3 (New York: North Holland, 1999).

55. For example, see Joshua D. Angrist and Victor Lavy, "Using Maimonides' Rule to Estimate the Effect of Class Size on Student Achievement," *Quarterly Journal of Economics,* vol. 114, no. 2 (1999), pp. 533–75; David N. Figlio and Jens Ludwig, "Sex, Drugs, and Catholic Schools: Private Schooling and Adolescent Non-Market Behaviors," Working Paper 7990 (Cambridge, Mass.: National Bureau of Economic Research, 2000); Joshua D. Angrist and Alan Krueger, "Instrumental Variables and the Search for Identification," *Journal of Economic Perspectives,* vol. 15, no. 4 (2001), pp. 69–87; Brian Jacob, "Accountability, Incentives, and Behavior: The Impact of High-Stakes Testing in the Chicago Public Schools," Working Paper 8968 (Cambridge, Mass.: National Bureau of Economic Research, 2002); Brian Jacob and Lars Lefgren, "Remedial Education and Student Achievement: A Regression-Discontinuity Analysis," Working Paper 8918 (Cambridge, Mass.: National Bureau of Economic Research, 2002); and Brian Jacob and Lars Lefgren, "The Impact of Teacher Training on Student Achievement: Quasi-Experimental Evidence from School Reform Efforts in Chicago," Working Paper 8916 (Cambridge, Mass.: National Bureau of Economic Research, 2002).

56. Thomas D. Cook, "Science Phobia: Why Education Researchers Reject Randomized Experiments," *Education Next* (Fall 2001), pp. 63–68, quote on p. 68.

57. Jeremy D. Finn and Charles M. Achilles, "Answers and Questions about Class Size: A Statewide Experiment," *American Education Research Journal*, vol. 28 (1990), pp. 557–77; Frederick Mosteller, "The Tennessee Study of Class Size in the Early School Grades," *The Future of Children: Critical Issues for Children and Families*, vol. 5 (1995), pp. 113–27; and Alan Krueger, "Experimental Estimates of Education Production Functions," *Quarterly Journal of Economics*, vol. 114, no. 2 (1999), pp. 497–532.

58. Cecilia E. Rouse, "Private School Vouchers and Student Achievement: An Evaluation of the Milwaukee Parental Choice Program," *Quarterly Journal of Economics*, vol. 113, no. 2 (1998), pp. 553–602.

59. Edward B. Fiske and Helen F. Ladd, *When School Compete: A Cautionary Tale* (Brookings, 2000).

60. Gary Solon, "Intergenerational Income Mobility in the U.S.," *American Economic Review*, vol. 82, no. 3 (1992), pp. 393–408; and David J. Zimmerman, "Regression toward Mediocrity in Economic Stature," *American Economic Review*, vol. 82, no. 3 (1992), pp. 409–29.

61. See Susan Mayer, *What Money Can't Buy: Family Income and Children's Life Chances* (Harvard University Press, 1997).

62. Meredith Phillips and others, "Family Background, Parenting Practices, and the Black-White Test Score Gap," in Christopher Jencks and Meredith Phillips, eds., *The Black-White Test Score Gap* (Brookings, 1998), pp. 103–48.

63. Jens Ludwig, Helen F. Ladd, and Greg J. Duncan, "Urban Poverty and Educational Outcomes," in William Gale and Janet Rothenberg Pack, eds., *Brookings-Wharton Papers on Urban Affairs* (Brookings, 2001), pp. 147–201.

64. Paul Jargowsky, *Poverty and Place* (New York: Russell Sage, 1997).

65. Edward L. Glaeser and Jacob L. Vigdor, *Racial Segregation in the 2000 Census: Promising News* (Brookings, Center on Urban and Metropolitan Policy, 2001).

Too Little Too Late: American High Schools in an International Context

WILLIAM H. SCHMIDT

In recent years, increasing attention has focused on the inadequate preparation of American students for future jobs as well as for life in general. This complaint is heard from both industry and higher education. The most recent National Assessment of Educational Progress (NAEP) reports continue to remind the public that a large majority of twelfth graders are below proficiency in most subject matter areas, including mathematics, science, U.S. history, civics, and geography. From 70 to 90 percent of high school seniors scored below the proficient level on each of these subject matter tests.[1] The results are somewhat better only in reading, with 60 percent of the students scoring below the proficient level.[2] The NAEP Governing Board defined proficiency as the level that all students should reach. In mathematics and science, the proportion of students below the proficient level was estimated to be around 80 percent.[3]

The concern of this paper is with the proficiency of U.S. twelfth graders in the areas of quantitative and scientific literacy. Developing proficiency in these two areas is certainly critical to the future success of graduating seniors, be they university-bound or headed immediately into the work force. For those who pursue higher education, mathematical competency in particular often operates as a gatekeeper, controlling not only entry to the more prestigious colleges and universities but also to the courses of study that are

I would like to acknowledge Richard Houang, Leland Cogan, and HsingChi Wang, senior researchers at Michigan State University, for their intellectual contributions to this article. This work was funded by the National Science Foundation through a grant (REC–9550107). However, I alone assume responsibility for the results and interpretation presented here.

available to students once admitted. As a result, a student's mathematical competencies ultimately influence even his or her choice of careers.

Given the increasingly complex and technological nature of the economy, the work force implications are also profound. What was once considered knowledge for the elite has now become essential for all. Many jobs in the new economy demand technological knowledge and skills based on the disciplines of mathematics, physics, biology, and chemistry.[4] For example, the U.S. economy's information technology sector has accounted for nearly one-third of the nation's economic growth over the past few years (before the most recent economic slowdown) and employed some five million people. Twenty percent of those five million were foreign-educated and came to the United States specifically to fill an unmet need in this sector because of inadequacies in basic mathematics and science in the U.S. education system.[5]

Even old-line industrial production no longer runs primarily on low-level skills and a strong back. Ever more increasingly, it involves computers, robotics, and other high-tech innovations, all dependent on a work force with a sophisticated knowledge base in mathematics and science.[6] Machine tooling is a good example. That work is now done by computer-numerically-controlled (CNC) manufacturing technology. Individuals operating this machinery need mathematical training that includes knowledge of calculus.[7] A Midwest think tank has estimated that 60 percent of the new jobs demand skills possessed by 20 percent of the current work force.[8]

Data sources other than NAEP also document the low levels of competency of high school graduates in both mathematics and science. Industry has responded by investing large amounts of money in reeducating the work force, not so much for specific jobs, but in basic literacy issues including numerical and scientific principles.[9]

Cross-national comparisons of the United States with other countries also provide useful data. Most recently, in 1995, the Third International Mathematics and Science Study (TIMSS) measured mathematics and science literacy of end-of-secondary-school students in twenty-two countries. The specialized knowledge of students taking more advanced courses in mathematics and physics was also tested.[10]

For both general literacy of all seniors and more technical knowledge for mathematics and physics majors, the performance of the United States was poor by comparison to other countries. U.S. students statistically outperformed only two countries, Cyprus and South Africa, on the literacy test.[11] This was true in both mathematics and science. U.S. fourth graders (also measured in TIMSS) were statistically second to only one country in science.[12] One implication of this downward trend in relative standing is that the causative factors most likely lie with the educational system and not with the nature of the students or associated demographics.

NAEP, TIMSS, and state assessment results have prompted numerous states to introduce additional high school graduation requirements centering on course taking as a way of addressing the problem. These requirements vary from minimum course requirements (such as all students must take algebra I and biology to graduate) to specifying the number of such mathematics and science courses required for a high school diploma (such as three years each of both mathematics and science without necessarily specifying which courses). Some states have also introduced mandatory high school graduation tests, which students must pass to receive their diploma. The key question from a policy perspective is whether such policy levers are the right ones to address the problems of poor student performance.

This paper traces the development of mathematical and scientific literacy over grade levels and examines the relationship of high school course taking to twelfth-grade literacy in mathematics and science. These issues are explored in an international context using data from TIMSS.

TIMSS

TIMSS, which was sponsored by the International Association for the Evaluation of Educational Achievement (IEA), is the largest cross-national study ever undertaken. A random sample of twelfth graders in each country (as end-of-secondary-school students were defined in the United States and in most other countries) took the literacy test, which included topics from both mathematics and science. The literacy test was not designed to measure what was taught and learned in the final year of secondary school. Instead it was designed to measure the cumulative knowledge of the students over all their years of schooling. In fact, it was explicitly designed not to measure what students were studying in their last year of secondary school—the point at which the test was given. As the authors responsible for the development of the literacy test wrote, "The role of the literacy study within TIMSS, therefore, is to ask whether school leavers can remember the mathematics and science they have been taught and can therefore apply this knowledge to the challenges of life beyond school."[13]

In addition to the literacy tests, twelfth-grade students completed questionnaires about their social class backgrounds, home environment, attitudes about school, future plans and aspirations, and course taking while in high school.

Scientific Literacy

Although not designed as a curriculum-based test, the TIMSS literacy test, in its development, was informed by the curriculum analysis done in TIMSS.[14] The question addressed here is, From which grade level (defined from an international point of view) is the content contained in this literacy test primarily drawn? Another way to phrase the question is, How difficult is the test in terms of the grade level at which the majority of the topics contained on the test are intended to be taught by most countries?

To address this issue, data from the analysis of country content standards for each grade were used. Using the content standards document for a country, ministry officials and curriculum specialists were asked to identify for each of forty-four topics in mathematics and seventy-nine topics in science the grade levels at which the topic was introduced, focused on, and completed.[15]

From these data each mathematics and science topic in each country was assigned a grade level. This index was derived as a weighted average of the grade level at which the greatest amount of instructional coverage was intended to occur and the grade level at which the topic was first introduced. This value was then averaged over all the TIMSS countries that provided data.

This index averaged over countries is considered a measure of international topic difficulty. Larger values for a topic indicate that the topic was typically meant to be introduced and covered most extensively at higher grades and therefore is more likely a difficult topic. Similarly, topics with smaller index values were typically dealt with in the earlier grades.

For the literacy test, the index value for each topic contained on the test was weighted by the proportion of items covering the topic. The weighted index values were summed over all topics on the test. This resulted in a value of 7.6 and 5.7 for the science and mathematics literacy tests, respectively. In other words, the TIMSS literacy test is mostly made up of content that was meant to be taught primarily at fifth through seventh grade across the "TIMSS world."

For some countries the intended grade level for the mathematics test content is even lower. For Singapore and South Korea, the number one and two countries in ranked performance at eighth grade (neither of which participated in the end-of-secondary-school portion of the study), the content difficulty index of the mathematics literacy tests was 5.0 and 4.8, respectively. The content difficulty index for each country is derived by using the country-specific values for each topic and then is weighted in a similar fashion as described for the overall international index.

In science, the top two countries at eighth grade were Singapore and the Czech Republic. Using their curricula to define the difficulty of the science literacy test resulted in values of 6.1 and 5.5, respectively. The TIMSS literacy test was not that difficult, at least by international standards. Difficulty is defined here in terms of intended content coverage; that is, content difficulty and not the more traditional psychometric characteristic of item difficulty based on student responses. The latter has at least as much to do with the cognitive demands of the item as with the complexity of the content from a disciplinary point of view.

The TIMSS test administered at the end of eighth grade (Population 2 in TIMSS parlance) was subjected to the same type of content analysis.[16] The international content difficulty index of the mathematics test content was intended to be covered at fifth grade (5.6) and the content of the science test was intended to be covered at seventh grade (7.5). As seen from these results, the intended coverage of the topics making up the eighth-grade test is about the same grade level as the Population 3 literacy test.

I do not necessarily intend this analysis to be critical of the TIMSS literacy test. It was developed through an internationally collaborative process. As U.S. states struggle with the definition of the content specifications for high school exit examinations, the resolution is often to aim the test at content covered in grades seven, eight, and nine (California is an example). Considering the content difficulty of the literacy test is critical when viewing the achievement results.

Literacy as Realized

The U.S. performance at twelfth grade completes a pattern of decline in the relative ranking of the United States from fourth grade on. In tables 1 and 2, data on the countries' rankings are presented for the mathematics and

Table 1. Results from the TIMSS Twelfth-Grade Mathematics Literacy Assessment

Nation	Average	Standard error
With average scores significantly higher than the United States		
Netherlands	69.6	(0.9)
Sweden	67.1	(0.8)
Denmark	65.7	(0.8)
Switzerland	64.0	(1.4)
Iceland	63.4	(0.5)
New Zealand	62.4	(1.0)
Australia	61.8	(2.1)
Norway	61.6	(0.8)
France	61.0	(1.0)
Canada	60.4	(0.8)
Slovenia	60.2	(1.8)
Austria	60.1	(1.1)
Germany	54.9	(1.3)
Hungary	52.7	(0.7)
With average score not significantly different from the United States		
Italy	50.7	(1.3)
Russian Federation	49.7	(1.5)
Lithuania	49.1	(1.6)
United States	49.0	(0.9)
Czech Republic	47.0	(2.8)
Israel	45.5	(2.9)
With average score significantly lower than the United States		
Cyprus	42.0	(1.1)
South Africa	26.0	(1.9)
Average of twenty-two countries	55.6	(1.5)

Note: TIMSS = Third International Mathematics and Science Study.

science literacy tests, respectively. Unlike rankings reported elsewhere, the metric for the comparison is average percent correct averaged over all the literacy items. These percentages can be interpreted in two ways. First, they are estimates of the percent of the population of students that can pass a typical item on the literacy test. Second, they are estimates of the percent of items on the literacy test that a typical student can pass (in the sampled population).[17]

For example, the international averages for mathematics and science indicate that a typical student in the TIMSS world, regardless of country

Table 2. Results from the TIMSS Twelfth-Grade Science Literacy Assessment

Nation	Average	Standard error
With average scores significantly higher than the United States		
Netherlands	66.4	(0.8)
Sweden	66.1	(0.7)
Iceland	64.2	(0.4)
Norway	63.1	(0.7)
New Zealand	61.8	(0.9)
Canada	61.5	(0.5)
Australia	60.8	(1.8)
Switzerland	60.1	(1.0)
Slovenia	58.6	(1.4)
Austria	58.2	(1.0)
Denmark	57.9	(0.7)
With average score not significantly different from the United States		
Germany	55.1	(0.9)
France	54.1	(1.2)
Czech Republic	53.1	(1.8)
United States	53.0	(0.7)
Russian Federation	52.6	(1.1)
Italy	49.6	(1.0)
Israel	47.8	(2.3)
With average score significantly lower than the United States		
Hungary	50.0	(0.5)
Lithuania	48.8	(1.1)
Cyprus	43.0	(0.7)
South Africa	29.9	(1.9)
Average of twenty-two countries	55.3	(1.2)

Note: TIMSS = Third International Mathematics and Science Study.

membership, could pass about half of the literacy items in both mathematics and science. From the literacy point of view, the international mean indicates that about half of the students in the TIMSS world could pass a typical item defining TIMSS mathematics or science literacy.

In the top-achieving country in both mathematics and science—the Netherlands—more than two-thirds of its students could pass a typical literacy item by the end of secondary school. For the United States, the comparable number is only one-half of the students. The statistical implication is that the United States has essentially the largest variation possible on a typical literacy item.

The difficulty in interpreting the above analysis is that a typical literacy item has little meaning if the goal of the analysis is to characterize literacy more precisely; that is, as literacy in different content areas of mathematics and science. In mathematics, such differences can be estimated in six more specific content areas: proportionality; functions and equations; data; measurement units; fractions and decimals; and perimeter, area, and volume.

The estimated proportion of U.S. students who can answer a typical item correctly in each subcategory varied from a low of 35 percent in perimeter, area, and volume to a high of 60 percent for measurement units. Although the relative ranking of the United States with respect to other countries is essentially the same in both cases, from a literacy point of view it is important to note that a majority (60 percent) of U.S. high school senior students could answer correctly a typical TIMSS item in the category of measurement units. The interpretation of this is heavily dependent on both the domain definition and the difficulties associated with the items used to operationalize the domain. If the domain and associated item difficulties represent a reasonable definition of what all students should know to be considered literate, then the 60 percent figure has important implications, as compared with a much smaller percentage (such as 35 percent for perimeter, area, and volume). However, because the item difficulties are not necessarily the same from one domain to the others, comparisons across domains are both tricky and risky.

In science, only three content areas can be estimated: energy and physical processes, environment and pollution, and human biology and health. Of these three, U.S. twelfth graders did best in human biology; 66 percent were able to answer correctly a typical item in this domain. They did most poorly in the physics domain.

The most informative analysis in determining what, from a literacy point of view, U.S. students know is to move to the items themselves. Assuming each item represents something important for students to know, one way to answer the question of U.S. literacy in an international context is to estimate the number of items for which a majority of the students in a country have answered the item correctly. If a 70 percent criterion is used—that is, more than 70 percent of the students in a country were able to answer at least 70 percent of the test items correctly—then no country's end-of-secondary-school students as a whole achieved literacy.

Tables 3 and 4 indicate these results for different criteria in terms of the percent of students who answer the item correctly for each of mathematics

Table 3. Number of Countries with Twelfth-Grade Students Passing More Than 70 Percent of the Mathematics Literacy Items at Different Item Difficulties

Country	Average item difficulty	Number of items	Percent of items with item difficulty				
			p > 0.9	*p > 0.8*	*p > 0.7*	*p > 0.6*	*p > 0.5*
Australia	61.8	45	0	9	44	58	67
Austria	60.1	45	2	11	38	58	73
Canada	60.4	45	0	11	36	56	67
Cyprus	42.0	43	0	0	9	16	37
Czech Republic	47.0	45	2	2	7	27	44
Denmark	65.7	45	2	20	53	69	78
France	61.0	45	0	18	44	64	71
Germany	54.9	45	0	4	20	49	67
Hungary	52.7	40	0	0	18	30	65
Iceland	63.4	45	2	16	47	62	76
Israel	45.5	45	0	0	2	18	44
Italy	50.7	45	0	2	9	36	53
Lithuania	49.1	45	0	2	9	29	56
Netherlands	69.6	45	9	38	58	71	80
New Zealand	62.4	45	2	11	44	53	69
Norway	61.6	45	0	9	36	60	73
Russian Federation	49.7	45	0	2	11	27	53
South Africa	26.0	45	0	0	0	0	4
Sweden	67.1	45	2	22	51	67	84
Switzerland	64.0	45	0	13	44	71	80
United States	49.0	45	0	2	7	36	56
Slovenia	60.2	45	2	4	38	60	67
Average	55.6	45	0	2	20	47	64
Number of countries with at least	50%	None	None	3	12	18
x percent of the items meeting	60%	None	None	None	8	14
the criterion	70%	None	None	None	2	8

and science. It is only when the criterion drops to 60 percent and only in mathematics that two countries emerge. In both Switzerland and the Netherlands, the majority of children (more than 60 percent) could answer at least 70 percent of the mathematics literacy items correctly. If the criterion drops still further to a simple majority (more than 50 percent) that passes an item, then eight countries in mathematics and five in science have achieved literacy. The United States is not among the eight or the five countries. Only five of the twenty-two countries have end-of-secondary-school students who are literate by this definition in both mathematics and science.

Table 4. Countries with Twelfth-Grade Students Passing More Than 70 Percent of the Science Literacy Items at Different Item Difficulties

Country	Average item difficulty	Number of items	Percent of items with item difficulty				
			$p > 0.9$	$p > 0.8$	$p > 0.7$	$p > 0.6$	$p > 0.5$
Australia	60.8	36	3	19	33	58	67
Austria	58.2	36	6	17	33	50	64
Canada	61.5	36	6	25	31	58	69
Cyprus	43.0	36	3	6	14	22	36
Czech Republic	53.1	36	11	17	22	42	53
Denmark	57.9	36	6	17	28	50	64
France	54.1	34	3	9	24	44	56
Germany	55.1	36	6	11	28	47	58
Hungary	50.0	34	6	12	15	32	50
Iceland	64.2	36	14	28	47	64	72
Israel	47.8	36	0	3	14	28	47
Italy	49.6	36	3	6	22	39	50
Lithuania	48.8	36	0	8	17	33	50
Netherlands	66.4	36	11	31	42	61	83
New Zealand	61.8	36	0	19	44	61	69
Norway	63.1	36	8	25	39	61	72
Russian Federation	52.6	36	3	8	22	39	56
South Africa	29.9	36	0	0	3	11	17
Sweden	66.1	36	14	33	39	64	81
Switzerland	60.1	35	3	17	37	51	71
United States	53.0	36	3	11	28	44	56
Slovenia	58.6	35	11	29	46	46	54
Average	55.3	36	3	11	25	42	64
Number of countries with at least 50 percent of the items meeting the criterion			None	None	None	10	19
Number of countries with at least 60 percent of the items meeting the criterion			None	None	None	5	10
Number of countries with at least 70 percent of the items meeting the criterion			None	None	None	None	5

Common Items

Common items appear on the TIMSS Population 2 (eighth-grade) test and the twelfth-grade literacy test. Their original presence was for psychometric purposes (scaling), but they can be used to ask the question of how the cohort of eighth graders performed relative to the cohort of twelfth graders, at least on some of the literacy items. The generalizations from this analysis are severely restricted and must be limited to the ten to fourteen

Figure 1. TIMSS Country Averages for Common Mathematics Items

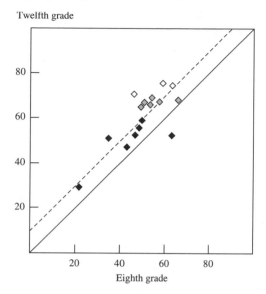

Twelfth grade

Eighth grade

Note: TIMSS = Third International Mathematics and Science Study.

items that were involved. Figures 1 and 2 represent graphically these results and indicate that on average countries only differed by about 10 percent higher scores in twelfth grade compared with eighth grade in terms of the percent of students who could correctly answer an item.

Little learning related to literacy as defined by the TIMSS common items has taken place, at least at the cohort level. In other words, what the cohort of students knew at the end of secondary school in science and mathematics was much the same as what they knew at the end of eighth grade. This was true at least as the ten common mathematics and fourteen common science items represented literacy. This assertion requires that an assumption be made about the two TIMSS cohorts. TIMSS data are not longitudinal in the traditional sense. The eighth- and twelfth-grade cohorts of students in 1995 were assumed to be similar, with the only major differences being four additional years of schooling and four more years of maturity. With this assumption, longitudinal cohort comparisons become reasonable.

Consider one of the common items on the concept of measurement units (see figure 3). This item was also present on the fourth-grade (Population 1) TIMSS test. The solid symbols and lines represent the grades at which the

Figure 2. TIMSS Country Averages for Common Science Items

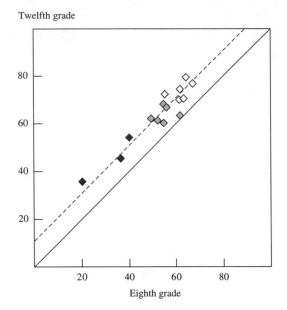

Note: TIMSS = Third International Mathematics and Science Study.

item was given. The outlined symbols and lines are linear extrapolations based on the grade levels at which the item was administered. For the United States, the 10 percent gain from eighth to twelfth grade is consistent with the average increase. Both the international average and the results for the Czech Republic, one of the highest-performing countries at eighth grade, indicate little or no gain from eighth to twelfth grade. The data for this item are consistent with the general pattern described for the ten common items.

How are the data for the measurement units item representative of the literacy test as a whole? The answer to this question cannot directly be determined because the literacy test was only administered at the twelfth grade. An idea of what the answer might be comes from additional data collected in the United States but based on the eighth-grade test instead of the twelfth-grade literacy test. The topic difficulty of that test was essentially the same as that for the literacy test.

In a set of seven Michigan districts, the eighth-grade TIMSS test was administered in grades seven through twelve to some twelve thousand students as a part of a special reform effort undertaken in 2001. Data were pro-

Figure 3. Example of a TIMSS Mathematics Common Item

L12. Four children measured the width of a room by counting how many paces it took them to cross it. The chart shows their measurements.

Who has the longest pace?

A. Stephen

B. Erlane

C. Ana

D. Carlos

Name	Number of paces
Stephen	10
Erlane	8
Ana	9
Carlos	7

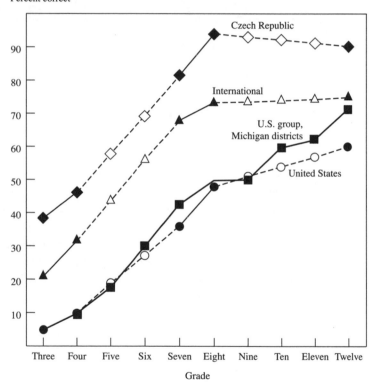

Note: TIMSS = Third International Mathematics and Science Study.

Figure 4. Total Score for TIMSS Population 2 Assessment across Grades Seven to Twelve

Percent correct

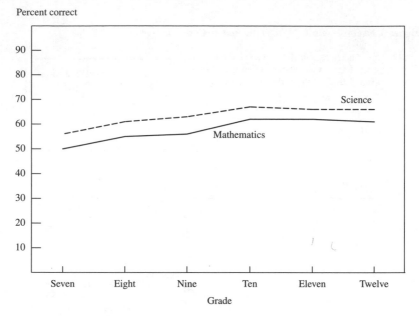

Grade

Note: TIMSS = Third International Mathematics and Science Study.

vided like those in figure 3 but not for the United States as a whole and not for an item on the literacy test. The data were the percent correct at each grade level averaged over all items on the eighth-grade test. In these Michigan districts, the performance of the students greatly mirrored that of the United States as a whole at those grades for which a national sample existed (grades three, four, seven, eight, and twelve). Thus the use of the data as representative of the nation, at least in terms of seventh- to twelfth-grade achievement on the eighth grade TIMSS test, may not be unreasonable. However, this must remain an untested assumption.

Figure 4 shows the test results and indicates a pattern similar to that in figure 3. The implications of figures 3 and 4 call into question the effectiveness of U.S. high schools at least in terms of further developing literacy in mathematics and science. A subtler implication concerns the importance of the middle school curriculum in developing basic literacy. The importance of the middle school curriculum and the highly repetitive, incoherent, and not very demanding nature of the U.S. middle school curriculum have been discussed elsewhere.[18]

High School Course Taking

The aggregate data results for the United States raise the question as to the relationship of high school course taking to basic quantitative and scientific literacy. The TIMSS data presented thus far permit generalizations relative only to cohorts of students and not to individual students. They are also derived from a literacy test based on content typically taught in the middle grades and not in high school.

The implication of the first of these two caveats is that it would be inappropriate based on these data to infer that no individual student acquires a greater degree of literacy in mathematics and science while attending high school. Unfortunately, the issue of learning or change from the eighth grade to the twelfth grade and its relationship to course taking cannot be directly addressed because the TIMSS data are not longitudinal at the individual student level.

It is also inappropriate to interpret the aggregate data results as implying that cohorts of students exiting high school possess no greater knowledge in mathematics or science than cohorts entering high school. This is only true for the mathematics and science topics found on a literacy test based on middle school content. For example, a cohort exiting high school clearly has more knowledge about calculus than does a cohort entering high school, simply because some students take calculus in high school.

The question of the relationship of high school course taking and achievement has been extensively explored over the past two decades. These studies show that the academic level of the courses taken and the quantity of courses taken within the discipline are both positively related to achievement.[19] The findings are unambiguous. The particular question addressed here is whether such a relationship exists for an internationally defined literacy test centered around middle school content.

The major findings of TIMSS also point to course taking as a likely factor related to student performance. Curriculum at the eighth grade is important both to country differences and to differences across classrooms within countries, especially within the United States.[20] TIMSS reports have also indicated how much more coherent, focused, and rigorous the curriculum is of the top-achieving countries, especially during the middle grades when compared with that of the United States.[21]

At the high school level the new curriculum issue that arises is selection bias. Put simply, it is the question of who takes what courses. In most U.S.

high schools, students are permitted to construct their own curriculum either by their own choices or through the influence of academic counselors. This is ostensibly done to recognize student differences in ability, life plans, and motivations. The result has led to the characterization of U.S. high schools as "shopping malls."[22] Students are not required to take specific sequences of courses but can pick and choose among alternatives, some of which might make sense sequentially while others might not. This approach assumes that such choices would be made rationally.

This aspect of the high school curriculum serves as a likely conjecture for the lack of a cohort gain in test results. If high school course taking reflects a somewhat random process across students within a cohort, then in the aggregate little or no growth in learning is likely to take place. This could be true even if, at the individual student level, course taking was related to twelfth-grade performance on the literacy test.

Several studies have characterized high school course taking in mathematics and science and have found great variability.[23] In one study, such course-taking patterns were somewhat unrelated to the traditional school tracks. The results indicated many students taking the more advanced course sequences were not in the college preparatory track.[24]

U.S. Course-Taking Patterns as Estimated from TIMSS

How many U.S. students take a mathematics course in their final year of high school? How does this compare with other countries? Slightly less than two-thirds of U.S. students took a mathematics course in their senior year (without regard to what that course was). This should not be taken to indicate the percent of U.S. high school students who take four years of mathematics, because some students take their only high school mathematics course as seniors. This estimate is low by international standards. In several countries, essentially all students—even those in the vocational tracks—take some type of mathematics course in their last year of secondary school. Only four other countries have a slightly lower percent of their students taking a mathematics course in their last year of secondary school than the United States.

In many of the TIMSS countries, all secondary students—no matter what track they are in—are required to take two, three, or four years of mathematics. The mathematics content that students study in a given year is common at least within a specific track.[25] Students have little choice, as usually only one mathematics or science course is offered per year for each track. Student choice exists only for some tracks in terms of whether to take an additional year of mathematics or science.

For the United States, which does not have such commonly sequenced requirements, the nature of the course is probably a more important indicator than some measure of quantity. Quantity in the United States, unlike in other countries, does not have any generalized meaning. For example, in U.S. middle schools (grades six through eight), different tracks representing different mathematics content are prevalent even though all students are taking three years of mathematics.[26] Those content distinctions have been shown to be related to achievement.[27]

In science, different courses are also available in the middle grades, and again it becomes important to know that not only virtually all middle grade students have three years of science but also what the science content is for those courses. For example, the curriculum for some middle school students but not others includes physical science.

Such differences in content exposure at the eighth grade were related to cross-national differences in achievement gain. In science, differences in content coverage accounted for as much as 70 percent of the variance across countries for some topics. For mathematics, the R^2 statistic ranged from around 10 percent to as much as 40 percent of the cross-country variation in gain for different tested topics.[28]

All of this implies that the number of courses taken is probably not a good indication of course taking relative to achievement. As a result, what follows focuses on the level or nature of the course taking, not the quantity. The course-taking behavior of U.S. students can be examined in many ways. I choose not to explore the courses taken in isolation from each other but as a pattern across all four areas—mathematics, physics, chemistry, and biology. I do so for substantive reasons: The three science disciplines are interrelated in terms of content, especially as new discoveries are incorporated into the curriculum; and mathematics serves as the language for all three sciences, especially as they move beyond their more descriptive aspects.

One could hypothesize, based on the literature as well as on the rhetoric coming from states and districts, that one of the most common course-taking patterns would be at least three years of mathematics and at least three years of science for college-bound high school students. The sequence would be two years of algebra and a course in geometry, as well as one year each of biology, chemistry, and physics.[29]

Less than one-third of all U.S. students take this pattern of courses or a more demanding one over their four years of high school. Even for the category of college preparatory students, which is estimated from the TIMSS data to contain around half of all high school students (55 percent), less than half (40 percent) take this or a more demanding pattern. The estimate drops to 15 percent for the general academic track and only 5 percent for vocational-technical students.

I collapsed the different courses taken into three levels of course taking for each of the four disciplines to achieve some simplicity in describing the myriad of course-taking patterns that existed in the 1994–95 school year. Even this attempt at simplification resulted in seventy-six distinct course-taking patterns (theoretically only eighty-one such patterns are possible).

For mathematics, the three levels chosen were (1) algebra II or less, (2) pre-calculus, analytical geometry, or trigonometry, or (3) calculus, including Advanced Placement (AP) calculus. For each of the sciences, the three levels were: (1) no course taken in the area, (2) the basic introductory course (biology I, physics I, or chemistry I) taken, and (3) a course requiring the introductory level course as a prerequisite, including the AP versions of biology, chemistry, and physics. In all cases the level described the most advanced course taken.

The fact that there are seventy-six different patterns for the combination of mathematics and science levels even at this level of aggregation reflects the absence of clear course standards for U.S. high school students. These data seem consistent with the analogy of the American high school as a "shopping mall." For three-fourths of all students, twelve patterns are needed to characterize their course taking, but for that other 25 percent some additional sixty patterns are necessary. The three most common course patterns were: algebra II or less, no physics, and the introductory chemistry and biology courses (19 percent); the same pattern with no chemistry course (19 percent); and a pattern identical to the first, only the students take an advanced biology course in addition to the introductory biology course (8 percent). This implies that nearly half of all students took no mathematics more advanced than a second course in algebra and absolutely no physics. When this is coupled with the fact that only about 30 percent of eighth-grade students study physical science, the low levels of science literacy are not surprising if literacy includes some basic knowledge in physics.[30]

Presumably the diversity in course taking would be reduced if only the college preparatory students were considered. This hypothesis is based on the notion that college entry requirements would enforce some type of homogeneity. The data on the course patterns taken by students in each of the three tracks are given in table 5. Unfortunately, there still are seventy patterns for this select group. Fifteen different ones were needed to characterize three-fourths of college-bound students. Even for these more academically elite students, large degrees of freedom in course taking were evident. The fact that three of the four most common patterns do not include even a basic physics course would seem to have important implications for literacy among even the college-educated—especially if they do not take a physics course in college.

The most common pattern for college-bound students might be expected to include a pre-calculus course (three or four years of mathematics, depending on whether algebra I was taken in eighth or ninth grade) and an introductory course in each of biology, chemistry, and physics (three years of science not including a general science course). Less than one-third of the college-bound high school seniors in 1995 had taken such a course of studies.

The most common pattern for the general academic track student had no chemistry or physics, only biology and algebra II (or less) taken by around one-fourth of the students. If the general academic track requirement was slightly different—three years of mathematics with a second course in algebra and the same three years of science—then only 15 percent of the students would meet it. Here there are still sixty-four different observed patterns. For the vocational-technical students, a little more direction is evident with forty-seven course-taking patterns. The most common pattern is the same as for the general track, but nearly half (43 percent) of all vocational students take that pattern.

If the college and university community had uniformly declared in the spring of 1995 that it would admit only students who had taken at least a basic introductory course in biology, physics, and chemistry and a pre-calculus or analytical geometry course, then less than 20 percent of the high school class of 1995 would have been eligible. If course taking was completely random across students for the high school class of 1995, then by chance alone 20 percent would be eligible for admission to college. As a result, one cannot rule out that in the aggregate the results would be the same if instead of academic advising or student choice the U.S. educational system simply randomly assigned students to different courses. For those in the college preparatory course of studies, less than 30 percent would have been eligible for college under this criterion.

Table 5. Course-Taking Patterns for the Three High School Tracks

Course-taking pattern	Patterns exhibited by 6 percent or more (percent)	Students (percent)	Number of math, biology, chemistry, physics patterns	Number of patterns describing 75 percent of students in track
General academic program		33.7	64	6
Algebra II, biology, no chemistry, no physics	27.1			
Algebra II, biology, chemistry, no physics	25.2			
Algebra II, advanced biology, chemistry, no physics	8.9			
Vocational/technical		11.6	47	3
Algebra II, biology, no chemistry, no physics	43.1			
Algebra II, biology, chemistry, no physics	17.0			
Algebra II, advanced biology, no chemistry, no physics	16.5			
Algebra II, no biology, no chemistry, no physics	7.4			
College preparatory program		54.7	70	15
Algebra II, biology, chemistry, no physics	14.2			
Algebra II, advanced biology, chemistry, no physics	8.8			
Pre-calculus, biology, chemistry, physics	8.6			
Algebra II, biology, no chemistry, no physics	7.5			

High School Course Taking and Literacy

Is the amazing amount of diversity in course taking related to the mathematical and scientific literacy of the U.S. high school population in TIMSS? Could the almost haphazard nature of the course-taking behavior of American students contribute to the apparent absence of cohort gain over the high school years as evidenced by the aggregate data results?

A regression model was fitted to the U.S. data at the student level relating course taking in mathematics and science to mathematics literacy achievement. This was done while controlling for socioeconomic status (SES) based on such measures as the number of home possessions and parents' education level. Age, gender, ethnicity, and college aspirations were also controlled for in the model.

The results of this analysis are summarized in table 6. The student background variables account for 23.7 percent of the variance in mathematics literacy across students. Adding the course-taking data more than doubles the percent of variance accounted for to 57.5 percent. Clearly differences in student achievement in literacy are related to background characteristics, but even when holding this constant, a significant relationship of achievement to course taking (opportunity to learn) is found. That added effect is slightly larger than that attributed to SES and other background characteristics by themselves.

The model does not control for general mathematical ability or for prior achievement, and, as such, selection bias can account for some of the apparent curriculum effects. Controlling for the large number of student background characteristics should reduce the amount of bias attributable to selection effects. Given that mathematics as a school subject is hierarchical, the high school course taking likely reflects prior content experience as well (such as that found in the middle school).

Interpreting the coefficients of the estimated model is particularly revealing. The way the model is parameterized, the intercept describes the expected achievement of a white male student who is taking calculus together with advanced science courses in physics, chemistry, and biology while still controlling for other factors such as age and SES. This particular parameterization is arbitrary and could be done differently.

Consider course taking in mathematics. Taking nothing more than an algebra I class over the four years of high school would yield a predicted literacy score some 130 points below that of taking calculus, with all else being

Table 6. Models Predicting U.S. Twelfth-Grade Students' TIMSS Mathematics Literacy Score

Parameter	Student background			Curriculum variables		
	Estimate	Standard error	Pr > | t |	Estimate	Standard error	Pr > | t |
Intercept	426.46	8.36	< .0001	582.04	7.49	< .0001
Student's background and college plan						
SES composite	0.94	0.09	< .0001	0.36	0.07	< .0001
Age	−29.35	2.30	< .0001	−13.95	1.75	< .0001
Age square	0.36	1.12	.7470	−0.94	0.84	.2636
Being female	−6.43	2.40	.0073	−7.93	1.80	< .0001
Being American Indian or Alaskan Native	−29.17	6.85	< .0001	−19.37	5.13	.0002
Being black	−81.48	3.81	< .0001	−61.10	2.89	< .0001
Being Hispanic	−39.20	3.88	< .0001	−30.31	2.92	< .0001
Being Asian or Pacific Islander	−11.13	5.45	.0412	−25.58	4.10	< .0001
Being white	0.00	—	—	0.00	—	—
Working	−6.21	5.07	.2204	−1.29	3.80	.7352
Working square	0.28	0.85	.7377	−0.15	0.64	.8128
Plan to major in						
Biological sciences	37.04	6.51	< .0001	6.31	4.96	.2031
Business	13.04	3.25	< .0001	5.01	2.44	.0403
Chemistry	31.45	9.62	.0011	−5.15	7.28	.4797
Computer sciences	21.78	5.28	< .0001	0.81	3.97	.8385
Earth sciences	25.47	9.93	.0104	6.65	7.45	.3723
Engineering	52.84	4.08	< .0001	18.01	3.13	< .0001
Heath occupations	−28.24	5.49	< .0001	−20.50	4.12	< .0001
Heath sciences	23.03	3.40	< .0001	0.79	2.61	.7630
Mathematics	22.91	9.27	.0136	−11.19	6.97	.1087
Physics	79.24	16.83	< .0001	42.38	12.62	.0008

(continued on next page)

the same (a white male student taking advanced courses in each of physics, chemistry, and biology). Looking at the results from the opposite direction, taking (1) geometry or algebra II or both, (2) statistics, or (3) trigonometry or pre-calculus or both in addition to algebra I would imply a predicted gain in literacy of approximately 30, 50, and 80 points, respectively. Again, these results are only suggestive of a general relationship (not necessarily causal) as the predictions assume the current U.S. curricular context.

Even science course taking affects achievement in mathematics literacy but, as might be expected, in a less pronounced fashion. The largest esti-

Table 6. Models Predicting U.S. Twelfth-Grade Students' TIMSS Mathematics Literacy Score *(continued)*

Parameter	Student background			Curriculum variables		
	Estimate	Standard error	Pr > |t|	Estimate	Standard error	Pr > |t|
Courses taken in high school						
Taken general math				−132.44	5.37	<.0001
Taken algebra I				−127.75	4.48	<.0001
Taken geometry				−101.45	3.54	<.0001
Taken algebra II				−100.35	3.38	<.0001
Taken statistics				−79.87	3.44	<.0001
Taken trigonometry				−49.13	5.42	<.0001
Taken pre-calculus				−45.84	3.14	<.0001
Taken calculus				0.00	—	—
Taken no physics or conceptual physics				−38.46	3.85	<.0001
Taken physics I				−11.21	3.86	.0036
Taken physics II or AP physics				0.00	—	—
Taken no biology				−4.95	4.41	.2610
Taken biology				8.42	1.94	<.0001
Taken second year biology, human anatomy, physiology				0.00	—	—
Taken no chemistry				−32.75	3.34	<.0001
Taken chemistry I				−12.59	2.80	<.0001
Taken chemistry II or AP chemistry				0.00	—	—

	R^2	df	Pr > F	R^2	df	Pr > F
Model fit	0.2365	20, 4681	<.0001	0.5747	33, 4668	<.0001

Note: TIMSS = Third International Mathematics and Science Study; SES = socioeconomic status; — = statistically fixed, therefore no defined standard error; AP = Advanced Placement.

mated effects are evident in terms of taking physics and chemistry, in which mathematics plays a more central role. For biology, the effect on mathematics literacy from course taking is negligible or nonexistent.

The background characteristic with the largest impact on literacy is the ethnicity of the student—in particular, being African American.[31] The estimated black-white gap for the TIMSS literacy test holding social class, age, and course taking constant is 60 points. This estimated effect is similar in magnitude to the curricular effect of taking statistics when contrasted with taking only algebra I. The estimated effect of taking calculus over taking only algebra I is more than twice as large as the black-white gap. The estimated curricular effects are as large as or larger than the SES and ethnicity variables. This calls into question those who argue it is the demographic background and not the type of schooling received that makes the largest difference for achievement.[32]

The estimated black-white effect when controlling only for the background variables (for example, SES) is some 20 points higher. So around 25 percent of the black-white difference may be related to differences in course-taking behavior. A closer examination of the course-taking data shows the nature of the differences between white and black students. Approximately half of the white students took pre-calculus or calculus (including analytical geometry and trigonometry). The corresponding number is around 30 percent for black students. Considering only those students who take the calculus course, the gap is even greater—17 percent versus 6 percent.

At the eighth grade what is often called an algebra class is likely not that, considering the type of textbook used. The same situation also might be true at the high school level, and such effects might be more pronounced for schools with high concentrations of minority students.[33] Thus the estimate for African American students taking advanced mathematics courses could be inflated considering the actual content of the course, no matter how it is labeled.

Policy Implications

The U.S. performance on the high school literacy test when contrasted with other countries is poor. This finding is even more striking when one considers that the international topic difficulty of the test is estimated to be only at the fifth- through seventh-grade level. Further, data from a set of districts that administered the eighth-grade TIMSS test at every grade from seventh through twelfth suggest little cohort growth in literacy over the high school years. These conclusions are supported by NAEP data that indicate U.S. high school students do not perform well in mathematics or science.

The TIMSS data show the powerful and strong relationship of curricular content to learning, both across countries and across classrooms within countries, especially in the United States. Much of the poor performance of the United States may be attributed to a poorly constructed curriculum that is not coherent from a disciplinary point of view and not intellectually rigorous from an international point of view. The high school data seem consistent with those results. Not only does the United States continue to drop in relative ranking, but this drop also appears to be related to the nature of the U.S. curriculum. From a policy perspective, however, new issues emerge.

Through the first eight years of schooling, students are exposed to the content their teacher chooses or to whatever content the track to which they are assigned dictates. In high school the tracking continues largely as an outgrowth of what was started in the middle grades. If that were the sole factor determining high school course taking, then there would be some small number of distinct course patterns—certainly not over seventy such patterns, which is what was found.

This observed reality I believe is the result of a policy that grants fourteen- and fifteen-year-olds the right to choose what courses they take. Just as elementary and middle schools have no real national standards in mathematics or science, high schools also have no national standards. Even for the college-bound, there do not appear to be any such standards. The result is a chaotic collection of course-taking patterns simulating a stochastic model in which it is assumed that course taking is a random process.

A take on the famous line from *One Flew Over the Cuckoo's Nest* seems appropriate here as students are put in charge of their own course selections. Choices seem to reflect not a coherent plan of study but a somewhat arbitrary collection of courses, perhaps to meet some vaguely stated requirements such as a stipulation as to the number of courses needed for graduation or college entrance.

The data are clear. Such choices make a difference as to what is achieved in terms of literacy. One could speculate based on the estimated statistical model that, if more students took more demanding courses, the U.S. average literacy test results would be more competitive internationally and the lack of growth across cohorts likely would not be observed. These, however, must remain conjectures given the limitations of the data. Developing a mathematically and scientifically literate society is dependent on a more sensible approach to the high school curriculum. This will not occur by chance or by student choice. I believe this will occur only through a carefully thought-out set of standards; that is, a limited number of course patterns instead of some seventy such patterns, even for those planning to attend college.

Apparently the "splintered vision" about which I have written (with others) not only characterizes the elementary and middle schools in the United-

States but also the high schools.[34] However, here the culprit seems to be the policy that permits choice by those with limited knowledge of how such choices could affect their futures and that fails to clearly stipulate what is important for all students in each of the different tracks to know.

Another policy implication, especially in light of the fact that the U.S. pattern of little or no gain from eighth grade to twelfth grade seems consistent with other countries, is that the middle school curriculum likely is very important in developing a literate society, especially if this curriculum is common for all students. Given earlier TIMSS results that paint the U.S. middle school curriculum as lacking coherence with little rigor and extreme variability in learning opportunities as a consequence of tracking policies, none of this bodes well for elevating the country's literacy in mathematics and science to internationally competitive levels or for reducing the black-white gap in the United States.

Both are critical, and I believe the data are compelling in their message. The future of American children is at stake as possibly is the economic strength of the nation. How much longer can needed talent be imported through manipulation of U.S. visa policies while the country fails to provide a proper education for its own people?

Comment by Iris C. Rotberg

The validity of research depends to a large extent on the validity of the assumptions on which it is based. Some of the assumptions in William H. Schmidt's paper have been tested and found to be accurate. Others have been tested and found to be questionable. For others, little evidence exists one way or the other. Examining the assumptions underlying the paper is useful, therefore, as a basis for interpreting the findings and assessing their implications for public policy. These assumptions also have general relevance because they appear frequently in the education research literature.

I begin with basic assumptions that have been tested and found to be valid. First, students who have studied the material covered by a test will get higher test scores than those who have not. It is difficult to do well on a calculus test if you have never studied calculus. Second, the paper assumes a selection bias—that is, some students are advised, inappropriately, to take less demanding courses. That advice, in turn, reduces the students' potential for high academic achievement and closes options they otherwise might have had. The important point is that schools have a responsibility to offer each child the strongest possible educational experience.

From these well-tested assumptions, the paper moves to a set of assumptions for which there is less support. First, the paper assumes that the Third International Mathematics and Science Study (TIMSS) provides the information needed to draw conclusions about the quality of education in participating countries. The main problem is that Schmidt uses TIMSS data as the basis for his analysis.[35] In my view, TIMSS is so flawed that implications cannot be drawn about the quality of education in any of the participating countries.[36] Rankings of countries in TIMSS are based on simple comparisons of test scores in the final year of secondary school, without any controls for the large differences between participating countries on a wide range of variables. Therefore, it is impossible to learn from the study how variables such as the following affected student selectivity and, in turn, test score rankings: participation and exclusion rates of both schools and students being tested; percent of the age cohort who dropped out of school and therefore did not take the test; percent of students taking advanced assessments; average age and grade of students taking the test; special concentrated programs for different students; practices with respect to the inclusion or exclusion of low-achieving students, language minority students, students with disabilities, apprenticeship programs, and entire regions of the country in the test comparisons; the mix of public and private schools, comprehensive and specialized schools, and academic and vocational schools; tracking and coaching practices; family socioeconomic status (SES); and the consistency between the education program and the test.

Each of these variables can be expected to play a significant role in the extent to which the students taking the test represent a highly select group, not the general student population. The TIMSS study did not conduct a multivariate analysis to provide information about the contribution of each variable to the test score rankings. The variables are so confounded that how any of them, individually or in combination, affected the test scores cannot be determined. The use of these data, therefore, does not contribute either to research knowledge or to informed public policy.

The difficulty of unraveling the TIMSS findings is illustrated by tables 1–3, which show the wide differences between countries on several of the major variables. The tables, which are adapted from data presented in the TIMSS report, also explicitly show that few of the participating countries

Table 1. TIMSS Scores on Assessments of Mathematics and Science General Knowledge, Advanced Mathematics, and Physics

Nation	Average mathematics score	Average science score	Average advanced mathematics score	Average physics score
Australia	522	527	525	518
Austria	518	520	436	435
Canada	519	532	509	485
Cyprus	446	448	518	494
Czech Republic	466	487	469	451
Denmark	547	509	522	534
France	523	487	557	466
Germany	495	497	465	522
Greece	—	—	513	486
Hungary	483	471	—	—
Iceland	534	549	—	—
Italy	476	475	474	—
Latvia	—	—	—	488
Lithuania	469	461	516	—
Netherlands	560	558	—	—
New Zealand	522	529	—	—
Norway	528	544	—	581
Russian Federation	471	481	542	545
Slovenia	512	517	475	523
South Africa	356	349	—	—
Sweden	552	559	512	573
Switzerland	540	523	533	488
United States	461	480	442	423
International average	500	500	501	501

Source: Adapted from data presented in Department of Education, National Center for Education Statistics, *Pursuing Excellence: A Study of U.S. Twelfth-Grade Mathematics and Science Achievement in International Context*, NCES 98–049 (Government Printing Office, 1998), figures 1, 5, 9, and 16.

Note: TIMSS = Third International Mathematics and Science Study. Nations not meeting international sampling and other guidelines are in italics. Canada and France met the guidelines for the advanced mathematics assessment; France and Norway, for the physics assessment. A dash (—) indicates that the nation did not participate in that assessment.

met the international sampling and other guidelines set forth by the TIMSS researchers.

Schmidt uses TIMSS data as the main basis for his findings and recommendations with respect to curriculum. Unfortunately, the study provides no guidance about curriculum or any other component of school systems. It serves, instead, primarily as a Rorschach test that reflects previously held views about U.S. schools.

Second, the paper assumes that the performance of U.S. schools declines from the fourth grade on. I do not know if the performance of U.S. schools

Table 2. TIMSS Sampling Data Participation and Exclusion Rates
Percent

Nation	Mathematics and science general knowledge assessment		Advanced mathematics assessment		Physics assessment	
	Combined participation rates	Exclusion rates	Combined participation rates	Exclusion rates	Combined participation rates	Exclusion rates
Australia	52	6	55	No data	54	No data
Austria	73	18	81	18	81	18
Canada	68	9	77	No data	73	No data
Cyprus	98	22	96	22	96	22
Czech Republic	92	No data	92	No data	92	No data
Denmark	49	2	49	No data	47	No data
France	69	1	77	No data	77	No data
Germany	80	11	78	11	82	11
Greece	—	—	87	No data	87	No data
Hungary	98	0	—	—	—	—
Iceland	74	0	—	—	—	—
Italy	62	30	68	30	77	50
Latvia	—	—	—	—	—	—
Lithuania	85	16	92	16	—	—
Netherlands	49	22	—	—	—	—
New Zealand	81	0	—	—	—	—
Norway	71	4	—	—	83	No data
Russian Federation	90	43	96	43	95	43
Slovenia	42	6	42	No data	43	No data
South Africa	65	0	—	—	—	—
Sweden	82	0	89	No data	89	No data
Switzerland	85	3	87	No data	87	No data
United States	64	4	67	No data	68	No data

Source: Adapted from data presented in Department of Education, National Center for Education Statistics, *Pursuing Excellence: A Study of U.S. Twelfth-Grade Mathematics and Science Achievement in International Context*, NCES 98–049 (Government Printing Office, 1998), tables A1.1, A1.2, and A1.3.

Note: TIMSS = Third International Mathematics and Science Study. The sampling plan established the following protocol for selecting schools and students to participate in the testing: (1) the sample was to be representative of at least 90 percent of students in the total population eligible for the study (that is, exclusion rates should be no greater than 10 percent); (2) the school participation rate without the use of replacement schools should be at least 50 percent; and (3) the combined participation rate (computed by multiplying the school and student rates after replacements) should be at least 75 percent or school and student participation rates each should be 85 percent. Nations not meeting international sampling and other guidelines are in italics. Canada and France met the guidelines for the advanced mathematics assessment; France and Norway, for the physics assessment. "No data" indicates that the nation participated, but the TIMSS report did not provide data on combined participation rates or exclusion rates. A dash (—) indicates that the nation did not participate in that assessment.

Table 3. TIMSS Data on School Completion Rates, Percent of Age Cohort Taking Advanced Subjects, Age and Grade of Participating Students, and Differentiation in Programs

Nation	Percent of twenty-five-to thirty-four-year-olds completing secondary education	Percent taking advanced assessments as proportion of age cohort		Average age of participating students	Grades of participating students	Extensive differentiation in programs for students with differing abilities or interests
		Advanced mathematics	Physics			
Australia	57	16	13	17.7	12	No
Austria	81	33	33	19.1	10–14	Yes
Canada	84	16	14	18.6	12–14	No
Cyprus	No data	9	9	17.7	12	Yes
Czech Republic	91	11	11	17.8	10–13	Yes
Denmark	69	21	3	19.1	12	Yes
France	86	20	20	18.8	11–13	Yes
Germany	89	26	8	19.5	12–13	Yes
Greece	No data	10	10	—	—	No data
Hungary	No data	—	—	17.5	10, 12	Yes
Iceland	No data	14	—	21.2	12–14	Yes
Italy	49	—	—	18.7	11–13	Yes
Latvia	No data	—	3	—	12	No data
Lithuania	No data	3	—	18.1	12	Yes
Netherlands	70	—	—	18.5	11–12	Yes
New Zealand	64	—	—	17.6	11–12	No
Norway	88	—	8	19.5	12	Yes
Russian Federation	No data	2	2	16.9	11	Yes
Slovenia	No data	75	39	18.8	11–12	Yes
South Africa	No data	—	—	20.1	12	No
Sweden	88	16	16	18.9	11–12	Yes
Switzerland	88	14	14	19.8	11–13	Yes
United States	87	14	14	18.1	12	No
International average	78	19	14	18.7	—	—

Source: Adapted from data presented in Department of Education, National Center for Education Statistics, *Pursuing Excellence: A Study of U.S. Twelfth-Grade Mathematics and Science Achievement in International Context*, NCES 98–049 (Government Printing Office, 1998), tables A5.7, A5.12, A5.13, and A5.14.

Note: TIMSS = Third International Mathematics and Science Study. Nations not meeting international sampling and other guidelines are in italics. Canada and France met the guidelines for the advanced mathematics assessment; France and Norway, for the physics assessment. A dash (—) indicates that the nation did not participate in that assessment. "No data" indicates that the nation participated, but the TIMSS report did not provide data on school completion rates or program differentiation.

declines between elementary school and high school, but the test score rankings do not inform the issue. Indeed, the TIMSS report presents data showing that the average age of the students taking the test in each country influences its relative performance between eighth grade and the final year of secondary school. In the general mathematics assessment, five countries ranked higher in the final year than in eighth grade, six (including the United States) ranked lower, and nine maintained their position. However, the TIMSS report points out that the countries that declined had the smallest average age gap between the two grades (3.5 years), whereas those that gained had the largest age gap (5.4 years). In short, the findings are an artifact of the research design: Students in some countries were older and had more years of schooling.

Third, the paper states that "the causative factors" [for the test score rankings] "most likely lie with the educational system and not with the nature of the students or associated demographics." That assumption is not supported by the current study or by the significant body of research that shows a strong relationship between low student achievement and poverty. TIMSS did not collect the data needed to quantify the relationship between student poverty and test scores in the international comparisons. However, Schmidt—after making the statement quoted above—goes on to demonstrate a significant correlation between SES and student achievement based on U.S. data. The countries participating in TIMSS differ substantially in rates of absolute and relative poverty, both of which can be expected to play a major role in the test score rankings. Furthermore, the United States ranks high in relative poverty.[37] Looking at the research literature more broadly, it is difficult to identify any other correlation in educational research that has been so consistent and pronounced as between poverty and low educational achievement. For example, the test score rankings of states on the National Assessment of Educational Progress (NAEP), the rankings of districts within states, or the rankings of schools within districts clearly show that correlation.

That does not mean children from low-income families cannot excel in school. Many overcome the odds and achieve at a high level. But the odds are not on their side, both because of poverty and because the schools they attend receive the fewest resources. Constance Clayton, the former superintendent of the Philadelphia public schools, put it this way: "We must face every day the realities of the unequal hand dealt to our children and to our schools."[38] Curriculum changes will not address these basic educational problems.

Fourth, the paper assumes that test score rankings are valid predictors of both a nation's productivity in science and technology and its economic strength. Student test scores have been used for almost fifty years to explain a variety of perceived crises. In the 1950s and 1960s, following the launch of *Sputnik*, U.S. analysts were concerned that the country might not be able to compete with the Soviet Union in technology. Later, shortages of scientists and engineers were predicted. That crisis was followed by a concern about competing economically with Japan. The rhetoric linked each of the perceived problems to international test score rankings. Yet, the United States has maintained a high level of productivity in science and technology, as measured by basic research, technological advances, and product development. Moreover, the economy has generally been strong, with one of the lowest unemployment rates in the world. Clearly, some U.S. schools have real problems. However, these problems will not be solved by making tenuous links between test score rankings on TIMSS and what the society perceives as its current crisis. Little evidence exists that the rankings of industrialized nations on international test score comparisons predict either a nation's productivity in science and technology or its economic strength.

Fifth, the paper states that "twenty percent of [the] five million [workers in the U.S. information technology sector] were foreign-educated and came to the United States specifically to fill an unmet need in this sector because of inadequacies in basic mathematics and science in the U.S. education system." While high school preparation in mathematics and science always leaves room for improvement, there is little evidence to draw a connection between staffing patterns in technological industries and the quality of curricula in U.S. schools. Do the data support a cause and effect relationship between U.S. schools and the participation of workers who were educated abroad? Is it possible, for example, that shortages of U.S. workers are caused by the fact that U.S. mathematicians prefer to become investment bankers or technology entrepreneurs, where the financial rewards are greater? Or, perhaps, the industries that report shortages are unable to find enough qualified U.S. residents at the salaries they choose to pay. Existing data do not provide evidence to choose among these, or other possible, interpretations.

Finally, the paper assumes that improving curricula and increasing and revising course requirements will address the most important educational problems. Schmidt hypothesizes that "much of the poor performance of the United States may be attributed to a poorly constructed curriculum that is not coherent from a disciplinary point of view and not intellectually rigorous from an international point of view." Perhaps, but the major educational problems in the United States occur in communities with high poverty rates and inadequate resources for education. It would be reassuring to believe that the most difficult educational problems could be addressed simply by revising curriculum, with little attention to the underlying causes of the problems. However, the evidence suggests that the problems are much deeper. They stem from poverty and the fact that the nation devotes the fewest educational resources to the students with the fewest resources. Quick fixes—whether more course requirements or more tests—will not address the basic issues. My concern is that, by focusing on what, at best, are marginal solutions, real problems are ignored.

Comment by Alan Siegel

The results of the Third International Math and Science Study (TIMSS) demonstrate the power of outstanding teaching and curricula and, by way of contrast, the weaknesses in the U.S. education system, which ill serves American society as a whole and its children in particular. Of the many failings, the quality of the textbooks is, evidently, the most severe. In terms of social institutions, the components in greatest need of redress are funding streams and assessment programs. From a procedural perspective, American educational ills stem, in no small part, from a complex K–12 infrastructure that has lost sight of the content that must be taught.

TIMSS

William H. Schmidt's study analyzes the decline of U.S. TIMSS results from fourth to eighth to twelfth grades and concludes that the causes of America's uniquely poor performance must lie within its education system. On the repeat test TIMSS-R, for example, American eighth graders were about at the international average. In contrast, 46 percent of all students in first-place Singapore were among the top 10 percent of students worldwide; only 9 percent of American youth were in this category. Three-fourths of Singapore's eighth graders placed among the top 25 percent of all students, whereas the United States had 28 percent who scored this well. Singapore had a whopping 93 percent of their students place among the top half of all test takers worldwide, while the United States had 61 percent. Only 1 percent of the students in Singapore placed among the bottom 25 percent of all students worldwide, as opposed to 22 percent for the United States. Moreover, South Korea, Hong Kong, Japan, and Flemish Belgium all had performances that were far beyond the achievement levels representative of the United States.

These are astonishing differences, and they are all the more remarkable because Singapore is a heterogeneous society with several different native languages and lessons are taught in yet another language—English. Although its society is far more orderly than that found in the United States, the majority of American classrooms are not so unruly that learning is materially reduced. This is not to deny the existence of horrific problems in some inner-city schools and serious problems of educational inequity. The point is that the lower-quality educational offerings that are endemic to many—but not all—of the low socioeconomic status (SES) schools cannot explain the mediocre performances of students at all achievement levels, the decline by grade level, or the astonishing performance differences between U.S. students and those from Singapore.

Schmidt's study explains that the twelfth-grade TIMSS questions concerned content matter that was, on average, at a grade level of 5.7. On this basic test, American students were at the bottom of the industrialized world; they managed to outperform only South Africa and Cyprus. On the more specialized advanced math test, they placed next to last; even Cyprus scored far better than the United States. The consequences are many.

Does Poor Performance Matter?

Former deputy secretary of education and Xerox chief executive officer David Kearns has estimated that corporate costs resulting from America's low-quality K–12 education system are more than $50 billion per year. Others have put forth a more conservative estimate of $30 billion.

In any case, corporate America has been relying on large numbers of foreign workers to meet the need for highly skilled math, science, and technology experts. These days, much of America's Yankee ingenuity is imported. The United States should have an education system that prepares far more Americans—including those of low socioeconomic status—for such jobs.

At present, the public school system is failing to meet this challenge. The education provided is often far too weak to allow U.S. graduates to take advantage of these opportunities.

Although how the best U.S. nuclear weapons designs wound up in China is unknown, there is a good chance that this security loss resulted, in part, from the shortage of native-born Americans qualified to support classified research.

Moreover, a new phenomenon soon will emerge—a reverse brain drain. By the beginning of 2003, the place with the highest starting salaries in computer science and the lowest taxes will be a brand-new national research and development center located in continental East Asia. Soon, some of the best American talent will be on the move, and the United States may pay yet another price for training so many from abroad.

Math Is for All Areas of the Economy

Sound mathematics is not just for high technology, engineering, medicine, science, business, and academics. For example, my sheet metal contractor, who fabricated the heating conduits for my house, made every piece I designed. However, I asked him to use his knowledge to design the one critical part, which connects a rectangular duct to an offset square opening some foot and a half away. Furthermore, airplane pilots rely on on-board computers to give all kinds of information from the ascent angle for altitude climbs to projections of fuel consumption. Commercial pilots must not only be able to perform the calculations when these systems fail, but they must also be able to recognize bogus computer projections that result from human operator errors. Every once in a while, someone enters erroneous data, and a plane slams into a mountain.

Building contractors and carpenters routinely substitute one structural element in an architectural plan for another. They need to know that a beam with a 12×4 cross section is 125 percent stronger than an 8×8, and they should know why. Plumbers need to know that the waste lines in your house should run at a 1 to 2 percent grade.

In some hospitals, registered nurses have to pass regularly scheduled math checkup exams. As you read the sample math questions from old National Assessment of Educational Progress (NAEP) exams, think about the answers you would want from your airplane pilot and from the person who might be measuring out your medication, making the units conversions, and making allowances for your weight and metabolic processing, and who might be your last line of defense against accidental overdose.

Math matters.

Is the U.S. Assessment System Adequate?

International math and science studies provide a remarkably sound reality check for judging how well the U.S. education infrastructure is meeting the needs of students. The TIMSS results demonstrate that the education system is failing its most important social obligation—to produce an educated citizenry able to function effectively in a workplace that is becoming increasingly technical, able to support an economy that (until recently) has been dominated by growth in the high-tech sectors, able to support a defense system that is overwhelmingly dependent on high technology, and able to make informed, societal decisions about economic, legal, political, and educational matters that all depend on mathematical, analytic, and scientific judgments.

President George W. Bush has challenged the nation to have high expectations and to provide proof of performance based on testing. Accordingly, it is appropriate to ask if the existing assessment system can determine how well the educational infrastructure is working. I would like to suggest that the answer is no.

There are many assessment programs, and I will be able to provide some precautionary comments about only a few of them. The first program to consider is the National Assessment of Educational Progress. Although the NAEP should be analyzed in depth, I will just offer some broad-brush comments about the exam based on the 133 sample twelfth-grade problems listed on the NAEP website.[39]

The following question has a rating of hard, which is the most challenging category for the NAEP.

> The postal rate is 25 cents for the first ounce and 20 cents for each additional ounce or part of an ounce. What would it cost to mail a package that weighs 6.8 ounces?
>
> $1.25 $1.40 $1.45 $1.70 $1.75

Evidently, the rating is right on target. More than 60 percent of U.S. twelfth graders could not round 6.8 up to 7 and add up 25 cents for the first ounce plus an additional 120 cents for the remaining six ounces. I am not certain how this problem ranks on an international level, but an uneducated guess would place this question around grade five. The next twelfth-grade problem reads:

> The population of the United States is approximately 250 million, and the national debt is approximately 4 trillion dollars. If this debt were divided equally among the population, what would be the debt, in dollars, per person?
>
> 16   1,600   16,000   1,600,000   16,000,000

This question depends upon two unrelated issues—knowing how many zeros are in a trillion and understanding the simplest principles underlying decimal placement in long division. Sixty-one percent of American students could not find the correct answer, but the entanglement of disparate subtopics means that no one can determine with certainty what part of the educational process failed. As for the grade-level ranking of the question—well, how can it matter?

Here is another question with a rating of hard.

> In a group of 1,200 adults, there are 300 vegetarians. What is the ratio of nonvegetarians to vegetarians in the group?
>
> 1 to 3   1 to 4   3 to 1   4 to 1   4 to 3

Only 25 percent of American twelfth graders found the correct answer. The NAEP website has commentary explaining the significance of each question. The discussion about this problem is as follows.

> Description: Express Ratio in Word Problem
>
> This question measures number sense, properties, and operations. This content area focuses on students' understanding of numbers (whole numbers, fractions, decimals, integers, real numbers, and complex numbers), operations, estimation, and applications to real-world situations. Students are expected to demonstrate an understanding of numerical relationships as expressed in ratios, proportions, and percents. Students are also expected to understand properties of numbers and operations, generalize from numerical patterns, and verify results. Number sense includes questions that address a student's understanding of relative size, equivalent forms of numbers, and use of numbers to represent attributes of real-world objects and quantities.
>
> This question also focuses on the subtopic of relating counting, grouping, and place value.
>
> This question measures students' conceptual understanding. Students demonstrate conceptual understanding in mathematics when they provide evidence that they can recognize, label, and generate examples of concepts; use and interrelate

models, diagrams, manipulatives, and varied representations of concepts; identify
and apply principles; know and apply facts and definitions; compare, contrast,
and integrate related concepts and principles; recognize, interpret, and apply the
signs, symbols, and terms used to represent concepts. Conceptual understanding
reflects a student's ability to reason in settings involving the careful application of
concept definitions, relations, or representations of either.

The vagueness, exaggerated importance, and ultimate irrelevance of this
discussion to the question are self-evident. For all of these words, little
effort is made to relate the question at hand to teaching goals or even a
grade level.

The following problems have a rating of easy.

Description: Solve Pair of Equations: $4 \times \square = \square$ and $3 \times \square = \square$

What number if placed in each box above would make both equations true?

0   1   2   4

Normally, a pair of equations would have two unknowns, and any one of a
few standard methods would be used to get the answer. Instead, this problem consists of two trivial equations with one unknown, but both have the
solution ? = 0. Another question reads:

Divide: $15 \overline{)30.45}$

Yet another is:

What is 2/3 of 15 marbles?

10 marbles   9 marbles   8 marbles   5 marbles

Of the twelfth-grade problems listed on the NAEP website, forty-seven are
rated easy; twenty-six, medium; and sixty, hard.

The arithmetic questions are extraordinarily easy. The fractions question
might be appropriate for a preindustrialized society with minimal education,
but not the United States. The NAEP questions reveal an apparent decision
to avoid finding out if the American education system is imparting the
understanding necessary to solve such basic problems as, say,

How much is 1/3 + 5/7 ?

These sample questions also display a remarkable absence of testing for
algebraic skills. Algebra is important because its symbolic expressiveness is
the most fundamental tool for modeling the real world. Asking if high
schoolers can plug zero into the pre-algebra problem $4 \times \square = \square$ and $3 \times \square$

= ☐ does not test algebraic reasoning. Of the 133 twelfth-grade problems listed for the years 1990, 1992, and 1996, I counted three that were at a level of algebra that can be interpreted as asking for an expression or formula. Two qualify as advanced; the third is the only one that requires a formula to be given. It reads:

> The length of a rectangle is 3 more than its width. If L represents the length, what is an expression for the width?
>
> $3 \div L$ $L \times 3$ $L + 3$ $L - 3$

The next problem is as challenging an equation as any of the sample NAEP postings. It simply asks students to find the square root of 729.

> If $n \times n = 729$, what does n equal?

The NAEP-supplied problem descriptions are overstated and seem to hide the weakness of the questions behind vague categorizations and intentions. For this question, the website explains:

> This question measures algebra and functions. This content area extends from work with simple patterns, to basic algebra concepts, to sophisticated analysis. Students are expected to use algebraic notation and thinking in meaningful con-texts to solve mathematical and real-world problems, addressing an increasing understanding of the use of functions. Other topics assessed include using open sentences and equations as representational tools and using the notion of equiva-lent representations to transform and solve number sentences and equations of increasing complexity.

It is not my intention to teach any math here, so I will skip the details. Years ago, I taught inner-city teenagers remedial mathematics. The students were sweet and attentive, but they knew very little. The course began with the addition of single-digit integers, and it progressed nicely. By the end of the year, I could assign problems such as

$$\frac{4}{3 - \dfrac{2}{4x - 3}} + 3 = 8$$

The structure of these kinds of equations is special. You can build in greater levels of reciprocals and still solve them by composing algebraic steps in a way that is akin to peeling an onion. Once the class members understood how to solve these problems, they had fun with them because they felt empowered. I recall starting one class with a warm-up problem of this type. A nineteen-year-old six-footer overflowed his desk as he sat working away at the exercise. The anchor tattooed on his ample biceps rippled as he wrote equation after equation and systematically peeled off the outermost of the operators that kept x hidden within complicated layers of arithmetic expressions. At last, when had he finished the inversions and had the right answer, he exclaimed, "Wow! I can blow away my sister at this stuff."

At that point, it was easy to explain that in the problem the 8 could just as well be the parameter A, and the 4 could be B, and so on. The solution method is exactly the same (as long as you do not rely on a calculator). The class understood. The rules of algebra allow letters free passage to any location where numbers are permitted. Well, almost anywhere, for they are not to be found on NAEP tests of understanding. The NAEP designers appear to believe that students should not, must not, or cannot be expected to understand the fundamentals of algebra.

Likewise, the four NAEP trigonometry problems sprinkled among the 133 questions are all immediate plug-ins. They are straightforward and require little more than an awareness of the most basic definitions. There is no testing of understanding.

To summarize, the NAEP twelfth-grade mathematics test is weaker than the TIMSS test and is immeasurably below the scope of, say, a Japanese high school entrance (not exit) exam. Very little high school material is covered, and the little that is tested tends to be remarkably shallow. Unfortunately, less than 30 percent of American twelfth-grade students earn scores that the National Assessment Governing Board has judged adequate to establish proficiency. Such a low percentage should be a source of national concern. I am particularly concerned because the test is far too weak to determine if students are proficient at basic high school mathematics.

The test also suffers from systemic weaknesses. Some of the problems can be solved by guess and check. The question $4 \times \square = \square$ and $3 \times \square = \square$, for example, can be solved by plugging in the first answer in the multiple choice selection. A typical SAT question for two equations in two unknowns is of the form:

Suppose x and y solve the two equations $2x + 5y = 3$ and $5x + 2y = 4$.

How much is $x + 2y$?

| 1 | $1\frac{1}{5}$ | $1\frac{1}{3}$ | $1\frac{2}{5}$ | $1\frac{2}{3}$ |

This question cannot be answered by testing the choices to see which one works. In contrast, the NAEP's sample arithmetic problems are much too simple. Moreover, many of the questions are stated with "friendly numbers," which often allow students to get the right answer even if they do not know enough to solve the problem in general. For example, the question that asks twelfth graders to divide 15 into 30.45 does not require an understanding of long division to get the answer.

The use of friendly number problems constitutes a serious compromise of the assessment value of the NAEP because many of the latest reform math programs teach computation only with friendly numbers. By design, the test is preventing researchers from using the NAEP to see if, as many content experts contend, fluency in arithmetic, fractions, and long division is a crucial prerequisite for fluency in algebra. There is simply no reason to avoid collecting data that could answer such an important question. The results do not have to be included in the scoring of the exam. Such apparent problem avoidance cannot possibly serve the national interest.

Math matters, and the failure to teach it properly matters more. Yet in its current form, the NAEP seems to have a structure that hides deficiencies in the U.S. educational system and thereby helps perpetuate them

Low expectations beget low performance. The main contribution of the TIMSS is that it reveals what is possible, how low the standards are, and how little mathematical knowledge is being passed on to the next generation.

The Nature of Mathematical Knowledge

Mathematics is layered and deep. Concepts recur over and over again in greater abstraction and greater sophistication. A person learns each new layer by understanding and internalizing it in terms of more concrete notions that he or she has already mastered. But if even a single level of this growing foundation is stripped away, then the next level might require a huge leap in understanding, which can leave most students lost and unable to progress.

For example, my colleagues all agree that a mastery of fractions is essential for learning algebra. The management of fractions is all about the collection of like items (such as sevenths) and the manipulation of expressions that change the representation without changing the value. But it is far easier to learn these notions in the concrete world of ratios of integers than in the symbolic formulations of algebra. Fractions and long division contain the rudiments of polynomial arithmetic. The carryover is huge. It includes factoring, least common multiples, and greatest common divisors—all best learned in the concrete world of integers and numerical ratios.

Fractions appear in a standard application of Ohm's law, which states that the current is the voltage divided by the resistance. The application says that for two resistors in parallel, the reciprocal of the total resistance is the sum of the reciprocals of the individual resistances (as stated on the left below). I recently saw a high school physics text that had been updated for the newer math programs. It included the more friendly formula (shown on the right below), in which the answer does not need any addition of fractions.

$$\frac{1}{R_{Tot}} = \frac{1}{R_1} + \frac{1}{R_2} \qquad\qquad R_{Tot} = \frac{R_1 R_2}{R_1 + R_2}$$

The alternative formulation, although 100 percent correct, is pedagogically unsound because it is devoid of physical interpretation. (The concise interpretation for the equation on the left is that conductance is additive for parallel resistors. In simpler language, take every term in the equation and multiply it by the voltage. Given Ohm's law, the total current thus is found by adding up the individual current in each of the parallel resistors.) To see the difference between the two formulations, take a moment to extend them to the case of three resistors. The first formula has a natural pattern that is correct and can be proven correct by observing that the total current through three parallel resistors is the sum of the three individual currents. The second formulation also has an extension to three resistors, but the natural pattern that most students would guess gives the wrong answer. This formulation is just plain worthless because it does not extend (as naturally) to more resistors in parallel.

Problem solving requires modeling to transform real-world problems into mathematical formulations. The best formulations are ones in which the mathematical representation is, in a sense, a direct translation from the physical world into mathematical equations. Students require sound basic skills if they are to manage this kind of material. The gateway to real-world problems includes all of algebra, which, in turn, requires a solid facility with the harder parts of arithmetic. Calculus and more advanced mathematics offer powerful problem formulation and problem-solving tools, but they will not be accessible to anyone who is not fluent in algebra. If the foundations of algebra and algebraic thinking are stripped away, then all that follows comes tumbling down.

Mathematics is relentlessly hierarchical. Issues of long division and polynomial arithmetic reappear in the fundamental theorem of algebra, in calculus, and yet again in more advanced topics. These higher-level abstractions turn out to have many important applications that range from elementary to advanced.[40]

And sound mathematics is not just for technical careers and academicians. Not one of the four high school reform programs I have studied contains enough geometry for the design problem that my sheet metal contractor had to solve.

A Confluence of Misjudgments

The issue of questionable content is by no means limited to the NAEP. Schmidt conjectures that some of the contemporary math textbooks might be below grade level and fail to teach the subjects they purport to cover. One of the new K–5 textbook series has fewer than thirty multiplication questions in which both the multiplier and the multiplicand have a digit that exceeds 5. Thus, 4×17 might be asked, but exercises as hard as 7×83 will be rare. One of the reform middle school programs omitted teaching how to divide fractions. In response to criticisms, the book company now covers the subject, but the real issues are: How could it have committed such an omission in the first place? What kind of education studies could have validated such a program?

Might some reform programs, in an effort to correct for the ills of rigid teaching, have gone much too far in yet another wrong direction? In some of the more radical programs, students are not taught the multiplication table, and they are not taught the standard place-column method for multiplication. In some schools in Manhattan's District 2, teachers must write multiplication problems in the form

$$37 \times 17 = ?$$

They are strongly discouraged from writing

$$\frac{37}{\times 17}$$

because this formulation is suggestive of systematic methods, which are seen as rigid.

Not too long ago, I saw a mother ask her fifth-grade daughter to compute 17×4. She thought about the problem for a while and then said that four was two times two. She said that 17×2 is. . . . She thought for a while. Her eyes rolled around. She thought some more and announced 34. She then said that $34 + 34$ is . . . , and the process repeated. She got the right answer (68), but the process had taken three subway stops (or more than three minutes). It was heartwarming to see her tough out the problem. It was very pleasing to see how proud she was of her answer. But it was gut wrenching to realize how little she knew and to know the difficulties she will encounter when she has to face more advanced material.

In one of the fifth-grade reform programs in Manhattan's District 2, the students are given a drawing depicting an empty bookcase that is five feet wide and has four shelves. Their homework assignment is to color the drawing to show the bookcase completely filled with books that are one-inch thick. In a middle school reform program, the class will be asked to keep a journal about their favorite number, and the students will be asked to write a sentence about each of the integers from one to twenty. In high school, students will learn to find the area of a figure by chopping it into little squares and counting up the number of pieces, but they might not learn why the area of a triangle is half the product of the base length and the height.

The rhetoric about higher-level problem solving not withstanding, these assignments are typical of the overall shallowness of some reform programs. In reality, the claims about high-level thinking are typified by a celebration of the ways students who are deprived of systematic skills can, given enough time, devise seat-of-the-pants tricks to compute, for example, 17×4.[41]

Similarly, one ninth-grade reform book has, scattered among its 515 pages, only 25 pages that even contain an equal sign. Of these, only pages 435 and 436 discuss solving equations. The totality of the information about algebra that is on these pages is depicted in box 1. The whole idea of emphasizing tricks and shortcuts over generally applicable techniques is completely backward but is consistent with some of the contemporary education theories about learning. Moreover, the book's content coverage is alarmingly thin, and the practice exercises are dumbed down in the extreme. The problems have no depth, and they give students no practice putting the basic concepts of algebraic manipulation together to solve more complex questions.

Some of these texts tend to avoid symbolic expressions and thereby avoid teaching one of the most powerful features of algebra. Students need to understand that the language of numbers extends to include unknowns such as x and parameters such as a, b, c, and so on. They need to be able to express relationships in abstract terms and to read them with ease. For

Box 1. A Year's Worth of Algebraic Equations for the Ninth Grade

Some such equations are easier to solve than others. Sometimes the particular numbers involved suggest tricks or shortcuts that make them easy to solve.

In each of the equations below, the letter x stands for an unknown number. Use any method you like to find the number x stands for, but write down exactly how you do it.

Be sure to check your answers and write down in detail how you find them.

$$\frac{x}{5} = 7 \qquad \frac{x}{6} = \frac{72}{24} \qquad \frac{x}{8} = \frac{11}{4} \qquad \frac{x}{7} = \frac{5}{3}$$

$$\frac{x+1}{3} = \frac{4}{6} \qquad \frac{5}{13} = \frac{19}{x} \qquad \frac{2}{x} = 6 \qquad \frac{9}{x} = \frac{x}{16}$$

example, in algebra, students should not only be able to solve an equation such as $y = 3x + 2$ for x to get the answer $x = (y - 2)/3$, but they should also understand the fundamental processes in general terms. That is, students should understand that the equation $cy = ax + b$ is just as easy to solve to get $x = (cy - b)/a$. In one of the ninth-grade reform textbooks, I could find only one exercise in which students need to divide by anything other than a number. This exception is not for a linear equation but is instead for the much more difficult exercise 7 on page 748, which says:

> Show how to derive the quadratic formula by applying completing the square to the general quadratic equation, $ax^2 + bx + c = 0$.

This question seems to be asking for a tremendous leap in skill given the text's limited use of exercises with symbolic coefficients. Moreover, the presentation on completing the square is likewise weak and thin. As is characteristic of these programs, the method is taught by example without (apart from a circumspect illustration) any explanation about why the key step was taken or any overview about how to determine the key step in general.

What happens if students do not see the pattern? What happens if a student is absent that day and has to learn the mathematics from the book? Where is the practice to reinforce the simple technique and to determine who understands and who does not? Where is the validation data to support the educational value of this problem? Where are the conceptual reinforcement exercises asking students to adapt the notion to similar but slightly different problems? The answer is that they are not to be found. Although many traditional textbooks also fail to provide concept reinforcement exercises, I do not believe that the educational failings of the past are sufficient reason for continuing such practices.

Sadly, I have just hinted at the failings within some of the reform programs. The new ideas about what math is and how learning takes place are supported by comparably flawed theories about cognitive psychology. Three distinguished cognitive psychologists—including a Nobel Prize winner—wrote a detailed critique showing how modern cognitive psychology has been systematically misapplied in the mathematics education literature.[42] They probably knew what they were talking about; some of the misrepresented findings were the product of their own research. Unfortunately, their paper is written with so much technical jargon that it is a tough, albeit illuminating, read. Perhaps the clearest sense of their concerns can be found in the accompanying discussion about the consequences of these theories. They cite a passage from a 1993 draft of the National Council of Teachers of Mathematics assessment standard for mathematics, which rejects the idea that mathematical knowledge is the consequence of mastering fundamental "concepts and skills" and learning how to put them together to solve more complex problems. Of this, J. R. Anderson, L. M. Reder, and H. A. Simon wrote:

> This false rejection of decomposition and decontextualization runs deep in modern mathematics education. . . . We can only say we find frightening the prospect of mathematics education based on such a misconceived rejection of componential analysis.

In other words, they are saying that learning requires teachers and textbooks to present fundamental concepts and to show how general principles and systematic methods can be applied to solve real-world problems. The authors are objecting to the current alternative, which is to present one or two examples without any explanation about how to solve a problem in general. Thus, for example, every multiplication problem is yet another challenge because students are deprived of systematic methods for place-based multiplication. Similar failings occur in the discussion of algebraic methods, in virtually all definitions, and throughout some of the latest textbooks.

Validation studies are also undermined by poor scientific methodology. For example, in comparative studies, the quality of the control programs, as can be inferred from TIMSS data, is likely to be far below a world-class standard. Controls for teaching skill are likewise problematic. Many statistical teaching studies show that specific education degrees and even advanced degrees are weak indicators of teaching skill, although experience has a stronger correlation.[43] The best data for measuring teaching quality are provided by the database for the Tennessee Value-Added Assessment System (TVAAS), which stores the yearly progress of individual students along with their specific classroom teachers. W. L. Sanders and J. C. Rivers used the TVAAS to show that the difference between having three good teachers in a row versus three poor teachers can be a swing of 50 percentile points.[44] Independent studies have confirmed these results.[45] It follows that teaching skill is an important control variable for comparative education studies. Unfortunately, the TVAAS is one of the few programs with the data necessary for such analyses.

Comparative studies should also report controls for spending. In New York City, for example, the direct expenditures can vary across the city by more than 50 percent ($15,000 versus $9,200 per student) for schools of comparable size and composition, and likewise the support for auxiliary instructional personnel exhibits comparable variability.

Moreover, most education studies are not open; that is, they do not publish enough information to permit an independent review to determine if the primary data support the findings. As for observational studies, evidence shows that even some of the best (open) research in this area can be so flawed that the findings can be contradicted by the study's own data.[46] In a sense, Anderson, Reder, and Simon have observed, via completely independent means, similar kinds of scientific weakness in the education literature.

Given these failings, the abdication of proper content coverage by the NAEP is extremely serious. The problem is further compounded by contemporary education practices that use achievement tests that are aligned with reform teaching programs. So if fundamental material has been stripped out of a curriculum, chances are that it will not be on the recommended achievement tests, and certainly not in the textbook validation study.

The questions on commercial tests are typically secret. However, teachers get to see them, and teachers may well be involved with the grading. For example, constructed-answer questions are graded by hand and are often graded within the very district where the exam is given. So the secrecy surrounding these examinations cannot prevent teaching to the test, but the security does prevent independent reviews of the questions and answers. Consequently, the examinations must be trusted to be competently designed with comprehensive coverage of grade-level appropriate content, vigilantly administered to ensure that the results measure actual progress, and diligently scored to present consistent, accurate achievement levels that can be monitored over a period of many years.

Unfortunately, growing evidence suggests that such trust has not yet been earned. Newspapers report significant cheating scandals in California, New York, and many places in between. Misdeeds include giving out old exams for practice, offering inappropriate help, allowing extra time, correcting mistakes, and providing an answer key. Accidents occur as well. In 1999, eighty-seven hundred New York City students were mistakenly forced to attend summer school because their tests were translated into achievement scores that were too low. In 2000 New York City's sixth-grade reading scores were so ridiculously high that the Board of Education removed them from its website, even though the test manufacturer claims that the adjusted achievement levels were correct. In 2000, forty-seven thousand Minnesota students received math test scores that were too low because of errors in the answer keys. The errors were discovered by a parent after he threatened to file a lawsuit if the testing company continued to deny him access to his daughter's test. (She had received a failing score but, he finally discovered, had actually passed the test.)

The issue of content is even more important for testing programs, and especially so because so many of the latest curriculum reforms are experimentally omitting and dumbing down basic mathematics. In some programs, trial and error is taught as a substitute for systematic analysis. Topics that do not mesh conveniently with these new ideas might be dropped from the curriculum or placed with little development at the end of a lengthy book with little likelihood that the material would be taught. Nevertheless, no one can expect the testing companies to offer world-class assessment tests, the book publishers to recommend that such products be used in conjunction with the programs they sell, or school boards to select the best testing program as a means of validating their education policies. And when achievement tests are designed and graded in secret, no means are available to assess the severity of the omissions and the general dumbing down of the assessment practices.

Reliable, high-quality standards assessment programs clearly do not exist. As a consequence, textbook publishers, state and local school administrators, and curriculum designers face little to no accountability. Teachers are placed in circumstances where the opportunity to teach is greatly compromised by weak programs. The absence of a sound assessment policy ensures that teachers will also be spared any accountability for their performance. However, the lack of accountability stops there. No matter what, the children will suffer for the mistakes of others and, in many cases, will pay for unsound education policy with a lifetime of limited employment opportunity. Evidently, the secrecy surrounding exams undermines their validity, enhances the possibility of misuse, and benefits test manufactures, scoring companies, and mathematics program designers far more than the recipients of these services.

Parents have a crucial need and absolute right to know how well their public schools are performing. Without solid assessment data, they are powerless to exert their rights via participatory democracy. Without reliable information, even the vote is debased. Similarly, school choice, for better or worse, will be all the worse if families lack the knowledge necessary to make those choices in an informed way. They deserve better.

Recommendations

I offer, by way of conclusion, a number of recommendations.

The international math and science studies should continue to receive federal support. Without them, no way would exist to determine how powerful a sound education system can be or how far short of this standard the latest reforms might be. It follows that, the poor performances of U.S. high school seniors notwithstanding, international testing of math and science at the twelfth-grade level should resume and testing should continue at grade four and eight.

The oversight structure for the NAEP should be reconfigured to emphasize content. The NAEP is presently mandated to be a consensus-based test and, as such, cannot begin to approach the level of a world-class standard. Only two practicing mathematicians are on the twenty-six-member 2004 NAEP Mathematics Steering Committee, and the committee is not entitled to see the exam questions. The NAEP should include a solidly content-based exam that can stand as an independent validity check of all instructional programs, both new and old. The test design must be sound. The oversight must be by a board of content experts empowered to conduct a scrupulous review of topics coverage and problem depth. Where possible, perhaps program managers in the research branches of the National Science Foundation could have a role in the oversight management.

Federally funded education studies should be subject to stringent requirements for open data.

Federal incentives should be used to foster open testing programs with questions and answers that are publicly available for independent review. Although this form of testing creates additional burdens for test designers, the educational system can ill afford to rely on assessment programs in which the examination quality is above any review process and mistakes might be likely to go uncorrected.[47] Even the NAEP can and should be a part of such a program with full postings of past tests.

Federal incentives should be used to foster the adoption of value-added assessment programs. Value-added testing clearly gives the best measure of achievement for every aspect of the education system—from students to teachers, program directors, and textbooks alike. Where feasible, value-added assessment should also be used in NAEP pilot studies designed to test a fixed set of schools over a number of consecutive years.

Federal incentives should encourage state, district, and school examination scores to be reported along with (and disaggregated by) the teaching programs used in the schools. There is no reason to shield inferior programs from the consequences of their own design failures, and even less reason to suppress performance-based evidence of successful reforms. In addition, the per student costs for various program implementations should be reported.

Federal incentives should encourage qualified content experts to participate in the design of sound assessment programs in general, and open assessment instruments in particular.

Federal incentives should foster pilot projects to develop and test open content–based, high-performance, low-stakes assessment programs. Reform cannot occur overnight, and students cannot be held accountable for levels of knowledge and understanding that transcend current classroom practice. A first step toward better programs should hold the programs, textbooks, and teaching to higher standards. One way to foster such reform might be to have comprehensive diagnostic testing in the beginning of each academic year, instead of the end. Such programs might provide a better measure of effective learning, might identify topics appropriate for intensive review, and might lead to wider social acceptance than high-stakes end-of-year examinations. When graduation depends on testing, the evidence suggests that political pressures are likely to undermine the comprehensiveness of the test and thereby weaken the utility of open assessment as a means of fostering a world-class K–12 education system.

Notes

1. The estimated percentage of students reaching the proficient level on each of these tests can be found in a series of reports by the Department of Education entitled *The Nation's Report Card*. For science and mathematics, the results are from the year 2000; history, 2001. The geography and civics results were collected in 1994 and 1998, respectively.

2. Sheida White, *The NAEP 1998 Reading Report Card: National and State Highlights* (Department of Education, Office of Educational Research and Improvement, National Center for Education Statistics, 1999).

3. J. S. Braswell and others, *The Nation's Report Card: Mathematics 2000* (Department of Education, Office of Educational Research and Improvement, National Center for Education Statistics, 2001); and *The Nation's Report Card: Science Highlights 2000* (Department of Education, Office of Educational Research and Improvement, National Center for Education Statistics, 2001).

4. "American Workers and Economic Change," statement by the Research and Policy Committee of the Committee for Economic Development, New York, 1996; Karen Larson, "Bridging the Gap: Developing a National System of Industry Skill Standards," National Alliance of Business, Washington, 1996; and Karen Larson, "The Employee—Then and Now," *Work America*, vol. 12, no. 1 (1996), for a summary that includes "American Workers and Economic Change," Larson, "Bridging the Gap," and other examples.

5. James Glanz, "Trolling for Brains in International Waters," *New York Times*, April 1, 2001, section 4, p. 3.

6. *The Formula for Success: A Business Leader's Guide to Supporting Math and Science Achievement* (Washington: Business Coalition for Education Reform, 1998).

7. Over a third of the companies surveyed indicated they were providing remedial education in mathematics. For a summary, see Michael E. Porter and Debra van Opstal, *U.S. Competitiveness 2001* (Washington: Council on Competitiveness, 2001), p. 50.

8. John Glenn, *Before It's Too Late: A Report to the Nation from the National Commission on Mathematics and Science Teaching for the 21st Century* (Department of Education, 2000).

9. Based on an interview with Richard W. Judy, Hudson Institute, April 19, 2000, as reported in Glenn, *Before It's Too Late*.

10. The Third International Mathematics and Science Study (TIMSS) is the largest international study of mathematics and science ever attempted. The tests were conducted for nine-year-olds, for thirteen-year-olds, and for students in their final year of secondary school, however that was defined by the country. The study involved comparing official curricula,

textbooks, teacher practices, and student achievement in up to fifty countries, depending on the particular comparison. The part of the study reported on here deals with the students in their last year of secondary school (Population 3). We use the U.S. designation for this group—twelfth graders—recognizing this as inadequate internationally. This population included a representative sample of all students in the last year of secondary school. This group, on which the analyses presented in this paper are based, was administered a literacy test covering both mathematics and science. The specialists were defined as those taking calculus, physics, or both. A representative sample of each of these three groups was chosen. They were administered the literacy test as well as tests appropriate to their specialization. The international results are presented in Ina V. S. Mullis and others, *Mathematics and Science Achievement in the Final Year of Secondary School* (Boston College, 1998). The conceptual model undergirding TIMSS is presented in William H. Schmidt and Curtis C. McKnight, "Surveying Educational Opportunity in Mathematics and Science: An International Perspective," *Educational Evaluation and Policy Analysis*, vol. 17 (1995), pp. 337–53.

11. Sayuri Takahira and others, *Pursuing Excellence: A Study of U.S. Twelfth-Grade Mathematics and Science Achievement in International Context* (Department of Education, National Center for Education Statistics, 1998).

12. William H. Schmidt and others, *Facing the Consequences: Using TIMSS for a Closer Look at U.S. Mathematics and Science Education* (Dordrect, Netherlands: Kluwer Academic Publishers, 1999).

13. Graham Orpwood and Robert A. Garden, *Assessing Mathematics and Science Literacy* (Vancouver, Canada: Pacific Educational Press, 1998), p. 11.

14. William H. Schmidt and others, *Many Visions, Many Aims,* vol. I: *A Cross-National Investigation of Curricular Intentions in School Mathematics* (Dordrect, Netherlands: Kluwer Academic Publishers, 1997); and William H. Schmidt and others, *Many Visions, Many Aims,* vol. II: *A Cross-National Investigation of Curricular Intentions in School Science* (Dordrect, Netherlands: Kluwer Academic Publishers, 1997). See also Graham Orpwood and Robert A. Garden, *Assessing Mathematics and Science Literacy,* vol. 4 (Vancouver, Canada: Pacific Educational Press, 1998).

15. The data collection technique is identified as generalized topic trace mapping (GTTM) and involves country curriculum experts using their own country's content standards and making judgments about grade-level placement for each topic contained in the TIMSS curriculum frameworks. The framework topics are identified in David Robitaille and others, *Curriculum Frameworks for Mathematics and Science* (Vancouver, Canada: Pacific Educational Press, 1993). A detailed description of the data collection procedure is found in William H. Schmidt and others, *Many Visions, Many Aims,* vols. I and II, appendix D.

16. *Pursuing Excellence: A Study of U.S. Eighth-Grade Mathematics and Science Teaching, Learning Curriculum, and Achievement in International Context* (Department of Education, National Center for Education Statistics, 1996).

17. Frederic M. Lord and Melvin R. Novick, *Statistical Theories of Mental Test Scores* (Addison-Wesley, 1968).

18. Schmidt and others, *Facing the Consequences;* and Leland S. Cogan, William H. Schmidt, and David E. Wiley, "Who Takes What Math and in Which Track? Using TIMSS to Characterize U.S. Students' Eighth-Grade Mathematics Learning Opportunities," *Educational Evaluation and Policy Analysis*, vol. 23 (Winter 2001), pp. 323–41.

19. These studies are not meant to be an exhaustive review of all such studies: William H. Schmidt, "High School Course Taking: Its Relationship to Achievement," *Journal of Curriculum Studies*, vol. 15 (1983), pp. 311–32; Barbara Schneider, Christopher B. Swanson, and Catherine Riegle-Crumb, "Opportunities for Learning: Course Sequences and Positional

Advantages, *Social Psychology of Education*, vol. 2 (1998), pp. 25–53; David Lee Stevenson, Kathryn S. Schiller, and Barbara Schneider, "Sequences of Opportunities for Learning," *Sociology of Education*, vol. 67 (1994), pp. 184–98; A. Gamoran, "The Stratification of High School Learning Opportunities," *Sociology of Education*, vol. 60 (1987), pp. 135–55; V. E. Lee, A. S. Bryk, and J. B. Smith, "A Multilevel Model of the Social Distribution of High School Achievement," *Sociology of Education*, vol. 62 (1989), pp. 172–92; V. E. Lee and A. S. Bryk, "Curriculum Tracking as Mediating the Social Distribution of High School Achievement," *Sociology of Education*, vol. 61 (1988), pp. 78–94; J. Oakes, *Keeping Track: How Schools Structure Inequality* (Yale University Press, 1985); S. W. Raudenbush, R. P. Fotiu, and Y. F. Cheong, "Inequality of Access to Educational Resources: A National Report Card for Eighth-Grade Math," *Educational Evaluation and Policy Analysis*, vol. 20, no. 4 (1998), pp. 253–68; L. V. Jones and others, "Mathematics and Science Test Scores as Related to Courses Taken in High School and Other Factors," *Journal of Educational Measurement*, vol. 23 (1986), pp. 197–208; V. E. Lee, R. G. Croninger, and J. B. Smith, "Course-Taking, Equity, and Mathematics Learning: Testing the Constrained Curriculum Hypothesis in U.S. Secondary Schools," *Educational Evaluation and Policy Analysis*, vol. 19, no. 2 (1997), pp. 99–121; K. A. Rasinski and J. West, *Eighth Graders' Reports of Courses Taken during the 1998 Academic Year by Selected Student Characteristics*, Report NCES 90–459 (Department of Education, National Center for Education Statistics, 1990); D. A. Rock and J. M. Pollack, *Mathematics Course-Taking and Gains in Mathematics Achievement*, Report NCES 95–714 (Department of Education, National Center for Education Statistics, 1995); P. A. Sebring, "Consequences of Differential Amounts of High School Coursework: Will the New Graduation Requirements Help?" *Educational Evaluation and Policy Analysis*, vol. 9 (1987), pp. 258–73; and Gary Natriello, Aaron M. Pallas, and Karl Alexander, "On the Right Track? Curriculum and Academic Achievement," *Sociology of Education*, vol. 62 (1989), pp. 109–18.

20. William H. Schmidt and others, *Why Schools Matter: A Cross-National Comparison of Curriculum and Learning* (San Francisco: Jossey-Bass, 2001).

21. Gilbert A. Valverde and William H. Schmidt, "Greater Expectations: Learning from Other Nations in the Quest for 'World-Class Standards' in U.S. School Mathematics and Science," *Journal of Curriculum Studies*, vol. 32 (2000), pp. 651–87.

22. Arthur G. Powell, Eleanor Farrar, and David K. Cohen, *The Shopping Mall High School: Winners and Losers in the Educational Marketplace* (Houghton Mifflin, 1985).

23. See, for example, William H. Schmidt, "High School Course Taking: A Study of Variation," *Journal of Curriculum Studies*, vol. 15 (1983), pp. 167–82; Joseph Murphy, Thomas R. Hull, and Allan Walker, "Academic Drift and Curriculum Debris: Analysis of High School Course-Taking Patterns and Its Implications for Local Policy Makers," *Journal of Curriculum Studies*, vol. 19 (1987), pp. 341–60; and David Lee Stevenson, Kathryn S. Schiller, and Barbara Schneider, "Sequences of Opportunities of Learning," *Sociology of Education*, vol. 67 (1994), pp. 184–98.

24. Stevenson, Schiller, and Schneider, "Sequences of Opportunities of Learning," pp. 184–98.

25. David Robitaille, ed., *National Contexts for Mathematics and Science Education: An Encyclopedia of the Education Systems Participating in TIMSS* (Vancouver, Canada: Pacific Educational Press, 1997).

26. Cogan, Schmidt, and Wiley, "Who Takes What Math and in Which Track?"

27. Schmidt and others, *Why Schools Matter.*

28. Schmidt and others, *Why Schools Matter.*

29. Ernest L. Boger, *High School: A Report on Secondary Education in America* (Harper and Row, 1983).

30. Schmidt and others, *Facing the Consequences.*

31. L. V. Hedges and A. Nowell, "Changes in the Black-White Gap in Achievement Test Scores," *Sociology of Education,* vol. 72. no. 2 (1999), pp. 111–35.

32. The popular interpretation of the Coleman report was that schools do not make a difference. The perception persists, despite challenges to this interpretation and other analyses that contradict it. See James S. Coleman and others, *Equity of Educational Opportunity* (Department of Education, National Center for Education Statistics, 1966); Erik A. Hanushek, "Outcomes, Incentives, and Beliefs: Reflections on Analysis of the Economics of Schools," *Educational Evaluation and Policy Analysis,* vol. 19 (1997), pp. 301–08; and Harold Wenglinsky, "How Money Matters: The Effect of School District Spending on Academic Achievement," *Sociology of Education,* vol. 70 (1997), pp. 221–37.

33. Cogan, Schmidt, and Wiley, "Who Takes What Math and in Which Track?"

34. William H. Schmidt, Curtis McKnight, and Senta Raizen, *A Splintered Vision: An Investigation of U.S. Science and Mathematics Education* (Dordrect, Netherlands: Kluwer Academic Publishers, 1997).

35. Department of Education, National Center for Education Statistics, *Pursuing Excellence: A Study of U.S. Twelfth-Grade Mathematics and Science Achievement in International Context,* NCES 98–049 (Government Printing Office, 1998).

36. The analysis of the Third International Mathematics and Science Study is based on Iris C. Rotberg, "Interpretation of International Test Score Comparisons," *Science,* May 15, 1998, pp. 1030–31. Tables 1–3 appeared at *Science* Online in connection with that article (www.sciencemag.org/feature/data/981368.shl [May 15, 1998]).

37. See, for example, McKinley L. Blackburn, *Comparing Poverty: The United States and Other Industrialized Nations* (Washington: American Enterprise Institute for Public Policy Research, 1997).

38. Iris C. Rotberg and James J. Harvey, *Federal Policy Options for Improving the Education of Low-Income Students,* vol. I: *Findings and Recommendations* (Washington: RAND, 1993), p. IV.

39. The National Assessment of Educational Progress (NAEP) website is nces.ed.gov/nationsreportcard/mathematics/ [November 6, 2002].

40. On September 9, 2002, I attended a lecture on one of the most significant discoveries in number theory in more than a decade. The result, which shows that fast tests exist to determine if a very large number is prime, was presented by one of the most distinguished mathematicians in the Courant Institute of New York University. He began by saying that the result, which was proven by two undergraduates and their college teacher, solved a problem that had been open for more than two hundred years. Moreover, the brilliant part of their work, he said, was an application of the most important topic in high school mathematics: polynomial long division. If this dynamic threesome can do the same for factoring, then the most important and most widespread security algorithm on the World Wide Web will be in ruins.

41. These overstatements are not that different from the exaggerated titles and problem descriptions provided on the NAEP website.

42. J. R. Anderson, L. M. Reder, and H. A. Simon, "Applications and Misapplications of Cognitive Psychology to Mathematics Education," *Texas Education Review,* vol. 1, no. 2 (Summer 2000), pp. 29–49, available at www.texaseducationreview.com [November 6, 2002]. See also act.psy.cmu.edu/personal/ja/papers/misapplied.html [November 6, 2002].

43. E. Hanushek, "The Impact of Differential Expenditures on School Performance," *Educational Researcher* (May 1989), pp. 45–62; and R. Ferguson, "Paying for Public Educa-

tion: New Evidence on How and Why Money Matters," *Harvard Journal of Legislation,* vol. 28 (1991), pp. 465–98.

44. W. L. Sanders and J. C. Rivers, *Cumulative and Residual Effects of Teachers on Future Student Academic Achievement* (Knoxville, Tenn.: Tennessee Value-Added Assessment System, 1996), available at mdk12.org/instruction/ensure/tva/tva_2.html [November 6, 2002].

45. E. A. Hanushek, J. F. Kain, and S. G. Rivkin, "Teachers, Schools, and Academic Achievement," NBER Working Paper 6691 (Cambridge, Mass.: National Bureau of Economic Research, August 1998), available at papers.nber.org/papers/w6691.pdf [November 6, 2002]; H. Jordan, R. Mendro, and D. Weerasinghe, "Teacher Effects on Longitudinal Student Achievers," *National Educational Longitudinal Study* (Department of Education, 1997); and J. Kain, *The Impact of Individual Teachers and Peers on Individual Student Achievement* (University of Texas at Dallas, Green Center for the Study of Science and Society, 1998).

46. J. W. Stigler and others, *The TIMSS Videotape Classroom Study: Methods and Findings from an Exploratory Research Project on Eighth-Grade Mathematics Instruction in Germany, Japan, and the United States*, NCES 99–074 (Department of Education, 1999), available at nces.ed.gov/pubsearch/pubsinfo.asp?pubid=1999074 [November 6, 2002]; J. W. Stigler and others, *The TIMSS Videotape Classroom Study: Eighth-Grade Mathematics Lessons: United States, Japan, and Germany*, video recording, ORAD 97–1023 (Department of Education, National Center for Education Statistics, 1997); J. W. Stigler and J. Hiebert, *The Teaching Gap: Best Ideas from the World's Teachers for Improving Education in the Classroom* (Free Press, 1999); and A. Siegel, "Effective Teaching and the TIMSS Observational Study," in W. M. Evers and H. J. Walberg, eds., *Testing Student Learning, Evaluating Teaching Effectiveness* (Stanford, Calif.: Hoover Institution, forthcoming). The last reference shows how a widely cited and remarkably open TIMSS observational study by Stigler and others systematically ignored the actual teaching of the students by the teachers and erroneously concluded that the students had independently discovered the very concepts their teacher had just reviewed.

47. Moreover, a comprehensive test is just a physical embodiment of a curriculum. For such tests, teaching to the test would seem to be desirable, and the reality is that teachers are just as able to teach to a weak testing program as a strong one. Ultimately, a sound curriculum is best confirmed by the results of a sound testing program.

Should America Be
More Like Them?
Cross-National High School
Achievement and U.S. Policy

DAVID P. BAKER

The modern comprehensive American high school, since its inception in the early twentieth century, has been considered alternately an organizational blessing and a bane on educational progress. Welcomed as an organizational advance through which the hodgepodge of schools in urban America could be made into an orderly pedagogical and administrative pyramid, the early modern high school was seen as an educational institution meeting the social and economic challenges of an increasingly diverse industrial-urban society.[1] The image of a rational, bureaucratic, large, and robust comprehensive high school was pushed forward through the middle of the twentieth century as a progressive and modernizing model for the entire nation.[2] However, by the second half of the century, as evidence of social decline, persistent poverty, racial disparities, and educational failure in urban communities became ever more obvious, the image of the urban comprehensive high school shifted from an exemplary model to a broken institution in need of reform.

The world's image of the American comprehensive high school has run a similar course over the twentieth century. The creation of a comprehensive and socially integrated secondary education was the cornerstone of U.S.

I wish to thank Diane Ravitch for organizing a stimulating policy conference; Stephen Heyneman and Jaekyung Lee for their insightful comments on the paper during the conference; and Brian Goesling and Maryellen Schaub for their assistance on earlier drafts.

education plans for reforming the defeated fascist regimes in Japan and Germany. It also had a significant influence on the development of modern secondary education systems throughout the world from the 1940s on.[3] Yet by the time the influential *A Nation at Risk* report was issued some forty years later, secondary education in the most politically and economically powerful nation in the world was declared internationally mediocre at best.[4] Ironically, many of the organizational features of the once-lauded American high school became the focus of intense speculation about how they might impede educational quality.

At the same time, international comparisons of American education have become popular and widespread in the reform debates of the last several decades. Many centerpieces of the current American reform movement were shaped through evidence and speculation on what other more educationally successful nations were doing that the United States was not. The growing volume of international studies and data available with which to compare the United States has influenced this policy trend. For example, the international data portfolio of the National Center on Education Statistics in the Department of Education has more than tripled since the 1980s and is slated to grow even more over the next decade.

As a consequence, many debates about what should be done to reform the American high school revolve around assessing U.S. national competitiveness in the world's educational progress. This is evidenced by both the Bush administration's early 1990s educational strategy and the Clinton administration's Goals 2000 (see Goal #5) and informally through two decades' worth of op-ed pieces on the international state of American education. So the question has become not only what would improve American secondary education, but also what is required to make it the best in the world? Making international competitiveness a main goal of educational reform has opened the door to wide speculation about what should be imported from other nations to improve secondary education. In other words, in American education policy circles an often-asked question over the past two decades has been: What is it that other nations do to make their mathematics and science education more effective than the United States and should it become more like theirs? Many suggestions have been put forward, and these continue to circulate within American policy debates as possible reasons that some nations do better than others in mathematics and science.

Specific features from other education systems that have intrigued American reformers of secondary education fit into five categories.

1. Create nationwide school and classroom climates that are conducive to teaching and learning.

2. Manage the nation's schools with enough local autonomy for accountability without too many centralized restrictions.

3. Motivate a nation's student body to study more and work harder to learn mathematics and science.

4. Develop and implement world-class mathematics and science curricula for a nation's secondary schools.

5. Train and motivate a national faculty in secondary mathematics and science to teach effectively, and provide them with the necessary school-based resources to do so.

Ironically, given their origin in international comparisons, many ideas for national reform have not undergone any serious cross-national testing of their ability to change a nation's standing in secondary education effectiveness.[5] Underlying the tendency to make national policy based on untested observations from cross-national data is the belief among the policy community that on the more microlevels, such as schools and students, the factors represented in the five reform categories are strongly related to a student's achievement, and empirical evidence supports this. The problem occurs with the leap to inferring that these factors will also answer the larger question of how the United States could change its overall level of international achievement competitiveness. A subtle, but problematic, shift in causal reasoning takes place when reform analysts move from speculation about what needs to happen at levels below the nation such as schools, classrooms, and students to what needs to happen at the national level. For example, no one would doubt that a demanding curriculum taught by an effective teacher in a school with resources leads to better achievement; or that a motivated student, other things equal, will learn more than an unmotivated one. Hence the assumption is that nations that do these things will have higher average achievement in subjects such as mathematics and science. But the question remains, How can nations make policy to do these things across large numbers of schools? This is often not known for sure, and further, as I show here, often national differences in aggregations of microfactors do not answer the question of what might cause cross-national differences in secondary education in mathematics and science.

Similarly, the average American high school is often assumed to be lacking in central aspects related to achievement in comparison to secondary education in other nations. Inferring backward from the United States' generally mediocre international performance, the assumption is that many American high schools are ineffective because of clear differences from high schools in more effective nations. Again, for most of the five reform speculations, this is rarely statistically tested and this unconfirmed assumption continues to have considerable impact on policy about how to move U.S. secondary education up in international rankings.

Finally, in a similar vein, in observing the international standing of the American high school, policymakers often note the diversity of students and schools within the large, localized U.S. education system. They assumed that this national feature causes special problems for certain populations of disadvantaged students, but again this has not been empirically examined cross-nationally.

Using the detailed, international data from the original 1994 Third International Mathematics and Science Study (TIMSS) and its replication in 1999, I explore these issues for a selected set of indicators for each of the five reform dimensions.[6] Although I focus on mathematics, much of what is described here could be applied to science as well. The analyses presented are based on a set of technical articles and papers in which indicators of these dimensions are examined and modeled in multivariate detail.[7] My colleagues and I have prepared these statistical analyses as part of a U.S. Department of Education–National Science Foundation jointly funded project providing theoretically based and policy-relevant secondary analysis of the 1994 TIMSS data set.

American High School from an International Perspective

Two questions are considered for each of the five secondary education reform issues: How much of a difference exists between the average American high school and the average across nations? Is the difference associated with cross-national achievement? The answers are summarized in table 1.

Reform Issue 1: Create nationwide school and classroom climates that are conducive to teaching and learning.

Many factors are conducive to a learning climate in schools and classrooms. Speculation on the state of American schools and classrooms focuses on an image of frequent disruptions by students resulting in a less effective learning climate. This includes the extreme image of the American high school as a violent and dangerous place. School disruption and vio-

Table 1. American High School from an International Perspective

School characteristic	How much of a difference exists between the average American high school and the average across nations?[a]	Is the difference associated with cross-national achievement?
School size	No	No
Math class size	No	No
Disruptive learning environment		
Eighth grade	No	Yes[b]
Twelfth grade	Small	No[c]
Degree of decentralized control of instruction and curriculum (eighth grade)	Large—more decentralized	No
Complexity of decision environment	Small—more complex	Yes—negative
Amount of instructional leadership	Large—less leadership	No
Daily assigned homework	Large—more homework	Yes—negative
Use of remedial shadow education	Large—less use	No—eighth grade; Yes—negative, twelfth grade
Classroom implementation curriculum (eighth grade)		
Number of topics covered	Small—more coverage	No
Repetition of topics	Small—more repetitious	No
Instructional resources (eighth grade)		
Absolute amount	No	Yes
Equity of distribution	No	Yes

Source: Third International Mathematics and Science Study, twelfth-grade general mathematics and eighth-grade data.
Note: Means, correlations, and other statistics and technical details of statistical tests are available from the author upon request.
a. Twelfth-grade nations are Australia, Austria, Canada, Cyprus, Czech Republic, Denmark, France, Germany, Hungary, Iceland, Italy, Lithuania, Netherlands, New Zealand, Norway, Russian Federation, Slovenia, South Africa, Sweden, Switzerland, and United States.
b. Eighth-grade effect vanishes after controlling for national funding level for education and resource inequality.
c. After extreme outlier, South Africa is removed.

lence have been topics of national concern throughout the last decade as shooting incidents have taken place in U.S. public schools. The impact of the media coverage of these occurrences is hard to measure, but reports of student and teacher fears of violence indicate that anxiety is widespread.[8] Even though some statistical reports show that levels of violence in U.S. schools have generally fallen since the early 1990s, concerns about school violence have increased, not only in the United States but in other nations as well.[9] Americans tend to perceive their public schools as sites of frequent violence and disruptions, and they probably believe that school violence occurs more here than in other nations. But how true is this and what effect do levels of student disruptions have on learning cross-nationally?

In an extensive analysis of these issues, Motoko Akiba, Gerald K. LeTendre, Brian Goesling, and I find that American eighth-grade classrooms typically are not disrupted by bullying and threats any more than the average across the other nations in TIMSS.[10] A substantial proportion of American eighth-grade teachers (40 percent) report regular classroom disruptions by students, but this proportion is still below the international average. Although considerable disruptive behavior occurs in the average American middle school, close to the same is occurring on average across other nations. Further, the number of students who report being bullied drops off by the twelfth grade in the United States. In the average American high school, 11 percent of students report being bullied, which is less than the international average of 15 percent. Furthermore, a similar drop-off from middle grades to high school happens in most other nations in the TIMSS study.

In terms of the cross-national relationship between levels of disruption and achievement, although my colleagues and I report a moderate bivariate association of .4 at the eighth grade, the analysis goes on to show that this relationship vanishes when national levels of educational resource equity and funding of education are taken into account. Not even an initial bivariate relationship exists between national achievement and national levels of student disruption in the twelfth grade. Also we find that levels of school disruption and everyday violent student behavior are not related to the level of adult violence across nations. Although, among wealthy nations, the United States has a very high adult violence rate, this does not translate into above average school disruption and everyday violence.

Reform Issue 2: Manage the nation's schools with enough local autonomy for accountability without too many centralized restrictions.

Effective management, local accountability, and lower centralized obstructions are ideas at the heart of much of the recent reform of mathematics and science education in the United States. The notion that, even in the midst of a localized administrative system, many American high schools have too many centralized restrictions (from districts, states, and the federal government) is a popular theme behind the movement for school-based management. The logic behind greater accountability and autonomy to meet curricular and instructional standards and goals is: (1) an effective degree of autonomy at the school level to make curricular and instructional decisions,

(2) a low degree to which other levels of the administrative system can influence (interfere with or complicate) these decisions, and (3) the degree to which the instructional process is under the management of schools. The origins of these prescriptions for more effective schooling are part of a long American policy debate about improving public services such as schools, and images from cross-national studies of schooling are intermixed into this discussion. An image has been created that, compared with schools in other nations, the American school is greatly hampered by ineffective management of curricular and instructional issues.

My colleagues and I have developed three indicators of national management of mathematics curriculum and instruction in schools. These suggest that the international image of the troubled administration of American middle and high schools is perhaps too simple. For example, M. Fernanda Astiz, Alexander Wiseman, and I, using a set of responses from principals, constructed a national measure of the degree to which principals versus central authorities have operational control over decisions and policies about mathematics and science curricula (degree of decentralized control).[11] The United States has the least centralized managerial process among all TIMSS nations. This is not just official policy, but also operational practice. Many American principals report that they have considerable control over curricular decisions. At the same time, however, a second measure of managerial complexity for schools shows that the American principal makes curricular and instructional decisions in a more complicated environment than is usual in other nations. In other words, although the American principal tends to have considerable autonomy compared with his or her counterpart in other nations, a number of other American stakeholders (both community and educational authorities) have some degree of influence on school decisions. But cross-nationally this is not as unusual as it might first sound. A widespread global trend in national educational systems also is found toward mixing centralized and decentralized administrative features together. This creates complexity for policymaking in many nations. In this respect the world of education governance may be moving more toward the United States. Wiseman constructed a third managerial measure and finds that the more complex managerial environment in the United States tends to decrease the amount of time and effort principals spend on direct management of instruction in their schools compared with the international average.[12]

The degree to which the indicators of national management of curriculum and instruction are related to national mathematics achievement further complicates the story. Cross-national variation in decentralization of administration is unrelated to national achievement. But, as Astiz, Wiseman, and I report, more centralized authority does lead to a smaller and more consistently implemented mathematics curriculum across nations' classrooms. Yet neither variation in centralization nor curricular consistency is related to cross-nation variation in achievement. Similarly, although the average American high school principal spends comparatively less time on management of instruction, cross-national variation in the level of instructional leadership is not related to national achievement. Furthermore, a relationship exists between national levels of stakeholders and national achievement, so that nations such as the United States, which tend to have more sources of influence on school decisions, have lower mathematics achievement. These results cast doubt on the notion that decentralization is always the best way to create more effective school management. Optimal international models for school management and achievement are not obvious at this point.

Reform Issue 3: Motivate a nation's student body to study more and work harder to learn mathematics and science.

Two features identified from other nations have received the lion's share of attention about ways to improve American high school students' motivation to study more and work harder to master mathematics at a higher level: (1) high-stakes testing and (2) more academic work outside school, through assigned homework and use of more formal tutoring and other methods know as shadow education. TIMSS affords three useful indicators of motivation and outside schoolwork at the national level.

First is homework. Nationally just over half of American high school students in mathematics have assigned homework every day, which is substantially larger than the international average of just under a third of students with daily homework. While this may be good news for proponents of frequent homework, nations with higher proportions of students assigned homework tend to have lower national mathematics achievement. Gerald LeTendre, Motoko Akiba, Alexander Wiseman, and I find that more homework is often assigned in classrooms to make up for deficient progress in class.[13] Too much homework, or misuse of homework in many classrooms, may be an indicator of ineffective teaching and a weak application of a curriculum within a nation.

In recent decades the world has seen growing use of tutoring services and related supplemental practices to help students learn the in-school curriculum. This institutional growth has been named shadow education because what goes on in these private services shadows formal school curricula and requirements. Although some nations, such as Japan and South Korea, have elaborate and highly publicized shadow education activities, shadow education was reported in all TIMSS nations. Motoko Akiba, Gerald LeTendre, Alexander Wiseman, and I find that shadow education is widespread, and sizable numbers of students in most nations use it to help them with mathematics.[14] Contrary to earlier speculation about shadow education, most students in most nations use it for remedial purposes (or to address deficits in instruction), not for enhancement. American students' use of shadow education follows this trend and usually is remedial. Furthermore, the overall use of such educational services in the United States is lower than the international average.

Some American educational reformers speculate that the widespread use of shadow education in other nations may lead to higher national achievement—for example, in Japan and South Korea. The main argument is that the presence of extensive shadow education will be positively associated with national achievement levels. The logic behind this idea is twofold. First, extensive shadow education represents extended academic training for a large proportion of the student population and hence has the potential to increase overall achievement. Second, shadow education is a consequence of a larger process that motivates intensive efforts in behalf of certain subjects (for example, mathematics) through such devices as preparing for high-stakes testing or other tightly linked accountability mechanisms.[15] A number of other nations in the mid-1990s, when the TIMSS data were collected, were using high-stakes testing. Although the United States has never had a national high-stakes test of the type found in these nations, since then high-stakes testing has grown as a local and state practice in the United States with the hope that it will increase student motivation to learn.

Internationally, however, not much support is found for this twofold argument as a means to increase national achievement. For eighth grade, my colleagues and I estimated a structural model of the direct effects of each of six detailed indicators of shadow education use in a nation on national mathematics achievement levels plus the indirect effect of high-stakes tests through shadow education. None of the six indicators of shadow education is associated with national variation in mathematics achievement, and the package of high-stakes tests and shadow education is not associated with variation in national achievement. The analysis also found no direct effect of high-stakes tests on national achievement.[16] At the high school level, wide use of shadow education (again, mostly remedial) is negatively associated with national achievement. These findings indicate that the speculation on national arrangements of high-stakes tests and wide use of shadow education to increase student effort and motivation may not be a cause of cross-national differences in achievement.

Reform Issue 4: Develop and implement world-class mathematics and science curricula for a nation's secondary schools.

A chief messages to emerge from the early reporting on TIMSS is that the United States should reform its mathematics and science curricula if it is to improve internationally. William H. Schmidt and his colleagues have published numerous reports that argue that the intended curricula (that is, the planned official curricula) in U.S. schools are too broad, repetitious, and not demanding enough for American students to compete effectively on a global scale.[17]

While I have already examined other factors related to curriculum, such as how decisions about it are made, two indicators of the implementation of the curriculum in eighth-grade general mathematics classrooms are of note. First, Gerald LeTendre, Alexander Wiseman, Erling Boe, Brian Goesling, and I find that the implemented mathematics curriculum in the average American classroom is slightly broader than the average in other nations, but this characteristic of curricula is not related to cross-national achievement.[18] Second, the same is true with the repetition of curricular topics. In the average American classroom there is slightly more repetition, but this characteristic is not related to cross-national achievement.

Reform Issue 5: Train and motivate a national faculty in secondary mathematics and science to teach effectively, and provide them with the necessary school-based resources to do so.

Although the TIMSS data have little to say about the training of mathematics and science teachers, they do contain a significant amount of information about the availability of instructional resources. These data provide information about school-level availability of resources such as budgets for teaching materials, in-classroom supplies, library service and quality, physical plant resources, adequate instructional space, and computer hardware and software. In addition to absolute levels of instructional resources, Brian Goesling, Gerald K. LeTendre, Inga Dora Sigfusdottir, and I developed a measure of instructional resource inequality between schools with which one can compare them cross-nationally.[19] In other words, a national system of education has large inequality of resources if the distribution across schools is highly uneven; for example, schools serving wealthier communities receive more resources than other schools. Taken together, the absolute and relative resource levels in nations are revealing.

Instructional resources available to the average American school are about the same as the average across the TIMSS nations.[20] Similarly, instructional resource inequality in the United States is about the same as in the average TIMSS nation. Both the absolute national level of instructional resources and the nature of their distribution throughout systems are significantly related to national achievement. Further, among the wealthy nations in the TIMSS study, the United States has comparatively high levels of resource inequalities in instructional resources across schools.

Educating Disadvantaged Students in America

A constant challenge facing American education is meeting the special education needs of an economically and culturally diverse society. A number of large, national studies over the past two decades has shown the growth of an American underclass in both urban and rural communities whose conditions are resistant to amelioration by general economic development in the United States.[21] While the so-called new economy has propelled wealth and opportunity for many, social and economic inequalities are widening. For example, even though there has been a worldwide reduction in income inequality between nations, there is a greater world pattern of within-nation inequality.[22]

Numerous critics of American schooling have pointed out the inferior educational opportunities for many disadvantaged youth living in urban and rural communities as well as the significant role limited educational opportunity plays in reproducing poverty.[23] Although, as a result, policy has focused on the poor quality of educational opportunities in public high schools serving disadvantaged students, all the educational improvements and reforms of the last forty years have had less impact on disadvantaged groups in the American society than on the mainstream. Race and social class gaps in achievement continue and remain entrenched within the system.[24]

With the TIMSS data I examined how well American schools educate students from several types of disadvantaged backgrounds compared with other nations. I selected two indicators of social and economic disadvantage—low education of the student's mother and living in a single-parent home. Although these family characteristics do not assure a disadvantaged home in every case, they often lead to a disadvantaged home life for many students. The proportion of students with uneducated mothers and single-parent homes in the U.S. twelfth-grade TIMSS sample is 11 percent and 15 percent, respectively (international means for wealthy nations are 29 percent and 11 percent, respectively).[25] Among the thirteen wealthy developed nations in the TIMSS twelfth-grade sample, American disadvantaged students learn considerably less general mathematics than similar disadvantaged students in other nations (see table 2). The American mean mathematics knowledge for both students with mothers with less than a high school education and from single-parent homes is strikingly low. Because the U.S. total sample of twelfth graders did not perform well, it is not a surprise that disadvantaged students in the United States also performed poorly. But it is also true that while the American total eighth-grade sample did as well as a number of other wealthy nations, American eighth-grade disadvantaged students finished last compared with similar students in other wealthy nations.[26]

To illustrate the ramifications of this poor educational record with needy students for national academic competitiveness, one can calculate the impact on the total American mean mathematics knowledge if the United States were to educate its disadvantaged students as well as other nations do. If the United States were as successful as Sweden in educating youth with mothers without a high school degree, the total mean would be improved by 14 points. If the United States did that and also did as well as Sweden does with youth whose mothers have just a high school degree, the U.S. mean would move to 488, which would put the United States beyond five wealthy nations that it currently performs below.[27] This is a simple exercise that can be played with any proportion of a distribution. But the message here is clear: Receiving a subpar education significantly adds to the risk of entering the ranks of the underclass, and being from a disadvantaged home in the United States places a youth at greater risk of poor educational performance than in many other nations. Moreover, these findings show that educational systems in other nations have ways to lessen the impact of disadvantaged backgrounds on school achievement. This is not to say that what is done in these nations is perfect or that no negative impact accrues from disadvantaged families. But these findings suggest that social

Table 2. Education of Disadvantaged Students in the United States from an International Perspective

Ranking of nation		*Ranking of nation*
Students with mothers without a high school degree (mean proportion in nation = 29 percent)	*Mathematics mean*	*Students from single-parent homes (mean proportion in nation = 11 percent)*
	560	Netherlands
	550	
Netherlands		Iceland
Sweden	540	Sweden
Denmark		
	530	Switzerland
Iceland		Australia
New Zealand	520	Norway, Denmark
Austria, Norway		Austria, Canada
Switzerland	510	
	International mean	New Zealand
France, Australia	500	
Canada		
	490	
	480	
		Germany
	470	
	460	
Germany	450	
	440	
United States		United States
	430	

Source: Third International Mathematics and Science Study, twelfth-grade general mathematics data.

and educational policies may be at work in other nations that could help in the United States in meeting the educational challenge of students from disadvantaged families.

What does an international perspective reveal about the policy areas that might be useful to examine in more detail with the aim of improving education for the most disadvantaged? I selected four national educational characteristics from the analyses of my colleagues' and my prior work that had a positive or negative association with cross-national mathematics achievement (see table 3). For each of these characteristics I calculated the national

Table 3. Comparison of U.S. High Schools Serving Students with Mothers without High School Degrees and Similar Schools in Other Wealthy Nations

Characteristic	Comparison
Instructional resources	U.S. schools have more shortages
Equitable distribution of resources	U.S. schools experience more resource inequalities
Daily assigned homework	U.S. schools assign substantially more
Complexity for local decisions about instruction and curriculum	U.S. schools have more stakeholders with influence on decisions

Source: Third International Mathematics and Science Study, twelfth-grade data.
Note: See table 2 for list of comparison nations.

mean for high schools in the United States and twelve other wealthy nations that enroll the most disadvantaged students (students with mothers who have less than a high school education).[28]

In each case, the schools that serve American disadvantaged students appear problematic in comparison to high schools in other nations. Schools that serve disadvantaged students in the United States tend to have lower absolute instructional resources and work in a system with greater resource inequalities overall as compared with schools for disadvantaged students in other nations. Given that the level of overall national wealth is similar among these nations, this is not just a function of national differences in wealth. For a wealthy nation, American high schools with disadvantaged students are far behind in supplying fundamental instructional resources.

Teachers in American high schools with disadvantaged students are almost three times more likely to assign daily homework than their counterparts working with disadvantaged students in other wealthy nations. Large amounts of assigned homework could indicate ineffective teaching and curriculum implementation. American principals of these schools are faced with a more complex environment (that is, greater numbers of stakeholders involved in decisions) in which to make local decisions about curriculum and instruction than their counterparts in other nations. This complexity leads to a decisionmaking process that is negatively related to achievement. Although these are just some of the possible causes of the poor international performance of American disadvantaged students in high school mathematics, they illustrate the massive challenge before the United States to improve education for a group of students and families that has continually been left behind.

Implications for American Educational Policy

Over the past century, the image of the American public high school has gone from an international model of effective secondary education to a symbol of the United States' educational crisis. How much these contrasting images match reality is not easy to determine. From an international perspective, the American high school clearly is not as negatively extreme in its practices and environment as some of its critics have suggested. However, American high schools fail to do some things high schools in other systems routinely do to advance mathematics achievement for students.

In considering U.S. schools internationally, one must keep in mind that significant global forces are at work to lessen cross-national differences in how schooling operates. The current global trend is toward convergence among structure and operation of the world's school systems. For example, in a 2001 paper, Gerald K. LeTendre, Motoko Akiba, Brian Goesling, Alexander W. Wiseman, and I use the TIMSS case-study transcripts and teachers survey and find substantial isomorphism among aspects of teaching in Germany, Japan, and the United States.[29] Another paper shows that a widespread single pattern of smaller school effects and larger family background effects on student mathematics achievement across all TIMSS nations is in part a function of the homogenizing of schooling through increasing state support of education.[30]

The analyses reviewed here suggest several conclusions about educational reform and the state of the American high school. First, that no single silver bullet can solve U.S. education problems is certainly true, if somewhat incomplete. Analyses of international data over the past several years suggest that a whole case of silver bullets may be required to make real changes in the international competitiveness of American secondary education. If concern about international rankings is not just rhetorical and the United States is truly dedicated to reforming mathematics and science education so that American students can be more competitive internationally, then educators and policymakers must realize that the international findings point to a need for a robust set of reforms instead of more singular approaches.

An example of this is the need to look beyond the messages about reform initially originating from TIMSS. A dominating policy message from earlier press releases and the earliest analyses of TIMSS is that the American mathematics and science curricula are broken and need reforming. I would certainly agree that the United States should reform its curricula along more effective standards; there is nothing to disagree with about this. And certainly comparative analysis has helped reveal alternative models for curricula. But subsequent analyses of TIMSS show how complex the whole picture is. Reforming key operational pieces of the American school such as the intended curricula or the accountability of instruction without more effective distribution of basic instructional resources, particularly to the schools that need resources the most, will not lead to significant national improvement. The same can be said of the current major reform idea of accountability and local control of instruction and learning. These are clearly good ideas, but to launch them without coordination with other reforms, such as resource and teacher quality improvement, will most likely not achieve much national change. Certainly the desperate conditions of education for disadvantaged American students will necessitate simultaneous reform on a number of fronts.

This kind of reform is not easy to accomplish. A key difficulty of American education policy reform is the task of making broad change palatable to the multilayered structure of districts, states, and federal government, intermixed with a vast array of powerful interest groups. Consequently it is necessary to push hard for any particular reform, and often this leads to simpler, stripped-down messages. American educational policy recommendations are aptly named reform movements, akin to political and social movement campaigns. To change policy in such an environment, simplified singular reforms, instead of more complex multiple reforms, have the best chance of successfully running the political maze of the U.S. educational system. This presents a formidable challenge to getting American education to adopt a broad integrated approach to reform suggested by international findings.

Looking across these analyses of TIMSS and other similar international data gives one concern about finding clear ways to make national policy. Some of the surprises found in research studies illustrate this best. For example, finding that large amounts of shadow education are remedial in most nations and that a positive relationship does not exist between substantial outside education and national achievement came as a surprise given the volume of speculation about the positive effects of enhancement shadow education in high-performing nations such as Japan and South Korea. Or, finding that widespread daily homework in a system is perhaps an indicator of weak instruction and curricular implementation seems at first a paradox, but upon further reflection makes sense. National teaching corps that use homework judiciously in the teaching process and less routinely (that is, nonritualistically) reflect a number of positive things about a national education system. And, finding that national rates of school disruption and everyday violence are more a function of the overall quality of schooling and not a function of adult violence in a nation suggests a host of policy implications that are not usually considered in terms of curbing school violence and student disruption.

Nations are nations, schools are schools, and students are students; causal factors at one level do not necessarily or automatically transfer to other levels. The full-scale implementation of secondary education in nations is a complex phenomenon, influenced by more than the simple linear aggregation of school-level or student-level factors. All levels of the system share processes, but the increasing organizational complexity as one moves organizationally further from the student adds entirely new dimensions that have an impact on the overall practice of education. The seemingly intractable problem of limited educational opportunities and poor academic outcomes of economically and racially disadvantaged students in the United States is a prime example of how elusive systemic solutions are. But at the same time, the United States has seen other nations do significantly better with their disadvantaged students. If nothing else, this provides some hope for more systemic national reforms.

Seen from an international perspective, the American high school and what goes on there suggest that education policy cannot be easily separated from other sectors of policy. For example, using the TIMSS data, Gillian Thompson shows that among European nations cross-national variation in family policy influences the detrimental effects of single-parent families on achievement.[31] Nations with more progressive economic family assistance policies tend to have a weaker connection between family problems and mathematics achievement. This is preliminary work that needs more development, but along with the other analyses presented here it suggests that broader policy reforms, such as coordinating education and family policy, will be needed to make significant national progress in secondary education of all American students.

Comment by Jaekyung Lee

David P. Baker makes a significant contribution to the understanding of cross-national education differences by synthesizing many studies that he and his colleagues have done with the Third International Mathematics and Science Study (TIMSS) data and by drawing policy implications from that synthesis. This paper not only addresses the issue of poor performance of the average American student from an international perspective, but also pays attention to the poorer achievement of disadvantaged students in the United States. Baker's paper provides a comprehensive look into school effect by combining a complex array of the TIMSS data on school input, process, context, and outcomes. However, the paper also reveals the limitations of the current TIMSS data, as well as limitations in Baker's studies as they relate to critical policy questions.

Issues of Selection for Review and Comparison

In reviewing and synthesizing past TIMSS studies, Baker selects almost exclusively his own studies without referencing other studies on the same topic. Providing a comprehensive and balanced literature review, including earlier international studies using non–TIMSS data as well as the studies of TIMSS data by other researchers, would have created a scholarly framework within which his findings could be better evaluated. In the comparative research field, different studies often produce findings that are not always congruent with each other. Much depends on which countries and variables are selected and how they are analyzed and compared.

Who is being compared with whom is critical in this kind of comparative study. The validity of selection and comparability is not discussed in this paper. Baker is not consistent in his selection of countries for comparison. In the first part of his paper, when examining average achievement, Baker includes all TIMSS countries for comparison. But in the second part of his paper, where he examines the achievement of disadvantaged students, Baker selects only developed, wealthy countries. Moreover, he uses both eighth- and twelfth-grade data for the former comparison but only twelfth-grade data for the latter comparison. It is not clear why he chose to use different sets of countries or grades for comparisons and how such different selection criteria might have influenced his findings and conclusions.

Missing Variables and Measurement Issues

The studies that Baker reviews use several indicators to measure school effects, but some important variables are missing in those analyses. To begin with, information on the rigor of the curriculum is lacking. Based on the TIMSS teacher survey results, Baker points out that the average U.S. eighth-grade math class has more coverage and repetition of topics and that these variables are not related to achievement variations across the TIMSS countries. Without considering other key instructional variables, however, how the breadth of instruction alone can be related to achievement outcomes is not clear. The level of implemented curriculum should have been considered. TIMSS curriculum studies showed that the U.S. curriculum is not only less focused but also less advanced.[32] Further, Baker's comparison of implemented curriculum is limited to the eighth-grade data, and inferring that the American high school is not much different from an international average based on the eighth-grade level data is misleading. Simply comparing the national averages also conceals substantial variations in the type of courses offered by American high schools and taken by their students.

Teacher quality and training are another important set of missing variables in Baker's review. He acknowledges that the TIMSS data provide little information on the training of teachers. In fact, teacher quality can be the most important factor that determines the quality of instruction. Even when teachers say that they cover the same thing to the same extent, their differences in content and pedagogical knowledge should result in significant variation in the quality of teaching and learning.

In addition to these kinds of key schooling variables, much broader cultural and institutional differences must be considered. East Asian countries such as Japan and South Korea could not have performed best without their traditional cultural influences: high expectations for academic achievement, high aspiration for college education, high level of parental engagement and support for learning, and highly homogeneous value system. These cultural forces interplay with or are reinforced by centralized institutional rules and arrangements that restrict student choices, impose fierce competition for a common goal (for example, entrance into top-tier universities), and reward academically successful students.

Private tutoring in Japan and South Korea reflects these forces and plays an important role in boosting academic achievement.[33] Although Baker argues that this out-of-school education variable (shadow education) generally does not explain cross-country variation in achievement, the variable measured by students' self-reported frequency and amount of after-school lessons may not capture the level of rigor and intensity that are strongly influenced by cultural and institutional forces. In a similar vein, his argument that high-stakes exams have no effect on national achievement needs further investigation. His analysis does not differentiate how high the stakes are and how competitive the exams are.[34]

In his analysis of equity, Baker uses two indicators of socioeconomic status (SES): mother's education and single-parent household. He argues that these family characteristics often lead to a disadvantaged home life for many students. One test of this argument is whether these are good predictors of student achievement. Common sense says yes. However, an analysis of the TIMSS data by D. Koretz and his colleagues shows the insignificant influence of mother's and father's education on student achievement in the United States.[35] They also find that the effects of mother's education in TIMSS were less than half the size compared with the results from the National Education Longitudinal Study. The reason for this is unknown, but the finding raises doubt about the reliability of students' self-reported parental education variable in TIMSS. Checking other indicators of SES such as the number of books available at home would be helpful.

Issues of Data Analysis and Potential Biases

Ecological fallacy means that the between-country relationship of variables cannot be used to suggest that the within-country relationship would be the same. In addition to cross-national analysis, unique predictors of academic achievement need to be identified country by country. For example, T. N. Postlethwaite observes that the relationship between whole class teaching and achievement is positive at the between-country level, whereas most countries have no relationship and some countries even have a negative relationship at the within-country level.[36] Baker also points out that causal relationship at one level does not necessarily transfer to other levels. This raises a question as to what would be the most appropriate level or unit of analysis to guide policymaking. The answer depends on at which level of a school system a given schooling variable can be best manipulated. Can highly decentralized countries such as the United States manipulate daily assigned homework? If the classroom is regarded as the most appropriate locus of control over homework, then classroom-level analysis of the relationship between homework and achievement should provide the most meaningful and informative results. This issue also relates to the question of whether the United States can be fairly compared with other countries that have a centralized national school system with more control over key schooling variables.

Furthermore, drawing causal inferences from cross-sectional data analysis is difficult. For example, Baker observes that the relationship between homework assignment and achievement is negative. Even though the analysis was done at the classroom level, the result may be interpreted in a different way: When students were not performing well, teachers were more likely to assign homework. The same can be said of the relationship between shadow education and achievement: Lower-performing students were more likely to seek private tutoring help. Because of these limitations, Baker's analysis of the TIMSS data does not provide clear answers about school effect. Despite the cross-sectional nature of TIMSS data, more analysis of achievement gains, instead of achievement status, is needed. Why does U.S. students' achievement deteriorate from the eighth grade to the twelfth grade relative to other countries? [37] Which countries improved student learning more than others at the eighth-grade level and why? By addressing these questions, observed achievement gains could be better related to education policies and policy effects could be better assessed.

Achievement Gap and Inequity

Baker's comparison of disadvantaged students' achievement deserves further analysis. The meaning of disadvantage may not be comparable from country to country. Do single-mother households in Europe have the same level of socioeconomic disadvantage as their counterparts in the United States? Even within the United States, disadvantage has several dimensions and the indicators may change as population changes over time. For example, students from a non–English language background have grown rapidly in the United States, and they face special disadvantages for schooling that other disadvantaged groups do not. More discussion about the nature and type of social or educational disadvantage in each country is needed.

Contrary to a popular belief, the U.S. distribution of academic achievement does not show any greater inequality than does an average country. In terms of variability within country as measured by standard deviation, U.S.

Figure 1. Average Eighth-Grade Math Scores by Living with Mother in South Korea and the United States

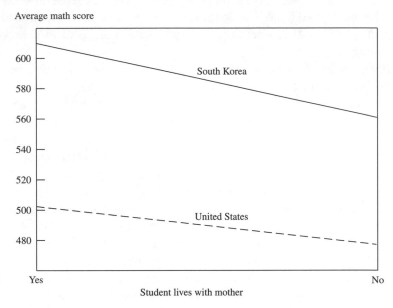

eighth graders are slightly above the international mean in mathematics and the United States does not have a large achievement gap.[38] It would be more meaningful to compare the achievement gap instead of the group average among the countries. How big is the gap between students from single-parent homes versus other students in the United States? How does the gap in the United States (not the average score of single-parent students) compare with the corresponding gap in other countries? For example, figure 1 and figure 2 show that the TIMSS eighth-grade math achievement gap between disadvantaged students and others in the United States, based on Baker's definition, is not different from South Korea. It would be more meaningful to relate the measure of the resource inequity to measures of achievement gap, instead of to the achievement of disadvantaged students.

Conclusion

The central question raised in Baker's paper is whether the United States can improve its performance by imitating what higher-performing countries do. Here performance concerns include both academic excellence and

Figure 2. Average Eighth-Grade Math Scores by Father's Highest Education Level in South Korea and the United States

Average math score

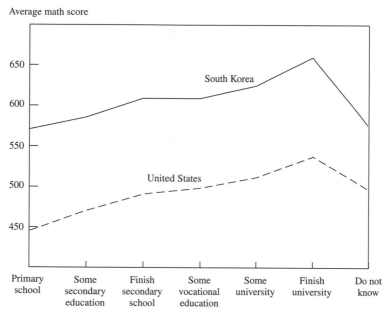

Father's highest education level

equity. The former is usually measured by the level of average achievement; the latter, by the size of the achievement gap. Full agreement has not been reached on what factors account for the higher average achievement of countries such as Japan and South Korea. Moreover, consensus has not been found on whether the United States has more or less equitable distribution of achievement.

What seems obvious, though, is that the United States has moved in the direction of following those higher-performing countries' path during the last two decades. However, what many people may not realize as well is that those higher-performing East Asian countries followed the opposite path (for example, destandardization, diversification, decentralization) during the same period of time, and the Eastern and Western school systems may become more alike over time.[39] U.S. educational reform goals must be reconsidered. Educators and policymakers should be thinking about ways to maintain the strengths of the American school system as much as ways to fix its weaknesses. A balancing act is in order.

Comment by Stephen P. Heyneman

Cross-national education survey research was first just an experiment, born by a chance visit of Torsten Husen from the University of Stockholm to the Comparative Education Center at the University of Chicago in the mid-1950s. There, Husen met C. Arnold Anderson, Mary Jean Bowman, and Benjamin Bloom, whose view was that the whole world should be seen as a single educational laboratory. From this meeting emerged the International Association for the Evaluation of Educational Achievement (IEA), which, for diplomatic reasons, was managed from Sweden. First results appeared in 1964. Since then, thirty-three cross-national studies have been conducted, twenty-nine of which were associated with IEA.

From the beginning a myriad of problems emerged—the logistics of such a massive enterprise, the complexities of agreeing on common definitions, methodologies, sampling and data management. These problems have been the focus of a great deal of official and unofficial assessments of the state of the art, which helped to generate a number of significant improvements in the standards expected for cross-national surveys.[40] In spite of this progress, doubts and skepticism remain.[41] These have generated carefully constructed replies.[42]

Early reviews of cross-national policy implications focused attention on better understanding of the generalizations associated with the influences on academic achievement. One of the most persistent generalizations is that the influence of the home is greater than the influence of the school itself.[43] Stephen P. Heyneman and William Loxley, however, found that the degree of this influence varies across nations and that the lower a nation's gross domestic product (GDP), the more influence the school seems to have.[44] This finding has been a principal rationale for the investment in school quality by the World Bank, United States Agency for International Development (USAID), United Nations Educational, Scientific, and Cultural Organization (UNESCO), and many other development assistance agencies. Although recent reanalyses have challenged the strength of the earlier findings, the current conclusions are that the influence of socioeconomic status on achievement is by no means uniform across nations, age or grade levels, gender, and subject matter.[45]

More recent policy reviews have tried to speculate on the meaning of these cross-national projects on local education policy within the United

States. William H. Schmidt and his colleagues, for instance, helped Americans focus on the weaknesses of having a splintered curriculum in which a scattering of topics is presented to students with insufficient attention to the progression, sequencing, and review found in more academically successful nations.[46]

David P. Baker has used cross-national studies to generate novel hypotheses across a wide variety of education policy characteristics. He finds that American school systems distribute school resources less fairly and are less able to educate the most disadvantaged students by comparison to other countries. He also uses cross-national studies to challenge common assumptions—for instance, that American schools are more likely to experience violence and classroom disruption. He finds that more homework is often a proxy for poor educational quality and that nations with effective family assistance policies are better able to overcome the handicap of social poverty. And he uses these cross-national studies as the basis for speculating that the reason American school systems have such significant policy difficulties stems from their public governance in which elections for education posts determine policy direction. Because political campaigns have a single and simplistic focus (sex education, get God back in school, more time on task, class size, and so on) that attracts voters for school board elections, the nature of American education reform seems to be as fractured as the sequencing in its curriculum.

The problems in Baker's paper are few, but not without importance. Baker seems to assume that remedial work (the main focus of homework) is somehow less than useful. The term *remedial* seems to imply something pejorative. But in any survey the interpretation of what remedial means may vary. It may imply work to make up for previous gaps in understanding, or it may imply work on the essential skill mechanisms within a curriculum. For instance, it may include craftsmanship skills, something many schools in the United States lack.

For example, one school I visited recently in Russia displayed a large number of drawings in a hallway. All were considered excellent, but all were of one thing: a half-empty glass of water on a table. I asked why all the drawings were of the same thing. The answer was that they represented an essential exercise that all students (not just art students) must master before they can go on to more creative expression, and the display was supposed to highlight the differences in which creativity could be expressed within a restricted task.

I wondered how many schools in the United States would have taken such a mundane task to such an honorable level. I wondered whether the average level of drawing among students in the United States was adversely affected by the lack of attention to the mundane craftsmanship skills necessary to draw well. Could the tendency to use homework as remedial work be a sign that American teachers were attempting to lay the necessary groundwork for the craft of math and science?

In much of Baker's discussion of school governance, only two sets of actors are mentioned as having legitimate claims to schools. This is a serious mistake often made by American education policy analysts. The discussion of school choice is distorted by suggesting that it is dichotomous, that it is a tension between parent and state. Three different sources of legitimate claims normally are made on the governance of schools and school systems. They are the state, the parents, and the education profession.[47] The fact that the education profession is often left out of discussions about school choice in the United States may be a reflection of the weakness of the education profession in determining the future of American education. But just because it may be a weak source of governance within the Untied States, one should not assume that it is weak elsewhere.

Baker observes that the degree of state control differs from one country to another, and between local and national authorities, but he does not point out that the level of control by the education profession differs as well. Key to understanding education governance issues across countries is to understand better that legitimate control over schools and school systems is not binary. In many instances, understanding about what is possible in terms of governance, and characterization of countries as being more pro–parent choice as opposed to more controlled by state authorities, is flawed by such a simplistic binary model.

Torsten Husen, C. Arnold Anderson, Mary Jean Bowman, and Benjamin Bloom should be proud today. Almost fifty years after their meeting, their dream of using the world as a research laboratory to better understand the process of education has been realized. Cross-national projects, which attempt to calibrate the degree of curriculum coverage and the influences on achievement, are a normal, regular, and permanent part of the world of education.

Baker's paper represents the best of this genre of new and innovative interpretations of what Bloom had in mind when he thought of the world of education as a single laboratory. He did not think that it was uniform or that identical principles or intervention strategies would emerge. Instead, he was energized by the possibility that all peoples could learn by looking at themselves through information systematically collected from around the world. This is what Baker's paper does so well.

Notes

1. David Tyack, *The One Best System: A History of American Urban Education* (Harvard University Press, 1974).

2. James Conant, *The American High School Today* (New York: Signet, 1959).

3. D. Baker and D. Holsinger, "Human Capital Formation and School Expansion in Asia: Does a Unique Regional Model Exist?" *International Journal of Comparative Sociology* (1996).

4. National Commission on Excellence in Education, A *Nation at Risk: The Imperative for Education Reform* (Government Printing Office, 1983).

5. In the initial official reports on the Third International Mathematics and Science Study (TIMSS), the Department of Education included preliminary bivariate analyses. More complex analyses slowly emerged after these reports were issued.

6. For a description of the TIMSS study and data, see International Association for the Evaluation of Educational Achievement, *User Guide for the TIMSS International Database: Primary and Middle School Years*, edited by Eugenio J. Gonzalez and Teresa A. Smith (Chestnut Hill, Mass.: TIMSS International Study Center, 1997).

7. As described in the technical papers, all associations between reform factors and national achievement reported here have been verified using various appropriate multivariate modeling techniques including estimation by ordinary least squares regression, Hierarchial Linear Models, and structural equations.

8. K. Maguire and A. L. Pastore, eds., "Sourcebook of Criminal Justice Statistics, 1998" (www.albany.edu/sourcebook [1998]).

9. Department of Education and Department of Justice, *1999 Annual Report on School Safety* (Government Printing Office, 2000); and M. D. Hinds, ed., *Violent Kids: Can We Change the Trend?* (New York: National Issues Forums Institute and Public Agenda, 2000).

10. Motoko Akiba and others, "Student Victimization: National and School System Effects on School Violence in Thirty-seven Nations," *American Education Research Journal* (forthcoming).

11. M. Fernanda Astiz, Alexander Wiseman, and David P. Baker, "Slouching towards Decentralization: Consequences of Globalization for Curricular Control in National Education Systems," *Comparative Education Review,* vol. 46, no. 1 (2002), pp. 66–88.

12. Alexander W. Wiseman, "Principals' Instructional Management Activity: A Cross-National Analysis of How School Environments Influence What School Principals Do," Ph.D. dissertation, Pennsylvania State University, Educational Theory and Policy Program, 2001.

13. Gerald LeTendre and others, "Homework and the Quality of Education: A Cross-National Exploration," Working Paper (Pennsylvania State University, Education Policy Studies Department, 2002).

14. David P. Baker and others, "Worldwide Shadow Education: Outside-School Learning, Institutional Quality of Schooling, and Cross-National Mathematics Achievement," *Educational Evaluation and Policy Analysis*, vol. 23, no. 1 (2001), pp. 1–17.

15. National Research Council, *High Stakes: Testing for Tracking, Promotion, and Graduation* (Washington: National Academy Press, 1999).

16. For modest evidence of an effect, see J. Bishop, *Do Curriculum-Based External Exit Exam Systems Enhance Student Achievement?* CPRE Research Report Series RR–40 (University of Pennsylvania, Graduate School of Education, Consortium for Policy Research in Education, 1998).

17. Because chapter 6, "American High Schools in an International Context" by William H. Schmidt, in this volume compares in detail the American twelfth-grade curricula with other nations, I do not pursue all the intricacies of this topic here. W. Schmidt and others, *Many Visions, Many Aims: A Cross-National Investigation of Curricular Intentions in School Mathematics* (Netherlands: Kluwer Academic Publishers, 1997).

18. Gerald LeTendre and others, "Classroom Implementation of National Curricula and Cross-National Patterns of Achievement," Working Paper (Pennsylvania State University, Education Policy Studies, 2002).

19. Brian Goesling and others, "The Institutional Context of Educational Stratification: Comparing School Resource Inequalities within Thirty-five Countries," paper presented at the annual meeting of the American Educational Research Association, New Orleans, Louisiana, April 2002.

20. My colleagues and I are currently undertaking this kind of analysis for the twelfth-grade sample. Preliminary results indicate a similar trend cross-nationally and for the United States.

21. W. Wilson, *The Truly Disadvantaged: The Inner City, the Underclass, and Public Policy* (University of Chicago Press, 1987).

22. Glenn Firebaugh, *The New Geography of Global Income Inequality* (Harvard University Press, 2002).

23. J. Kozol, *Savage Inequalities* (Crown Publishers, 1991).

24. George Farkas, "Racial Disparities and Discrimination in Education: What Do We Know, How Do We Know It, and What Do We Need to Know?" workshop paper on Measuring Disparities in Education, National Research Council, Division of Behavioral and Social Sciences and Education, Committee on National Statistics, Washington, D.C., July 1, 2002.

25. While the United States has a high stop-out rate (around 20 percent) by age eighteen, it offers a number of ways to obtain a high school diploma. As a result, the United States has one of the highest high school completion rates in the world in cohorts aged twenty-four to twenty-eight.

26. David P. Baker, Gerald LeTendre, and Brian Goesling, "Educational Resource Inequalities among American Schools and Cross-National Differences," Working Paper (Pennsylvania State University, Education Policy Studies Department, 2002).

27. Similar results are found for other indicators of student disadvantage.

28. I took the quartile of schools that had the largest proportion of students with mothers with less than high school education.

29. Gerald K. LeTendre and others, "Teachers' Work: Institutional Isomorphism and Cultural Variation in the U.S., Germany, and Japan," *Educational Researcher,* vol. 30 (2001), pp. 3–15.

30. David P. Baker, Brian Goesling, and Gerald K. LeTendre, "Socio-Economic Status, School Quality, and National Economic Development: A Cross-National Analysis of the 'Heyneman-Loxley Effect' on Mathematics and Science Achievement," *Comparative Education Review,* vol. 46, no. 3 (2002), pp. 291–313.

31. Gillian Thompson, "Does Family Policy Environment Mediate the Effect of Single-Parenthood on Children's Academic Achievement? A Study of Fourteen European Coun-

tries," paper presented at the annual meeting of the Comparative and International Society, Orlando, Florida, March 2002.

32. What makes such diffuse curriculum worse is that it is less challenging. The topics being taught in U.S. eighth-grade math classrooms were at a seventh-grade level compared with other countries. See National Center for Education Statistics, *Pursuing Excellence: A Study of U.S. Eighth-Grade Mathematics and Science Teaching, Learning, Curriculum, and Achievement in International Context* (Department of Education, 1996); and W. H. Schmidt, C. C. McKnight, and S. T. Raizen, *A Splintered Vision: An Investigation of U.S. Science and Mathematics Education* (Boston: Kluwer Academic Publishers, 1997).

33. See J. Lee, "Missing Links in International Education Studies: Can We Compare the U.S. with East Asian Countries?" *International Electronic Journal for Leadership in Learning,* vol. 3, no. 18 (1999), available at www.acs.ucalgary.ca/~iejll/volume3/lee.html [April 2002].

34. See M. A. Eckstein and H. J. Noah, *Secondary School Examinations: International Perspectives on Policies and Practice* (Yale University Press, 1993).

35. See D. Koretz, D. McCaffrey, and T. Sullivan, "Predicting Variations in Mathematics Performance in Four Countries Using TIMSS," *Educational Policy Analysis Archives,* vol. 9, no. 34 (2001), available at epaa.asu.edu/epaa/v9n34 [April 2002].

36. T. N. Postlethwaite, "Overview of Issues in International Achievement Studies," paper prepared for a lecture at Oxford University, Department of Education, 1997.

37. Another limitation of the Third International Mathematics and Science Study data is that the achievement test score is not on a developmental scale so an absolute amount of learning gain from the eighth grade to the twelfth grade cannot be examined. Moreover, differences in twelfth-grade students' age level among countries make the comparison difficult. But comparison can be limited to countries that participated in both grades and have the same age level of students as the United States.

38. See also Koretz, McCaffrey, and Sullivan, "Predicting Variations in Mathematics Performance in Four Countries Using TIMSS."

39. See J. Lee, "School Reform Initiatives as Balancing Acts: Policy Variation and Educational Convergence among Japan, Korea, England, and the United States," *Educational Policy Analysis Archives,* vol. 9, no. 13 (2001), available at epaa.asu.edu/epaa/v9n13.html [April 2002]; and R. Rothstein, "Weighing Students' Skills and Attitudes," *New York Times,* May 16, 2001, p. A25.

40. I. Olkin and D. T. Searls, "Statistical Aspects of International Assessments of Science Education," paper presented at the conference on Statistical Standards for International Assessments in Pre-College Science and Mathematics, Washington, D.C., 1985; D. Horvitz, "Improving the Quality of International Education Surveys," draft prepared for the Board on International Comparative Studies in Education, 1992; E. A. Medrich and J. E. Griffith, *International Mathematics and Science Assessments: What Have We Learned?* (Department of Education, Office of Educational Research and Improvement, 1992); H. Goldstein, *Interpreting International Comparisons of Student Achievement* (Paris: United Nations Educational, Scientific, and Cultural Organization, 1995); T. N. Postlethwaite, *International Studies of Academic Achievement: Methodological Issues* (University of Hong Kong, 1999); Robert L. Linn, "The Measurement of Student Achievement in International Studies," in National Research Council, *Methodological Advances in Cross-National Surveys of Educational Achievement* (Washington: National Academy Press, 2002), pp. 27–58; Ronald R. Chromy, "Sampling Issues in Design, Conduct, and Interpretation of International Comparative Studies of School Achievement," in National Research Council, *Methodological Advances in Cross-National Surveys of Educational Achievement* (Washington: National

Academy Press, 2002), pp. 80–117; Claudia Buchmann, "Measuring Family Background in International Studies of Education: Conceptual Issues and Methodological Challenges," in National Research Council, *Methodological Advances in Cross-National Surveys of Educational Achievement* (Washington: National Academy Press, 2002), pp. 150–98; Robert E. Floden, "The Measurement of the Opportunity to Learn," in National Research Council, *Methodological Advances in Cross-National Surveys of Educational Achievement* (Washington: National Academy Press, 2002), pp. 231–67; Marshall S. Smith, "Drawing Inferences for National Policy from Large-Scale Cross-National Education Surveys," in National Research Council, *Methodological Advances in Cross-National Surveys of Educational Achievement* (Washington: National Academy Press, 2002), pp. 295–321; Brian Rowen, "Large-Scale, Cross-National Surveys of Educational Achievement: Promises, Pitfalls, and Possibilities," in National Research Council, *Methodological Advances in Cross-National Surveys of Educational Achievement* (Washington: National Academy Press, 2002), pp. 321–53; National Research Council, *Summary Report of the Conference on October 16-17, 1985 (Draft),* Committee on National Statistics, Commission on Behavioral and Social Sciences and Education (Washington: National Academy Press, 1985); National Research Council, *A Framework and Principles for International Comparative Studies in Education,* Board on International Comparative Studies in Education, edited by Norman M. Bradburn and Dorothy M. Gilford, Commission on Behavioral and Social Sciences and Education (Washington: National Academy Press, 1990); National Research Council, *International Comparative Studies in Education: Descriptions of Selected Large-Scale Assessments and Case Studies,* Board on International Comparative Studies in Education, Commission on Behavioral and Social Sciences and Education (Washington: National Academy Press, 1995); and M. O. Martin, K. Rust, and R. J. Adams, *Technical Standards for IEA Studies* (Amsterdam, Netherlands: International Association for the Evaluation of Educational Achievement, 1999).

41. I. Rotberg, "I Never Promised You First Place," *Phi Delta Kappan* (December 1990), pp. 296–303.

42. N. Bradburn and others, "A Rejoinder to 'I Never Promised You First Place,'" *Phi Delta Kappan* (June 1991), pp. 774–77.

43. James S. Coleman and others, *Equality of Educational Opportunity* (Department of Health, Education, and Welfare, Office of Education, 1966).

44. Stephen P. Heyneman and William Loxley, "The Effect of School Quality on Academic Achievement across Twenty-nine High- and Low-Income Countries," *American Journal of Sociology,* vol. 88, no. 6 (May 1983), pp. 1162–94.

45. David P. Baker, Brian Goesling, and Gerald K. LeTendre, "Socioeconomic Status, School Quality, and National Economic Development: A Cross-National Analysis of the 'Heyneman-Loxley' Effect," *Comparative Education Review* (forthcoming).

46. William H. Schmidt and others, *Why Schools Matter: A Cross-National Comparison of Curriculum and Learning* (New York: Jossey-Bass, 2001).

47. Amy Gutmann, *A Democratic Education* (Princeton University Press, 1999).

Accelerating Advancement in School and Work

HILARY PENNINGTON

Current efforts to reform the American high school face a number of complex realities. Among the most significant are the far-reaching economic and demographic changes in the United States over the past several decades. The restructuring of the economy has made some education beyond high school the new prerequisite for middle-class jobs, raising the bar for what levels of skill all students must acquire. At the same time, demographic changes mean that the most rapidly growing segments of the student population—now and into the future—are those whom the education system serves least well.

High schools today must meet the dual challenge of preparing all students to function at higher levels and performing better for those least well served. Their task is not simply to help most students graduate with a minimal level of competence, but also to ensure that all students leave high school college-ready (that is, able to enter college without needing remediation). This is true both for students who will enter college immediately after high school and for those who will enter the work force but need ongoing education over time to advance economically.

The standards-based reform movement provides a strong foundation for meeting these challenges, especially because of its emphasis on setting higher and clearer expectations for what students need to know and be able to do. Although standards-based reforms have steadily raised achievement at the elementary and middle school levels, they have not yet succeeded in significantly improving outcomes for the increasingly heterogeneous students who stay in high school, let alone for the many who drop out before earning a diploma.

The problem is not just a failing of high schools but also of the secondary education system in general, whose large, one-size-fits-all high schools and underfinanced second-chance programs are ill equipped to deal with the diverse circumstances of high school youth. The secondary education system has to serve, among others, ninth graders reading below the sixth-grade level and needing accelerated literacy acquisition, low-performing youth taking general track courses that do not prepare them for college or work, students whose primary language is not English, out-of-school youth needing a way to get into college and onto career paths, students who desire advanced technical education, students of all income groups ready for more advanced academic challenges, and average students trying simply to get by. Too many young people drift anonymously through this system—bored, alienated, and unsure of their future direction.

A one-size-fits-all institution designed for the twentieth century cannot serve the different needs of all young people well in a new era. Meeting the twenty-first century's challenges will require more than tinkering around the edges of high schools as they currently are configured. It will require a fundamental restructuring of the secondary school system, both within schools and between schools and the world around them.

Yet most current high school reform efforts remain narrow, working backward from high school graduation and focusing on the experience of students within the four walls of the school. State accountability measures encourage this narrow focus, stressing student performance on high school exit exams, while ignoring the equally important question of how well young people fare in their lives and in the labor market several years out from high school.

In *Transforming the American High School*, a 2001 report from Jobs for the Future and the Aspen Institute, former assistant secretary for elementary and secondary education Michael Cohen argues for a more radical approach.

> The current education system, including high schools, provides students with a constant amount of time and a single approach for learning—and produces unacceptably large variations in student performance. The only way to get all students up to common, high performance standards is to flip this formulation on its head. We must provide students with multiple learning options and pathways and varied lengths of time to complete high school and gain the skills necessary to enter postsecondary education without remediation.[1]

In many ways, this argument calls for a return to the original intent of standards-based reform efforts in the early 1990s, when leading advocates saw higher standards and varied lengths of time in which to achieve them as part of an integrated reform agenda. The National Center for Education and the Economy's report *America's Choice*, for example, argued strongly for a competency-based system of multiple pathways in which time would be the variable and the achievement of a core set of academic and applied learning standards would be the constant.[2] Students would have the opportunity to move into apprenticeships, college-level classes, or other postsecondary options upon reaching a basic standard.

Yet these strands were separated as the reform efforts progressed. Defining standards and assessments in core academic disciplines became the dominant focus, and many now argue that state assessment and accountability systems are creating greater standardization of educational approaches. Efforts to achieve greater academic rigor through more relevant approaches to teaching and learning and to include work-based internships and apprenticeships as an alternative, high-status route to college and careers have evolved into a separate movement that includes Tech Prep, school-to-work, service learning, and similar initiatives. Varying the time and pathways to college and careers has proved to be the most difficult dimension to change.

The policy debate about high school reform needs to reengage these ideas. As one step in that direction, this paper has three purposes: first, to demonstrate why improving young people's transition to college and careers must be central to high school reform efforts, and how achieving this will require a fundamental restructuring of the secondary education system toward more deliberate variation in pedagogy, time, and institutional arrangements; second, to identify emerging strategies for such a restructuring; and third, to highlight the policy challenges involved in bringing such approaches to meaningful scale.

What this paper advocates must be read against a backdrop of discouraging research findings about the limited impact on high school performance of a variety of highly touted reform efforts, including recent experiments such as comprehensive school designs and charter schools. The proposals must also be seen in the context of resistance to the centralized standards and clearly articulated pathways that distinguish the secondary systems of the nations of Europe and Asia. There is no silver bullet. Yet the question remains: What is the best way to proceed in the American context—and what strategies worth trying have the best chance of succeeding?

Improving Transitions to Postsecondary Education and Work

Education beyond high school is critical to economic and individual success. The economy has changed. Most jobs require education beyond high school, and the skills required for jobs that can support a family are the same as those required for college.[3] Among others, these skills include the ability to read at high levels, solve semistructured problems, communicate effectively orally and in writing, and work in diverse groups.

The economic returns from gaining a postsecondary education are clear. A college graduate earns 70 percent more than a high school graduate, and the growing income disparity in the United States relates closely to educational attainment. Even one year of postsecondary education increases lifetime earnings.[4] Conversely, the unemployment rate for high school dropouts is four times the rate for college graduates.[5] A person who enters the work force with little education will find it difficult, if not impossible, to catch up.

In effect, two years of postsecondary education has become the minimum that young people must achieve if they are to enter jobs that pay enough to form and sustain a family. While not all young people will or should enter college directly after high school, all will need some postsecondary education at some point if they are to progress in the labor market.

Despite the importance of some postsecondary education to labor market success, too few youth make it to or through college. While three-fourths of high school graduates now go to college, over half fail to complete a degree and one-third never see their sophomore year. This number does not include the unacceptably large, and growing, number of young people who drop out before graduating from high school—the 5.4 million out-of-school youth in America.

Urban areas face particularly urgent challenges. Close to half the schools in the thirty-five largest U.S. cities have weak promotion power (that is, the capacity to hold and promote students from ninth through twelfth grade). Nearly 50 percent of the students in these schools do not graduate in four years.[6]

Serious problems also exist with completion at the postsecondary level. Only half of those who enroll on a four-year campus receive a degree within six years.[7] The numbers are worse at two-year colleges, where half of all young people enroll. Of students who entered public two-year postsecondary institutions in 1995–96, only 31 percent completed a certificate degree within three years of enrollment.[8]

College completion rates are especially problematic for low-income and minority youth. A young person whose family income is under $25,000 has less than a 6 percent chance of earning a four-year college degree.[9] This even pertains to those who are academically strong. A national study of the factors determining college success found that, while three-fourths of upper-income students who scored in the top 20 percent on a basic skills test earned four-year degrees, only 36 percent of low-income students who achieved the same high test scores earned a degree.[10]

The statistics are equally dismaying for young people of color. Nearly 29 percent of Hispanic youth and 12.6 percent of black youth age sixteen to twenty-four have dropped out of school, compared with 7.3 percent of whites.[11] The Education Trust reports that African American and Latino seventeen-year-olds read at the same level as white thirteen-year-olds. Marta Tienda's longitudinal study found that only 6 percent of youth from these groups complete a four-year college degree.[12] Part of the reason is that minority youth are substantially more likely to be enrolled in two-year postsecondary institutions. In 1991, 55 percent of Hispanics enrolled in higher education and 43 percent of blacks were in community colleges.[13]

A significant contributing factor to low college completion rates is the large numbers of freshmen entering college in need of remediation. In 1995, 29 percent of all college freshmen and more than 40 percent of those in colleges with high minority enrollment were required to take remedial courses in math, reading, or writing and, as a result, were more likely to leave college without completing a degree.[14]

Young people without strong skills or postsecondary credentials are struggling in the labor market. Large majorities of employers report that high school graduates are not well prepared for work in their companies. And young people face a tough struggle in the labor market. Andrew Sum and his colleagues report that "in 1998, nearly three out of ten families headed by a person under the age of 30 were poor or near poor, versus only 10 percent for those families with a head 30 or older." The recession of the early 2000s only exacerbated these difficulties, with young adults accounting for 95 percent of the net loss of employment in the country in 2000.[15]

Again, these problems are particularly acute for minority and low-income youth. One-fourth of young African American men and one-third of African American women age sixteen to twenty-three experience prolonged periods of disconnectedness in the labor market (that is, for twenty-six weeks out of any calendar year, they are not enrolled in school, not employed, or not in the military, and they are not married to someone who is employed, in school, or in the military). In comparison, less than 10 percent of white youth experience a period of disconnectedness. Individuals who are disconnected are ten times more likely to be poor later in their lives as those who were never disconnected.[16]

The changing demographics create a strong imperative to do better. The United States is experiencing one of the biggest demographic shifts in its history, and much of the growth is in school-age population. By 2015, the traditional college population (eighteen to twenty-four years old) will increase by over four million. White youth are projected to remain the majority, growing by 800,000, or 4 percent, but minority youth are expected to grow by 3.5 million, or 40 percent. Hispanic youth alone will account for about half the coming boom in this age group.[17] According to the Hudson Institute's *Workforce 2020* report, almost all of the net new labor market entrants over the next two decades will be children of color.[18] If current education attainment levels persist, a large percentage of minority youth will not complete a postsecondary credential.

Taken together, these trends indicate a problem with youth transitions to postsecondary education and careers. At a time when high schools should be a pathway to opportunity for all students, they are routes to nowhere for many. Too many young people leave high school ill prepared for the demands of adulthood in an increasingly complex economy and spend their next decade drifting in and out of postsecondary education and low-end jobs.

Creating a Better Framework

Defining the goal for high school performance in terms of the numbers of students who pass high school exit exams, as most states and districts currently do, is far from sufficient if the broader problem of educating young people beyond high school is to be addressed effectively. What if the objectives were to double the numbers of young people who complete postsecondary education and to close the gap by income and race? How would a system designed to accomplish these objectives differ from the existing system?

Part of the answer lies in the structure of the education system itself:

strengthening the relationship between secondary and postsecondary education and reconfiguring the use of time within and between the two. One overarching principle to guide efforts to build a more effective secondary system should be to encourage multiple pathways to and through college. The objective should be to create a high-performing system of multiple pathways that presumes all students will learn to a set of commonly agreed upon high standards—but through different pedagogical approaches, by different institutional arrangements, and in different amounts of time. The system would create deliberate variability to attain greater consistency in the results. It would recognize the differences in student needs and encourage customized approaches to meeting them—using learning in and out of school to engage and motivate students. It would promote competency, not seat time, as the currency for academic progression.

Continued implementation of standards-based reform efforts is central to this objective. A system of multiple pathways without a common standard risks recreating or perpetuating the equity problems that plague the systems today. But, the work of building multiple pathways to college should not wait until the United States is closer to achieving a standards-based education system. A key short-term priority should be linking the multiple pathways that already exist much more tightly to college; that is, to the academic standards required for entry into credit-bearing, college-level courses in technical or academic subjects.

A second principle is to accelerate advancement through high school and the first two years of college, especially for young people who are poor and of color. At a minimum, this means ensuring that the transition happens better (fewer youth fall through the cracks and more enter and complete postsecondary education) and helping the progression happen faster (so that most young people have completed a first postsecondary credential by age twenty-six). Accomplishing this will require rethinking the use of time in the education system, with grades eleven and twelve and the first two years of postsecondary education being particularly fertile ground for change.

The transition of young Americans from high school to postsecondary education and work takes too long. Young people are stuck in an education system built on the assumption of seat time measured in Carnegie units—four years of high school leading to two or four years of college—which they presumably will complete sequentially, although increasingly they do not.

This is problematic for both low- and high-performing youth. For example, if a young person drops out before graduating from high school, she essentially loses access to some or all public funding for her education. If she reenrolls in an alternative school or a general equivalency diploma (GED) program, she often must do so at her own expense, at education centers that are desperately under-equipped compared with the public schools, and her progress is likely to be painfully slow. Worse still, the existing second-chance system does not act as a feeder into postsecondary institutions; the two are disconnected.

At the other end of the spectrum, the transition time is also too slow for students who are on track in school and can achieve high school exit-level competence in the tenth grade, the year when most states first administer the assessments that determine high school graduation. The senior year in the United States is largely wasted, with colleges essentially accepting students for admission on the basis of their junior year transcript and students typically completing most of their required coursework in their junior year.

Many questions remain to be answered if high school reform efforts are to incorporate the principles of multiple pathways and accelerated advancement, including: Will the standards movement, as currently being implemented, ensure the combination of choice and equity that must exist? How can the academic progress of students who start high school with low levels of literacy and math proficiency be accelerated? Can students remediate and accelerate at the same time? If a goal is to have students graduate from high school college-ready, what does that mean for the level of rigor and intellectual challenge their high school education must entail? If the system is to allow young people to move on to college or work after having demonstrated competency as early as the tenth grade (the level at which most state high school exit exams are set), what should the subsequent four years of schooling look like? Should grades nine to twelve and the first two years of postsecondary education, or eleven and twelve and the first two years of postsecondary education, be permanently collapsed? At what point should students be encouraged to choose specialization? Do changes in the economy mean that a universal system of fourteen years of public education should be instituted? What reconfiguration of time and routes would be necessary to finance such a system, given the cost constraints of state and federal budget deficits?

Toward Effective Schools or Learning Environments

Historically, the United States has dealt with the challenges of preparing high school youth for adulthood through a tracked education system: college prep, general track, and vocational education. The dominant trend over the past few decades has been to eliminate the general track and try to raise the academic quality of vocational education and college prep courses. In general, the results have been mixed.

In part because of the standards movement, emphasis on college prep has grown—increasingly defining the standard that all students must achieve. New York State's recently imposed requirement that all students must take Regents exams to graduate from high school is an example of this.

Efforts to abolish the general track are progressing slowly but surely. Attempts to increase the academic rigor of vocational education are also progressing slowly, and they have produced uneven results to date. Much of traditional vocational education remains resistant to change, and the current emphasis on the academic disciplines severely constrains the time and resources available for vocational classes. In addition, changes in skill requirements mean that much specialized technical education now takes place at the postsecondary level, leaving unresolved the question of what vocational technical education at the secondary level should entail. Facing declining enrollments, many districts have cut back vocational course offerings and, as a consequence, a valuable option has been reduced.

The tendency now is to address the challenges of academic preparation and youth transitions through whole school change efforts, not tracks. High school reform efforts in this regard can be grouped into three strands. Some districts have embraced whole school reform to improve the performance of existing high schools (regardless of their size) through the implementation of standards-based curricula, upgrading the academic core, and so on. Others have reconfigured existing schools—often by breaking large high schools into smaller units and by developing specialized themes or focuses for each of these units. A good example of this kind of change are career academies—specialized houses or schools within bigger high schools that group students together for intensive academic and experiential preparation within broad career clusters. At the same time, many small, new high schools have been created by state charter legislation, citywide initiatives such as Boston's Pilot School and Chicago's Small Schools Initiative, and foundation leveraging of public and private dollars such as New York City's New Century Schools Initiative. The schools are more costly in per pupil expenditure, but not necessarily in cost per graduate.[19] Often all of these reforms can be found in the same district.

A fourth strand of reform deserves greater attention—a movement toward what might best be called blended institutions. These schools have moved further than most traditional high schools to create specialized approaches in response to particular needs of specific populations. They have embraced different pedagogies, instructional environments, and uses of time to help their students advance toward the completion of college credentials and positive life outcomes.

In discussing these effective learning environments, I draw on research I and my colleagues conducted since 2000 through the Jobs for the Future's From the Margins to the Mainstream Initiative.[20] The schools and programs we explore fall into three basic categories. Some are diploma-granting institutions, such as small or alternative schools. Others identify themselves as contributing to positive youth development and include a range of arts, internship, community development, and service learning programs that young people look to for sanctuary and challenge in their discretionary hours. A smaller group bridges grades eleven and twelve and the first two years of postsecondary education, offering college credits (and potentially a two-year degree or credential), usually in combination with a GED or high school diploma program (see figure 1).

These categories, however, are far from distinct. Many of the most promising are blended institutions that cross boundaries most high school reform discussions do not acknowledge—between secondary and postsecondary, between in-school and out-of-school time, and between school and work. While such models are far from the dominant breed of high school, they are important as high-quality options for some schools and for what they suggest about reforming the rest.

Multiple Pathway Learning Environments

In the schools profiled below, which have highly focused, rigorous learning environments, the young people are known well, engage in work that matters to them, and demonstrate their learning through performance and

Figure 1. Categories of Effective Learning Environments

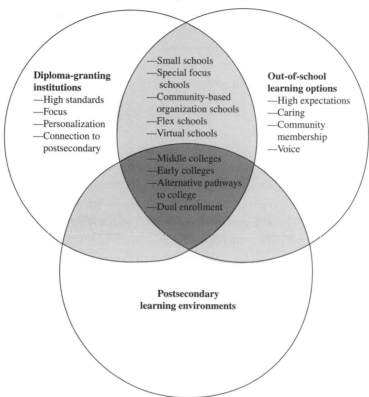

competency-based assessments in addition to more traditional forms of assessment. Several key features about their design stand out—important not only because they contribute to the schools' success in raising student achievement, but also because they are features that the current policy environment at the district and state levels does little to encourage. In fact, many argue that current policies and incentives do the opposite. In particular these schools offer high cognitive challenge through teaching that balances remediation and acceleration; creative use of time and learning outside of schools; more kinds of opportunities and supports for young people, especially in urban environments where youth lack access to the kinds of experience that middle-class children are more likely to receive as a matter of course; and improved linkages to postsecondary education.

These high schools, like many other urban high schools, work with students who enter ninth grade far behind in their literacy and math skills. Yet the schools handle students' need for remediation by giving them complex cognitive work to do at the same time as working to improve their basic skills. The Fenway High School in Boston, Massachusetts, is a good example. The Fenway achieves impressive results for urban students by combining a rigorous curriculum, learning outside of school, and relationships with adults.

Now in its nineteenth year, the Fenway sends 90 percent of its diverse student body to college, and its students excelled on the 2001 Massachusetts Comprehensive Assessment System (MCAS) tests. Eighty-eight percent of Fenway students passed the English portion, and 79 percent passed the math portion on their first try. These results exceeded the statewide average pass rates and were higher than any other urban high school in the state that accepts a broad range of students, including charter schools such as City on a Hill. In addition to exceeding all their urban peers, Fenway students as a group scored higher than many of those at suburban schools in the state.

One of Boston's pilot schools, the Fenway enjoys significant flexibility in its budgeting and staffing. It allows students to choose a theme-based learning family, which serves as their intellectual and personal home for four years, and provides an integrated curriculum, a strong advisory system, and extended learning opportunities in the community, including external panel reviews of student work. The Fenway provides rigorous intellectual work for its students, regardless of their starting point. For example, it requires all freshmen to take a humanities seminar built around essential questions such as, What does it mean to be human? In addition, all freshmen take a fundamentals of literacy course in which they build vocabulary and learn the strategies of good readers.

In contrast, the high school remediation efforts that many urban students usually encounter return to tried-and-true traditional approaches to teaching that ignore much of what the last several decades of cognitive research has shown about how development and learning occur. Traditional learning theory called for starting with basic skills and then moving to more complex ones. But cognitive science research has shown that learners become engaged by tackling cognitive challenges. Many high schools defer hands-on experience on principle (and out of concern about helping students pass state tests), moving to specialization after a foundation of general knowledge has been formed. Yet, for many young people, only the process of specializing, of going deeply into something, makes school relevant. This suggests a need for approaches that pursue both rigor and relevance—remediation and acceleration—at the same time.

The Fenway is not alone in demonstrating positive results from this strategy. Reformers are learning that part of the problem, particularly with youth who are seriously alienated from school, may be that they are underchallenged. The American Youth Policy Forum conducted an extensive review of programs that have succeeded in closing the achievement gap between races.[21] Three of the most common characteristics of successful programs are that they provide students with small, personal learning communities; demand rigorous, high-quality work; and give students extensive supports. High Schools That Work, with its emphasis on providing career-bound students with an upgraded academic core, and Talent Development High School, with its emphasis on accelerated literacy acquisition provided through extended time during and after the school day for ninth graders, are considered successful programs.

Another good example is Advancement Via Individual Determination (AVID), which targets underachieving young people with grades of "C" or below for participation in Advanced Placement courses, providing them with study skills, tutoring support, and role models. AVID has grown from thirty-two students in one high school to more than sixty-five thousand students in more than twelve hundred schools in twenty-one states and fourteen foreign countries. Over 92 percent of its students enroll in college, a figure nearly one-third higher than national averages.

The Met, in Providence, Rhode Island, is designed to change the nature of the learning experience by utilizing many resources outside the school to foster students' cognitive and personal development. Founded in 1996, the Met is small and personal, with two schools of 110 students each. The Met has one-third the dropout rate, one-third the absentee rate, and one-eighteenth the suspension rate of other Providence high schools. Of the first graduating classes, 85 percent went directly to college and 82 percent were still in college two years later.

The school has radically redesigned the use of time and resources to allow a highly individualized, learner-driven education. With input from their parents and a teacher-adviser, each student designs a personal learning plan, reviewed and revised quarterly, to plot progress toward the skills, knowledge, and personal qualities required for postsecondary success. Starting in the ninth grade, Met students spend two days per week at internships that they select according to their interests. Internships are based on the premise that adolescents learn best when they are deeply engaged in real-world settings. The goal is to create motivated learners, not to prepare students for specific careers.

Students study fewer topics but in far more depth. They work closely with adults, instead of learning only with same-age peers. They do not take tests. They give public exhibitions of what they have learned, and they receive detailed narratives written by their teachers, not letter grades.

Despite the effectiveness of strategies such as these, the ways in which states and districts are implementing standards makes it difficult for many high schools to organize learning outside the classroom. Many districts and some states have increased course requirements in traditional academic disciplines. In most cities, few after-school or out-of-school learning experiences are available, and they are not well coordinated with school-based reforms. Although recent years have seen increasing recognition of the ways in which community resources can help strengthen learning and youth development during the school day and in the hours when young people are not in school, these efforts have been slow to grow, especially at the high school level.[22]

Nevertheless, in a few places, public-private partnerships, such as the 21st Century Community Learning Centers, and citywide initiatives, such as the New York Beacons and Chicago Afterschool Matters, are bringing new resources into youth development initiatives. Accumulating evidence shows that participation in community-based youth programs promotes positive outcomes for all age groups.

Boston is organizing work-based learning experiences for young people on a large scale, through the efforts of the school district and the Boston Private Industry Council (PIC), which has played a leadership role in supporting a major restructuring of all fifteen comprehensive high schools in the city along school-to-career principles. The PIC has organized hundreds of employers, with the number of employer partners engaged in the most intensive partnerships, career pathways, rising from forty-six in 1995–96 to more than two hundred in 1999–2000.

Students participating in these school-to-career programs have structured work-based learning plans that allow for formal feedback on their progress toward broad performance competencies such as critical thinking and teamwork. Students' performance at the work site is linked to a database at the district so that the PIC and the Boston public schools can track the impact of students' participation in school-to-career activities on their academic performance. The data suggest that students who participate in intensive school-to-career experiences have better attendance and college-going rates than their peers and that they do as well as or slightly better than non-school-to-career students on the state MCAS and district Stanford Achievement Test, Ninth Edition, assessments.

The Boston public schools and the PIC also jointly sponsor three summer programs that give students work experience and intensive academic coaching through internships at companies such as Verizon and the Federal Reserve Bank. These show significant success in engaging students, including those who are most at risk of not passing state standards, with an average learning gain in seven weeks of 1.2 grades. This is a promising way of organizing community resources outside the school to achieve more time for reaching standards and to provide urban youth with access to work experience and supportive adults.

The schools profiled here encourage a different kind of relationship between secondary and postsecondary institutions. The Fenway and the Met take direct responsibility for whether their students go to college and how they do there. The schools provide intensive support to their graduates at least through their first year in college and have jointly hired an evaluator to do a detailed, longitudinal analysis of how their graduates do once they leave. Washtenaw Technical Middle College (WTMC) and Portland Community College (PCC) go further—representing new kinds of institutions that blend high school and postsecondary education. Linkages between high school and postsecondary education are critical for the goals of multiple pathways and accelerated advancement, and these linkages have been growing over the past decade.

Washtenaw Technical Middle College, in Ann Arbor, Michigan, illustrates successful strategies for raising student achievement and accelerating their acquisition of postsecondary credentials. Housed at the campus of Washtenaw Community College, it is the only public secondary school in Michigan to be chartered through a community college as a result of the state's charter school legislation. WTMC has combined high school and college courses so that graduating students can earn a high school diploma and a certificate or an associate in arts (AA) degree simultaneously.

Once enrolled at WTMC, students move through five phases, from four high school core classes to credit-level Washtenaw Community College courses and career pathways. Students, who must have at least five high school credits to enroll in WTMC, begin by taking core transition courses—English, math, science, and social studies. In addition, they enroll in Career Focus, a series of seminars developed by WTMC to help students meet the requirements for technical programs and credit courses offered at the community college in answer to the high failure rate (43 percent) of WTMC students in college courses during the school's first year of operation. An analysis of the failures revealed that students did not lack ability but needed specific skills and behaviors to make a successful transition to college-level courses.

The curriculum has brought results. WTMC students are now the best-performing group on campus. Their pass rate in college-level courses has improved to 80 percent.

Portland Community College, in Portland, Oregon, is another example of an institution that links secondary and postsecondary education in new ways. More than two thousand students enroll at PCC, making it the largest high school in Portland. PCC's multiple entry points allow students with as low as third-grade reading and math skills to enroll in noncredit and developmental (remedial) education courses that link directly to credit-based career education programs. Eighty percent of the out-of-school youth who enter PCC's high school completion program continue their education in the program, earn a diploma or a GED, return to a high school program, or obtain employment while simultaneously gaining college credits.

Attempts to strengthen the connections between secondary and postsecondary education also include significant work to align these two systems better at the state level. One of the most promising efforts is the P–16 movement, led by organizations such as the Education Trust and the Education Commission of the States and foundations such as the Pew Charitable Trusts. The assumption here is that aligning the practices of, and relationships among, educational institutions at various levels will expand the numbers, qualifications, and diversity of those who go on to college. Over a dozen states now have formal P–16 partnership efforts.

The experience in New York shows the potential impact on young people of increased alignment between high school and college. The state now requires all young people to take state Regents exams to qualify for a high school diploma and has eliminated all remedial programs at the four-year postsecondary level. Fueled in part by policy changes at the state level, New York City has built partnerships between district high schools and postsecondary institutions. For example, tens of thousands of students in New York

City are engaged in the College Now Program, a partnership between the public schools and the City University of New York (CUNY). The CUNY system gives its placement exams for credit-bearing courses to eleventh graders in schools participating in the program. Students who pass those exams can immediately enter a dual-enrollment program and start to take credit-bearing courses in any CUNY institution. As a result, they leave high school much further along, reducing the time and cost of a postsecondary degree. Eleventh graders who take those exams and fail know it at the beginning of eleventh grade and can immediately start taking remedial education courses. They can take those course not just in their high schools, which may not have very good resources and have not done very well by them but also in the CUNY system. All 17 CUNY campuses and all 161 high schools in the city are participating. College Now is reaching thirteen thousand students, of whom more than ten thousand are registered for dual-credit courses. College Now students accumulate credits more quickly, have better attendance rates, and outscore their peers on the state Regents exams.

Advanced Placement courses and dual enrollment are also strategies for helping students achieve postsecondary credentials. Increasing numbers of states and some districts enable students to enroll simultaneously in high school and college courses and to receive credit for both. Some are expanding Advanced Placement offerings. Such programs save money for families and reward students who meet performance standards. New York, Utah, and Washington have extensive postsecondary-option programs. For example, Utah's New Century scholarship program offers a 75 percent scholarship to a four-year state college or university to students who graduate from high school with an associate in arts degree.

High school students enrolled in Washington state's Running Start program do very well upon transfer to the state college and university system, and the state estimated a savings of $36.9 million during the 1999–2000 school year, with students saving an additional $13.6 million in tuition costs.

So far, data from dual-enrollment programs suggest two things. First, dual enrollment does not necessarily accelerate degree completion. Young people who can earn college credit while in high school still must make sense of a confusing array of courses at both the high school and college levels, and often the credits they earn do not transfer fully. Second, dual-enrollment programs appear to benefit primarily students from rigorous high schools and from middle- to upper-middle-class families. Yet accelerated advancement may have the greatest economic and educational benefit for the students for whom it is least accessible.

In the spring of 2002, the Gates, Carnegie, Ford, and Kellogg Foundations announced a $40+ million, five-year initiative designed to test that possibility. It will create seventy early college high schools—small high schools from which students leave with a diploma, a two-year associate in arts degree, or sufficient college credits to enter a four-year liberal arts program as a sophomore or junior. By changing the structure of the high school years and compressing the number of years to the AA, early college high schools have the potential to improve high school and college graduation rates and to prepare students better for entry into high-skill careers. At these schools, no transition will take place between high school and college. Students can earn an AA within the same small institution in which they do high school work.

More than most school start-up projects, these early college high schools cross into relatively unexplored territory: They are based on the notions that learning can be accelerated for adolescents and that high school and college—two separate and often incompatible learning environments—can be combined. While the schools face a challenging task, some experience exists on which to build. For example, Bard College has expanded from the success of its affiliated high school, Simon's Rock in Great Barrington, Massachusetts, to initiate an early college high school in New York City. The Bard Early College High School has restructured the four high school years and the traditional curriculum so that every student can graduate with a two-year associate in arts degree or enough college credits to enter a four-year, liberal arts program as a sophomore or junior. This school accepts highly motivated students, selected on the basis of their transcripts, writing samples, and interviews. It emphasizes advanced writing and thinking skills through a series of workshops and core seminars. With the assistance of the Woodrow Wilson National Fellowship Foundation, the Bard model is being expanded to create nine schools.

Another partner in this national project, the Middle College High School National Consortium, will start eight new early college high schools on community college campuses and redesign twelve existing middle colleges. Situated on community college campuses, the more than thirty middle colleges around the country target low-performing youth and offer, among other things, a combination of rigorous coursework, extensive supports and personalization, and internships in the community. Cece Cunningham, principal of LaGuardia Middle College High School, describes the "power of place" to raise student achievement and aspiration.

Based on the successful middle college model, the new early college high schools will have a maximum of one hundred students per grade and a teaching environment that stresses small learning communities and student-teacher interactions. Students will follow an accelerated path leading to a high school diploma and an AA degree in five years. The ninth- and tenth-grade years will entail high school courses, with intensive support in literacy and math; the eleventh- and twelfth-grade years will blend high school and college-level courses; and the next year will be solely college-level courses. Students will be taught by both high school and community college faculty.

Implications for Public Policy

Many barriers remain to moving from a smorgasbord of options to a system of multiple pathways to college held to a common standard of performance and available at a scale commensurate with the need. The schools highlighted here are fragile and experience failure as well as success. Too often, they operate at the margins of their systems and attract skepticism or even hostility from other schools and district leaders. Few school districts have either a strategy or effective mechanisms for learning from their innovative and promising experience. As a result, even the most successful schools often serve more to release pressure for broader systemic reform than to inform and help accelerate change. The strategies for which this paper argues are not prominent either in practice or in current debates about education policy.

At the community level, most schools are hampered in their ability to create better supports for young people and are burdened by a lack of financial resources, inefficient organizational structures, and poor communication channels with other institutions. It is rare to find academic, after-school, summer, and youth development programs aligned in ways that enable them to collaborate efficiently. Cognitively challenging and engaging projects offered by youth development programs, for example, are ignored in favor of more traditional forms of homework help in after-school hours. Little discussion is held about how learning outside the school building might count for high school credit. Postsecondary institutions and high schools also remain poorly connected. Often district and state policies fail to encourage the continuity across schools, postsecondary institutions, and youth providers that would produce greater effectiveness and scale. Few states have implemented comprehensive strategies for encouraging multiple pathways through high school into college.[23]

In light of these realities, any serious effort to build a system of diverse pathways to college and careers will have to address complex issues regarding standards, accountability, and governance if it is to achieve significant impact.

Standards, Assessment, and Credentialing Learning

Building a system of multiple pathways for high school students will require recalibrating views about standards and assessments. A pressing task is the need for closer alignment between high school exit requirements and exams and the entrance requirements to credit-bearing college courses of study and career jobs.

Unfortunately, most current state assessments have been designed to test student mastery of subject matter content in the high school academic disciplines. They are not aligned to college entrance and work requirements. The American Diploma Project—a collaboration between Achieve Inc., the Education Trust, the National Alliance for Business, and Fordham University, in partnership with the states of Indiana, Kentucky, Massachusetts, Nevada, and Texas—is beginning to take on this task. It is working to identify the literacy and math skills necessary for entry into credit-bearing college courses and work at high-performance workplaces.

Oregon was the first state to adopt competency-based certificates of initial mastery (CIM) and certificates of advanced mastery (CAM) as part of an overall comprehensive vision based on the 1990 National Center on Education and the Economy *America's Choice* report. That publication urged the development of a system in which young people were able to leave high school as early as grade ten, providing they had reached the CIM. Partly in response to this vision, the state university system moved to a competency-based admissions process, the Proficiency-Based Admissions Standards System (PASS), under which the state colleges and universities would admit students by their performance on assessments for the CIM and CAM. While adopting these new approaches, the state also kept its standard high school graduation requirements and the high school diploma in place, creating inevitable problems that the state is currently moving to address.

Another pressing task for states as they review and improve their standards and assessment systems is the need to develop more competency-based or performance-based assessments that can help move away from the construct of seat time. Effective assessments should be multiple and authentic, and they could allow significant flexibility in how performance is demonstrated in subjects other than literacy and math, including upgraded course requirements and end-of-course exams.

Credentialing will also need to reward learning inside school and out. The Minnesota Credits for Learning statute, for example, requires schools to offer students credit for work completed outside of school that demonstrably achieves state academic standards. Most states have a long way to go before their standards and assessments encourage project-based learning and other strategies proven to engage young people and to reflect real-world application of knowledge in the new basic skills.

Financing

By definition, the kinds of blended institutions that cross traditional boundaries between high school and postsecondary institutions, and between leaning in school and out, raise complex issues about financing. Some of the blended schools profiled here have combined several different funding streams. For example, by serving youth and adults, Horizonte in Salt Lake City can draw on both district per pupil budgeting and the unusually high level of state dollars available for adult high school completion and English as a Second Language. As a dropout recovery and prevention program, the alternative pathway at Portland Community College gets average daily attendance money for its students. As students move into college coursework, they become eligible for Pell grants as well.

However, financing schools in this patchwork way consumes valuable time and energy on the part of school leaders. Some districts allow schools to have more control and flexibility in their budgets. Part of what the Fenway, for example, has been able to achieve stems from its status as a pilot school, part of a network of schools created in 1994 through the Boston teachers union contract to promote increased options within the school district. The pilot schools are public schools, not charters, but they differ from traditional Boston public schools in that they receive significant autonomy over budget, staffing, school day and school year calendar, curriculum, and governance.

Wisconsin and Minnesota have allowed state money to follow vulnerable youth through children-at-risk statutes that enable public school districts to contract with private, nonprofit, nonsectarian agencies to educate children who meet the statute's criteria for being at risk. Enacted in the mid-1980s, these statutes create a more stable funding stream for private, nonprofit agencies or community-based alternative schools. Districts with large numbers of dropouts and youth who meet the statute's criteria for being at risk are required to let students choose alternative education environments. Contracted providers are considered partnership schools under the Milwaukee public school system and receive per pupil funding at 80 percent of the average per pupil expenditure. In Milwaukee today, alternative education programs are responsible for 20 percent of the high school graduates. Similarly, about thirty community-based alternative schools operate within the Minneapolis public school system under this legislation, also reported to be responsible for 20 percent of high school graduates.[24]

Despite unresolved controversies over vouchers, more experimentation must be encouraged with flexible funding at the high school level, particularly for those youth who have dropped out or who are trapped in consistently underperforming high schools. In addition to allowing money to follow students, public policy should provide incentives to encourage students to enroll in learning environments that have proven their effectiveness with young people, either because they incorporate productive design elements or because they demonstrate convincing evidence of success.

Ultimately, the implications for the financing and structure of a system of multiple pathways are much bigger.

> As more students cross the boundaries between once completely separate systems, and as learning takes place more frequently in different institutional settings (e.g., workplaces, youth development organizations, on-line), often with different cost structures, states will need to reexamine how these various systems are financed and the nature of incentives being created for both students and for systems.[25]

Curriculum and Teacher Capacity

An effective system of multiple pathways must address issues of curriculum and teacher capacity. The quality of teachers and the rigor and coherence of academic curriculum are among the few strategies consistently shown to work in raising the academic achievement of high school students.

The multiple pathways agenda brings some unique opportunities and challenges in this regard to improve curriculum and teaching.

On one hand, the kinds of blended institutions profiled here have the ability to draw on a much greater range of teachers than do traditional schools, from the college faculty associated with early college high schools to the community and business partners involved in expanding out-of-school learning opportunities. On the other hand, this approach to teaching will face many barriers to adoption, including resistance from teachers unions and fundamental changes in how schools of education function.

Accountability

Creating multiple pathways in the routes to college will require redefining state accountability measures (at both the secondary and postsecondary levels) accordingly. States should consider supplementing existing accountability measures (how students perform on state tests and high school graduation requirements) by looking at how well students do in their transitions to work and further education. How many students went on directly to college? How many of them needed remediation? How many returned after freshman year? How many have completed a postsecondary degree? How many graduates are employed? What are their wages?

In New York, New Visions for Public Schools is partnering with CUNY to commission the creation of a unified database that will collect information on remediation, course taking, and other measures of student success by school. Its goal is to get high schools to think about and feel responsible for the success of their graduates. Sixty percent of New York City high school graduates who pursue college do so at CUNY, and the same percentage of the teachers and school leaders in the city's public schools come from CUNY. Because most students attend publicly funded postsecondary institutions in their states, it would be possible to do a similar analysis elsewhere.

The larger issue of how accountability for institutions of postsecondary education gets defined matters greatly to the ideas proposed here. Few incentives currently are offered for postsecondary institutions to involve themselves with high school reform or to change their practices to succeed better at helping an increasingly diverse student population complete college degrees. As greater numbers of students expect access to college, state legislators are likely to exert more pressure on postsecondary institutions for improved performance.

A number of additional issues must be resolved if states are to move toward accountability measures that cross the boundaries between high school, college, and work. How can states hold these different systems mutually accountable? How can they determine adequate yearly progress when students may take courses offered by local colleges or online providers? Answering some of these questions will require states to collect longitudinal data on students. Many states have the technical ability to do this through tracking student records and unemployment insurance records, but only a handful (including Florida, Illinois, and Texas) have begun to do so.

Some would argue that in the U.S. market-based system, data can become a de facto standard; that is, if sufficient data about institutional performance are collected and reported over time, consumers' choice will be rationalized. There is no reason not to begin tracking longitudinal data about students in a much more concerted way. An additional priority should be developing systems that allow for data to cross state lines to track students who graduate from school in one state and are employed in a neighboring one.

Finally, the issue of accountability raises the challenge of the limits and extent of state responsibility for public education. Given the changes in the nature of economic opportunity, should public education be universal through the first several years of postsecondary education? Would such a shift be affordable without fundamentally reconfiguring the delivery system and the time and ways to earn degrees? States such as Georgia and Maryland have begun to consider this question.

Governance

The ideas put forward here also challenge the notions of governance. If states align high school exit requirements with the entry-level requirements for college work and career jobs, will they need an overarching board that aligns education from kindergarten through four years of postsecondary education? If districts encourage deliberate variation in the kinds of secondary options available to students, how should this system be governed?

Paul Hill and his colleagues argue for consideration of several new models for governance of school districts, including three that would be relevant to the multiple pathways agenda.[26] The first envisions a structure in which a strong chief executive officer manages a portfolio of distinctive schools, each of which has made a contract with the district around a particular school design and specific anticipated results. This structure would encourage multiple pathways. The second calls for a superintendent and school board to create a diverse system of public schools through contracts—the diverse providers model. These could include arts organizations, community organizations, other nonprofits, and so on. The third urges experimentation with community partnerships. In this model, the entire educational resources of the community would be available to the children: internships, service learning opportunities, museums, community-based organizations. A community education board, instead of a school board, would be responsible for mobilizing all community resources—in schools, community organizations, workplaces, the faith community, postsecondary institutions, and so on—on behalf of the children.

Conclusion

The past decade has seen explosive growth in diverse learning options for young people, including new schools, vouchers, charter laws, and distance learning and dual-enrollment options that are blurring the lines between secondary and postsecondary institutions. The ways in which students move across and between the institutions of work and learning differ dramatically from what the systems originally assumed. One could argue that the United States already is creating multiple pathways to adulthood for its adolescents. A system is lacking that ensures that this expansion of options is occurring in the best way possible if the long-term goal is equity and the improved performance of the system for all young people.

If the challenges of reform continue to be defined solely as a problem of improving the existing high schools, a major opportunity will be missed to reconfigure the secondary schooling system for the demands of the twenty-first century. The conversation must be expanded so that it is truly about what is next—the transition to college and careers.

Comment by Sheila E. Murray

A long-standing consensus exists that traditional comprehensive high schools no longer prepare students for the world that has changed around them. Policymakers and parents point to poor student performance on standardized exams and rising educational costs; employers are concerned that recent high school graduates do not have the skills to be productive in technologically advanced markets; recent high school graduates require remedial mathematics and English courses; and students regularly complain that school experiences are trivial, contrived, and meaningless. Despite the widespread agreement, research and efforts to reform high schools have been slowed by the view that reform should begin with children just entering the educational system because changes at the high school level come too late for struggling students.

Hilary Pennington recommends a restructuring of secondary and post-secondary education through a system of multiple pathways to college. In addition, she maintains that this restructuring must be accompanied by clear, uniform standards for all pathways that prepare young people well for college or careers and must build upon reform strategies such as personalization, relevance, and flexible time for graduation.

The strategies proposed in this paper are substantial; they require major changes in institutions and in behavior. The stakes, as Pennington suggests, are high. For many at-risk adolescents, high schools are a pathway to nowhere. Thus, it is important to look critically at the available research evidence and to take advantage of insights gleaned from other major reforms.

Rigorous Evaluations of Small-Scale Programs

The paper describes several reform experiments currently under way that have been successful in improving college matriculation for disadvantaged students. As informative as the successes have been, many reasons can be cited that a few innovative experiments are not a sound basis for transforming high schools. For example, multiple reform strategies are going on at the Fenway High School. Isolating which strategy works and which does not or why is difficult.

Education policies are often critiqued on the basis of the strength or weakness of the research behind them. Policies with high stakes must be based on rigorous research. This would suggest a more substantial research effort for reform, including independent, third-party evaluations using the most appropriate research design. The research for many of the strategies in this paper (for example, standards, personalization, relevance, and flexible time) is based on newly implemented policies (standards) or small-scale experiments (for example, small learning communities and flexible time).

The research on these programs is largely descriptive, as many of the reforms were adopted without an evaluation component that followed students well beyond high school graduation through college and into their early labor market experiences.

In addition, little of the research supporting these programs incorporates an evaluation of their cost-effectiveness. No indication is made of the costs associated with implementing these programs on a larger scale. Teacher shortages after the implementation of the California class-size reduction suggests that small-scale experiments can easily run into constraints when they are implemented quickly on a large scale.

Lessons from Other Major Reforms

Changes in the behavior and tasks in any organization are difficult. This is especially true as pathways to college and career are changed because of the many sectors of the economy that would be affected. Not only would curriculum, management, and financing of the high school change in Pennington's proposal, but the behavior and tasks of universities, employers, and federal, state, and local governments would as well. More important, the proposed changes would require parents and students to take additional risks with newly organized schools and degrees. This would require substantial buy-in from each participant and important safeguards for students.

As research on comprehensive reform suggests, buy-in is difficult to achieve. Many changes advocated by design teams in the New American Schools program, for example, met considerable resistance and were heavily dependent on support by districts and principals. More important, a high level of coherence was necessary. All participants needed to understand how changes in their tasks and behavior fit within the design of the reform.[27]

Political buy-in at the state and local level is also important. The proposed reforms rely heavily on the willingness of states to target resources toward poor schools. Experience from over three decades of school finance reforms suggests that effort to redistribute education resources from wealthy to poor school districts met with considerable political opposition. For example, W. N. Evans, S. E. Murray, and R. M. Schwab find that school finance reforms that are initiated by legislatures have no effect on the disparity of resources between districts.[28] Instead, only redistribution at the behest of the courts is successful in reducing within-state inequality in total education spending.

As Marc Tucker points out, change in the system would require well-established structures that are "simple enough and stable enough to be understood and negotiated by everyone, everywhere." This is particularly true for students and employers. The countries cited by Tucker have well-established skill standards and certificate programs. Because these are not in place in the United States, much of the risk for a nontraditional program will be borne by the students. This imposes a cost to the student and should be considered when comparing programs to the status quo.

Finally, the proposal suggests using standards to ensure that students are learning. Unfortunately, the experience with standards-based reform is relatively new, and much confusion and controversy surround the use of these standards. For example, to receive Title I resources the 1994 and 2001 amendments of the Elementary and Secondary Act require states to adopt content and performance standards, to align assessments to these standards, and to inform schools and districts. Compliance with these provisions in Title I schools alone has been slow.[29] In addition, content standards have not been uniform. In Kentucky, where the state legislature was required by the courts to provide an adequate education, curriculum changes to adhere with the content standards were voluntary and thus schools vary widely in their curriculum. Moreover, Kentucky and other states regularly revise their standards and assessment systems. Thus additional safeguards seem to be needed to ensure that students do not suffer from weak programs.

Conclusion

The proposals put forth by Pennington to restructure the U.S. system for secondary education are important new directions for policymakers, employers, educators, parents, and students. The movement to transform the American high school has been forwarded considerably by the positive examples Pennington cites. As these experiments are taken to the next level, serious discussions about transforming the high school experience are necessary because, as Pennington's examples suggest, experiences in high school are not too late to help struggling students.

Comment by Marc Tucker

Hilary Pennington does a fine job of laying out the current state of high school reform in the United States from the perspective of the transition from school, on the one hand, to postsecondary education and careers, on the other.

She describes a fascinating collage of experiments, in which many kinds of distinctions start to blur. High schools offer college programs. Colleges offer high school programs. Academic and vocational goals are combined in the same programs and course. Programs are offered by some things that look like schools and others that do not. And so on.

This picture is both exciting and disturbing. It is exciting because it gives one the feeling that the wraps are at long last being taken off. A system that has patently failed is being challenged as it needs to be. People with interesting and appealing ideas for its rebirth and renewal are being given funds and scope to try out their plans and proposals. It is disturbing because what is most needed is a system and this rampant experimentation and the blurred boundaries could produce something that feels like bewildering chaos to its participants. By way of explaining what I mean by a system, I will provide a composite sketch of the way a number of other advanced industrialized nations organize education for the years in which U.S. students attend high school.

In those countries, all students take more or less the same curriculum for their first nine or ten years, set to the same standards, and then they go their own way. Until recently, those ways were typically very separate, but, in the last few years, that has been less and less true. Now students who have elected gymnasium (the route to university) for their upper secondary path are increasingly making a lateral move afterward to pick up a vocational credential. Similarly, governments are making it much easier for students who start in the upper secondary vocational curriculum to add enough demanding academic courses to qualify for university exams, formerly open only to gymnasium students. Some nations also are creating new paths to the university entrance exams that are just as demanding as the traditional gymnasium but composed of courses that in many cases are built around problems and projects.

These countries are responding to the same pressures the United States is—the drying up of low-skill jobs and the enormous resulting political pressure to provide postsecondary education to virtually everyone—but they have some important advantages.

First, many of these countries have done a much better job than the United States has in the first nine or ten years of the education process. The effects are most visible in the bottom half of the distribution, where students typically achieve at far higher levels than the U.S. lower half. That means that they are better prepared for gymnasium and for a vocational education that requires serious intellectual effort.

Second, in most of these countries, a national school leaving exam serves also as a college (they would say university) entrance exam. There are very few private universities, so it is clear how well a student has to do to go to university, thereby providing a powerful motivation to achieve. In the United States, one can go to most institutions called colleges with no more than a high school diploma, the requirements for which are typically minimal.

Third, these countries have a much stronger tradition of vocational education, typically accompanied by a national system of occupational skills standards and strong employer participation. In most of northern Europe, students who do not meet the skills standards simply cannot get a job in their chosen occupation, so students planning to enter the work force after what the United States calls high school have strong incentives to take tough courses and work hard in school. Employers play multiple roles in the process of training students for their chosen occupations, assessing them against the standards and, in many other ways, easing the transition from school to work.

One other feature of these other systems is important to note. When students go from gymnasium or its equivalent to university, they are not entering the equivalent of the American college. They are entering professional school. These students have finished their general education (including the experience American students are supposed to get in the first two years of college) in gymnasium. Gymnasium typically begins in the tenth or eleventh year of schooling and lasts three years. Thus university typically begins in the thirteenth or fourteenth year, whereas, in the U.S. system, professional education can begin anywhere from the junior year of college to the first year of graduate school. From the standpoint of system efficiency, these other—mostly European—nations have managed to create a system that produces the same or better outcomes while saving the cost of one to three years of expensive university education.

Systems so constructed have many advantages. They are, among other things, (1) effective, in terms of producing a total population that is as highly skilled as that of any other nation and, no less important, able to learn quickly what it needs to learn to adjust quickly to changes of all kinds as they come; (2) flexible, in terms of enabling people to pursue enormously varied objectives and to change their minds along the way; and (3) admirably efficient, in terms of the total cost in time and money needed to produce a person with a given qualification.

Certain features of these systems are worth noting. They depend on having clearly demarcated parts of the system and on clear, universal standards that serve as gateways for moving from one part of the system to another—in particular from lower secondary education to upper secondary education, from upper secondary education to university, and from upper secondary vocational education into the labor market. The existence of these gates provides strong incentives for students at every level of the system to take tough courses and study hard, so they can reach their goals, which can only be won by doing exactly that.

Second, these systems invest heavily in assessment, which is typically done by having real people examine the extended work product of the students and comparing it with the standards.

Third, the countries that use systems of this sort are paying more and more attention to guidance, finding ways to help students understand their options and identify those that suit them.

Fourth, though these systems are dynamic, undergoing constant change, they are not an endless amorphous experiment. The governments that use such systems believe that it is important to have structures that guarantee similar opportunities for students throughout the whole nation, structures that are simple enough and stable enough to be understood and negotiated by everyone, everywhere.

The United States should not copy the system of any other nation and probably could not, even if it wanted to. But when you have fallen a long way behind the leaders, it is not out of order to take a look at the way that leaders get results before going off in another direction. No doubt, some Americans will take umbrage at the idea that the United States is not the leader, but the evidence is too overwhelming to ignore. The Third International Mathematics and Science Study studies showed not only that U.S. high school students are far behind the pack in general science and general math, but that they are even further behind in advanced math and science.

The more recent Program for International Assessment studies place the United States, at best, in the middle of the pack, far behind the leaders. American graduate schools are the best in the world, attracting students from every quarter of the globe, but as many as half of the lower division of U.S. college students would not qualify for admission to postsecondary educational institutions in much of the rest of the industrialized world. And no one I have ever met believes that the United States is competitive in vocational education.

So I would like to offer a modest proposal for an American adaptation of the international system I have described. It is intended to enable the United States to reach the goals related to quality, flexibility, and efficiency. The National Center on Education and the Economy, of which I am president, devised this schema to organize its America's Choice high school design, but the proposal could also be adopted by a state as the basis of its formal kindergarten through postsecondary education policy.

The first step would be to create a state standard for entrance into the bottom tier of the state higher education institutions: ready to take credit-bearing courses. In particular, and at a minimum, meeting this standard would certify that the person has the skills in reading, writing, and mathematics needed to do college-level work in those and other subjects. States would issue a certificate to students who meet this standard. The expectation would be that this standard would be met by the time a student was sixteen years old or at the end of the tenth grade. There are two reasons to do this. First, most other advanced nations expect their students to complete the common curriculum by this age, and there is no reason that it should take longer to do that in the United States than elsewhere. Second, if most students are expected to reach this goal by the end of their sophomore year, that will leave two or more years for students who have not reached that goal by the end of their sophomore year to do so before they have to leave high school. The aim, as Pennington noted in her paper, is to set a fixed standard, a standard that some students may take longer to reach than others.

The second step is to develop assessments adequate to make this determination. This is no small step. The only way to find out whether someone has the skills and knowledge to write an essay that meets the standard of college-level work is to ask that person to write such an essay and read it and critically evaluate it. This is so when it comes to the way students taking the Advanced Placement tests are assessed, tests that cost $75 per student per subject to take, but not when it comes to the typical state assessments at the tenth-grade level, on which much less is spent. Furthermore, virtually all experts on the subject agree that high-stakes systems of the sort that I refer to here should be based on multiple modes of assessment. The Cambridge University examination system includes not only end-of-course and end-of-sequence exams, but its scores are also based on teacher grades on teacher-assigned work that are checked by professional assessors. These tests do not cost as much as the Advanced Placement tests, but they are much more expensive than the typical state high-stakes tenth-grade test.

The third step is to create the tools, policies, and support systems that will enable U.S. high schools to get their students to the standard just described. This will entail identifying schools whose students are in danger of failing to meet this standard and requiring those schools to use a comprehensive school reform program that includes a standard curriculum and a soundly conceived program of technical assistance and professional development needed to implement that curriculum as well as all the associated safety net programs the students in those schools probably need.

By standard curriculum, I mean a single curriculum in which most of the courses are required and are designed to get the students to the standard. This means no general track, no vocational track, no career academies (that is, a program with a career education focus), and no distractions. It may mean the use of career themes or work-based learning for some students, not for the purpose of providing technical skills, but for the purpose of providing a motivation to continue their academic studies. These programs may employ a traditional pedagogy or a highly innovative one, but they exist for one purpose only—to get their students to the certificate standard just mentioned.

Notwithstanding the success stories in Pennington's paper, experience teaches that getting virtually all U.S. high school sophomores to this standard will take a Herculean effort. Astonishingly little research has been done in the last fifty years on the problems of low-performing high school students and even less on developing curriculum for them that works. The nation needs to greatly increase the effort it is making on this front to get results on the scale needed.

The next step is to carefully define in policy the options that are available to students who reach the new certificate standard. Those at the National Center on Education and the Economy who have been working on this problem over the last twelve years are convinced that qualifying students should then begin some form of college. If the standard that a student has met qualifies him or her for college-level work, then why not send that student to college?

But, as Pennington's paper points out, students need not leave high school to embark on college, though they should have that option. Students who get their certificate and want to pursue a program leading to a two-year technical degree or certificate ought to leave the high school and go straight to a community or technical college offering such a program. Everything from programs in welding and auto mechanics to programs in software systems management, hotel and restaurant management, cardiovascular technology and technical, graphics and design fall into this category. Few high schools in the United States can afford the equipment (which has to be constantly updated) and the faculty needed for such programs. The institutions that should have these programs are the community and technical colleges and that is where students who want to pursue such programs should be sent.

States that elect to go down the path I am suggesting may turn around, however, to discover that their community colleges (many states do not have separate systems of technical colleges) are jettisoning their technical programs in favor of their general education programs, which are cheaper to operate, do not require that students have strong reading, writing, and math skills (though they should), and lead to a more prestigious position on the academic pecking order. The implication is that many states may have to strengthen the capacity of their community colleges to offer strong two-year technical programs to make this aspect of this proposal work.

What is missing and badly needed in the community and technical college system are national standards for the technical occupations and assessments to gauge when those standards have been met. The National Skill Standards Board, chartered to develop such a system, apparently will not do so before it sunsets. Some states are working on them, but state standards are no substitute for a national system. Absent these standards, the colleges set their own standards, which vary widely, producing a situation in which employers do not know what degree and certificate holders can do and degree and certificate holders have a hard time marketing themselves to employers for the same reason. Standards are the key to a successful school to work transition in all the nations in which such standards are in use.

But what about the students who do not choose to leave their high school to pursue a technical program at the local community or technical college? How many options these students have and the nature of the options will depend on the size and location of the school and the preferences of the community, but the common feature would be that all of the options would represent some form of going to college in high school. Among the examples of such programs would be the International Baccalaureate (IB) program. It was conceived as the embodiment of a European gymnasium program set to a high European standard. Even the most selective of American selective colleges admit IB diploma holders as college sophomores. Another alternative would be a demanding program that is based on the admission requirements of the highest level of the state university system and that includes a substantial number of Advanced Placement courses, another way to enter college with a head start. A third option would be a program set to a high academic standard but employing a pedagogy heavily based on problems and projects. The National Center on Education and the Economy will be working on the development of such a curriculum over the next few years. Other options are described in Pennington's paper. Some high schools may be able to offer only one such option. Others might be able to offer many. Most options will take advantage of the faculty resident in the school, but others might be virtual, available from the World Wide Web.

All of these programs will terminate in examinations, too. Some are designed as an integral part of the upper secondary program the student is participating in. Others will be given by the institutions the student intends to attend next. But the states could contribute greatly to a smooth transition if they developed assessments for the purpose of establishing standards for transferring into the sophomore or junior year of the state university system. Then all high schools would make sure that their students were prepared for those examinations and assessments, as a minimum standard for the end of the upper secondary programs. These standards would apply to students who took their upper secondary program in community or technical colleges as well as those who took their program in the high schools, and so all students would be on an equal footing, no matter what path they had chosen. Individual postsecondary institutions and individual programs within those institutions could impose additional requirements, but the core performance requirements in the public institutions would be known by everyone and common across the board.

Students electing to stay in a high school to participate in its upper division program would experience a different social environment than was the case in their lower division program. It would feel more like college, less like the traditional high school, with more responsibility and fewer restrictions—more grown up. The high school will have to do this just to compete with the community and technical colleges, but it should want to anyway.

Two quick points need to be made on finance. First, Great Britain has found a way to deal with the problem to which Pennington referred regarding the dropout statistics in higher education. Great Britain gives its further education colleges (similar to U.S. community colleges) a sign-up fee when a student matriculates and a certain amount in each year thereafter, but most of the compensation does not come to the college until the student has received his or her degree. There is much more mobility among college students in the United States than in Great Britain, but it would be possible and useful to adapt the British system to the United States by deferring some of the compensation to the postsecondary institutions the student attends until a degree is awarded, whether the student attends only one such institution or several.

Second, many American community colleges are giving up offering technical programs because they are more expensive than academic ones. The Danes have solved this problem by funding their institutions based on the full-time equivalent students in their programs, but the amount given each student varies, depending on the expense of offering the particular program in which that student is enrolled. This is made easier by the fact that the Danes have a national skill standards system that defines their vocational program offerings nationwide.

Much of what I have described was foreshadowed in Pennington's paper. On a few minor matters, I have chosen to argue, at least by implication, with some of the propositions offered, but, in the main, my aim has been to tease out the structural implications and give form to the kind of system that might emerge from the trends that Pennington described. At the same time, I have cautioned against too much enthusiasm for an age of experimentation that fails to provide the people who will use the U.S. school system enough structure to get what they want and need from it.

Notes

1. Michael Cohen, *Transforming the American High School: New Directions for State and Local Policy* (Boston: Jobs for the Future; and Washington: Aspen Institute, 2001).

2. National Center on Education and the Economy, *America's Choice: High Skills or Low Wages! The Report of the Commission on the Skills of the American Workforce* (Rochester, N.Y., June 1990).

3. Richard Murnane and Frank Levy, *Teaching the New Basic Skills* (New York: Free Press, 1996).

4. Anthony P. Carnevale and Donna M. Desrochers, *Help Wanted . . . Credentials Required: Community Colleges in the Knowledge Economy* (Princeton, N.J.: Educational Testing Service; and Washington: American Association of Community Colleges, 2001).

5. Andrew Sum and others, *The National Economic Downturn and Deteriorating Youth Employment Prospects: The Case for a Young Adult Jobs Stimulus Program* (Northeastern University, Center for Labor Market Studies, November 2001).

6. Michael Nettles and Nellie Letger, "Prepared for Dropouts in America," paper prepared for a forum convened by Harvard University, Graduate School of Education, Civil Rights Project and Achieve Inc., Boston, Massachusetts, 2001.

7. National Commission on the High School Senior Year, *Raising Our Sights: No High School Senior Left Behind* (Princeton, N.J.: Woodrow Wilson National Fellowship Foundation, October 2001).

8. Carnevale and Desrochers, *Help Wanted.*

9. Advisory Committee on Student Financial Assistance, *Access Denied: Restoring the Nation's Commitment to Equal Educational Opportunity* (Washington: Advisory Committee on Student Financial Assistance, 2001).

10. Sum and others, *The National Economic Downturn and Deteriorating Youth Employment Prospects.*

11. National Commission on the High School Senior Year, *Raising Our Sights.*

12. Marta Tienda, "The New Labor Markets: Implications for the Nation's Young People," in *Promoting Educational Excellence in the New Economy: The Challenges for National Policy,* proceedings of the Aspen Institute Congressional Program, Eighth Conference, vol. 16, no. 2, February 16-19, 2001.

13. Carnevale and Desrochers, *Help Wanted.*

14. National Center for Education Statistics. *The Condition of Education 1997,* NCES 97–388 (Department of Education, 1997).

15. Sum and others, *The National Economic Downturn and Deteriorating Youth Employment Prospects.*

16. Paul Hill and others, *It Takes a City: Getting Serious about Urban School Reform* (Brookings, 1999).

17. Carnevale and Desrochers, *Help Wanted.*

18. Richard Judy and Carol D'Amico, *Workforce 2020* (Indianapolis, Ind.: Hudson Institute, 2000).

19. Barbara Lawrence and others, *Dollars and Sense: The Cost-Effectiveness of Small Schools* (Cincinnati, Ohio: Knowledge Works Foundation, 2000).

20. From the Margins to the Mainstream Initiative is supported by grants from the Carnegie Corporation of New York, the John D. and Catherine T. MacArthur Foundation, the W. K. Kellogg Foundation, the Charles Stewart Mott Foundation, and Atlantic Philanthropies. At a critical moment in the growing movement to improve high schools, this multiyear initiative looks for solutions and strategies outside of the one-size-fits-all traditional high school. The project seeks practical answers to the question of how school systems can take advantage of breakthrough possibilities offered by emerging, powerful learning environments inside and outside of the school building, school day, and school year. Jobs for the Future will publish the results of the research and analysis in more depth in a white paper and in other materials being prepared by project director Adria Steinberg and other Jobs for the Future staff members.

21. Sonia Jurich and Steve Estes, *Raising Academic Achievement for America's Youth: A Study of Twenty Successful Programs* (Washington: American Youth Policy Forum, 2000).

22. National Research Council and the Institute of Medicine, *Community Programs to Promote Youth Development* (Washington: National Academy Press, 2002).

23. This material draws on forthcoming publications being prepared by Adria Steinberg and other Jobs for the Future staff members for the From the Margins to the Mainstream Initiative.

24. Stephanie M. Smith and Jean G. Thomases, *CBO Schools: Profiles in Transformational Education* (Washington: Academy for Education Development, Center for Youth Development and Policy Research, 2001).

25. Cohen, *Transforming the American High School,* p. 21.

26. Hill and others, *It Takes a City.*

27. M. Berends, S. J. Bodilly, and S. N. Kirby, *New American Schools Facing the Challenges of Whole-School Reform: New American Schools after a Decade,* MR 1498–EDU (Santa Monica, Calif.: RAND, 2002).

28. W. N. Evans, S. E. Murray, and R. M. Schwab, "School Houses, Court Houses, and State Houses after *Serrano,*" *Journal of Policy Analysis and Management,* vol. 16, no. 1 (1997).

29. Department of Education, *High Standards for All Students: A Report from the National Assessment of Title I on Progress and Challenges since the 1994 Reauthorization* (Washington, 2001).